IFRS Explained

First edition 2012
Fifth edition December 2016

ISBN 9781 5097 0271 8
Previous ISBN 9781 4727 4022 9
eISBN 9781 5097 0322 7

British Library Cataloguing-in-Publication Data
A catalogue record for this book is available from the British Library

Published by

BPP Learning Media Ltd
BPP House, Aldine Place
142-144 Uxbridge Road
London W12 8AA

www.bpp.com/learningmedia

Printed in the United Kingdom by

RICOH UK Limited
Unit 2
Wells Place
Merstham
RH1 3LG

Your learning materials, published by BPP Learning Media Ltd, are printed on paper obtained from traceable sustainable sources.

A note about copyright

Dear Customer

What does the little © mean and why does it matter?

Your market-leading BPP books, course materials and e-learning materials do not write and update themselves. People write them on their own behalf or as employees of an organisation that invests in this activity. Copyright law protects their livelihoods. It does so by creating rights over the use of the content.

Breach of copyright is a form of theft – as well as being a criminal offence in some jurisdictions, it is potentially a serious beach of professional ethics.

With current technology, things might seem a bit hazy but, basically, without the express permission of BPP Learning Media:

- Photocopying our materials is a breach of copyright

- Scanning, ripcasting or conversion of our digital materials into different file formats, uploading them to facebook or e-mailing them to your friends is a breach of copyright

You can, of course, sell your books, in the form in which you have bought them – once you have finished with them. (Is this fair to your fellow students? We update for a reason.) Please note the e-products are sold on a single user licence basis: we do not supply 'unlock' codes to people who have bought them secondhand.

And what about outside the UK? BPP Learning Media strives to make our materials available at prices students can afford by local printing arrangements, pricing policies and partnerships which are clearly listed on our website. A tiny minority ignore this and indulge in criminal activity by illegally photocopying our material or supporting organisations that do. If they act illegally and unethically in one area, can you really trust them?

IFRS

Contents

Part B: Single entity financial statements

3 Presentation of published financial statements

4 Accounting for tangible non-current assets

5 Intangible assets and goodwill

6 Reporting financial performance

7 Revenue and inventories

Part D: Specialised standards

20 Share-based payment

21 Employee benefits

22 Foreign currency translation

23 Accounting for agriculture and mineral resources

Introduction

This book is intended for those with basic accounting knowledge who now wish to get familiar with IFRS. We have dealt with the standards under topic headings and the aim has been to show how the provisions of the standards are applied in practice. Rather than detailed cross-references to sections and sub-sections, we have concentrated on bringing out the key points and showing examples and workings where applicable.

We have explained in some detail the preparation of IFRS financial statements including consolidated financial statements. Many readers will already be familiar with consolidation procedures, but may find it useful to go through the basics before taking account of those issues peculiar to IFRS, such as non-controlling interest at fair value.

We have omitted two standards dealing with financial reporting by financial institutions:

- IAS 26 *Accounting and reporting by retirement benefit plans*
- IFRS 4 *Insurance contracts*

These are complex standards and knowledge of them is not required by most preparers of financial statements.

Part A

The regulatory and conceptual framework

The IASB and the regulatory framework

1 Impact of globalisation

The current reality is that the world's capital markets operate more and more freely across borders. The impacts of rapid globalisation are epitomised by the words of Paul Volker, Chairman of the IASC Foundation Trustees in November 2002, in a speech to the World Congress of Accountants.

> 'Developments over the past year and more have strongly reinforced the logic of achieving and implementing high-quality international accounting standards. In an age when capital flows freely across borders, it simply makes sense to account for economic transactions, whether they occur in the Americas, Asia, or Europe, in the same manner. Providing improved transparency and comparability will certainly help ensure that capital is allocated efficiently. Not so incidentally, generally accepted international standards will reduce the cost of compliance with multiple national standards.'

As the modern business imperative moves towards the globalisation of operations and activities, there is an underlying commercial logic that also requires a truly global capital market. Harmonised financial reporting standards are intended to provide:

- A platform for wider investment choice
- A more efficient capital market
- Lower cost of capital
- Enhanced business development

Globally, users of financial statements need **transparent** and **comparative information** to help them **make economic decisions**.

From 2005, EU listed companies have been required to use IFRS in preparing their consolidated financial statements. This is an important step towards eventual harmonisation with the USA.

2 International Accounting Standards Board (IASB)

The International Accounting Standards Board is an independent, privately-funded accounting standard setter based in London. Contributors include major accounting firms, private financial institutions, industrial companies throughout the world, central and development banks, and other international and professional organisations.

In March 2001 the IASC (International Accounting Standards Committee) Foundation was formed as a not-for-profit corporation incorporated in the USA. The IASC Foundation is the parent entity of the IASB. In July 2010 it changed its name to the IFRS Foundation.

From April 2001 the IASB assumed accounting standard setting responsibilities from its predecessor body, the International Accounting Standards Committee (IASC).

The members of the IASB come from a number of countries and have a variety of backgrounds with a mix of auditors, preparers of financial statements, users of financial statements and an academic.

The objectives of the IFRS Foundation are:

(a)   To develop, in the public interest, a single set of high quality, understandable, enforceable and globally accepted financial reporting standards based upon clearly articulated principles. These standards should require high quality, transparent and comparable information in financial statements and other financial reporting to help investors, other participants in the world's capital markets and other users of financial information make economic decisions.

(b)   To promote the use and rigorous application of those standards.

(c)   In fulfilling the objectives associated with (a) and (b), to take account of, as appropriate, the needs of a range of sizes and types of entities in diverse economic settings.

(d)   To promote and facilitate adoption of International Financial Reporting Standards (IFRSs), being the standards and interpretations issued by the IASB, through the convergence of national accounting standards and IFRSs.

Structure of the IASB

The structure of the IASB can be illustrated by the following diagram:

IFRS Foundation

The IFRS Foundation is made up of 22 Trustees, who essentially monitor and fund the IASB, the IFRS Advisory Council and the IFRS Interpretations Committee. The Trustees of the IFRS Foundation are responsible for the governance and oversight of the International Accounting Standards Board (IASB).

The Trustees are not involved in any technical matters relating to the Standards. This responsibility rests solely with the IASB.

The Trustees are accountable to the Monitoring Board, a body of publically accountable markets authorities.

Trustees are appointed for a renewable term of three years. Each Trustee is expected to have an understanding of, and be sensitive to, international issues relevant to the success of an international organisation responsible for the development of high quality global accounting standards for use in the world's capital markets and by other users.

Six of the Trustees must be selected from the Asia/Oceania region, six from Europe, six from North America, one from Africa, one from South America and two from the rest of the world

IFRS Advisory Council

The IFRS Advisory Council provides a formal vehicle for further groups and individuals with diverse geographic and functional backgrounds to give advice to the Board and, at times, to advise the Trustees. It comprises about 50 members and meets at least 3 times a year. It is consulted by the IASB on all major projects and its meetings are open to the public. It advises the IASB on the prioritisation of its work and on the implications of proposed standards for users and preparers of financial statements.

IFRS Interpretations Committee

The Interpretations Committee provides timely guidance on the application and interpretation of International Financial Reporting Standards. It deals with newly identified financial reporting issues not specifically addressed in IFRSs, or issues where unsatisfactory or conflicting interpretations have developed, or seem likely to develop.

Scope and authority of IFRSs

The IASB achieves its objectives primarily by developing and publishing IFRSs and promoting the use of those standards in general purpose financial statements and other financial reporting.

IFRSs set out **recognition, measurement, presentation and disclosure requirements** dealing with transactions and events that are important in general purpose financial statements. IFRSs are based on the IASB *Conceptual Framework for Financial Reporting*, which:

- Addresses the **concepts** underlying the information presented in general purpose financial statements

- Facilitates the **consistent** and logical formulation of IFRSs

- Provides a basis for the use of judgement in resolving accounting issues

IFRSs are designed to apply to the general purpose financial statements and other financial reporting of all profit-oriented entities.

General purpose financial statements are directed towards the common information needs of a wide range of users; for example, shareholders, suppliers, employees and the public at large. The objective of financial statements is to provide information about the financial position, performance and cash flows of an entity that is useful to those users in making economic decisions.

A complete set of financial statements includes:

- A statement of financial position

- A statement of profit or loss and other comprehensive income

- A statement of all changes in equity, showing only owner changes in equity (non-owner changes are in the statement of comprehensive income)

- A statement of cash flows

- Accounting policies and explanatory notes

- Comparative information

The term 'financial statements' includes a complete set of financial statements prepared for an interim or annual period, and condensed financial statements for an interim period. In the interest of timeliness and cost, and to avoid repeating information previously reported, an entity may provide less information in its interim financial statements than in its annual financial statements. IAS 34 *Interim financial reporting* prescribes the minimum content of complete or condensed financial statements for an interim period.

Many of the IASs produced by the old IASC allowed entities to make a choice between 'benchmark treatments' and 'allowed alternatives'. By contrast, the IASB has shifted the emphasis away from allowing entities a choice between accounting treatments, and is reconsidering all those IASs where choices are permitted. Its objective is either to reduce the number of options available to choose from, or to eliminate the element of choice altogether. This is in line with the IASB's emphasis on reporting like transactions and events in a like way, and reporting different transactions and events differently.

Any limitation of scope of an IFRS will be made clear in the standard.

IFRS due process

IFRSs are developed through an international due process that involves accountants, financial analysts and other users of financial statements, the business community, stock exchanges, regulatory and legal authorities, academics and other interested individuals and organisations from around the world. The IASB consults the IFRS Advisory Council in public meetings on major projects, agenda decisions and work priorities, and discusses technical matters in meetings that are open to public observation.

The overall agenda of the IASB will initially be set by discussion with the Advisory Council. The process for developing an individual standard would involve the following steps:

step 1	During the early stages of a project, IASB may establish an **Advisory Committee** to give advice on issues arising in the project. Consultation with the Advisory Committee and the Standards Advisory Council occurs throughout the project. There may also be consultation with another standard setter such as the FASB.
step 2	IASB may develop and publish **Discussion Papers** for public comment.
step 3	Following the receipt and review of comments, IASB would develop and publish an **Exposure Draft** for public comment.
step 4	Following the receipt and review of comments, the IASB would issue a final **International Financial Reporting Standard**.

Interpretation of IFRSs

The IFRS Interpretations Committee assists the IASB by improving existing Standards. The Interpretations Committee has two main responsibilities:

- Review, on a timely basis, newly identified financial reporting issues not specifically addressed in IFRSs

- Clarify issues where unsatisfactory or conflicting interpretations have developed, or seem likely to develop in the absence of authoritative guidance, with a view to reaching a consensus on the appropriate treatment

The Interpretations Committee also helps the IASB move towards international harmonisation by working with its equivalent national-level bodies (such as the UITF in the UK).

The Interpretations Committee, like the IASB itself, adopts a **principle-based approach**. Its intention is to provide guidance that is in line with the rest of the IFRSs. It therefore bases itself, like each of the individual Standards, first and foremost on the IASB *Conceptual Framework*. It will then look at any relevant IFRSs for principles applying the *Conceptual Framework* to that particular area.

The Interpretations Committee develops its interpretations through a due process of consultation and debate which includes making Draft Interpretations available for public comment.

Comment periods

The IASB issues each Exposure Draft of a Standard and discussion documents for public comment, with a normal comment period of 120 days. In certain circumstances, the Board may expose proposals for a much shorter period. However, such limited periods would be used only in extreme circumstances. Draft Interpretations are normally exposed for a 90-day minimum comment period.

3 Generally Accepted Accounting Practice (GAAP)

The expression GAAP may or may not have statutory or legal authority or definition, depending on the country involved, eg it does not have statutory authority in the UK, but does so in the USA.

GAAP is in fact a **dynamic concept** and changes constantly as circumstances alter through new legislation, standards and practice.

The problem of what is 'generally accepted' is not easy to settle, because new practices will obviously not be generally adopted yet. The criteria for a practice being 'generally accepted' will depend on factors such as whether the practice is addressed by financial reporting standards or legislation, and whether other companies have adopted the practice. Most importantly perhaps, the question should be whether the practice is consistent with the needs of the users and the objective of financial reporting and whether it is consistent with the 'true and fair' concept.

True and fair view (or presented fairly)

It is a requirement of both national legislation (in some countries, eg the UK) and International Standards on Auditing that the financial statements should give a **true and fair view of** (or **'present fairly, in all material respects'**) the financial position of the entity as at the end of the financial year and its profit or loss for the period.

The terms 'true and fair view' and 'present fairly, in all material aspects' are not defined in accounting or auditing standards. Despite this, a company may depart from any of the provisions of accounting standards if these are inconsistent with the requirement to give a true and fair view. This is commonly referred to as the **'true and fair override'**. It has been treated as an important **loophole** in the law in different countries and has been the cause of much argument and dissatisfaction within the accounting profession.

4 Other international influences

European Commission (EC)

The EC regulations form one part of a broader programme for the harmonisation of company law in member states. The commission is uniquely the only organisation to produce international standards of accounting practice which are legally enforceable, in the form of directives which must be included in the national legislation of member states.

However, the EC has also acknowledged the role of the IASB in harmonising world-wide accounting rules and it promotes the use of IFRS worldwide.

United Nations (UN)

The UN has a Commission and Centre on Transnational Reporting Corporations, through which it gathers information concerning the activities and reporting of multinational companies. The UN processes are highly political and probably reflect the attitudes of the governments of developing countries to multinationals.

International Federation of Accountants (IFAC)

The IFAC is a private sector body established in 1977 and which now consists of almost 200 professional accounting bodies from over 100 different countries. The IFAC's main objective is to co-ordinate the accounting profession on a global scale by issuing and establishing international standards on auditing, management accounting, ethics, education and training.

In November 2011 the IASB and the IFAC announced agreement in the form of a Memorandum of Understanding to strengthen their co-operation in developing private and public sector accounting standards.

Organisation for Economic Co-operation and Development (OECD)

The OECD supports the work of the IASB but also undertakes its own research into accounting standards via ad hoc working groups. For example, in 1976 the OECD issued guidelines for multinational companies on financial reporting and non-financial disclosures. The OECD appears to work on behalf of developed countries to protect them from extreme proposals of the UN. The OECD has also entered the debate on corporate governance.

International Organisation of Securities Commissions (IOSCO)

IOSCO is the representative of the world's securities markets regulators. High quality information is vital for the operation of an efficient capital market, and differences in the quality of the accounting policies and their enforcement between countries leads to inefficiencies between markets. IOSCO has been active in encouraging and promoting the improvement and quality of IFRSs over the last ten years. IOSCO issued a report in May 2000 which recommended to all its members that they allow multinational issuers to use IFRSs, as supplemented by reconciliation, disclosure and interpretation where necessary to address outstanding substantive issues at a national or regional level.

IASB staff and IOSCO continue to work together to resolve outstanding issues and to identify areas where new IASB standards are needed.

In September 2013, IOSCO and the IASB announced joint protocols under which they will strengthen their co-operation in support of their commitment to the highest standards of global financial reporting.

Financial Accounting Standards Board (FASB)

The US standard-setter, the FASB and the IASB have been undertaking a project of harmonisation between US GAAP and IFRS.

In September 2002, both parties acknowledged their commitment to the process of developing accounting standards that can be used for domestic and international purposes. Both the FASB and the IASB have worked together to make amendments to current accounting standards in the short term, and to work together on a long term basis to ensure new standards issued are compatible.

The FASB is an important influence on the current and future work of the IASB. IFRS 15 *Revenue from contracts with customers* and IFRS 16 *Leases* are the results of joint IASB/FASB projects.

5 Scope and application of IFRSs

Any limitation of the applicability of a specific IAS/IFRS is made clear within that standard. IASs/IFRSs are **not intended to be applied to immaterial items, nor are they retrospective**. Each individual IAS/IFRS lays out its scope at the beginning of the standard.

Within each individual country **local regulations** govern, to a greater or lesser degree, the issue of financial statements. These local regulations include accounting standards issued by the national regulatory bodies and/or professional accountancy bodies in the country concerned.

IFRSs **concentrate on essentials** and are designed not to be too complex, otherwise they would be impossible to apply on a worldwide basis.

IFRSs do not override local regulations on financial statements. Users applying IFRS should simply disclose the fact where IFRSs are complied with in all material respects. Members of the IASB in individual countries will attempt to persuade local authorities, where current regulations deviate from IASs/IFRSs, that the benefits of harmonisation make local change worthwhile.

The development of an IFRS involves an **open, public process of debating technical issues** and evaluating input sought through several mechanisms. Opportunities for interested parties to participate in the development of IFRS would include, depending on the nature of the project:

(a)   Participation in the development of views as a member of the **IFRS Advisory Council**

(b)   Participation in **advisory groups**

(c)   Submission of a **comment letter** in response to a **discussion document**

(d)   Submission of a **comment letter** in response to an **Exposure Draft**

(e)   Participation in **public hearings**

(f)   Participation **in field visits and field tests**

The IASB publishes an annual report on its activities during the past year and priorities for next year. This report provides a basis and opportunity for comment by interested parties. In addition, it has recently changed its Constitution so that it is required to undertake a public consultation on its future technical agenda every three years. The IASB reports on its technical projects on its website. It also publishes a report on IASB decisions immediately after each IASB meeting in its newsletter *IASB Update*.

6 Progress towards global harmonisation

Worldwide effect of IFRS and the IASB

The IASB, and before it the IASC, has now been in existence for more than 30 years, therefore it is worth looking at the effect it has had in that time.

As far as Europe is concerned, the consolidated financial statements of many of Europe's top multinationals are already prepared in conformity with national requirements, EC directives and IFRS. These developments have been given added impetus by the internationalisation of capital markets. As discussed, IFRS has been implemented in the EU since 2005 for listed companies, and there is an established 'endorsement' process for the adoption of new standards.

The IASB and the Accounting Standards Board of Japan (ASBJ) have been working together to achieve convergence of IFRSs and Japanese Generally Accepted Accounting Practice (GAAP) since 2005. This work was formalised in 2007 with the Tokyo Agreement. Since 2010, certain qualifying listed companies in Japan have been allowed to use IFRSs as designated by the Financial Services Agency of Japan (FSAJ) in their consolidated financial statements, in lieu of Japanese GAAP.

IFRSs may not be used in statutory separate financial statements.

Although Japan has considered potential mandatory adoption of IFRS by public companies for some time, a decision is yet to be made. Currently, Japan is promoting greater use of IFRSs based on voluntary adoption. For example, the ASBJ is considering approving 'endorsed IFRS' which would be available for voluntary adoption by Japanese companies.

In America, the Securities and Exchange Commission (SEC) agreed in 1993 to allow foreign issuers (of shares, etc) to follow IAS/IFRS treatments on certain issues, including cash flow statements under IAS 7. The overall effect is that, where an IAS/IFRS treatment differs from US GAAP, these treatments are acceptable. Domestic issuers are required to apply US GAAP. The SEC is now supporting the IASB because it wants to attract foreign listings and, as discussed, the FASB is engaged in a long-term convergence project with the IASB.

In certain countries, the application of IFRS is **mandatory** for all domestic listed companies. The following provides an example of some of the countries, but the list is not exhaustive: Barbados, Cyprus, Georgia, Jamaica, Jordan, Kenya, Kuwait, Malawi, Mauritius, Nepal, Peru, Serbia and Trinidad and Tobago.

Countries that implemented IFRS for the 2005 European ruling in respect of the consolidated financial statements of public listed companies include Austria, Belgium, Czech Republic, Denmark, Estonia, Finland, France, Germany, Greece, Hungary, Iceland, Ireland, Italy, Liechtenstein, Lithuania, Luxembourg, Netherlands, Norway, Poland, Portugal, Slovenia, Slovak Republic, Spain, Sweden and the United Kingdom.

Harmonisation in Europe

The objective of the European Commission (EC) is to build a fully integrated, globally competitive market. A key element of this is the harmonisation of company law across the member states. In line with this the **EC aims to establish a level playing field for financial reporting,** supported by an effective enforcement regime. The commission is uniquely the only organisation whose accounting standards are legally enforceable, in the form of directives which must be included in the national legislation of member states. However, the directives have been criticised as they might become constraints on the application of worldwide standards, and may bring accounting standardisation and harmonisation into the political arena.

The EC adopted a regulation under which from 2005 consolidated financial statements of listed companies were required to comply with IFRS. The implications of this measure are far reaching. However, member states currently have the discretion to extend the implementation of IFRS to include non-listed companies.

In 2009 the IASB issued the IFRS for SMEs (small and medium-sized entities) and this is an important step toward the introduction of IFRS for all companies.

Many commentators believe that in the light of the EC's commitment to IFRS it is only a matter of time before national standard-setting bodies are, in effect, replaced by the IASB, with national standards falling into disuse. However, the IASB will continue to need input and expertise from valued national standard-setters.

IFRS in the USA

Convergence between IFRS and US GAAP is **one of the bigger issues** in the global implementation of IFRS. At present, all US entities must file accounts prepared under US GAAP. However, in 2002 the IASB and its US equivalent, the FASB (Financial Accounting Standards Board) agreed to harmonise their work plans, and to work towards reducing the differences between IFRS and US GAAP.

In **2008 the Securities and Exchange Commission (SEC) issued a 'roadmap'** for the use of IFRS, proposing the eventual mandatory use of IFRS for all US public companies by 2014. At present, only overseas issuers of securities are allowed to file accounts under IFRS (without having to provide a reconciliation to US GAAP).

The SEC's 'roadmap' allowed some companies the option of using IFRS from 2010. It envisaged phasing in IFRS by requiring companies to file accounts under both IFRS and US GAAP for the two years 2012–2014, after which accounts would be prepared under IFRS alone.

This has not played out in practice and the pace of convergence has slowed over the past few years. The SEC's draft strategic plan for 2014–2018 states within its objectives:

'Due to the increasingly global nature of the capital markets, the agency will work to promote higher quality financial reporting worldwide and will consider, among other things, whether a single set of high-quality global accounting standards is achievable.'

This appears to be a step backwards from its previous roadmap. However, 2014 saw the publication of IFRS 15 *Revenue from contracts with customers* and IFRS 16 *Leases*, which are the result of IASB/FASB collaborations.

Rules-based versus principles-based financial reporting standards

US GAAP is an example of a rules-based approach. It consists of a large number of specific accounting standards, and each standard contains a large number of rules (as well as exceptions to the rules), attempting to prescribe treatments for every possible situation that might arise. However, in 2002 the incoming chairman of the **FASB** signalled his support for a **shift to a principles-based approach**:

'I understand the US environment where there has been such a proliferation of rules. I like the principles-based approach but some people have exaggerated the differences. You are always going to have rules but the question is: 'Where do I start?' You can never have a rule for everything and at that point you have to go back to principles.'

Bob Hertz, FASB Chairman (*Financial Times, 27 May 2002*)

A principles-based approach, such as that used in developing IFRSs, is one where the individual standards can be clearly seen to be applications of the approach to accounting adopted by the standards as a whole. Thus each individual IAS/IFRS applies the IASB *Conceptual Framework*, and each standard is an individual reflection of the whole. Specificity at the level of detail is sacrificed for clarity in terms of the overall approach.

Accountants working under **IFRS** are required to use **more professional judgement** than under a rules-based approach. There may not be a specific rule that applies to the event that they need to report, so they need to use judgement in applying the principles contained in the relevant IFRS. It is the view of the IASB that this will result in better quality financial reporting. Accounts will have to be **true to the overall principles of IFRS**, rather than to an individual rule that may not be appropriate for the event being reported, and which may therefore result in an accounting treatment that is not true to the intentions of IFRS as a whole.

UK Accounting Standards Board convergence approach

The convergence process between UK GAAP and IFRS began in 2003 but was subsequently paused. During that time, UK standards did not keep pace with business changes and with evolving types of transaction, particularly with regard to financial instruments. The FRC undertook a consultation process over a number of years and decided that the optimum solution was a transition to an IFRS-based framework. Over the course of 2012 and 2013 it issued three new standards:

- FRS 100 *Application of financial reporting requirements* – issued November 2012

- FRS 101 *Reduced disclosure framework* – issued November 2012

- FRS 102 *The financial reporting standard applicable in the UK and Republic of Ireland* – issued March 2013

The FRC subsequently issued the following, mandatory from 1 January 2016:

- FRS 102 Section 1A – applicable for small entities.

- FRS 103 *Insurance contracts*

- FRS 104 *Interim financial reporting*

- FRS 105 *The financial reporting standard applicable to the micro-entities regime*

FRS 100 provides rules and guidance on how to select the appropriate accounting framework for a particular entity or group.

FRS 101 provides a reduced disclosure framework for qualifying entities, such as subsidiaries of groups reporting their individual entity financial statements under EU adopted IFRS.

FRS 102 replaces the majority of UK accounting standards, adopts an IFRS-based framework and improves accounting for financial instruments. It is based on the IFRS for SMEs, amended to ensure compliance with company law. It is intended for all UK entities other than those applying the FRSSE, or listed companies preparing group financial statements, who are already required to report under full IFRS. Such companies will still be allowed to apply FRS 101 or FRS 102 in preparing their individual entity financial statements.

FRS 102 Section 1A replaces the provisions of the FRSSE as they apply to small entities.

FRS 105 replaces the provisions of the FRSSE as they apply to micro-entities.

UK companies currently reporting under IFRS will be allowed to move to FRS 101 or 102 if they are reporting under IFRS on a voluntary basis. Those companies required to report under IFRS (consolidated financial statements of a listed company) will continue to do so.

FRS 102 has 35 chapters based mainly on the IFRS for SMEs with some cross-reference to full IFRS. The disclosure requirements are less than for full IFRS. Some of the key changes that will impact UK companies on moving to FRS 102 are:

- New requirements for financial instruments, bringing all derivatives on balance sheet measured at fair value through profit or loss

- More intangible assets to be recognised separately from goodwill when there is a business combination

- Useful life of goodwill and intangible assets not to exceed five years when no reliable estimate can be made

- Merger accounting only permitted in limited cases

The new standards were mandatory for accounting periods beginning on or after 1 January 2015.

7 Benefits of and barriers to global harmonisation

Benefits of global harmonisation

The benefits of harmonisation will be based on the benefits to users and preparers of accounts, as follows:

(a) Investors, both individual and corporate, would gain confidence by being able to evaluate the comparable financial results of different companies internationally as well as nationally when making investment decisions.

(b) Multinational companies would benefit from harmonisation for many reasons including the following:

(i) Better access would be gained to foreign investor funds.

(ii) Management control would be improved, because harmonisation would aid internal communication of financial information.

(iii) Appraisal of foreign entities for take-overs and mergers would be more straightforward.

(iv) It would be easier to comply with the reporting requirements of overseas stock exchanges.

(v) Preparation of group accounts would be less complex.

(vi) A reduction in audit costs might be achieved.

(vii) Transfer of accounting staff across national borders would be simpler.

(c) Governments of developing countries would save time and money if they could adopt international standards and, if these were used internally, governments of developing countries could attempt to control the activities of foreign multinational companies in their own country. These companies could not 'hide' behind foreign accounting practices which may be difficult to understand.

(d) Tax authorities. It would be easier to calculate the tax liability of investors, including multinationals who receive income from overseas sources.

(e) Regional economic groups usually promote trade within a specific geographical region. This would be aided by common accounting practices within the region.

(f) Large international accounting firms would benefit as accounting and auditing would be more straightforward if similar accounting practices existed throughout the world.

Barriers to harmonisation

(a) Different purposes of financial reporting. In some countries the purpose is solely for tax assessment, while in others it is for investor decision-making.

(b) Different legal systems. These prevent the development of certain accounting practices and restrict the options available.

(c) Different user groups. Countries have different ideas about who the relevant user groups of financial reporting are and their respective importance. In the USA investor and creditor groups are given prominence, while in Europe employees enjoy a higher profile.

(d) Needs of developing countries. Developing countries are obviously behind in the standard setting process and they need to first develop the basic standards and principles already in place in most developed countries.

(e) Nationalism is demonstrated in an unwillingness to accept another country's standard.

(f) Cultural differences result in objectives for financial reporting and accounting systems differing from country to country.

(g) Unique circumstances. Some countries may be experiencing unusual circumstances which affect all aspects of everyday life and impinge on the ability of companies to produce proper reports, for example hyperinflation, civil war, currency restriction and so on.

(h) The lack of strong accountancy bodies. Many countries do not have strong independent accountancy or business bodies which would support better standards and greater harmonisation.

8 IFRS 1: First-time adoption of International Financial Reporting Standards

IFRS 1 sets out the precise way in which companies should implement a change from local accounting standards (their previous GAAP) to IFRS. One of the main reasons for issuing a new standard was that listed companies in the EU were required to prepare their consolidated financial statements in accordance with IFRS from 2005 onwards.

The standard is intended to ensure that an entity's first IFRS financial statements contain high quality information that: is transparent for users and comparable over all periods presented; provides a suitable starting point for accounting under IFRS; and can be generated at a cost that does not exceed the benefits to users.

Definitions

IFRS 1 defines the following terms:

> **Date of transition to IFRSs.** The beginning of the earliest period for which an entity presents full comparative information under IFRSs in its first IFRS financial statements.
>
> **Deemed cost.** An amount used as a surrogate for cost or depreciated cost at a given date.
>
> **Fair value.** The price that would be received
>
> **First IFRS financial statements.** The first annual financial statements in which an entity adopts International Financial Reporting Standards (IFRSs), by an explicit and unreserved statement of compliance with IFRSs.
>
> **Opening IFRS statement of financial position.** An entity's statement of financial position (published or unpublished) at the date of transition to IFRSs.
>
> **Previous GAAP.** The basis of accounting that a first time adopter used immediately before adopting IFRSs. *(IFRS 1: Appendix A)*

IFRS 1 **only applies** where an entity prepares IFRS financial statements **for the first time**. Changes in accounting policies made by an entity that already applies IFRSs should be dealt with by applying either IAS 8 or specific transitional requirements in other standards.

Making the transition to IFRS

An entity should:

(a)   Select accounting policies that comply with IFRSs at the reporting date for the entity's first IFRS financial statements

(b) Prepare an opening IFRS statement of financial position at the date of transition to IFRSs. This is the starting point for subsequent accounting under IFRSs

(c) Disclose the effect of the change in the financial statements

Example: Reporting date and opening IFRS statement of financial position

A listed company has a 31 December year end and will be required to comply with IFRSs from 1 January 2012.

What is the date of transition to IFRSs?

The company's first IFRS financial statements will be for the year ended 31 December 2012.

IFRS 1 requires that at least one year's comparative figures are presented in the first IFRS financial statements. The comparative figures will be for the year ended 31 December 2011.

Therefore **the date of transition to IFRSs is 1 January 2011** and the company prepares an opening IFRS statement of financial position at this date.

Preparing the opening IFRS statement of financial position

IFRS 1 (para. 10) states that in its opening IFRS statement of financial position an entity shall:

(a) Recognise all assets and liabilities whose recognition is required by IFRSs

(b) Not recognise items as assets or liabilities if IFRSs do not permit such recognition

(c) Reclassify items that it recognised under previous GAAP as one type of asset, liability or component of equity, but are a different type of asset liability or component of equity under IFRSs

(d) Apply IFRS in measuring all recognised assets and liabilities

This involves restating the statement of financial position prepared at the same date under the entity's previous GAAP so that it complies with IASs and IFRSs in force at the first reporting date. In our example above, the company prepares its opening IFRS statement of financial position at 1 January 2011, following accounting policies that comply with IFRSs in force at 31 December 2012.

The accounting policies that an entity uses in its opening IFRS statement of financial position may differ from those it used for the same date using its previous GAAP.

The resulting adjustments are recognised directly in retained earnings (in equity) at the date of transition. (This is because the adjustments arise from events and transactions before the date of transition to IFRS.)

Exemptions from other IFRSs

An entity may elect to use any or all of a range of exemptions. These enable an entity not to apply certain requirements of specific accounting standards retrospectively in drawing up its opening IFRS statement of financial position. Their purpose is to ensure that the cost of producing IFRS financial statements does not exceed the benefits to users.

Business combinations

IFRS 3 need not be applied retrospectively to business combinations that occurred before the date of the opening IFRS statement of financial position. This has the following consequences:

(a)   Combinations keep the same classification (eg acquisition, uniting of interests) as in the previous GAAP financial statements.

(b)   All acquired assets and liabilities are recognised other than:

(i)   Some financial assets and financial liabilities derecognised under the previous GAAP (derivatives and special purpose entities must be recognised)

(ii)   Assets (including goodwill) and liabilities that were not recognised under previous GAAP and would not qualify for recognition under IFRSs

Any resulting change is recognised by adjusting retained earnings (ie equity) unless the change results from the recognition of an intangible asset that was previously subsumed within goodwill.

(c)   Items which do not qualify for recognition as an asset or liability under IFRSs must be excluded from the opening IFRS statement of financial position. For example, intangible assets that do not qualify for separate recognition under IAS 38 must be reclassified as part of goodwill.

(d)   The carrying amount of goodwill in the opening IFRS statement of financial position is the same as its carrying amount under previous GAAP. However, goodwill must be tested for impairment at the transition date.

9 IFRS 14: Regulatory deferral accounts

Many governments regulate the supply and pricing of particular types of activity by private entities, including utilities such as gas, electricity and water. Rate regulation allows suppliers to recover their costs in the prices they charge to customers and is also designed to protect the interests of customers. The recovery of some costs may therefore be deferred in order to keep prices stable and suppliers usually keep track of these deferred amounts in separate regulatory deferral accounts until they are recovered.

The established practice of most entities that already apply IFRS is not to recognise these regulatory account balances, but to allow the amounts to simply flow through profit or loss as they arise. However, entities reporting under different jurisdictions do recognise these deferred amounts.

The IASB has a comprehensive project to consider the issue of rate regulation and published a Discussion Paper in September 2014. In the meantime, it has issued IFRS 14 as an interim Standard under which first-time adopters of IFRS are permitted to continue to recognise deferred amounts in accordance with their previous GAAP requirements both on initial adoption of IFRS and subsequently. In order to facilitate comparison with entities that do not recognise these deferred amounts, deferral account balances must be presented separately.

IFRS 14 is effective from an entity's first IFRS financial statements for periods beginning on, or after, 1 January 2016, with early application allowed. It is permitted, but not required, to be applied. As noted, an entity which is already reporting under IFRS cannot apply IFRS 14.

IFRS 14 effectively provides an exemption from paragraph 11 of IAS 8 *Accounting policies, changes in accounting estimates and errors*, which requires the entity to consider the requirements of IFRS and of the *Conceptual Framework* when setting its accounting policies. When applying IFRS 14, an entity is additionally considering the requirements of its previous GAAP.

Financial statement presentation

Regulatory deferral account balances and movement in balances will be presented as follows:

Statement of financial position

Two line items:

- Regulatory deferral account debit balances – after total assets
- Regulatory deferral account credit balances – after total liabilities

Statement of profit or loss and other comprehensive income

Two line items:

- Movement in regulatory deferral account balances related to profit or loss
- Movement in regulatory deferral account balances related to OCI

Interactions with other IFRSs

IFRS 14 will impact upon other standards as follows:

- IAS 10 *Events after the reporting period* – some events after the reporting period may affect the recognition and measurement of deferral account balances.

- IAS 12 *Income taxes* – deferral account balances may give rise to deferred tax assets and liabilities and associated movements in deferred tax. These amounts are all presented separately from other deferred tax amounts in the financial statements alongside the related regulatory deferral account balances.

- IAS 33 *Earnings per share* – entities reporting deferral account balances are required to present an additional basic and diluted earnings per share which excludes the impact of deferral account balances.

- IAS 36 *Impairment of assets* – regulatory deferral account balances are included in the relevant cash-generating units and treated in the same way as other assets and liabilities when allocating impairment losses.

- IFRS 3 *Business combinations* – where an entity applies IFRS 14, regulatory deferral account balances may be recognised in respect of an acquiree regardless of whether the acquiree itself recognised such balances.

- IFRS 5 *Non-current assets held for sale and discontinued operations* – the measurement requirements of IFRS 5 do not apply to regulatory deferral account balances and therefore amounts disclosed in respect of discontinued operations and disposal groups will need to exclude related IFRS 14 balances.

- IFRS 10 *Consolidated financial statements* and IAS 28 *Investments in associates and joint ventures* – the entity's accounting policies in respect of regulatory deferral account balances must be applied in its consolidated financial statements and in accounting for investments in associates and joint ventures, notwithstanding that its investees may not have recognised regulatory deferral accounts in their financial statements.

Disclosure

The disclosure objectives of the standard are to identify clearly the nature of, and risks associated with, the rate regulation. Information should be disclosed regarding the rate-setting process, the identity of the regulator and risks and uncertainties associated with the deferral account balances. Disclosures also allow users to assess the effects of rate regulation on the entity's financial statements.

Conceptual framework for financial reporting

2

1 The need for a conceptual framework

A **conceptual framework**, in the field we are concerned with, is a statement of generally accepted theoretical principles which form the frame of reference for financial reporting. These theoretical principles provide the basis for the development of new accounting standards and the evaluation of those already in existence.

Although it is theoretical in nature, a conceptual framework for financial reporting has highly practical final aims.

The **danger of not having a conceptual framework** is demonstrated in the way some countries' standards have developed over recent years; standards tend to be produced in a **haphazard and fire-fighting way**. Where an agreed framework exists, the standard-setting body acts as an architect or designer, rather than a fire-fighter, building accounting rules on the foundation of sound, agreed basic principles.

The lack of a conceptual framework also means that fundamental principles are tackled more than once in different standards, thereby producing **contradictions** and **inconsistencies** in basic concepts. This leads to ambiguity and it affects the true and fair concept of financial reporting.

Another problem with the lack of a conceptual framework has become apparent in the USA. The large number of highly detailed standards produced by the Financial Accounting Standards Board (FASB) has created a financial reporting environment governed by **specific rules rather than general principles**. This would be avoided if a cohesive set of principles were in place.

A conceptual framework can also bolster standard-setters **against political pressure** from various 'lobby groups' and interested parties. Such pressure would only prevail if it was acceptable under the conceptual framework.

Advantages and disadvantages of a conceptual framework

Advantages

(a) The situation is **avoided** whereby standards are being developed on a **patchwork** basis, where a particular accounting problem is recognised as having emerged, and resources were then channelled into standardising accounting practice in that area, without regard to whether that particular issue was necessarily the most important issue remaining at that time without standardisation.

(b) As stated above, the development of certain standards (particularly national standards) have been subject to considerable political interference from interested parties. Where there is a conflict of interest between user groups on which policies to choose, policies deriving from a conceptual framework will be **less open** to criticism that the standard-setter buckled to **external pressure**.

(c) Some standards may concentrate on the **statement of profit or loss** whereas some may concentrate on the **valuation of net assets** (statement of financial position).

Disadvantages

(a) Financial statements are intended for a variety of users, and it is not certain that a single conceptual framework can be devised which will suit all users.

(b) Given the diversity of user requirements, there may be a need for a variety of accounting standards, each produced for a different purpose (and with different concepts as a basis).

(c) It is not clear that a conceptual framework makes the task of preparing and then implementing standards any easier than without a framework.

2 The IASB Conceptual Framework

The IASB *Framework for the Preparation and Presentation of Financial Statements* was produced in 1989 and is gradually being replaced by the new *Conceptual Framework for Financial Reporting*. This is the result of an IASB/FASB joint project, which was being carried out in phases; however, this ceased in 2010 due to other priorities within the organisations. Since 2012, the IASB has reactivated the programme but is working alone to consider the remaining elements of the *Conceptual Framework*.

The first phase, comprising Chapters 1 and 3, was published in September 2010. Chapter 2, entitled 'The reporting entity', has not yet been published. The current version of the Conceptual Framework includes the remaining chapters of the 1989 Framework as Chapter 4.

The *Conceptual Framework for Financial Reporting* is currently as follows:

In 2015, two Exposure Drafts (ED/2015/3 *Conceptual Framework for Financial Reporting* and ED/2015/4 *Updating References to the Conceptual Framework*) were published. These covered reviews of the following key areas:

- Elements of the financial statements
- The reporting entity
- Presentation
- Disclosure

No formal changes have been made to the *Conceptual Framework* as a result of these exposure drafts as the IASB is reviewing the comments at this time.

The Introduction to the *Conceptual Framework* points out the fundamental reason why financial statements are produced worldwide, ie to **satisfy the requirements of external users**, but that practice varies due to the individual pressures in each country. These pressures may be social, political, economic or legal, but they result in variations in practice from country to country, including the form of statements, the definition of their component parts (assets, liabilities etc), the criteria for recognition of items and both the scope and disclosure of financial statements.

It is these differences which the IASB wishes to narrow by **harmonising** all aspects of financial statements, including the regulations governing their accounting standards and their preparation and presentation.

The preface emphasises the way **financial statements are used to make economic decisions** and thus financial statements should be prepared to this end. The types of economic decisions for which financial statements are likely to be used include the following:

- Decisions to buy, hold or sell equity investments
- Assessment of management stewardship and accountability
- Assessment of the entity's ability to pay employees
- Assessment of the security of amounts lent to the entity
- Determination of taxation policies
- Determination of distributable profits and dividends
- Inclusion in national income statistics
- Regulations of the activities of entities

Any additional requirements imposed by **national governments** for their own purposes should not affect financial statements produced for the benefit of other users.

The *Conceptual Framework* recognises that financial statements can be prepared using a **variety of models**. Although the most common is based on historical cost and a nominal unit of currency (ie pound sterling, US dollar), the *Conceptual Framework* can be applied to financial statements prepared under a range of models.

Purpose and status

The Introduction gives a list of the purposes of the *Conceptual Framework* (IASB, 2010).

(a) To assist the Board in the **development of future IFRSs** and in its review of existing IFRSs.

(b) To assist the Board in **promoting harmonisation** of regulations, accounting standards and procedures relating to the presentation of financial statements by providing a basis for reducing the number of alternative accounting treatments permitted by IFRSs.

(c) To assist **national standard-setting bodies** in developing national standards.

(d) To assist **preparers of financial statements** in applying IFRSs and in dealing with topics that have yet to form the subject of an IFRS.

(e) To assist **auditors** in forming an opinion as to whether financial statements comply with IFRSs.

(f) To assist **users of financial statements** in interpreting the information contained in financial statements prepared in compliance with IFRSs.

(g) To provide those who are interested in the work of the IASB with **information** about its approach to the formulation of IFRSs.

The *Conceptual Framework* is not an IFRS and so does not overrule any individual IFRS. In the (rare) case of conflict between an IFRS and the *Conceptual Framework*, the **IFRS will prevail**.

Scope

The *Conceptual Framework* deals with:

(a) The **objective** of financial statements

(b) The **qualitative characteristics** that determine the usefulness of information in financial statements

(c) The **definition, recognition and measurement** of the elements from which financial statements are constructed

(d) Concepts of **capital and capital maintenance**

Users and their information needs

Users of accounting information consist of investors, employees, lenders, suppliers and other trade creditors, customers, government and their agencies and the public. Their needs are as follows.

(a) **Investors** are the providers of risk capital.

    (i) Information is required to help make a decision about buying or selling shares, taking up a rights issue and voting.

    (ii) Investors must have information about the level of dividend, past, present and future and any changes in share price.

    (iii) Investors will also need to know whether the management has been running the company efficiently.

    (iv) As well as the position indicated by the financial statements and earnings per share (EPS), investors will want to know about the liquidity position of the company, the company's future prospects, and how the company's shares compare with those of its competitors.

(b) **Employees** need information about the security of employment and future prospects for jobs in the company, and to help with collective pay bargaining.

(c) **Lenders** need information to help them decide whether to lend to a company. They will also need to check that the value of any security remains adequate, that the interest repayments are secure, that the cash is available for redemption at the appropriate time and that any financial restrictions (such as maximum debt/equity ratios) have not been breached.

(d) **Suppliers** need to know whether the company will be a good customer and pay its debts.

(e) **Customers** need to know whether the company will be able to continue producing and supplying goods.

(f) **Government's** interest in a company may be one of creditor or customer, as well as being specifically concerned with compliance with tax and company law, ability to pay tax and the general contribution of the company to the economy.

(g) The **public** at large would wish to have information for all the reasons mentioned above, but it could be suggested that it would be impossible to provide general purpose accounting information which was specifically designed for the needs of the public.

Financial statements cannot meet all these users' needs, but financial statements which meet the **needs of investors** (providers of risk capital) will meet most of the needs of other users.

The *Conceptual Framework* emphasises that the preparation and presentation of financial statements is primarily the **responsibility of an entity's management**. Management also has an interest in the information appearing in financial statements.

3 The objective of general purpose financial reporting

The Conceptual Framework states that:

> 'The objective of general purpose financial reporting is to provide information about the reporting entity that is useful to existing and potential investors, lenders and other creditors in making decisions about providing resources to the entity.' (IASB, 2010: p.7)

These users need information about:

- The **economic resources of the entity**
- The **claims against the entity**
- Changes in the entity's **economic resources and claims**

Information about the entity's **economic resources and the claims against it** helps users to assess the entity's liquidity and solvency and its likely needs for additional financing.

Information about a reporting entity's financial performance (the **changes in its economic resources and claims**) helps users to understand the return that the entity has produced on its economic resources. This is an indicator of how efficiently and effectively management has used the resources of the entity and is helpful in predicting future returns.

The *Conceptual Framework* makes it clear that this information should be prepared on an **accruals basis**.

> **Accruals basis.** The effects of transactions and other events are recognised when they occur (and not as cash or its equivalent is received or paid) and they are recorded in the accounting records and reported in the financial statements of the periods to which they relate. *(Conceptual Framework)*

Financial statements prepared under the accruals basis show users past transactions involving cash and also obligations to pay cash in the future and resources which represent cash to be received in the future.

Information about a reporting entity's cash flows during a period also helps users assess the entity's **ability to generate future net cash inflows** and gives users a better understanding of its operations.

4 Underlying assumption

> Going concern is the underlying assumption in preparing financial statements.

Going concern

> **Going concern.** The entity is normally viewed as a going concern, that is, as continuing in operation for the foreseeable future. It is assumed that the entity has neither the intention nor the necessity of liquidation or of curtailing materially the scale of its operations. *(Conceptual Framework)*

It is assumed that the entity has no intention to liquidate or curtail major operations. If it did, then the financial statements would be prepared on a **different (disclosed) basis.**

5 Qualitative characteristics of useful financial information

> **Qualitative characteristics.** The attributes that make financial information useful to users. *(Conceptual Framework)*

Chapter 3 of the *Conceptual Framework* distinguishes between **fundamental** and **enhancing** qualitative characteristics, for analysis purposes. **Fundamental** qualitative characteristics distinguish useful financial reporting information from information that is not useful or misleading. **Enhancing** qualitative characteristics distinguish more useful information from less useful information.

The two fundamental qualitative characteristics are **relevance** and **faithful representation**.

Relevance

> **Relevance.** Relevant information is capable of making a difference in the decisions made by users. It is capable of making a difference in decisions in decisions if it has **predictive value, confirmatory value** or both. *(Conceptual Framework)*

The relevance of information is affected by its **nature** and its **materiality**.

> **Materiality.** Information is material if omitting it or misstating it could influence decisions that users make on the basis of financial information about a specific reporting entity. *(Conceptual Framework)*

Faithful representation

> **Faithful representation.** Financial reports represent **economic phenomena** in words and numbers. To be useful, financial information must not only represent relevant phenomena but must **faithfully represent** the phenomena that it purports to represent. *(Conceptual Framework)*

To be a faithful representation information must be **complete, neutral** and **free from error**.

A **complete** depiction includes all information necessary for a user to understand the phenomenon being depicted, including all necessary descriptions and explanations.

A **neutral** depiction is without bias in the selection or presentation of financial information. This means that information must not be manipulated in any way in order to influence the decisions of users.

Free from error means there are no errors or omissions in the description of the phenomenon and no errors made in the process by which the financial information was produced. It does not mean that no inaccuracies can arise, particularly where estimates have to be made.

Substance over form

This is **not a separate qualitative characteristic** under the *Conceptual Framework*. The IASB says that to do so would be redundant because it is **implied in faithful representation**. Faithful representation of a transaction is only possible if it is accounted for according to its **substance and economic reality**.

Enhancing qualitative characteristics

Comparability

> **Comparability.** Comparability is the qualitative characteristic that enables users to identify and understand similarities in, and differences among, items. Information about a reporting entity is more useful if it can be compared with similar information about other entities and with similar information about the same entity for another period or date. *(Conceptual Framework)*

Consistency, although related to comparability, **is not the same**. It refers to the use of the same methods for the same items (ie consistency of treatment) either from period to period within a reporting entity or in a single period across entities.

The **disclosure of accounting policies** is particularly important here. Users must be able to distinguish between different accounting policies in order to be able to make a valid comparison of similar items in the accounts of different entities.

Comparability is **not the same as uniformity**. Entities should change accounting policies if those policies become inappropriate.

Corresponding information for preceding periods should be shown to enable comparison over time.

Verifiability

Verifiability. Verifiability helps assure users that information faithfully represents the economic phenomena it purports to represent. It means that different knowledgeable and independent observers could reach consensus that a particular depiction is a faithful representation. *(Conceptual Framework)*

Timeliness

Timeliness. Timeliness means having information available to decision-makers in time to be capable of influencing their decisions. Generally, the older information is the less useful it is. *(Conceptual Framework)*

Information may become less useful if there is a delay in reporting it. There is a **balance between timeliness and the provision of reliable information**.

If information is reported on a timely basis when not all aspects of the transaction are known, it may not be complete or free from error.

Conversely, if every detail of a transaction is known, it may be too late to publish the information because it has become irrelevant. The overriding consideration is how best to satisfy the economic decision-making needs of the users.

Understandability

Understandability. Classifying, characterising and presenting information clearly and concisely makes it understandable. *(Conceptual Framework)*

Financial reports are prepared for users who have a reasonable knowledge of business and economic activities and who review and analyse the information diligently. Some phenomena are inherently complex and cannot be made easy to understand. Excluding information on those phenomena might make the information easier to understand, but without it those reports would be incomplete and therefore misleading. Therefore matters should not be left out of financial statements simply due to their difficulty as even well-informed and diligent users may sometimes need the aid of an advisor to understand information about complex economic phenomena.

The cost constraint on useful financial reporting

This is a pervasive constraint, not a qualitative characteristic. When information is provided, its benefits must exceed the costs of obtaining and presenting it. This is a **subjective area** and there are other difficulties: others, not the intended users, may gain a benefit; also the cost may be paid by someone other than the users. It is therefore difficult to apply a cost-benefit analysis, but preparers and users should be aware of the constraint.

6 The elements of financial statements

Transactions and other events are grouped together in broad classes and in this way their financial effects are shown in the financial statements. These broad classes are the elements of financial statements. The *Conceptual Framework* lays out these elements as follows.

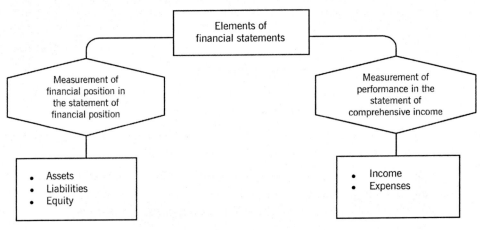

A process of **sub-classification** then takes place for presentation in the financial statements, eg assets are classified by their nature or function in the business to show information in the best way for users to take economic decisions.

Financial position

We need to define the three terms listed under this heading above.

> **Asset.** A resource controlled by an entity as a result of past events and from which future economic benefits are expected to flow to the entity.
>
> **Liability.** A present obligation of the entity arising from past events, the settlement of which is expected to result in an outflow from the entity of resources embodying economic benefits.
>
> **Equity.** The residual interest in the assets of the entity after deducting all its liabilities. *(Conceptual Framework)*

These definitions are important, but they do not cover the **criteria for recognition** of any of these items. This means that the definitions may include items which would not actually be recognised in the financial statements because they fail to satisfy recognition criteria particularly, as we will see below, the **probable flow of any economic benefit** to or from the business.

Whether an item satisfies any of the definitions above will depend on the **substance and economic reality** of the transaction, not merely its legal form.

Performance

Profit is used as a **measure of performance**, or as a basis for other measures (eg EPS). It depends directly on the measurement of income and expenses, which in turn depend (in part) on the concepts of capital and capital maintenance adopted.

The elements of income and expense are therefore defined.

> **Income.** Increases in economic benefits during the accounting period in the form of inflows or enhancements of assets or decreases of liabilities that result in increases in equity, other than those relating to contributions from equity participants.

> **Expenses.** Decreases in economic benefits during the accounting period in the form of outflows or depletions of assets or incurrences of liabilities that result in decreases in equity, other than those relating to distributions to equity participants.

Both **revenue** and **gains** are included in the definition of income. **Revenue** arises in the course of ordinary activities of an entity. Gains include those arising on the disposal of non-current assets. The definition of income also includes **unrealised gains** such as gains on revaluation of marketable securities.

Part A 2: Conceptual framework for financial reporting

7 Recognition of the elements of financial statements

Items which meet the definition of assets or liabilities may still not be recognised in financial statements because they must also meet certain **recognition criteria**.

> **Recognition.** The process of incorporating in the financial statements an item that meets the definition of an element and satisfies the following criteria for recognition:
>
> (a) It is probable that any future economic benefit associated with the item will flow to or from the entity; and
>
> (b) The item has a cost or value that can be measured with reliability.
>
> *(Conceptual Framework)*

Regard must be given to **materiality**.

Probability of future economic benefits

Probability here means the **degree of uncertainty** that the future economic benefits associated with an item will flow to or from the entity. This must be judged on the basis of the **characteristics of the entity's environment** and the **evidence available** when the financial statements are prepared.

Reliability of measurement

The cost or value of an item, in many cases, **must be estimated**. The *Conceptual Framework* states, however, that the use of reasonable estimates is an essential part of the preparation of financial statements and does not undermine their reliability. Where no reasonable estimate can be made, the item should not be recognised, although its existence should be disclosed in the notes, or other explanatory material.

Items may still qualify for recognition **at a later date** due to changes in circumstances or subsequent events.

Recognition of items

We can summarise the recognition criteria for assets, liabilities, income and expenses, based on the definition of recognition given above.

Item	Recognised in	When
Asset	The statement of financial position	It is probable that the future economic benefits will flow to the entity and the asset has a cost or value that can be measured reliably
Liability	The statement of financial position	It is probable that an outflow of resources embodying economic benefits will result from the settlement of a present obligation and the amount at which the settlement will take place can be measured reliably
Income	The statement of profit or loss and other comprehensive income	An increase in future economic benefits related to an increase in an asset or a decrease of a liability has arisen that can be measured reliably
Expenses	The statement of profit or loss and other comprehensive income	A decrease in future economic benefits related to a decrease in an asset or an increase of a liability has arisen that can be measured reliably

8 Measurement of the elements of financial statements

Measurement. The process of determining the monetary amounts at which the elements of the financial statements are to be recognised and carried in the statement of financial position and statement of comprehensive income.

(Conceptual Framework)

This involves the selection of a particular **basis of measurement**. A number of these are used to different degrees and in varying combinations in financial statements. They include the following.

Historical cost. Assets are recorded at the amount of cash or cash equivalents paid or the fair value of the consideration given to acquire them at the time of their acquisition. Liabilities are recorded at the amount of proceeds received in exchange for the obligation, or in some circumstances (for example, income taxes), at the amounts of cash or cash equivalents expected to be paid to satisfy the liability in the normal course of business.

Current cost. The amount of cash or cash equivalents that would have to be paid if the same or an equivalent asset was acquired currently.

Realisable (settlement) value.

–   **Realisable value.** The amount of cash or cash equivalents that could currently be obtained by selling an asset in an orderly disposal

–   **Settlement value.** The undiscounted amounts of cash or cash equivalents expected to be paid to satisfy the liabilities in the normal course of business

Present value. A current estimate of the present discounted value of the future net cash flows in the normal course of business.   (*Conceptual Framework*)

Historical cost is the most commonly adopted measurement basis, but this is usually combined with other bases, eg inventory is carried at the lower of cost and net realisable value.

Part B

Single entity financial statements

Presentation of published financial statements

3

1 IAS 1: Presentation of financial statements

The main objective of IAS 1 is:

> 'to prescribe the basis for presentation of general purpose financial statements, in order to ensure comparability both with the entity's own financial statements of previous periods and with the financial statements of other entities.' (IAS 1: para. 1)

IAS 1 applies to all **general purpose financial statements** prepared in accordance with IFRS, ie those intended to meet the needs of users who are not in a position to demand reports tailored to their specific needs.

The **objective of financial statements** is to provide information about the financial position, performance and cash flows of an entity that is useful to a wide range of users in making economic decisions. They also show the result of **management stewardship** of the resources of the entity.

In order to fulfil this objective, financial statements must provide information about the following aspects of an entity's results:

- Assets
- Liabilities
- Equity
- Income and expenses (including gains and losses)
- Contributions by and distributions to owners in their capacity as owners
- Cash flows

This information, along with other information in the notes, assists users in predicting the entity's **future cash flows** and, in particular, their timing and certainty.

Responsibility for the preparation and presentation of an entity's financial statements rests with the **board of directors** (or equivalent).

Components of financial statements

A complete set of financial statements includes the following components.

- A statement of financial position as at the end of the reporting period

- A statement of profit or loss and other comprehensive income for the reporting period

- A statement of changes in equity for the reporting period

- A statement of cash flows for the reporting period

- Notes, comprising a summary of significant accounting policies and other explanatory information

- A statement of financial position as at the beginning of the earliest comparative period when an entity applies an accounting policy retrospectively or makes a retrospective restatement of items in its financial statements, or when it reclassifies items in its financial statements

In addition, IAS 1 encourages, but does not require, a **financial review** by management (which is not part of the financial statements), explaining the main features of the entity's performance and position, and the principal uncertainties it faces. The report may include a review of the following.

(a) **Factors/influences determining performance**: changes in the environment in which the entity operates, the entity's response to those changes and their effect, and the entity's policy for investment to maintain and enhance performance, including its dividend policy

(b) Entity's **sources of funding**, the policy on **gearing** and its **risk management policies**

(c) **Strengths and resources** of the entity whose value is not reflected in the statement of financial position under IFRSs

Entities are encouraged to produce any other reports and statements which may aid users.

Fair presentation and compliance with IFRS

Most importantly, financial statements should present fairly the financial position, financial performance and cash flows of an entity. **Compliance with IFRS** is presumed to result in financial statements that achieve a fair presentation.

The following points expand on this principle.

(a) **Compliance with IFRS** should be disclosed

(b) **All relevant IFRS** must be followed if compliance with IFRS is disclosed

(c)   Use of an **inappropriate accounting treatment** cannot be rectified either by disclosure of accounting policies or notes/explanatory material

IAS 1 (para. 15–19) states what is required for a fair presentation.

step 1	Selection and application of **accounting policies**
step 2	**Presentation of information** in a manner which provides relevant, reliable, comparable and understandable information
step 3	**Additional disclosures** where required

The IAS then goes on to consider certain important assumptions which underpin the preparation and presentation of financial statements, which we might call fundamental assumptions.

Going concern

> The entity is normally viewed as a **going concern**, that is, as continuing in operation for the foreseeable future. Financial statements are prepared on a going concern basis unless management intends to liquidate the entity or to cease trading.

This assumption is based on the notion that, when preparing a normal set of accounts, it is always expected that the business will **continue to operate** in approximately the same manner for the foreseeable future (at least the next 12 months should be considered). In particular, the entity will not go into liquidation or scale down its operations in a material way. The main significance of the going concern assumption is that the assets of the business **should not be valued at their 'break up' value**, which is the amount that they would sell for if they were sold off piecemeal and the business were thus broken up.

If the going concern assumption is not followed, that fact must be disclosed, together with:

- The **basis** on which the financial statements have been prepared
- The **reasons** why the entity is not considered to be a going concern

Accrual basis of accounting

> Accrual basis of accounting. Items are recognised as assets liabilities, equity, income and expenses when they satisfy the definition and recognition criteria for those elements in the *Framework*.   (*IAS 1: para. 28*)

Entities should prepare their financial statements on the basis that transactions are recorded in them, not as the cash is paid or received, but as the revenues or expenses are **earned or incurred** in the accounting period to which they relate.

According to the accrual assumption, then, in computing profit revenue earned must be matched against the expenditure incurred in earning it.

Consistency of presentation

To maintain consistency, the presentation and classification of items in the financial statements should **stay the same from one period to the next. There are two exceptions**.

(a) There is a significant change in the **nature of the operations** or a review of the financial statements presentation indicates a **more appropriate presentation**

(b) A change in presentation is **required by an IFRS**

Materiality and aggregation

All material items should be **disclosed** in the financial statements.

Amounts which are **immaterial** can be aggregated with amounts of a similar nature or function and need not be presented separately.

> **Materiality.** Omissions or misstatement of items are material if they could, individually or collectively, influence the economic decisions of users taken on the basis of the financial statements. Materiality depends on the size and nature of the omission or misstatement judged in the surrounding circumstances. The size or nature of the item, or a combination of both, could be the determining factor.
>
> *(IAS 1: para. 7)*

An error which is too trivial to affect anyone's understanding of the accounts is referred to as **immaterial**. In preparing accounts it is important to assess what is material and what is not, so that time and money are not wasted in the pursuit of excessive detail.

Determining whether or not an item is material is a very **subjective exercise**. There is no absolute measure of materiality. It is common to apply a convenient rule of thumb (for example to define material items as those with a value greater than 5% of the net profit disclosed by the accounts). But some items disclosed in accounts are regarded as particularly sensitive and even a very small misstatement of such an item would be regarded as a material error. An example in the accounts of a limited liability company might be the amount of remuneration paid to directors of the company.

The assessment of an item as material or immaterial may **affect its treatment in the accounts**. For example, the statement of profit or loss of a business will show the expenses incurred by the business grouped under suitable captions (heating and lighting expenses, rent and local taxes etc); but in the case of very small expenses it may be appropriate to lump them together under a caption such as 'sundry expenses', because a more detailed breakdown would be inappropriate for such immaterial amounts.

In assessing whether or not an item is material, it is not only the amount of the item which needs to be considered. The **context** is also important.

(a)   If a statement of financial position shows non-current assets of $2 million and inventories of $30,000 an error of $20,000 in the depreciation calculations might not be regarded as material, whereas an error of $20,000 in the inventory valuation probably would be. In other words, the total of which the erroneous item forms part must be considered.

(b)   If a business has a bank loan of $50,000 and a $55,000 balance on bank deposit account, it might well be regarded as a material misstatement if these two amounts were displayed on the statement of financial position as 'cash at bank $5,000'. In other words, incorrect presentation may amount to material misstatement even if there is no monetary error.

Users are assumed to have a personal knowledge of business and economic activities and accounting and a willingness to study the information with reasonable diligence.

Offsetting

IAS 1 does not allow **assets and liabilities to be offset** against each other unless such a treatment is required or permitted by another IFRS.

Income and expenses can be offset only when:

(a)   An IFRS requires/permits it; or

(b)   Gains, losses and related expenses arising from the same/similar transactions are not material (aggregate).

Comparative information

IAS 1 requires comparative information to be disclosed for the previous period for all **numerical information**, unless another IAS permits/requires otherwise. Comparatives should also be given in narrative information where helpful.

Comparatives should be **reclassified** when the presentation or classification of items in the financial statements is amended (see IAS 8: Chapter 6).

Disclosure of accounting policies

There should be a specific section for accounting policies in the notes to the financial statements and the following should be disclosed there:

(a)   **Measurement bases** used in preparing the financial statements

(b)   Each **specific accounting policy** necessary for a proper understanding of the financial statements

To be clear and understandable it is essential that financial statements should disclose the accounting policies used in their preparation. This is because **policies may vary**, not only from entity to entity, but also from country to country. As an aid to users, all the major accounting policies used should be disclosed in the same place.

2 Structure and content of financial statements

An amendment to IAS 1 was published in June 2011. This amendment changed the name of the full statement from 'statement of comprehensive income' to 'statement of profit or loss and other comprehensive income'. The statement down to 'Profit (loss) for the year', which had previously been referred to as the 'income statement', then became the 'statement of profit or loss'. We have used the revised terminology in this text, but you will still probably meet 'income statement' and 'statement of comprehensive income' in other publications or articles.

IAS 1 *Presentation of financial statements* gives substantial guidance on the form and content of published financial statements. The standard looks at the statement of financial position and statement of profit or loss and other comprehensive income (the statement of cash flows is covered by IAS 7). First of all, some general points are made about financial statements.

Profit or loss for the year

The statement of profit or loss and other comprehensive income is the most significant indicator of a company's financial performance. So it is important to ensure that it is not misleading.

IAS 1 stipulates that all items of income and expense recognised in a period shall be included in profit or loss unless a **Standard** or an **Interpretation** requires otherwise.

Circumstances where items may be excluded from profit or loss for the current year include the correction of errors and the effect of changes in accounting policies. These are covered in IAS 8.

How items are disclosed

IAS 1 specifies disclosures of certain items in certain ways.

- Some items must appear on the face of the statement of financial position or statement of profit or loss and other comprehensive income.

- Other items can appear in a **note to the financial statements** instead.

- **Recommended formats** are given which entities may or may not follow, depending on their circumstances.

Obviously, disclosures specified by **other standards** must also be made, and we will mention the necessary disclosures when we cover each statement in turn. Disclosures in both IAS 1 and other standards must be made either on the face of the statement or in the notes unless otherwise stated, ie disclosures cannot be made in an accompanying commentary or report.

Identification of financial statements

As a result of the above point, it is most important that entities **distinguish the financial statements** very clearly from any other information published with them. This is because all IFRSs/IASs apply **only** to the financial statements (ie the main statements and related notes), so readers of the annual report must be able to differentiate between the parts of the report which are prepared under IFRSs, and other parts which are not.

The entity should **identify each** financial statement and the notes very clearly. IAS 1 also requires disclosure of the following information in a prominent position. If necessary it should be repeated wherever it is felt to be of use to the reader in his understanding of the information presented.

- **Name** of the reporting entity (or other means of identification)

- Whether the accounts cover the **single entity** only or a group of entities

- The **date of the end of the reporting period** or the period covered by the financial statements (as appropriate)

- The **presentation currency**

- The **level of rounding** used in presenting amounts in the financial statements

Judgement must be used to determine the best method of presenting this information. In particular, the standard suggests that the approach to this will be very different when the financial statements are communicated electronically.

The **level of rounding** is important, as presenting figures in thousands or millions of units makes the figures more understandable. The level of rounding must be disclosed, however, and it should not obscure necessary details or make the information less relevant.

Reporting period

It is normal for entities to present financial statements **annually** and IAS 1 states that they should be prepared at least as often as this. If (unusually) the end of an entity's reporting period is changed, for whatever reason, the period for which the statements are presented will be less or more than one year. In such cases the entity should also disclose:

(a)   The **reason(s) why** a period other than one year is used; and

(b)   The fact that the comparative figures given **are not in fact comparable**.

For practical purposes, some entities prefer to use a period which **approximates to a year**, eg 52 weeks, and the IAS allows this approach as it will produce statements not materially different from those produced on an annual basis.

Timeliness

If the publication of financial statements is delayed too long after the reporting period, their usefulness will be severely diminished. The standard states that entities should be able to produce their financial statements **within six months** of the end of the reporting period. An entity with consistently complex operations cannot use this as a reason for its failure to report on a timely basis. Local legislation and market regulation imposes specific deadlines on certain entities.

3 Statement of financial position

IAS 1 discusses the distinction between current and non-current items in some detail, as we shall see in the next section. First of all we can look at the **suggested format** of the statement of financial position (given in an appendix to the standard) and then look at further disclosures required.

Statement of financial position example

The example given by IAS 1 is as follows.

XYZ GROUP – STATEMENT OF FINANCIAL POSITION AT 31 DECEMBER

	20X9 $'000	20X8 $'000
Assets		
Non-current assets		
Property, plant and equipment	350,700	360,020
Goodwill	80,800	91,200
Other intangible assets	227,470	227,470
Investments in associates	100,150	110,770
Investments in equity instruments	142,500	156,000
	901,620	945,460

	20X9 $'000	20X8 $'000
Current assets		
Inventories	135,230	132,500
Trade receivables	91,600	110,800
Other current assets	25,650	12,540
Cash and cash equivalents	312,400	322,900
	564,880	578,740
Total assets	1,466,500	1,524,200
Equity and liabilities		
Equity attributable to owners of the parent		
Share capital	650,000	600,000
Retained earnings	243,500	161,700
Other components of equity	10,200	21,200
	903,700	782,900
Non-controlling interest	70,050	48,600
Total equity	973,750	831,500
Non-current liabilities		
Long-term borrowings	120,000	160,000
Deferred tax	28,800	26,040
Long-term provisions	28,850	52,240
Total non-current liabilities	117,650	238,280
Current liabilities		
Trade and other payables	115,100	187,620
Short-term borrowings	150,000	200,000
Current portion of long-term borrowings	10,000	20,000
Current tax payable	35,000	42,000
Short-term provisions	5,000	4,800
Total current liabilities	315,100	454,420
Total liabilities	492,750	692,700
Total equity and liabilities	1,466,500	1,524,200

IAS 1 (revised) specifies various items which must appear on the face of the statement of financial position as a minimum disclosure.

(a)   Property, plant and equipment
(b)   Investment property
(c)   Intangible assets
(d)   Financial assets (excluding amounts shown under (e), (h) and (i))
(e)   Investments accounted for using the equity method
(f)   Biological assets
(g)   Inventories
(h)   Trade and other receivables
(i)   Cash and cash equivalents
(j)   Assets classified as held for sale under IFRS 5
(k)   Trade and other payables
(l)   Provisions

(m)   Financial liabilities (other than (j) and (k))

(n)   Current tax liabilities and assets as in IAS 12

(o)   Deferred tax liabilities and assets

(p)   Liabilities included in disposal groups under IFRS 5

(q)   Non-controlling interests

(r)   Issued capital and reserves

Any **other line items,** headings or sub-totals should be shown on the face of the statement of financial position when it is necessary for an understanding of the entity's financial position.

The example shown above is for illustration only (although we will follow the format in this book). The IAS, however, does not prescribe the order or format in which the items listed should be presented. It simply states that they **must be presented separately** because they are so different in nature or function from each other.

Whether additional items are presented separately depends on judgements based on the assessment of the following factors.

(a)   **Nature and liquidity of assets and their materiality**. Thus goodwill and assets arising from development expenditure will be presented separately, as will monetary/non-monetary assets and current/non-current assets.

(b)   **Function within the entity**. Operating and financial assets, inventories, receivables and cash and cash equivalents are therefore shown separately.

(c)   **Amounts, nature and timing of liabilities**. Interest-bearing and non-interest-bearing liabilities and provisions will be shown separately, classified as current or non-current as appropriate.

The standard also requires separate presentation where **different measurement bases** are used for assets and liabilities which differ in nature or function. According to IAS 16, for example, it is permitted to carry certain items of property, plant and equipment at cost or at a revalued amount.

Information presented either on the face of the statement of financial position or by note

Further **sub-classification** of the line items listed above should be disclosed either on the face of the statement of financial position or in the notes. The classification will depend upon the nature of the entity's operations. As well as each item being sub-classified by its nature, any amounts payable to or receivable from any **group company or other related party** should also be disclosed separately.

The sub-classification details will in part depend on the requirements of IFRSs. The size, nature and function of the amounts involved will also be important and the factors listed above should be considered. **Disclosures** will vary from item to item and IAS 1 gives the following examples.

(a) **Property, plant and equipment** are classified by class as described in IAS 16, *Property, plant and equipment*.

(b) **Receivables** are analysed between amounts receivable from trade customers, other members of the group, receivables from related parties, prepayments and other amounts.

(c) **Inventories** are sub-classified, in accordance with IAS 2 *Inventories*, into classifications such as merchandise, production supplies, materials, work in progress and finished goods.

(d) **Provisions** are analysed showing separately provisions for employee benefit costs and any other items classified in a manner appropriate to the entity's operations.

(e) **Equity capital and reserves** are analysed showing separately the various classes of paid in capital, share premium and reserves.

The standard then lists some **specific disclosures** which must be made, either on the face of the statement of financial position or in the related notes.

(a) **Share capital disclosures** (for each class of share capital)

    (i) Number of shares authorised

    (ii) Number of shares issued and fully paid, and issued but not fully paid

    (iii) Par value per share, or that the shares have no par value

    (iv) Reconciliation of the number of shares outstanding at the beginning and at the end of the year

    (v) Rights, preferences and restrictions attaching to that class including restrictions on the distribution of dividends and the repayment of capital

    (vi) Shares in the entity held by the entity itself or by related group companies

    (vii) Shares reserved for issuance under options and sales contracts, including the terms and amounts

(b) Description of the nature and purpose of **each reserve** within owners' equity

Some types of entity have no share capital, eg partnerships. Such entities should disclose information which is **equivalent** to that listed above. This means disclosing the movement during the period in each category of equity interest and any rights, preferences or restrictions attached to each category of equity interest.

4 The current/non-current distinction

An entity must present **current** and **non-current** assets as separate classifications on the face of the statement of financial position. A presentation based on liquidity should only be used where it provides more relevant and reliable information, in which case all assets and liabilities must be presented broadly **in order of liquidity**.

In either case, the entity should disclose any portion of an asset or liability which is expected to be recovered or settled **after more than twelve months**. For example, for an amount receivable which is due in instalments over 18 months, the portion due after more than twelve months must be disclosed.

The IAS emphasises how helpful information on the **operating cycle** is to users of financial statements. Where there is a clearly defined operating cycle within which the entity supplies goods or services, then information disclosing those net assets that are continuously circulating as **working capital** is useful.

This distinguishes them from those net assets used in the long-term operations of the entity. Assets that are expected to be realised and liabilities that are due for settlement within the operating cycle are therefore highlighted.

The liquidity and solvency of an entity is also indicated by information about the **maturity dates** of assets and liabilities. IFRS 7 *Financial instruments: disclosures* requires disclosure of maturity dates of both financial assets and financial liabilities. (Financial assets include trade and other receivables; financial liabilities include trade and other payables.) In the case of non-monetary assets, eg inventories, such information is also useful.

Current assets

An asset should be classified as a **current asset** when it:

- Is expected to be realised in, or is held for sale or consumption in, the normal course of the entity's operating cycle; or

- Is held primarily for trading purposes or for the short-term and expected to be realised within twelve months of the end of the reporting period; or

- Is cash or a cash equivalent asset which is not restricted in its use.

All other assets should be classified as non-current assets.   (*IAS 1: para. 66*)

Non-current assets includes tangible, intangible, operating and financial assets of a long-term nature. Other terms with the same meaning can be used (eg 'fixed', 'long-term').

The term 'operating cycle' has been used several times above and the standard defines it as follows.

The operating cycle of an entity is the time between the acquisition of assets for processing and their realisation in cash or cash equivalents.   (*IAS 1: para. 68*)

Current assets therefore include inventories and trade receivables that are sold, consumed and realised as part of the normal operating cycle. **This is the case even where they are not expected to be realised within twelve months**.

Current assets will also include **marketable securities** if they are expected to be realised within twelve months after the reporting period. If expected to be realised later, they should be included in non-current assets.

Current liabilities

A liability should be classified as a **current liability** when it:

- Is expected to be settled in the normal course of the entity's operating cycle; or

- Is held primarily for the purpose of trading; or

- Is due to be settled within twelve months after the reporting period; or

- The entity does not have an unconditional right to defer settlement of the liability for at least twelve months after the reporting period.

All other liabilities should be classified as non-current liabilities. (*IAS 1: para. 69*)

The categorisation of current liabilities is very similar to that of current assets. Thus, some current liabilities are part of the **working capital** used in the normal operating cycle of the business (ie trade payables and accruals for employee and other operating costs). Such items will be classed as current liabilities **even where they are due to be settled more than twelve months after the end of the reporting period**.

There are also current liabilities which are not settled as part of the normal operating cycle, but which are due to be settled within twelve months of the end of the reporting period. These include bank overdrafts, income taxes, other non-trade payables and the current portion of interest-bearing liabilities. Any interest-bearing liabilities that are used to finance working capital on a long-term basis, and that are not due for settlement within twelve months, should be classed as **non-current liabilities**.

A **non-current financial liability** due to be **settled within twelve months** of the end of the reporting period should be classified as a **current liability**, even if an agreement to refinance, or to reschedule payments, on a long-term basis is completed after the end of the reporting period and before the financial statements are authorised for issue.

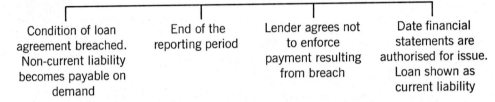

| End of the reporting period | Agreement to refinance on long-term basis | Date financial statements authorised for issue | Settlement date <12 months after end of the reporting period therefore current liability |

A **non-current financial liability** that is payable on **demand** because the entity **breached** a **condition** of its loan agreement should be classified as **current** at the end of the reporting period even if the **lender** has agreed **after the end of the reporting period**, and **before** the financial statements are **authorised for issue, not** to **demand payment** as a consequence of the breach.

| Condition of loan agreement breached. Non-current liability becomes payable on demand | End of the reporting period | Lender agrees not to enforce payment resulting from breach | Date financial statements are authorised for issue. Loan shown as current liability |

However, if the **lender** has **agreed** by the **end of the reporting period** to provide a **period of grace** ending **at least twelve months after the end of the reporting period** within which the entity can rectify the breach and during that time the lender cannot demand immediate repayment, the liability is classified as **non-current**.

5 Statement of profit or loss and other comprehensive income

IAS 1 allows income and expense items to be presented either:

(a)   In a single statement of profit or loss and other comprehensive income; or

(b)   In two statements: a separate statement of profit or loss and statement of other comprehensive income.

The format for a single statement of profit or loss and other comprehensive income is shown as follows in the standard. The section down to 'profit for the year' can be shown as a separate 'statement of profit or loss' with an additional 'statement of other comprehensive income'.

XYZ GROUP – STATEMENT OF PROFIT OR LOSS AND OTHER COMPREHENSIVE INCOME FOR THE YEAR ENDED 31 DECEMBER 20X7

	20X9 $'000	20X8 $'000
Revenue	390,000	355,000
Cost of sales	(245,000)	(230,000)
Gross profit	145,000	125,000
Other income	20,667	11,300
Distribution costs	(9,000)	(8,700)
Administrative expenses	(20,000)	(21,000)
Other expenses	(2,100)	(1,200)
Finance costs	(8,000)	(7,500)
Share of profit of associates	35,100	30,100
Profit before tax	161,667	128,000
Income tax expense	(40,417)	(32,000)
Profit for the year from continuing operations	121,250	96,000
Loss for the year from discontinued operations	–	(30,500)
Profit for the year	121,250	65,500
Other comprehensive income:		
Items that will not be reclassified to profit or loss:		
Gains on property revaluation	933	3,367
Investments in equity instruments	(24,000)	26,667
Actuarial gains (losses) on defined benefit pension plans	(667)	1,333
Share of gain(loss) on property revaluation of associates	400	(700)
Income tax relating to items that will not be reclassified	5,834	(7,667)
	(17,500)	23,000
Items that may be reclassified subsequently to profit or loss		
Exchange differences on translating foreign operations	3,934	9,467
Financial assets through other comprehensive income	1,400	1,200
Cash flow hedges	(667)	(4,000)
Income tax relating to items that may be reclassified	(1,167)	(1,667)
	3,500	5,000
Other comprehensive income for the year, net of tax	(14,000)	28,000
Total comprehensive income for the year	107,250	93,500
Profit attributable to:		
Owners of the parent	97,000	52,400
Non-controlling interest	24,250	13,100
	121,250	65,500
Total comprehensive income attributable to		
Owners of the parent	85,800	74,800
Non-controlling interest	21,450	18,700
	107,250	93,500
Earnings per share (in currency units)	0.46	0.30

Part B 3: Presentation of published financial statements

Companies are given the option of presenting this information in two statements as follows:

XYZ GROUP – STATEMENT OF PROFIT OR LOSS FOR THE YEAR ENDED 31 DECEMBER

	20X9 $'000	20X8 $'000
Revenue	390,000	355,000
Cost of sales	(245,000)	(230,000)
Gross profit	145,000	125,000
Other income	20,667	11,300
Distribution costs	(9,000)	(8,700)
Administrative expenses	(20,000)	(21,000)
Other expenses	(2,100)	(1,200)
Finance costs	(8,000)	(7,500)
Share of profit of associates	35,100	30,100
Profit before tax	161,667	128,000
Income tax expense	(40,417)	(32,000)
Profit for the year from continuing operations	121,250	96,000
Loss for the year from discontinued operations	–	(30,500)
Profit for the year	121,250	65,500
Profit attributable to:		
Owners of the parent	97,000	52,400
Non-controlling interest	24,250	13,100
	121,250	65,500

XYZ GROUP – STATEMENT OF PROFIT OR LOSS AND OTHER COMPREHENSIVE INCOME FOR THE YEAR ENDED 31 DECEMBER

	20X9 $'000	20X8 $'000
Profit for the year	121,250	65,500
Other comprehensive income:		
Items that will not be reclassified to profit or loss:		
Gains on property revaluation	933	3,367
Investments in equity instruments	(24,000)	26,667
Actuarial gains (losses) on defined benefit pension plans	(667)	1,333
Share of gain(loss) on property revaluation of associates	400	(700)
Income tax relating to items that will not be reclassified	5,834	(7,667)
	(17,500)	23,000
Items that may be reclassified to profit or loss:		
Exchange differences on translating foreign operations	5,334	10,667
Cash flow hedges	(667)	(4,000)
Income tax relating to items that may be reclassified	(1,167)	(1,667)
	3,500	5,000
Other comprehensive income for the year, net of tax	(14,000)	28,000
Total comprehensive income for the year	107,250	93,500
Total comprehensive income attributable to		
Owners of the parent	85,800	74,800
Non-controlling interest	21,450	18,700
	107,250	93,500

6 Statement of profit or loss

There are two methods of presenting information in the statement of profit or loss.

Nature of expense method

Expenses are not reallocated amongst various functions within the entity, but are aggregated in the statement of profit or loss **according to their nature** (eg purchase of materials, depreciation, wages and salaries, transport costs). This is by far the easiest method, especially for smaller entities.

Function of expense/cost of sales method

This method is more widely used. Expenses are classified according to their function as part of cost of sales, distribution or administrative activities. This method often gives **more relevant** information for users, but the allocation of expenses by function requires the use of judgement and can be arbitrary. Consequently, perhaps, when this method is used, entities should disclose **additional** information on the nature of expenses, including staff costs, and depreciation and amortisation expense.

Which of the above methods is chosen by an entity will depend on historical and industry factors, and also the **nature of the organisation**. Under each method, there should be given an indication of costs which are likely to vary (directly or indirectly) with the level of sales or production. The choice of method should fairly reflect the main elements of the entity's performance.

Examples of separate statements of profit or loss

XYZ GROUP STATEMENT OF PROFIT OR LOSS FOR THE YEAR ENDED 31 DECEMBER

Illustrating the classification of expenses by function

	20X9 $'000	20X8 $'000
Revenue	X	X
Cost of sales	(X)	(X)
Gross profit	X	X
Other income	X	X
Distribution costs	(X)	(X)
Administrative expenses	(X)	(X)
Other expenses	(X)	(X)
Finance costs	(X)	(X)
Share of profit of associates	X	X
Profit before tax	X	X
Income tax expense	(X)	(X)
Profit for the year	X	X
Profit attributable to:		
Owners of the parent	X	X
Non-controlling interest	X	X
	X	X

Illustrating the classification of expenses by nature

	20X9 $'000	20X8 $'000
Revenue	X	X
Other operating income	X	X
Changes in inventories of finished goods and work in progress	(X)	X
Work performed by the entity and capitalized	X	X
Raw material and consumables used	(X)	(X)
Employee benefits expense	(X)	(X)
Depreciation and amortisation expense	(X)	(X)
Impairment of property, plant and equipment	(X)	(X)
Other expenses	(X)	(X)
Finance costs	(X)	(X)
Share of profit of associates	X	X
Profit before tax	X	X
Income tax expense	(X)	(X)
Profit for the year	X	X
Profit attributable to:		
Owners of the parent	X	X
Non-controlling interest	X	X
	X	X

Information presented in the statement of profit or loss

The standard lists the following as the minimum to be disclosed on the face of the statement of profit or loss.

(a) Revenue

(b) Finance costs

(c) Share of profits and losses of associates and joint ventures accounted for using the equity method

(d) Tax expense

(e) A single amount comprising the post-tax profit or loss of discontinued operations and the post-tax gain or loss recognised on measurement to fair value less costs to sell or on disposal of the assets of the discontinued operation

(f) Profit or loss

The following items must be disclosed in the statement as allocations of profit or loss for the period.

(a) Profit or loss attributable to non-controlling interest
(b) Profit or loss attributable to owners of the parent

Income and expense items can be offset when, and only when:

(a)   It is permitted or required by an IFRS; or

(b)   Gains, losses and related expenses arising from the same or similar transactions and events are immaterial, in which case they can be aggregated.

Information presented either in the statement or in the notes

An analysis of expenses must be shown either in the statement of profit or loss (as above, which is encouraged by the standard) or by note, using a classification based on either the nature of the expenses or their function. This **sub-classification of expenses** indicates a range of components of financial performance; these may differ in terms of stability, potential for gain or loss and predictability.

Dividends

IAS 1 also requires disclosure of the amount of **dividends per share** for the period covered by the financial statements. This shown on the face of the statement of profit or loss.

Further points

(a)   All requirements previously set out in other Standards for the presentation of particular line items in the statement of financial position and statement of profit or loss are now dealt with in IAS 1. These line items are: biological assets; liabilities and assets for current tax and deferred tax; and pre-tax gain or loss recognised on the disposal of assets or settlement of liabilities attributable to discontinued operations.

(b)   An entity must disclose, in the summary of significant accounting policies and/or other notes, the **judgements** made by management in **applying** the **accounting policies** that have the **most** significant effect on the amounts of items recognised in the financial statements.

(c)   An entity must disclose in the notes information regarding **key assumptions** about the **future**, and other sources of **measurement uncertainty**, that have a significant **risk of** causing a **material adjustment** to the carrying amounts of assets and liabilities within the **next financial year**.

7 Changes in equity

This is the format of the statement of changes in equity

XYZ GROUP – STATEMENT OF CHANGES IN EQUITY FOR THE YEAR ENDED 31 DECEMBER 20X9

	Share capital	Retained earnings	Equity instruments	Revaluation surplus	Total	Non-controlling interest	Total equity
	$'000	$'000	$'000	$'000	$'000	$'000	$'000
Balance at 1 January 20X8	600,000	118,100	1,600	–	719,700	29,800	749,500
Changes in accounting policy	–	400	–	–	400	100	500
Restated balance	600,000	118,500	1,600	–	720,100	29,900	750,000
Changes in equity							
Dividends	–	(10,000)	–	–	(10,000)	–	(10,000)
Total comprehensive income for the year	–	53,200	16,000	1,600	70,800	18,700	89,500
Balance at 31 December 20X8	600,000	161,700	17,600	1,600	780,900	48,600	829,500
Changes in equity for 20X9							
Issue of share capital	50,000	–	–	–	50,000	–	50,000
Dividends	–	(15,000)	–	–	(15,000)	–	(15,000)
Total comprehensive income for the year	–	96,600	(14,400)	800	83,000	21,450	104,450
Transfer to retained earnings	–	200	–	(200)	–	–	–
Balance at 31 December 20X9	650,000	243,500	3,200	2,200	898,900	70,050	968,950

Note that where there has been a change of accounting policy necessitating a retrospective restatement, the adjustment is disclosed for each period. So, rather than just showing an adjustment to the balance b/f on 1.1.X9, the balances for 20X8 are restated.

Gains and losses on cash flow hedges or on the translation of foreign operations would be shown in additional columns.

8 Notes to the financial statements

The notes to the financial statements will **amplify** the information given in the statement of financial position, statement of profit or loss and other comprehensive income, statement of cash flows and statement of changes in equity. We have already noted above the information which the IAS allows to be shown by note rather than in the statements. To some extent, then, the contents of the notes will be determined by the level of detail shown on the **face of the statements**.

The notes to the financial statements should perform the following functions.

(a) Provide information about the **basis on which the financial statements were prepared** and which specific accounting policies were chosen and applied to significant transactions/events

(b) Disclose any information, not shown elsewhere in the financial statements, which is required by **IFRSs**

(c) Show any additional information that is relevant to understanding which is not shown elsewhere in the financial statements

The way the notes are presented is important. They should be given in a **systematic manner** and **cross referenced** back to the related figure(s) in the statement of financial position, statement of profit or loss and other comprehensive income, statement of cash flows or statement of changes in equity.

Notes to the financial statements will amplify the information shown therein by giving the following.

(a) More **detailed analysis** or breakdowns of figures in the statements
(b) **Narrative information** explaining figures in the statements
(c) **Additional information**, eg contingent liabilities and commitments

IAS 1 suggests a **certain order** for notes to the financial statements. This will assist users when comparing the statements of different entities.

(a) Statement of **compliance** with IFRSs

(b) Statement of the **measurement basis** (bases) and accounting policies applied

(c) **Supporting information** for items presented in each financial statement in the same order as each line item and each financial statement is presented

(d) Other disclosures, eg:

(i) Contingent liabilities, commitments and other financial disclosures
(ii) Non-financial disclosures

The order of specific items may have to be varied occasionally, but a systematic structure is still required.

Presentation of accounting policies

The accounting policies section should describe the following.

(a)   The **measurement basis** (or bases) used in preparing the financial statements

(b)   The **other accounting policies** used, as required for a proper understanding of the financial statements

This information may be shown in the notes or sometimes as a **separate component** of the financial statements.

The information on measurement bases used is obviously fundamental to an understanding of the financial statements. Where **more than one basis is used**, it should be stated to which assets or liabilities each basis has been applied.

Other disclosures

An entity must disclose in the notes:

(a)   The amount of dividends proposed or declared before the financial statements were authorised for issue but not recognised as a distribution to owners during the period, and the amount per share

(b)   The amount of any cumulative preference dividends not recognised

IAS 1 ends by listing some **specific disclosures** which will always be required if they are not shown elsewhere in the financial statements.

(a)   The domicile and legal form of the entity, its country of incorporation and the address of the registered office (or, if different, principal place of business)

(b)   A description of the nature of the entity's operations and its principal activities

(c)   The name of the parent entity and the ultimate parent entity of the group

9 Small and medium-sized entities (SMEs)

It could be argued that company financial statements should be of two types:

(a)   'Simple' ones for small companies with fewer regulations and disclosure requirements

(b)   'Complicated' ones for larger companies with extensive and detailed requirements

This is sometimes called the **big GAAP/little GAAP** divide.

This has been an area of discussion in IFRS accounting for many years. Many jurisdictions have their own standard for small and medium sized entities which reduce the reporting requirements for these entities. There was no guidance on this area from the IASB until 2009.

IFRS for SMEs

In July 2009 the IASB published its *International Financial Reporting Standard for SMEs*. This was the result of a project going back to 2003 in which an Exposure Draft had been field tested with the participation of 116 small companies in 20 countries.

The final IFRS for SMEs is a stand-alone document – users do not need to refer back to the full IFRSs. It applies to unquoted entities. Many of the principles in full IFRS for recognising and measuring the elements of financial statements have been simplified and topics not relevant to SMEs have been omitted. Substantially fewer disclosures are required. To further reduce the reporting burden, revisions to the IFRS for SMEs will be limited to once every three years.

Omitted topics

- Earnings per share
- Interim financial reporting
- Segment reporting
- Special accounting for assets held for sale

There are some options available under full IFRS which are not included in the IFRS for SMEs. Some of these are:

- The revaluation model for PPE and intangible assets (now allowed by a specific amendment in 2014)
- The accounting policy choice between cost and fair value models for investment property
- The various options for treatment of government grants

Recognition and measurement

These are the main simplifications to the recognition and measurement principles in full IFRS:

- Recognition of investment property is to be measured at cost less depreciation and impairment separately on the face of the statement of financial position.

- **Goodwill** is amortised over its useful life or ten years, rather than being subjected to impairment reviews.

- **Investments in associates and joint ventures** can be measured at cost unless there is a published price quotation.

- **Research and development costs** must both be recognised as expenses.

- **Borrowing costs** must be recognised as expenses.

- **PPE and intangible assets** do not need an annual review as per IAS 16/IAS 38. A review is only required if indications suggest that useful life etc have changed.

- A number of changes to **defined benefit plans**:

  - All past service cost to be recognised immediately in profit or loss

  - All actuarial gains and losses to be recognised immediately either in profit or loss or other comprehensive income

  - The projected unit credit method to be used only if it can be done without undue cost or effort

- No separate **held-for-sale** classification as per IFRS 5. Instead, holding assets for sale will be treated as an impairment indicator.

- **Biological assets** are to be held at fair value through profit or loss only when fair value can be determined without undue cost or effort. Otherwise the cost-depreciation-impairment model is used.

- **Share-based payment** expense is measured at the directors' best estimate of fair value if market prices are not available.

[These issues are all covered according to full IFRS in the relevant chapters of this text.]

10 IAS 34: Interim financial reporting

Governments, stock exchanges and regulators may require entities whose shares or loan notes are publicly traded to publish interim financial reports.

The following definitions are used in IAS 34.

> **Interim period** is a financial reporting period shorter than a full financial year.
>
> **Interim financial report** means a financial report containing either a complete set of financial statements (as described in IAS 1) or a set of condensed financial statements (as described in this standard) for an interim period. *(IAS 34: para. 4)*

The standard does not make the preparation of interim financial reports **mandatory**, taking the view that this is a matter for governments, securities regulators, stock exchanges or professional accountancy bodies to decide within each country. The IASB does, however, strongly recommend to governments, etc, that interim financial reporting should be a requirement for companies whose equity or debt securities are **publicly traded**. The specific recommendations are that:

(a) An interim financial report should be produced by such companies for **at least the first six months of their financial year** (ie a half year financial report).

(b)   The report should be **available no later than 60 days** after the end of the interim period.

Thus, a company with a year ending 31 December would be required as a minimum to prepare an interim report for the half year to 30 June and this report should be available before the end of August.

Minimum components

The proposed standard specifies the minimum component elements of an interim financial report.

- Condensed statement of financial position
- Condensed statement of profit or loss and other comprehensive income
- Condensed statement of changes in equity
- Condensed statement of cash flows
- Selected note disclosures

The rationale for requiring only condensed statements and selected note disclosures is that entities need not duplicate information in their interim report that is contained in their report for the previous financial year. Interim statements should focus more on new events, activities and circumstances.

Form and content

Where **full financial statements** are given as interim financial statements, IAS 1 should be used as a guide, otherwise IAS 34 specifies minimum contents.

The **condensed statement of financial position** should include, as a minimum, each of the major components of assets, liabilities and equity as were in the statement of financial position at the end of the previous financial year, thus providing a summary of the economic resources of the entity and its financial structure.

The **condensed statement of profit or loss and other comprehensive income** should include, as a minimum, each of the component items of income and expense as are shown in profit or loss for the previous financial year, together with the earnings per share and diluted earnings per share.

The **condensed statement of cash flows** should show, as a minimum, the three major sub-totals of cash flow as required in statements of cash flows by IAS 7, namely: cash flows from operating activities, cash flows from investing activities and cash flows from financing activities.

The **condensed statement of changes in equity** should include, as a minimum, each of the major components of equity as were contained in the statement of changes in equity for the previous financial year of the entity.

Selected explanatory notes

IAS 34 states that **relatively minor changes** from the most recent annual financial statements need not be included in an interim report. However, the notes to interim report should include the following (unless the information is contained elsewhere in the report).

- A statement that the **same accounting policies and methods of computation** have been used for the interim statements as were used for the most recent annual financial statements. If not, the nature of the differences and their effect should be described. (The accounting policies for preparing the interim report should only differ from those used for the previous annual accounts in a situation where there has been a change in accounting policy since the end of the previous financial year, and the new policy will be applied for the annual accounts of the current financial period.)

- Explanatory comments on the **seasonality or 'cyclicality'** of operations in the interim period. For example, if a company earns most of its annual profits in the first half of the year, because sales are much higher in the first six months, the interim report for the first half of the year should explain this fact

- The **nature and amount** of items during the interim period affecting assets, liabilities, capital, net income or cash flows, that are unusual, due to their nature, incidence or size

- The **issue or repurchase** of equity or debt securities

- Nature and amount of any **changes in estimates** of amounts reported in an earlier interim report during the financial year, or in prior financial years if these affect the current interim period

- **Dividends paid** on ordinary shares and the dividends paid on other shares

- **Segmental results** for the business segments or geographical segments of the entity (see IFRS 8)

- Any **significant events since the end of the interim period**

- Effect of the acquisition or disposal of subsidiaries during the interim period

- Any significant change in a **contingent liability or a contingent asset** since the date of the last annual statement of financial position

The entity should also disclose the fact that the interim report has been produced in compliance with IAS 34 on interim financial reporting.

The following are examples of the types of disclosures required:

(a) Write-down of inventories to net realisable value and the reversal of such a write-down

(b) Recognition of a loss from the impairment of property, plant and equipment, intangible assets, or other assets, and the reversal of such an impairment loss

(c)   Reversal of any provisions for the costs of restructuring

(d)   Acquisitions and disposals of items of property, plant and equipment

(e)   Commitments for the purchase of property, plant and equipment

(f)   Litigation settlements

(g)   Corrections of fundamental errors in previously reported financial data

(h)   Any debt default or any breach of a debt covenant that has not been corrected subsequently

(i)   Related party transactions

Periods covered

The standard requires that interim financial reports should provide financial information for the following periods or as at the following dates.

- **Statement of financial position data** as at the end of the current interim period, and comparative data as at the end of the most recent financial year

- **Statement of profit or loss and other comprehensive income data** for the current interim period and cumulative data for the current year to date, together with comparative data for the corresponding interim period and cumulative figures for the previous financial year

- **Statement of cash flows data** should be cumulative for the current year to date, with comparative cumulative data for the corresponding interim period in the previous financial year

- **Data for the statement of changes in equity** should be for both the current interim period and for the year to date, together with comparative data for the corresponding interim period, and cumulative figures, for the previous financial year

Materiality

Materiality should be assessed in relation to the interim period financial data. It should be recognised that interim measurements **rely to a greater extent on estimates** than annual financial data.

Recognition and measurement principles

A large part of IAS 34 deals with recognition and measurement principles, and guidelines as to their practical application. The **guiding principle** is that an entity should use the **same recognition and measurement principles in its interim statements as it does in its annual financial statements**.

This means, for example, that a cost that would not be capitalised in the year-end statement of financial position should not be capitalised in the statement of financial position for an interim period. Similarly, an accrual for an item of income or expense for a transaction that has not yet occurred (or a deferral of an item of income or expense for a transaction that has already occurred) is inappropriate for interim reporting, just as it is for year-end reporting.

Applying this principle of recognition and measurement may result, in a subsequent interim period or at the year-end, in a remeasurement of amounts that were reported in a financial statement for a previous interim period. The nature and amount of any significant remeasurements should be disclosed.

Revenues received occasionally, seasonally or cyclically

Revenue that is received as an occasional item, or within a seasonal or cyclical pattern, should not be anticipated or deferred in interim financial statements, if it would be inappropriate to anticipate or defer the revenue for the annual financial statements. In other words, the principles of revenue recognition should be applied consistently to the interim reports and year-end reports.

Costs incurred unevenly during the financial year

These should only be anticipated or deferred (ie treated as accruals or prepayments) if it would be appropriate to anticipate or defer the expense in the annual financial statements. For example, it would be appropriate to anticipate a cost for property rental where the rental is paid in arrears, but it would be inappropriate to anticipate part of the cost of a major advertising campaign later in the year, for which no expenses have yet been incurred.

The standard goes on, in an appendix, to deal with **specific applications** of the recognition and measurement principle. Some of these examples are explained below, by way of explanation and illustration.

Payroll taxes or insurance contributions paid by employers

In some countries these are assessed on an annual basis, but paid at an uneven rate during the course of the year, with a large proportion of the taxes being paid in the early part of the year, and a much smaller proportion paid later on in the year. In this situation, it would be appropriate to use an estimated average annual tax rate for the year in an interim statement, not the actual tax paid. This treatment is appropriate because it reflects the fact that the taxes are assessed on an annual basis, even though the payment pattern is uneven.

Cost of a planned major periodic maintenance or overhaul

The cost of such an event later in the year must not be anticipated in an interim financial statement unless there is a legal or constructive obligation to carry out this work. The fact that a maintenance or overhaul is planned and is carried out annually is not of itself sufficient to justify anticipating the cost in an interim financial report.

Other planned but irregularly-occurring costs

Similarly, these costs such as charitable donations or employee training costs, should not be accrued in an interim report. These costs, even if they occur regularly and are planned, are nevertheless discretionary.

A year-end bonus should not be provided for in an interim financial statement unless there is a constructive obligation to pay a year-end bonus (eg a contractual obligation, or a regular past practice) and the size of the bonus can be reliably measured.

The same principle applies to holiday pay. If holiday pay is an enforceable obligation on the employer, then any unpaid accumulated holiday pay may be accrued in the interim financial report.

Non-mandatory intangible assets

The entity might incur expenses during an interim period on items that might or will generate non-monetary intangible assets. IAS 38 *Intangible assets* requires that costs to generate non-monetary intangible assets (eg development expenses) should be recognised as an expense when incurred unless the costs form part of an identifiable intangible asset. Costs that were initially recognised as an expense cannot subsequently be treated instead as part of the cost of an intangible asset. IAS 34 states that interim financial statements should adopt the same approach. This means that it would be inappropriate in an interim financial statement to 'defer' a cost in the expectation that it will eventually be part of a non-monetary intangible asset that has not yet been recognised: such costs should be treated as an expense in the interim statement.

Depreciation

Depreciation should only be charged in an interim statement on non-current assets that have been acquired, not on non-current assets that will be acquired later in the financial year.

Tax on income

An entity will include an expense for income tax (tax on profits) in its interim statements. The tax rate to use should be the estimated average annual tax rate for the year. For example, suppose that in a particular jurisdiction, the rate of tax on company profits is 30% on the first $200,000 of profit and 40% on profits above $200,000. Now suppose that a company makes a profit of $200,000 in its first half year, and expects to make $200,000 in the second half year. The rate of tax to be applied in the interim financial report should be 35%, not 30%, ie the expected average rate of tax for the year as a whole. This approach is appropriate because income tax on company profits is charged on an annual basis, and an effective annual rate should therefore be applied to each interim period.

As another illustration, suppose a company earns pre-tax income in the first quarter of the year of $30,000, but expects to make a loss of $10,000 in each of the next three quarters, so that net income before tax for the year is zero. Suppose also that the rate of tax is 30%. In this case, it would be inappropriate to anticipate the losses, and the tax charge should be $9,000 for the first quarter of the year (30% of $30,000) and a negative tax charge of $3,000 for each of the next three quarters, if actual losses are the same as anticipated.

Where the tax year for a company does not coincide with its financial year, a separate estimated weighted average tax rate should be applied for each tax year, to the interim periods that fall within that tax year.

Some countries give entities tax credits against the tax payable, based on amounts of capital expenditure or research and development, etc. Under most tax regimes, these credits are calculated and granted on an annual basis; therefore it is appropriate to include anticipated tax credits within the calculation of the estimated average tax rate for the year, and apply this rate to calculate the tax on income for interim periods. However, if a tax benefit relates to a specific one-time event, it should be recognised within the tax expense for the interim period in which the event occurs.

Inventory valuations

Within interim reports, inventories should be valued in the same way as for year-end accounts. It is recognised, however, that it will be necessary to rely more heavily on estimates for interim reporting than for year-end reporting.

In addition, it will normally be the case that the net realisable value of inventories should be estimated from selling prices and related costs to complete and dispose at interim dates.

Use of estimates

Although accounting information must be reliable and free from material error, it may be necessary to sacrifice some accuracy and reliability for the sake of timeliness and cost-benefits. This is particularly the case with interim financial reporting, where there will be much less time to produce reports than at the financial year end. The proposed standard therefore recognises that estimates will have to be used to a greater extent in interim reporting, to assess values or even some costs, than in year-end reporting.

An appendix to IAS 34 gives some examples of the use of estimates.

(a) **Inventories**. An entity might not need to carry out a full inventory count at the end of each interim period. Instead, it may be sufficient to estimate inventory values using sales margins.

(b) **Provisions**. An entity might employ outside experts or consultants to advise on the appropriate amount of a provision, as at the year end. It will probably be inappropriate to employ an expert to make a similar assessment at each interim date. Similarly, an entity might employ a professional valuer to revalue fixed assets at the year end, whereas at the interim date(s) the entity will not rely on such experts.

(c) **Income taxes**. The rate of income tax (tax on profits) will be calculated at the year end by applying the tax rate in each country/jurisdiction to the profits earned there. At the interim stage, it may be sufficient to estimate the rate of income tax by applying the same 'blended' estimated weighted average tax rate to the income earned in all countries/jurisdictions.

The principle of **materiality** applies to interim financial reporting, as it does to year-end reporting. In assessing materiality, it needs to be recognised that interim financial reports will rely more heavily on estimates than year-end reports. Materiality should be assessed in relation to the interim financial statements themselves, and should be independent of 'annual materiality' considerations.

Accounting for tangible non-current assets

4

1 IAS 16: Property, plant and equipment

IAS 16 should be followed when accounting for property, plant and equipment unless another international accounting standard requires a **different treatment**.

IAS 16 **does not apply** to the following.

(a)   Biological assets, apart from bearer biological assets (see below)

(b)   Mineral rights and mineral reserves, such as oil, gas and other non-regenerative resources

However, it does apply to property, plant and equipment used to develop these assets.

Bearer biological assets

Following an amendment to IAS 41, plant-based bearer biological assets, especially plantation trees such as grape vines, rubber trees and oil palms, are now classified under IAS 16. This amendment applies to plants which are solely used to grow produce over several periods and are not themselves consumed, being usually scrapped when no longer productive. They are measured at **accumulated cost** until maturity and then become subject to depreciation and impairment charges

Definitions

The standard gives a large number of definitions. Note that the definition of 'fair value' has now been amended by IFRS 13.

Property, plant and equipment are tangible items that:

- Are held for use in the production or supply of goods or services, for rental to others, or for administrative purposes; and

- Are expected to be used during more than one period.

Cost is the amount of cash or cash equivalents paid or the fair value of the other consideration given to acquire an asset at the time of its acquisition or construction.

Residual value is the estimated amount that an entity would currently obtain from disposal of the asset, after deducting the estimated costs of disposal, if the asset were already of the age and in the condition expected at the end of its useful life.

Entity specific value is the present value of the cash flows an entity expects to arise from the continuing use of an asset and from its disposal at the end of its useful life, or expects to incur when settling a liability.

Fair value is the price that would be received to sell an asset or paid to transfer a liability in an orderly transaction between market participants at the measurement date. *(IFRS 13: para. 9)*

Carrying amount is the amount at which an asset is recognised after deducting any accumulated depreciation and accumulated impairment losses.

An impairment loss is the amount by which the carrying amount of an asset exceeds its recoverable amount.

Depreciation is the systematic allocation of the depreciable amount of an asset over its useful life.

Useful life is one of two things.

- The period over which an asset is expected to be available for use by the entity, or

- The number of production or similar units expected to be obtained from the asset by the entity. *(IAS 16: para. 6)*

Recognition

In this context, recognition simply means incorporation of the item in the entity's accounts, in this case as a non-current asset. The recognition of property, plant and equipment depends on two criteria.

Recognition

Recognition means incorporation of the item in the entity's financial statements, in this case as a non-current asset. The recognition of property, plant and equipment depends on two criteria:

(a) It is probable that **future economic benefits** associated with the asset will flow to the entity

(b) The cost of the asset to the entity can be **measured reliably**

These recognition criteria apply to **subsequent expenditure** as well as costs incurred initially. There are no longer any separate criteria for recognising subsequent expenditure.

Major components or spare parts, should also be recognised as property, plant and equipment.

For very **large and specialised items**, an apparently single asset should be broken down into its composite parts. This occurs where the different parts have different useful lives and different depreciation rates are applied to each part, eg an aircraft, where the body and engines are separated as they have different useful lives.

Once an item of property, plant and equipment qualifies for recognition as an asset, it will initially be **measured at cost**.

Components of cost

The standard lists the components of the cost of an item of property, plant and equipment.

- **Purchase price**, less any trade discount or rebate

- **Import duties** and non-refundable purchase taxes

- **Directly attributable costs** of bringing the asset to working condition for its intended use, eg:
    - The cost of site preparation
    - Initial delivery and handling costs
    - Installation costs
    - Testing
    - Professional fees (architects, engineers)

- Initial estimate of the unavoidable cost of dismantling and removing the asset and restoring the site on which it is located

The revised IAS 16 provides **additional guidance on directly attributable** costs included in the cost of an item of property, plant and equipment.

(a) These costs bring the asset to the location and working conditions necessary for it to be capable of operating in the manner intended by management, including those costs to test whether the asset is functioning properly.

(b) They are determined after deducting the net proceeds from selling any items produced when bringing the asset to its location and condition.

The revised standard also states that income and related expenses of operations that are incidental to the construction or development of an item of property, plant and equipment should be recognised in profit or loss.

The following costs **will not be part of the cost** of property, plant or equipment unless they can be attributed directly to the asset's acquisition, or bringing it into its working condition.

- Administration and other general overhead costs
- Start-up and similar pre-production costs
- Initial operating losses before the asset reaches planned performance

All of these will be recognised as an **expense** rather than an asset.

In the case of **self-constructed assets**, the same principles are applied as for acquired assets. If the entity makes similar assets during the normal course of business for sale externally, then the cost of the asset will be the cost of its production under IAS 2 *Inventories*. This also means that abnormal costs (wasted material, labour or other resources) are excluded from the cost of the asset. An example of a self-constructed asset is when a building company builds its own head office.

Expenditure incurred in replacing or renewing a component of an item of property, plant and equipment must be **recognised in the carrying amount of the item**. The carrying amount of the replaced or renewed component must be derecognised. A similar approach is also applied when a separate component of an item of property, plant and equipment is identified in respect of a major inspection to enable the continued use of the item.

Measurement subsequent to initial recognition

The standard offers two possible treatments here, essentially a choice between keeping an asset recorded at **cost** or revaluing it to **fair value**.

Cost model	Revaluation model
Carry the asset at its cost less any accumulated depreciation and any accumulated impairment loss.	• Carry the asset at a revalued amount, being its fair value at the date of the revaluation less any subsequent accumulated impairment losses. • Revaluations shall be made regularly enough so that the carrying amount approximates to fair value at the reporting date.

IAS 16 specifies that the revaluation model is available only if the fair value of the asset can be measured reliably.

Revaluation model

The **market value** of land and buildings usually represents fair value, assuming existing use and line of business. Such valuations are usually carried out by professionally qualified valuers.

In the case of **plant and equipment**, fair value can also be taken as **market value**. Where a market value is not available, however, depreciated replacement cost should be used. There may be no market value where types of plant and equipment are sold only rarely or because of their specialised nature (ie they would normally only be sold as part of an ongoing business).

The frequency of valuation depends on the **volatility of the fair values** of individual items of property, plant and equipment. The more volatile the fair value, the more frequently revaluations should be carried out. Where the current fair value is very different from the carrying value then a revaluation should be carried out.

Most importantly, when an item of property, plant and equipment is revalued, **the whole class of assets to which it belongs should be revalued**.

All the items within a class should be **revalued at the same time**, to prevent selective revaluation of certain assets and to avoid disclosing a mixture of costs and values from different dates in the financial statements. A rolling basis of revaluation is allowed if the revaluations are kept up to date and the revaluation of the whole class is completed in a short period of time.

How should any **increase in value** be treated when a revaluation takes place? The debit will be the increase in value in the statement of financial position, but what about the credit? IAS 16 requires the increase to be credited to a **revaluation surplus** (ie part of owners' equity), unless the increase is reversing a previous decrease which was recognised as an expense. To the extent that this offset is made, the increase is recognised as income; any excess is then taken to the revaluation surplus.

Example: Revaluation gain

B Co has an item of land carried in its books at $13,000. Two years ago a slump in land values led the company to reduce the carrying value from $15,000. This was taken as an expense in profit or loss. There has been a surge in land prices in the current year, however, and the land is now worth $20,000.

How do we account for the revaluation in the current year?

The double entry is:

DEBIT	Asset value (statement of financial position)	$7,000	
CREDIT	Profit or loss		$2,000
	Revaluation surplus		$5,000

The case is similar for a **decrease in value** on revaluation. Any decrease should be recognised as an expense, except where it offsets a previous increase taken as a revaluation surplus in owners' equity. Any decrease greater than the previous upwards increase in value must be taken as an expense in profit or loss.

Example: Revaluation and depreciation

A company bought an asset for $10,000 at the beginning of 20X6. It had a useful life of five years. On 1 January 20X8 the asset was revalued to $15,000. The expected useful life has remained unchanged (ie three years remain). How is this accounted for?

On 1 January 20X8 the carrying value of the asset is $10,000 – (2 × ($10,000 ÷ 5)) = $6,000. For the revaluation:

DEBIT	Asset value	$9,000	
CREDIT	Revaluation surplus		$9,000

The depreciation for the next three years will be $15,000 ÷ 3 = $5,000, compared to depreciation on cost of $10,000 ÷ 5 = $2,000. So each year, the extra $3,000 can be treated as part of the surplus which has become realised:

DEBIT	Revaluation surplus	$3,000	
CREDIT	Retained earnings		$3,000

This is a movement on owners' equity, not a profit or loss item.

Cost model: Depreciation

The standard states that:

- The **depreciable amount** of an item of property, plant and equipment should be allocated on a systematic basis over its useful life.

- The **depreciation method** used should reflect the pattern in which the asset's economic benefits are consumed by the entity.

- The **depreciation charge** for each period should be recognised as an expense unless it is included in the carrying amount of another asset.

Land and buildings are dealt with separately even when they are acquired together because land normally has an unlimited life and is therefore not depreciated. In contrast buildings do have a limited life and must be depreciated. Any increase in the value of land on which a building is standing will have no impact on the determination of the building's useful life.

Depreciation is usually treated as an **expense**, but not where it is absorbed by the entity in the process of producing other assets. For example, depreciation of plant and machinery can be incurred in the production of goods for sale (inventory items).

In such circumstances, the depreciation is included in the cost of the new assets produced.

Review of useful life

The following factors should be considered when **estimating the useful life** of a depreciable asset.

- Expected physical **wear and tear**
- **Obsolescence**
- Legal or other **limits on the use** of the assets

Once decided, the useful life should be **reviewed at least every financial year** end and depreciation rates adjusted for the current and future periods if expectations vary significantly from the original estimates.

The effect of the change should be disclosed in the accounting period in which the change takes place.

The assessment of useful life requires **judgement** based on previous experience with similar assets or classes of asset. When a completely new type of asset is acquired (ie through technological advancement or through use in producing a brand new product or service) it is still necessary to estimate useful life, even though the exercise will be much more difficult.

The standard also points out that the physical life of the asset might be longer than its useful life to the entity in question. One of the main factors to be taken into consideration is the **physical wear and tear** the asset is likely to endure. This will depend on various circumstances, including the number of shifts for which the asset will be used, the entity's repair and maintenance programme and so on. Other factors to be considered include obsolescence (due to technological advances in production or due to a reduction in demand for the product the asset produces) and legal restrictions, eg length of a related lease.

Review of depreciation method

The **depreciation method** should also be reviewed at least at each financial year end and, if there has been a significant change in the expected pattern of economic benefits from those assets, the method should be changed to suit this changed pattern. When such a change in depreciation method takes place the change should be accounted for as a change in accounting estimate and the depreciation charge for the current and future periods should be adjusted.

Impairment of asset values

An **impairment loss** should be treated in the same way as a **revaluation decrease** ie the decrease should be **recognised as an expense**. However, a revaluation decrease

Part B 4: Accounting for tangible non-current assets

(or impairment loss) should be charged directly against any related revaluation surplus to the extent that the decrease does not exceed the amount held in the revaluation surplus in respect of that same asset.

A **reversal of an impairment** loss should be treated in the same way as a **revaluation increase**, ie a revaluation increase should be recognised as income to the extent that it reverses a revaluation decrease or an impairment loss of the same asset previously recognised as an expense.

Retirements and disposals

When an asset is permanently **withdrawn from use, or sold or scrapped**, and no future economic benefits are expected from its disposal, it should be withdrawn from the statement of financial position.

Gains or losses are the difference between the estimated net disposal proceeds and the carrying amount of the asset. They should be recognised as income or expense in the profit or loss.

An entity is required to **derecognise the carrying amount** of an item of property, plant or equipment that it disposes of on the date the **criteria for the sale of goods** in IFRS 15 *Revenue from contracts with customers* would be met. This also applies to parts of an asset.

An entity cannot classify as revenue (ie in profit or loss) a gain it realises on the disposal of an item of property, plant and equipment.

Disclosure

The standard has a long list of disclosure requirements, for each class of property, plant and equipment.

(a) **Measurement bases** for determining the gross carrying amount (if more than one, the gross carrying amount for that basis in each category)

(b) **Depreciation methods** used

(c) **Useful lives** or depreciation rates used

(d) **Gross carrying amount** and accumulated depreciation (aggregated with accumulated impairment losses) at the beginning and end of the period

(e) **Reconciliation** of the carrying amount at the beginning and end of the period showing:

   (i) Additions

   (ii) Disposals

   (iii) Acquisitions through business combinations (see Chapter 17)

(iv)   Increases/decreases during the period from revaluations and from impairment losses

(v)   Impairment losses recognised in profit or loss

(vi)   Impairment losses reversed in profit or loss

(vii)   Depreciation

(viii)   Net exchange differences (from translation of statements of foreign entity)

(ix)   Any other movements

2 IAS 20: Accounting for government grants and disclosure of government assistance

It is common for entities to receive government grants for various purposes (grants may be called subsidies, premiums, etc). They may also receive other types of assistance which may be in many forms. The treatment of government grants is covered by IAS 20 *Accounting for government grants and disclosure of government assistance.*

Prior to the issue of IAS 20, government grants provided companies with an easy way to ramp up profits. In some cases grants would be credited to revenue in full, as soon as they were received. IAS 20 was issued to remedy this abuse.

IAS 20 does **not** cover the following situations.

- Accounting for government grants in financial statements reflecting the effects of **changing prices**

- Government assistance given in the form of **'tax breaks'**

- Government acting as **part-owner** of the entity

These definitions are given by the standard, as amended by IFRS 13.

> **Government.** Government, government agencies and similar bodies whether local, national or international.
>
> **Government assistance.** Action by government designed to provide an economic benefit specific to an entity or range of entities qualifying under certain criteria.
>
> **Government grants.** Assistance by government in the form of transfers of resources to an entity in return for past or future compliance with certain conditions relating to the operating activities of the entity. They exclude those forms of government assistance which cannot reasonably have a value placed upon them and transactions with government which cannot be distinguished from the normal trading transactions of the entity.
>
> **Grants related to assets.** Government grants whose primary condition is that an entity qualifying for them should purchase, construct or otherwise acquire non-current assets. Subsidiary conditions may also be attached restricting the type or location of the assets or the periods during which they are to be acquired or held.
>
> **Grants related to income.** Government grants other than those related to assets.
>
> **Forgivable loans.** Loans which the lender undertakes to waive repayment of under certain prescribed conditions. *(IAS 20: para. 3)*
>
> **Fair value.** The price that would be received to sell an asset, or paid to transfer a liability in an orderly transaction between market participants at the measurement date. *(IFRS 13: para. 9)*

There are many **different forms** of government assistance: both the type of assistance and the conditions attached to it will vary. Government assistance may have encouraged an entity to undertake something it would not otherwise have done.

How will the receipt of government assistance affect the financial statements?

(a)   An appropriate method must be found to account for any **resources transferred**.

(b)   The extent to which an entity has **benefited** from such assistance during the reporting period should be shown.

An entity should not recognise government grants (including non-monetary grants at fair value) until it has **reasonable assurance** that:

- The entity will comply with any **conditions** attached to the grant
- The entity will **actually receive** the grant

Even if the grant has been received, this does not prove that the conditions attached to it have been or will be fulfilled.

It makes no difference in the treatment of the grant whether it is received in cash or given as a reduction in a liability to government, ie the **manner of receipt is irrelevant**.

Any related **contingency** should be recognised under *IAS 37 Provisions, contingent liabilities and contingent assets*, once the grant has been recognised.

In the case of a **forgivable loan** (as defined in the key terms above) from government, it should be treated in the same way as a government grant when it is reasonably assured that the entity will meet the relevant terms for forgiveness.

Accounting treatment of government grants

There are two methods which could be used to account for government grants, and the arguments for each are given in IAS 20.

> **Capital approach.** The grant is credited directly to shareholders' funds.
>
> **Income approach.** The grant is credited to profit or loss over one or more periods.

The standard gives the following arguments in support of each method.

Capital approach

(a)   The grants are a **financing device**, so should go through the statement of financial position. In profit or loss they would simply offset the expenses which they are financing. No repayment is expected by the Government, so the grants should be credited directly to shareholders' interests.

(b)   Grants are **not earned**, they are incentives without related costs, so it would be wrong to take them to profit or loss.

Income approach

(a)   The grants are **not received from shareholders** so should not be credited directly to shareholders' interests.

(b)   Grants are **not given or received for nothing**. They are earned by compliance with conditions and by meeting obligations. There are therefore associated costs with which the grant can be matched in profit or loss as these costs are being compensated by the grant.

(c)   Grants are an extension of **fiscal policies** and so as income taxes and other taxes are charged against income, so grants should be credited to income.

IAS 20 requires grants to be recognised under the income approach, ie grants are recognised as income over the relevant periods to match them with related costs which they have been received to compensate. This should be done on a systematic basis. **Grants should not, therefore, be credited directly to shareholders' interests**.

It would be against the accruals assumption to credit grants to income on a receipts basis, so a **systematic basis of matching** must be used. A receipts basis would only be acceptable if no other basis was available.

Part B 4: Accounting for tangible non-current assets

It will usually be easy to identify the **costs related to a government grant,** and thereby the period(s) in which the grant should be recognised as income, ie when the costs are incurred. Where grants are received in relation to a depreciating asset, the grant will be recognised over the periods in which the asset is depreciated and in the same proportions.

In the case of **grants for non-depreciable assets,** certain obligations may need to be fulfilled, in which case the grant should be recognised as income over the periods in which the cost of meeting the obligation is incurred. For example, if a piece of land is granted on condition that a building is erected on it, then the grant should be recognised as income over the building's life.

There may be a **series of conditions** attached to a grant, in the nature of a package of financial aid. An entity must take care to identify precisely those conditions which give rise to costs which in turn determine the periods over which the grant will be earned. When appropriate, the grant may be split and the parts allocated on different bases.

An entity may receive a grant as compensation for expenses or losses which it has **already incurred.** Alternatively, a grant may be given to an entity simply to provide immediate financial support where no future related costs are expected. In cases such as these, the grant received should be recognised as income of the period in which it becomes receivable.

Presentation of grants related to assets

There are two choices here for how government grants related to assets (including non-monetary grants at fair value) should be shown in the statement of financial position.

(a)   Set up the grant as **deferred income**
(b)   **Deduct the grant** in arriving at the carrying amount of the asset

Whichever of these methods is used, the **cash flows** in relation to the purchase of the asset and the receipt of the grant are often disclosed separately because of the significance of the movements in cash flow.

Example

On 1 January 20X8, X Co purchased a non-current asset for cash of $100,000 and received a grant of $20,000 towards the cost of the asset. X Co's accounting policy is to treat the grant as deferred income. The asset has a useful life of five years.

What will be the accounting entries to record the asset and the grant in the year ended 31 December 20X8?

Acquisition of the asset and receipt of the grant on 1 January 20X8:

| DEBIT | Non-current assets | $100,000 |
| CREDIT | Cash | $100,000 |

– to record the asset at its cost

| DEBIT | Cash | $20,000 |
| CREDIT | Deferred income | $20,000 |

– to record the receipt of the grant

In the year ended 31 December 20X8 the asset is depreciated and a portion of the grant is released to profit or loss:

DEBIT	Depreciation expense ($100,000 / 5 years)	$20,000
CREDIT	Accumulated depreciation	$20,000
DEBIT	Deferred income ($20,000 / 5 years)	$4,000
CREDIT	Operating expenses	$4,000

The release of the deferred income is matched to the depreciation expense, so the net effect is an expense of **$16,000** relating to the asset.

If X Co had deducted the grant from the carrying amount of the asset, the net expense would have been:

	$	
Cost of asset	100,000	
Less grant received	(20,000)	
Carrying amount	80,000	
Depreciation (80,000 / 5 years)	16,000	Same result

Presentation of grants related to income

These grants are a credit to profit or loss, but there is a choice in the method of disclosure.

Method (a)	**Method (b)**
	Income approach
Present as a separate credit or under a general heading, eg 'other income'	Deduct from the related expense

Some would argue that offsetting income and expenses in profit or loss for the year is not good practice. Others would say that the expenses would not have been incurred had the grant not been available, so offsetting the two is acceptable. Although both methods are acceptable, disclosure of the grant may be necessary for a **proper understanding** of the financial statements, particularly the effect on any item of income or expense which is required to be separately disclosed.

Repayment of government grants

If a grant must be repaid it should be accounted for as a revision of an accounting estimate (see IAS 8 Chapter 6).

Repayment of a grant related to income	Repayment of a grant related to an asset
• Apply first against any unamortised deferred income set up in respect of the grant • Any excess should be recognised immediately as an expense	• Increase the carrying amount of the asset or reduce the deferred income balance by the amount repayable • The cumulative additional depreciation that would have been recognised to date in the absence of the grant should be immediately recognised as an expense

It is possible that the circumstances surrounding repayment may require a review of the **asset value** and an impairment of the new carrying amount of the asset.

Disclosure is required of the following.

- **Accounting policy** adopted, including method of presentation

- **Nature and extent** of government grants recognised and other forms of assistance received

- **Unfulfilled conditions and other contingencies** attached to recognised government assistance

The IASB is intending to amend IAS 20 but the project is currently deferred. It is unhappy with the following aspects:

- Grants being treated as a deferred credit when there is no liability. This is not consistent with the Conceptual Framework

- IAS 20 allows alternative treatments, which does not enhance comparability

- The option to deduct the grant from the carrying amount of the asset results in understatement of assets

SIC 10 Government assistance – no specific relation to operating activities

In some countries government assistance to entities may be aimed at encouragement or long-term support of business activities either in certain regions or industry sectors. Conditions to receive such assistance may not be specifically related to the operating activities of the entity. Examples of such assistance are transfers of resources by governments to entities which:

(a)   Operate in a particular industry
(b)   Continue operating in recently privatised industries
(c)   Start or continue to run their business in underdeveloped areas

The issue is whether such government assistance is a 'government grant' within the scope of IAS 20 and, therefore, should be accounted for in accordance with this standard.

Government assistance to entities meets the definition of government grants in IAS 20, even if there are no conditions specifically relating to the operating activities of the entity other than the requirement to operate in certain regions or industry sectors. Such grants should therefore not be credited directly to equity.

3 IAS 40: Investment property

IAS 40 was published in March 2000 and revised in 2008. Its objective is to prescribe the accounting treatment for investment property and related disclosure requirements.

Consider the following definitions (from IAS 40 apart from 'fair value').

Investment property is property (land or a building – or part of a building – or both) held (by the owner or by the lessee under a lease) to earn rentals or for capital appreciation or both, rather than for:

(a)   Use in the production or supply of goods or services or for administrative purposes, or

(b)   Sale in the ordinary course of business

Owner-occupied property is property held by the owner (or by the lessee under a lease) for use in the production or supply of goods or services or for administrative purposes.   *(IAS 40: para. 5)*

Fair value is the price that would be received to sell and asset or paid to transfer a liability in an orderly transaction between market participants at the measurement date.   *(IFRS 13: para. 9)*

Cost is the amount of cash or cash equivalents paid or the fair value of other consideration given to acquire an asset at the time of its acquisition or construction.

Carrying amount is the amount at which an asset is recognised in the statement of financial position.

A property interest that is held by a lessee under an **operating lease** may be classified and accounted for as an **investment property**, if and only if the property would otherwise meet the definition of an investment property and the lessee uses the IAS 40 **fair value model**. This classification is available on a property-by-property basis.

Examples of investment property include:

(a) **Land held for long-term capital appreciation** rather than for short-term sale in the ordinary course of business

(b) A **building** owned by the reporting entity and **leased out**

A company owns a piece of land. The directors have not yet decided whether to build a factory on it for use in its business or to keep it and sell it when its value has risen.

Would this be classified as an investment property under IAS 40?

Yes under IAS 40 para 8. If an entity has not determined that it will use the land either as an owner-occupied property or for short-term sale in the ordinary course of business, the land is considered as being held for capital appreciation.

Below are examples of things that are **not investment property** under IAS 40.

Type of non-investment property	Applicable IAS
Property intended for sale in the ordinary course of business	IAS 2 *Inventories*
Property being constructed or developed on behalf of third parties	IFRS 15 *Revenue from contracts with customers*
Owner-occupied property	IAS 16 *Property, plant and equipment*
Property leased to another entity	IFRS 16 *Leases*

Investment property should be recognised as an asset when two conditions are met.

(a) It is probable that the future economic benefits that are associated with the investment property will flow to the entity

(b) The cost of the investment property can be measured reliably

Initial measurement

An investment property should be measured initially at its **cost**, including transaction costs.

A property interest held under a lease and classified as an investment property shall be accounted for in accordance with IFRS 16.

Measurement subsequent to initial recognition

IAS 40 requires an entity to **choose between two models**.

- **The fair value model**
- **The cost model**

Whatever policy it chooses should be applied to **all of its investment property**.

Fair value model

(a) After initial recognition, an entity that chooses the **fair value model** should measure all of its investment property at fair value, except in the extremely rare cases where this cannot be measured reliably. In such cases it should apply the IAS 16 cost model.

(b) A gain or loss arising from a change in the fair value of an investment property should be recognised in net profit or loss for the period in which it arises.

Unusually, the IASB allows a fair value model for non-financial assets. This is not the same as a revaluation, where increases in carrying amount above a cost-based measure are recognised as revaluation surplus. Under the fair-value model all changes in fair value are recognised in profit or loss.

IFRS 13 *Fair value measurement,* issued in May 2011 deleted much of the guidance provided in IAS 40 in respect of the determination of fair value. Instead the requirements of IFRS 13 apply in measuring the fair value of investment properties. This standard requires that the following are considered in determining fair value:

(a) The asset being measured

(b) The principal market (ie that where the most activity takes place) or where there is no principal market, the most advantageous market (ie that in which the best price could be achieved) in which an orderly transaction would take place for the asset

(c) The highest and best use of the asset and whether it is used on a standalone basis or in conjunction with other assets

(d) Assumptions that market participants would use when pricing the asset

Having considered these factors, IFRS 13 provides a hierarchy of inputs for arriving at fair value. It requires that level 1 inputs are used where possible:

Level 1 Quoted prices in active markets for identical assets that the entity can access at the measurement date

Level 2 Inputs other than quoted prices that are directly or indirectly observable for the asset

Level 3 Unobservable inputs for the asset

More detail

Level 1 inputs are prices quoted in active markets for items identical to the asset (in this case investment property) being measured. Active markets are ones where transactions take place with sufficient frequency and volume for pricing information to be provided.

In general IFRS 13 requires in respect of non-financial assets that fair value is decided on the basis of the **highest and best use of the asset as determined by a market participant.** Highest and best use is determined from the perspective of market participants, even if the reporting entity intends a different use. For example, an entity may intend to use assets acquired in a business combination differently from how other market participants might use them. If, however, there is no evidence to suggest that the current use of an asset is not its highest and best use an entity does not need to carry out an exhaustive search for other potential uses.

The 'highest and best use' requirement would appear not to contradict point (b) below, because it requires a market participant rather than solely the knowledge of the entity.

IFRS 13 does not specifically mention investment property. However, KPMG *(Real Estate Newsletter, July 2011),* has expressed the opinion that the 'highest and best use' requirement is unlikely to change the valuation of investment property:

> 'The real estate sector is used to dealing with alternative use value. For example an existing commercial property which could generate additional value through conversion into a residential development would be valued based on the higher amount if there is reasonable certainty over the planning being gained.'

The guidance which remains in IAS 40 is as follows.

(a) Double counting should be prevented in deciding on the fair value of the assets. For example, elevators or air conditioning, which form an integral part of a building should be incorporated in the investment property rather than recognised separately.

(b)   According to the definition in IAS 36 *Impairment of assets,* fair value is not the same as 'value in use'. The latter reflects factors and knowledge as relating solely to the entity, while the former reflects factors and knowledge applicable to the market.

(c)   In those uncommon cases in which the **fair value of an investment property cannot be determined reliably** by an entity, the cost model in IAS 16 must be employed until the investment property is disposed of. **The residual value must be assumed to be zero.**

Cost model

The cost model is the **cost model in IAS 16**. Investment property should be measured at **depreciated cost, less any accumulated impairment losses**. An entity that chooses the cost model should **disclose the fair value of its investment property**.

Once the entity has chosen the fair value or cost model, it should apply it to all of its investment property. It **should not change from one model to the other unless the change will result in a more appropriate presentation**. IAS 40 states that it is highly unlikely that a change from the fair value model to the cost model will result in a more appropriate presentation.

Transfers

Transfers to or from investment property should **only** be made **when there is a change in use**. For example, owner occupation commences so the investment property will be treated under IAS 16 as an owner-occupied property.

When there is a transfer from investment property carried at fair value to owner-occupied property or inventories, the property's cost for subsequent accounting under IAS 16 or IAS 2 should be its fair value at the date of change of use.

Conversely, an owner-occupied property may become an investment property and need to be carried at fair value. An entity should apply IAS 16 up to the date of change of use. It should treat any difference at that date between the carrying amount of the property under IAS 16 and its fair value as a revaluation under IAS 16.

An investment property should be derecognised on disposal or when it is permanently withdrawn from use and no future economic benefits are expected from its disposal.

Any **gain or loss** on disposal is the difference between the net disposal proceeds and the carrying amount of the asset. It should generally be **recognised as income or expense in profit or loss**.

Disclosure requirements

These relate to:

- Choice of fair value model or cost model
- Whether property interests held under leases are included in investment property
- Criteria for classification as investment property
- Assumptions in determining fair value
- Use of independent professional valuer (encouraged but not required)
- Rental income and expenses
- Any restrictions or obligations

An entity that adopts the fair value model must also disclose a reconciliation of the carrying amount of the investment property at the beginning and end of the period.

4 IAS 36: Impairment of assets

There is an established principle that assets should not be carried at more than their recoverable amount. An entity should write down the carrying value of an asset to its recoverable amount if the carrying value of an asset is not recoverable in full. IAS 36 puts in place a detailed methodology for carrying out impairment reviews and related accounting treatments and disclosures.

IAS 36 applies to all tangible, intangible and financial assets **except** inventories, assets arising from construction contracts, deferred tax assets, assets arising under IAS 19 *Employee benefits* and financial assets within the scope of IAS 32 *Financial instruments: presentation*. This is because those IASs already have rules for recognising and measuring impairment. Note also that IAS 36 does not apply to non-current assets held for sale, which are dealt with under IFRS 5 *Non-current assets held for sale and discontinued operations*.

> **Impairment.** A fall in the value of an asset, so that its 'recoverable amount' is now less than its carrying amount in the statement of financial position.
>
> **Carrying amount.** Is the net value at which the asset is included in the statement of financial position (ie after deducting accumulated depreciation and any impairment losses). *(IAS 36: para. 6)*

The basic principle underlying IAS 36 is relatively straightforward. If an asset's value in the accounts is higher than its realistic value, measured as its 'recoverable amount', the asset is judged to have suffered an impairment loss. It should therefore be reduced in value, by the amount of the impairment loss. The amount of the **impairment loss** should be **written off against profit** immediately.

The main accounting issues to consider are therefore as follows.

(a)   How is it possible to **identify when** an impairment loss may have occurred?
(b)   How should the **recoverable amount** of the asset be measured?
(c)   How should an 'impairment loss' be **reported in the accounts**?

Identifying a potentially impaired asset

An entity should assess at each year end whether there are any indications of impairment to any assets. The concept of **materiality** applies, and only material impairment needs to be identified.

If there are indications of possible impairment, the entity is required to make a formal estimate of the **recoverable amount** of the assets concerned.

IAS 36 suggests how **indications of a possible impairment** of assets might be recognised. The suggestions are based largely on common sense.

(a)   **External sources of information**

    (i)   A fall in the asset's market value that is more significant than would normally be expected from passage of time over normal use.

    (ii)   A significant change in the technological, market, legal or economic environment of the business in which the assets are employed.

    (iii) An increase in market interest rates or market rates of return on investments likely to affect the discount rate used in calculating value in use.

    (iv)   The carrying amount of the entity's net assets being more than its market capitalisation.

(b)   **Internal sources of information**: evidence of obsolescence or physical damage, adverse changes in the use to which the asset is put, or the asset's economic performance

Even if there are no indications of impairment, the following assets must **always** be tested for impairment annually.

(a)   An intangible asset with an **indefinite useful life**
(b)   **Goodwill** acquired in a business combination

Measuring the recoverable amount of the asset

What is an asset's recoverable amount?

> The **recoverable amount of an asset** should be measured as the higher value of:
>
> (a) The asset's fair value less costs of disposal; and
>
> (b) Its value in use. *(IAS 36: para. 6)*

An asset's fair value less costs to sell is the amount net of selling costs that could be obtained from the sale of the asset. Selling costs include sales transaction costs, such as legal expenses.

(a) If there is **an active market** in the asset, the net selling price should be based on the **market value,** or on the price of recent transactions in similar assets.

(b) If there is **no active market** in the assets it might be possible to **estimate** a net selling price using best estimates of what 'market participants' might pay in an orderly transaction.

Net selling price **cannot** be reduced, however, by including within selling costs any **restructuring or reorganisation expenses**, or any costs that have already been recognised in the accounts as liabilities.

The concept of 'value in use' is very important.

> The **value in use** of an asset is measured as the present value of estimated future cash flows (inflows minus outflows) generated by the asset, including its estimated net disposal value (if any) at the end of its expected useful life. *(IAS 36: para. 6)*

The cash flows used in the calculation should be **pre-tax cash flows** and a **pre-tax discount rate** should be applied to calculate the present value.

The calculation of **value in use** must reflect the following:

(a) An estimate of the **future cash flows** the entity expects to derive from the asset

(b) Expectations about **possible variations** in the amount and timing of future cash flows

(c) The **time value of money**

(d) The price for bearing the **uncertainty** inherent in the asset, and

(e) **Other factors** that would be reflected in pricing future cash flows from the asset

Calculating a value in use therefore calls for estimates of future cash flows, and the possibility exists that an entity might come up with over-optimistic estimates of cash flows. IAS 36 (para. 33) therefore states the following.

(a)   Cash flow projections should be based on **'reasonable and supportable' assumptions**.

(b)   Projections of cash flows, normally up to a maximum period of five years, should be based on the most **recent budgets or financial forecasts**.

(c)   Cash flow projections beyond this period should be obtained by extrapolating short-term projections, using either a **steady or declining growth rate** for each subsequent year (unless a rising growth rate can be justified). The long term growth rate applied should not exceed the average long term growth rate for the product, market, industry or country, unless a higher growth rate can be justified.

Composition of estimates of future cash flows

These should include the following:

(a)   Projections of **cash inflows** from **continuing use** of the asset

(b)   Projections of **cash outflows** necessarily incurred to **generate the cash inflows** from continuing use of the asset

(c)   **Net cash flows** received/paid on **disposal** of the asset at the end of its useful life

There is an underlying principle that future cash flows should be estimated for the asset in its current condition. Future cash flows relating to restructurings to which the entity is not yet committed, or to future costs to add to, replace part of, or service the asset are excluded.

Estimates of future cash flows should exclude the following:

(a)   Cash inflows/outflows from financing activities
(b)   Income tax receipts/payments

The amount of net cash inflow/outflow on **disposal** of an asset should assume an orderly transaction.

Foreign currency future cash flows should be forecast in the currency in which they will arise and will be discounted using a rate appropriate for that currency. The resulting figure should then be translated into the reporting currency at the spot rate at the end of the reporting period.

The **discount rate** should be a current pre-tax rate (or rates) that reflects the current assessment of the time value of money and the risks specific to the asset. The discount rate should not include a risk weighting if the underlying cash flows have already been adjusted for risk.

Recognition and measurement of an impairment loss

The rule for assets at historical cost is:

> If the recoverable amount of an asset is less than its carrying amount, the carrying amount of the asset shall be reduced to its recoverable amount. That reduction is an impairment loss. An impairment loss shall be recognised immediately in profit or loss *(IAS 36: para. 59-60)*

The rule for assets held at a revalued amount (such as property revalued under IAS 16) is:

> Any impairment loss on a revalued asset shall to be treated as a revaluation decrease in accordance with that Standard. *(IAS 36: para. 60)*

In practice this means:

- To the extent that there is a revaluation surplus held in respect of the asset, the impairment loss should be charged to revaluation surplus

- Any excess should be charged to profit or loss

If it is not possible to calculate the recoverable amount for an individual asset, the recoverable amount of the asset's cash generating unit should be measured instead.

> A cash generating unit is the smallest identifiable group of assets for which independent cash flows can be identified and measured. *(IAS 36: para. 6)*

How would a cash generating unit be identified?

Here are two possibilities.

(a) A mining company owns a private railway that it uses to transport output from one of its mines. The railway now has no market value other than as scrap, and it is impossible to identify any separate cash inflows with the use of the railway itself. Consequently, if the mining company suspects an impairment in the value of the railway, it should treat the mine as a whole as a cash generating unit, and measure the recoverable amount of the mine as a whole.

(b) A bus company has an arrangement with a town's authorities to run a bus service on four routes in the town. Separately identifiable assets are allocated to each of the bus routes, and cash inflows and outflows can be attributed to each individual route. Three routes are running at a profit and one is running at a loss. The bus company suspects that there is an impairment of assets on the loss-making route. However, the company will be unable to close the loss-making route, because it is under an obligation to operate all four routes, as part of its contract with the local authority. Consequently, the company should treat all four bus routes together as a cash generating unit, and calculate the recoverable amount for the unit as a whole.

If an active market exists for the output produced by the asset or a group of assets, this asset or group should be identified as a cash generating unit, even if some or all of the output is used internally.

Cash generating units should be identified consistently from period to period for the same type of asset unless a change is justified.

The group of net assets less liabilities that are considered for impairment should be the same as those considered in the calculation of the recoverable amount.

Goodwill and the impairment of assets

Goodwill acquired in a business combination does not generate cash flows independently of other assets. It must be **allocated** to each of the acquirer's **cash-generating units** (or groups of cash-generating units) that are expected to benefit from the synergies of the combination. Each unit to which the goodwill is so allocated should:

(a)   Represent the **lowest level** within the entity at which the goodwill is monitored for internal management purposes

(b)   Not be **larger than a reporting segment** determined in accordance with IFRS 8 *Operating segments* (Chapter 15)

It may be impractical to complete the allocation of goodwill before the first reporting date after a business combination, particularly if the acquirer is accounting for the combination for the first time using provisional values. The initial allocation of goodwill must be completed before the end of the first reporting period after the acquisition date.

There are two situations to consider.

(a)   Where goodwill has been allocated to a cash-generating unit

(b)   Where it has not been possible to allocate goodwill to a specific cash-generating unit, but only to a group of units

A cash-generating unit to which goodwill has been allocated is tested for impairment annually. The **carrying amount** of the unit, including goodwill, is compared **with the recoverable amount**. If the carrying amount of the unit exceeds the recoverable amount, the entity must recognise an impairment loss.

Where goodwill relates to a cash-generating unit but has not been allocated to that unit, the unit is tested for impairment by **comparing its carrying amount** (excluding goodwill) **with its recoverable amount**. The entity must recognise an impairment loss if the carrying amount exceeds the recoverable amount.

The annual impairment test may be performed at any time during an accounting period, but must be performed at the **same time every year**.

Corporate assets

Corporate assets are group or divisional assets such as a head office building, computer equipment or a research centre. Essentially, corporate assets are assets that do not generate cash inflows independently from other assets, hence their carrying amount cannot be fully attributed to a cash-generating unit under review.

In testing a cash generating unit for impairment, an entity should identify all the corporate assets that relate to the cash-generating unit.

(a)   If a portion of the carrying amount of a corporate asset **can be allocated** to the unit on a reasonable and consistent basis, the entity compares the carrying amount of the unit (including the portion of the asset) with its recoverable amount.

(b)   If a portion of the carrying amount of a corporate asset **cannot be allocated** to the unit on a reasonable and consistent basis, the entity:

   (i)   Compares the carrying amount of the unit (excluding the asset) with its recoverable amount and recognises any impairment loss

   (ii)   Identifies the smallest group of cash-generating units that includes the cash-generating unit to which the asset belongs and to which a portion of the carrying amount of the asset can be allocated on a reasonable and consistent basis

   (iii)   Compares the carrying amount of that group of cash-generating units (including the portion of the asset allocated to the group of units) with the recoverable amount of the group of units and recognises any impairment loss

Accounting treatment of an impairment loss

If, and only if, the recoverable amount of an asset is less than its carrying amount in the statement of financial position, an impairment loss has occurred. This loss should be **recognised immediately**.

(a)   The asset's **carrying amount** should be reduced to its recoverable amount in the statement of financial position.

(b)   The **impairment loss** should be recognised immediately in profit or loss (unless the asset has been revalued in which case the loss is treated as a revaluation decrease).

After reducing an asset to its recoverable amount, the **depreciation charge** on the asset should then be based on its new carrying amount, its estimated residual value (if any) and its estimated remaining useful life.

An impairment loss should be recognised for a **cash generating unit** if (and only if) the recoverable amount for the cash generating unit is less than the carrying amount in the statement of financial position for all the assets in the unit. When an impairment loss is recognised for a cash generating unit, the loss should be allocated between the assets in the unit in the following order:

(a)   First, to the goodwill allocated to the cash generating unit

(b)   Then to all other assets in the cash-generating unit, on a pro rata basis

In allocating an impairment loss, the carrying amount of an asset should not be reduced below the highest of:

(a)   Its fair value less costs to sell

(b)   Its value in use (if determinable)

(c)   Zero

Any remaining amount of an impairment loss should be recognised as a liability if required by other IFRSs.

Example 1: Impairment loss

A company that extracts natural gas and oil has a drilling platform in the Caspian Sea. It is required by legislation of the country concerned to remove and dismantle the platform at the end of its useful life. Accordingly, the company has included an amount in its accounts for removal and dismantling costs, and is depreciating this amount over the platform's expected life.

The company is carrying out an exercise to establish whether there has been an impairment of the platform.

(a)   Its carrying amount in the statement of financial position is $3m.

(b)   The company has received an offer of $2.8m for the platform from another oil company. The bidder would take over the responsibility (and costs) for dismantling and removing the platform at the end of its life.

(c)   The present value of the estimated cash flows from the platform's continued use is $3.3m.

(d)   The carrying amount in the statement of financial position for the provision for dismantling and removal is currently $0.6m.

What should be the value of the drilling platform in the statement of financial position, and what, if anything, is the impairment loss?

Fair value less costs of disposal	=	$2.8m
Value in use	=	PV of cash flows from use less the carrying amount of the provision/liability
	=	$3.3m – $0.6m
	=	$2.7m
Recoverable amount	=	Higher of these two amounts, ie $2.8m
Carrying amount	=	$3m
Impairment loss	=	$0.2m

The carrying amount should be reduced to $2.8m.

Example 2: Impairment loss

A company has acquired another business for $4.5m: tangible assets are valued at $4.0m and goodwill at $0.5m.

An asset with a carrying amount of $1m is destroyed in a terrorist attack. The asset was not insured. The loss of the asset, without insurance, has prompted the company to assess whether there has been an impairment of assets in the acquired business and what the amount of any such loss is.

The recoverable amount of the business (a single cash generating unit) is measured as $3.1m.

There has been an impairment loss of $1.4m ($4.5m – $3.1m).

The impairment loss will be recognised in profit or loss. The loss will be allocated between the assets in the cash generating unit as follows.

(a) A loss of $1m can be attributed directly to the uninsured asset that has been destroyed.

(b) The remaining loss of $0.4m should be allocated to goodwill.

The carrying amount of the assets will now be $3m for tangible assets and $0.1m for goodwill.

Reversal of an impairment loss

The annual assessment to determine whether there may have been some impairment should be **applied to all assets**, including assets that have already been impaired in the past.

In some cases, the recoverable amount of an asset that has previously been impaired might turn out to be **higher** than the asset's current carrying value. In other words, there might have been a reversal of some of the previous impairment loss.

(a)   The reversal of the impairment loss should be **recognised immediately** as income in profit or loss.

(b)   The carrying amount of the asset should be increased to its **new recoverable amount**.

> An impairment loss recognised for an asset in prior years should be reversed if, and only if, there has been a change in the estimates used to determine the asset's recoverable amount since the last impairment loss was recognised.
>
> *(IAS 36: para. 114)*

The asset cannot be revalued to a carrying amount that is higher than its value would have been if the asset had not been impaired originally, ie its **depreciated carrying value** had the impairment not taken place. Depreciation of the asset should now be based on its new revalued amount, its estimated residual value (if any) and its estimated remaining useful life.

An exception to this rule is for **goodwill**. An impairment loss for goodwill should not be reversed in a subsequent period.

Disclosure

IAS 36 calls for substantial disclosure about impairment of assets. The information to be disclosed includes the following.

(a)   For each class of assets, the amount of **impairment losses recognised** and the amount of any **impairment losses recovered** (ie reversals of impairment losses)

(b)   For each individual asset or cash generating unit that has suffered a **significant impairment loss**, details of the nature of the asset, the amount of the loss, the events that led to recognition of the loss, whether the recoverable amount is fair value less costs to sell or value in use, and if the recoverable amount is value in use, the basis on which this value was estimated (eg the discount rate applied)

An entity may receive monetary or non-monetary compensation from third parties for the impairment or loss of items of property, plant and equipment. The compensation may be used to restore the asset. Examples include:

•   Reimbursement by insurance companies after an impairment of items of plant and equipment

•   Physical replacement of an impaired or lost asset

The accounting treatment is as follows.

(a) Impairments of items of property, plant and equipment should be recognised under IAS 36, disposals should be recognised under IAS 16.

(b) Monetary or non-monetary compensation from third parties for items of property etc that were impaired, lost or given up, should be included in profit or loss.

(c) The cost of assets restored, purchased, constructed as a replacement or received as compensation should be determined and presented under IAS 16.

5 IAS 23: Borrowing costs

IAS 23 *Borrowing costs* was revised in March 2007. Previously it gave a choice of methods in dealing with borrowing costs: capitalisation or expense. The revised standard requires capitalisation.

Only two definitions are given by the standard.

> **Borrowing costs.** Interest and other costs incurred by an entity in connection with the borrowing of funds.
>
> **Qualifying asset.** An asset that necessarily takes a substantial period of time to get ready for its intended use or sale. *(IAS 23: para. 5)*

The standard lists what may be **included in borrowing costs**.

- Interest expense calculated using the effective interest rate method as per IAS 39 (now per IFRS 9)

- Finance charges in respect of leases recognised in accordance with IAS 17 (now IFRS 16)

- Exchange differences arising from foreign currency borrowings to the extent that they are regarded as an adjustment to interest costs

Depending on the circumstances, any of the following may be qualifying assets.

- Inventories
- Manufacturing plants
- Power generation facilities
- Intangible assets
- Investment properties

Financial assets and inventories that are manufactured or otherwise produced over a short period of time are **not qualifying assets**. Assets that are ready for their intended use or sale when purchased are not qualifying assets.

Recognition

Borrowing costs should be capitalised if they are directly attributable to the acquisition, construction or production of a qualifying asset as part of its cost. Other borrowing costs are expensed as incurred.

Those borrowing costs directly attributable to the acquisition, construction or production of a qualifying asset are costs that **would have been avoided** had the expenditure on the qualifying asset not been made. This is obviously straightforward where funds have been borrowed for the financing of one particular asset.

Difficulties arise, however, where the entity uses a **range of debt instruments** to finance a wide range of assets, so that there is no direct relationship between particular borrowings and a specific asset. For example, all borrowings may be made centrally and then lent to different parts of the group or entity. Judgement is therefore required, particularly where further complications can arise (eg foreign currency loans).

Once the relevant borrowings are identified, which relate to a specific asset, then the **amount of borrowing costs eligible for capitalisation** will be the actual borrowing costs incurred on those borrowings during the period, *less* any investment income on the temporary investment of those borrowings. It would not be unusual for some or all of the funds to be invested before they are actually used on the qualifying asset.

Example

On 1 January 20X9 a company borrowed $1.5m to finance the production of two assets, both of which were expected to take a year to build. Production started during 20X9. The loan facility was drawn down on 1 January 20X9, and was utilised as follows, with the remaining funds invested temporarily.

	Asset A $'000	Asset B $'000
1 January 20X9	250	500
1 July 20X9	250	500

The loan rate was 9% and the company can invest surplus funds at 7%.

Ignoring compound interest, what are the borrowing costs which may be capitalised for each of the assets and consequently the cost of each asset as at 31 December 20X9?

	Asset A $	Asset B $
Borrowing costs:		
To 31 December 20X9		
$500,000/$1,000,000 × 9%	45,000	90,000
Less investment income:		
To 30 June 20X9 $250,000/$500,000 × 7% × 6/12	(8,750)	(17,500)
	36,250	72,500
Cost of assets		
Expenditure incurred	500,000	1,000,000
Borrowing costs	36,250	72,500
	536,250	1,072,500

In a situation where **borrowings are obtained generally**, but are applied in part to obtaining a qualifying asset, then the amount of borrowing costs eligible for capitalisation is found by applying the 'capitalisation rate' to the expenditure on the asset.

The **capitalisation rate** is the weighted average of the borrowing costs applicable to the entity's borrowings that are outstanding during the period, excluding borrowings made specifically to obtain a qualifying asset. However, there is a cap on the amount of borrowing costs calculated in this way: it must not exceed actual borrowing costs incurred.

Sometimes one overall weighted average can be calculated for a group or entity, but in some situations it may be more appropriate to use a weighted average for borrowing costs for **individual parts of the group or entity**.

Example

A company had the following loans in place at the beginning and end of 20X6.

	1 January 20X6 $	31 December 20X6 $
10% Bank loan repayable 20X8	120	120
9.5% Bank loan repayable 20X9	80	80
8.9% debenture repayable 20X7	–	150

The 8.9% debenture was issued to fund the construction of a qualifying asset (a piece of mining equipment), construction of which began on 1 July 20X6.

On 1 January 20X6, the company began construction of a qualifying asset, a piece of machinery for a hydro-electric plant, using existing borrowings. Expenditure drawn down for the construction was: $30m on 1 January 20X6, $20m on 1 October 20X6.

What are the borrowing costs to be capitalised for the hydro-electric plant machine?

Capitalisation rate = weighted average rate

$$= (10\% \times \frac{120}{120+80}) + (9.5\% \times \frac{80}{120+80})$$

$$= 9.8\%$$

Borrowing costs = ($30m × 9.8%) + ($20m × 9.8% × 3/12)

= $3.43m

Commencement of capitalisation

An entity can start to capitalise borrowing costs on the **commencement date**. This is the date when the following conditions are met:

(a)   Expenditure on the asset is being incurred

(b)   Borrowing costs are being incurred

(c)   Activities are undertaken that are necessary to prepare the asset for its intended use or sale

Expenditure must result in the payment of cash, transfer of other assets or assumption of interest-bearing liabilities. **Deductions from expenditure** will be made for any progress payments or grants received in connection with the asset. IAS 23 allows the **average carrying amount** of the asset during a period (including borrowing costs previously capitalised) to be used as a reasonable approximation of the expenditure to which the capitalisation rate is applied in the period. Presumably more exact calculations can be used.

Activities necessary to prepare the asset for its intended sale or use extend further than physical construction work. They encompass technical and administrative work prior to construction, eg obtaining permits. They do not include holding an asset when no production or development that changes the asset's condition is taking place, eg where land is held without any associated development activity.

Cessation of capitalisation

Once substantially all the activities necessary to prepare the qualifying asset for its intended use or sale are complete, then capitalisation of borrowing costs should cease. This will normally be when **physical construction of the asset is completed**, although minor modifications may still be outstanding.

The asset may be completed in **parts or stages**, where each part can be used while construction is still taking place on the other parts. Capitalisation of borrowing costs should cease for each part as it is completed. The example given by the standard is a business park consisting of several buildings.

Disclosures

The following should be disclosed in the financial statements in relation to borrowing costs.

(a)   Amount of borrowing costs **capitalised during the period**

(b)   **Capitalisation rate** used to determine the amount of borrowing costs eligible for capitalisation

1 IAS 38: Intangible assets

IAS 38 *Intangible assets* was originally published in September 1998. It has recently been revised to reflect changes introduced by the revision of IFRS 3 *Business combinations*. The objectives of the standard are:

(a) To establish the criteria for when an intangible asset may or should be **recognised**

(b) To specify how intangible assets should be **measured**

(c) To specify the **disclosure requirements** for intangible assets

IAS 38 applies to all intangible assets with certain **exceptions**: deferred tax assets (IAS 12), leases that fall within the scope of IFRS 16, financial assets, insurance contracts, assets arising from employee benefits (IAS 19), non-current assets held for sale, and mineral rights and exploration and extraction costs for minerals (although **some** of this material **is covered** by IAS 38). It does **not** apply to goodwill acquired in a business combination, which is dealt with under IFRS 3.

Definition

The definition of an intangible asset is a key aspect of the standard, because the rules for deciding whether or not an intangible asset may be **recognised** in the accounts of an entity are based on the definition of what an intangible asset is.

> An **intangible asset** is an identifiable non-monetary asset without physical substance The asset must be:
>
> (a) Controlled by the entity as a result of events in the past, and
>
> (b) Something from which the entity expects future economic benefits to flow.
>
> *(IAS 38: para. 8)*

Examples of items that might be considered as intangible assets include computer software, patents, copyrights, motion picture films, customer lists, franchises and fishing rights. An item should not be recognised as an intangible asset, however, unless it **fully meets the definition** in the standard. The guidelines go into great detail on this matter.

An intangible asset must be identifiable in order to distinguish it from goodwill. With non-physical items, there may be a problem with 'identifiability'.

(a)   If an intangible asset is **acquired separately through purchase**, there may be a transfer of a legal right that would help to make an asset identifiable.

(b)   An intangible asset may be identifiable if it is **separable**, ie if it could be rented or sold separately. However, 'separability' is not an essential feature of an intangible asset.

Another element of the definition of an intangible asset is that it must be under the control of the entity as a result of a past event. The entity must therefore be able to enjoy the future economic benefits from the asset, and prevent the access of others to those benefits. A **legally enforceable right** is evidence of such control, but is not always a necessary condition.

(a)   Control over **technical knowledge or know-how** only exists if it is protected by a **legal right**.

(b)   The skill of employees, arising out of the benefits of **training costs**, are most unlikely to be recognisable as an intangible asset, because an entity does not control the future actions of its staff.

(c)   Similarly, **market share and customer loyalty** cannot normally be intangible assets, since an entity cannot control the actions of its customers.

Expected future economic benefits

An item can only be recognised as an intangible asset if economic benefits are expected to flow in the future from ownership of the asset. Economic benefits may come from the **sale** of products or services, or from a reduction in expenditures (cost savings).

An intangible asset, when recognised initially, must be measured at **cost**. It should be recognised if, and only if, **both** the following occur.

(a)   It is probable that the **future economic benefits** that are attributable to the asset will **flow to the entity**.

(b)   The **cost can be measured reliably**.

Management has to exercise its judgement in assessing the degree of certainty attached to the flow of economic benefits to the entity. External evidence is best.

(a) If an intangible asset is **acquired separately**, its cost can usually be measured reliably as its purchase price (including incidental costs of purchase such as legal fees, and any costs incurred in getting the asset ready for use).

(b) When an intangible asset is acquired as **part of a business combination** (ie an acquisition or takeover), the cost of the intangible asset is its fair value at the date of the acquisition.

IFRS 3 explains that the fair value of intangible assets acquired in business combinations can normally be measured with sufficient reliability to be **recognised separately** from goodwill.

IFRS 13 requires that the following are considered in determining fair value:

(a) The asset or liability being measured.

(b) The principal market (ie that where the most activity takes place) or where there is no principal market, the most advantageous market (ie that in which the best price could be achieved) in which an orderly transaction would take place for the asset or liability.

(c) The highest and best use of the asset or liability and whether it is used on a standalone basis or in conjunction with other assets or liabilities.

(d) Assumptions that market participants would use when pricing the asset or liability.

IFRS 13 provides a hierarchy of inputs for arriving at fair value. It requires that level 1 inputs are used where possible:

Level 1 Quoted prices in active markets for identical assets that the entity can access at the measurement date

Level 2 Inputs other than quoted prices that are directly or indirectly observable for the asset

Level 3 Unobservable inputs for the asset

In accordance with IAS 20, intangible assets acquired by way of government grant and the grant itself may be recorded initially either at cost (which may be zero) or fair value.

Internally generated goodwill

The standard deliberately precludes recognition of internally generated goodwill because it requires that, for initial recognition, the cost of the asset rather than its fair value should be capable of being measured reliably and that it should be identifiable and controlled. Thus you do not recognise an asset which is subjective and cannot be measured reliably.

Research and development costs

Research activities by definition do not meet the criteria for recognition under IAS 38. This is because, at the research stage of a project, it cannot be certain that future economic benefits will probably flow to the entity from the project. There is too much uncertainty about the likely success or otherwise of the project. **Research costs should therefore be written off as an expense as they are incurred**.

Examples of research costs

(a) Activities aimed at obtaining new knowledge

(b) The search for, evaluation and final selection of, applications of research findings or other knowledge

(c) The search for alternatives for materials, devices, products, processes, systems or services

(d) The formulation, design evaluation and final selection of possible alternatives for new or improved materials, devices, products, systems or services

Development

Development costs **may qualify** for recognition as intangible assets provided that the following **strict criteria** can be demonstrated.

(a) The technical feasibility of completing the intangible asset so that it will be available for use or sale

(b) Its intention to complete the intangible asset and use or sell it

(c) Its ability to use or sell the intangible asset

(d) How the intangible asset will generate probable future economic benefits. Among other things, the entity should demonstrate the existence of a market for the output of the intangible asset or the intangible asset itself or, if it is to be used internally, the usefulness of the intangible asset

(e) Its ability to measure the expenditure attributable to the intangible asset during its development reliably

In contrast with research costs development costs are incurred at a later stage in a project, and the probability of success should be more apparent. Examples of development costs include the following.

(a) The design, construction and testing of pre-production or pre-use prototypes and models

(b) The design of tools, jigs, moulds and dies involving new technology

(c) The design, construction and operation of a pilot plant that is not of a scale economically feasible for commercial production

BPP
LEARNING MEDIA

(d)   The design, construction and testing of a chosen alternative for new or improved materials, devices, products, processes, systems or services

The standard **prohibits** the recognition of **internally generated brands, mastheads, publishing titles and customer lists** and similar items as intangible assets. These all fail to meet one or more (in some cases all) the definition and recognition criteria and in some cases are probably indistinguishable from internally generated goodwill.

Cost of an internally generated intangible asset

The costs allocated to an internally generated intangible asset should be only costs that can be **directly attributed** or allocated on a reasonable and consistent basis to creating, producing or preparing the asset for its intended use. The principles underlying the costs which may or may not be included are similar to those for other non-current assets and inventory.

The cost of an internally generated intangible asset is the sum of the **expenditure incurred from the date when** the intangible asset first **meets the recognition criteria**. If, as often happens, considerable costs have already been recognised as expenses before management could demonstrate that the criteria have been met, this earlier expenditure should not be retrospectively recognised at a later date as part of the cost of an intangible asset.

Example

A company is developing a new production process. During 20X9, expenditure incurred was $100,000, of which $90,000 was incurred before 1 December 20X9 and $10,000 between 1 December 20X9 and 31 December 20X9. The company can demonstrate that, at 1 December 20X9, the production process met the criteria for recognition as an intangible asset. The recoverable amount of the know-how embodied in the process is estimated to be $50,000.

How should the expenditure be treated?

At the end of 20X9, the production process is recognised as an intangible asset at a cost of $10,000. This is the expenditure incurred since the date when the recognition criteria were met, that is 1 December 20X9. The $90,000 expenditure incurred before 1 December 20X9 is expensed, because the recognition criteria were not met. It will never form part of the cost of the production process recognised in the statement of financial position.

All expenditure related to an intangible which does not meet the criteria for recognition either as an identifiable intangible asset or as goodwill arising on an acquisition should be **expensed as incurred**. The IAS gives examples of such expenditure.

- Start up costs
- Training costs
- Advertising costs
- Business relocation costs

Prepaid costs for services, for example advertising or marketing costs for campaigns that have been prepared but not launched, can still be recognised as a **prepayment**.

Measurement subsequent to initial recognition

The standard allows two methods of valuation for intangible assets after they have been first recognised.

Applying the **cost model**, an intangible asset should be **carried at its cost**, less any accumulated amortisation and less any accumulated impairment losses.

The **revaluation model** allows an intangible asset to be carried at a revalued amount, which is its **fair value** at the date of revaluation, less any subsequent accumulated amortisation and any subsequent accumulated impairment losses.

(a)   The fair value must be able to be measured reliably with reference to an **active market** in that type of asset.

(b)   The **entire class** of intangible assets of that type must be revalued at the same time (to prevent selective revaluations).

(c)   If an intangible asset in a class of revalued intangible assets cannot be revalued because there is **no active market** for this asset, the asset should be carried at its **cost less any accumulated amortisation and impairment losses**.

(d)   Revaluations should be made with such **regularity** that the carrying amount does not differ from that which would be determined using fair value at the reporting date.

The guidelines state that there **will not usually be an active market** in an intangible asset; therefore the revaluation model will usually not be available. For example, although copyrights, publishing rights and film rights can be sold, each has a unique sale value. In such cases, revaluation to fair value would be inappropriate. A fair value might be obtainable however for assets such as fishing rights or quotas or taxi cab licences.

Where an intangible asset is revalued upwards to a fair value, the amount of the revaluation should be credited directly to equity under the heading of a **revaluation surplus**.

However, if a revaluation surplus is a **reversal of a revaluation decrease** that was previously charged against income, the increase can be recognised as income.

Where the carrying amount of an intangible asset is revalued downwards, the amount of the **downward revaluation** should be charged as an expense against income, unless the asset has previously been revalued upwards. A revaluation decrease should be first charged against any previous revaluation surplus in respect of that asset.

Example

An intangible asset is measured by a company at fair value. The asset was revalued upwards by $400 in 20X8, and there is a revaluation surplus of $400 in the statement of financial position. At the end of 20X9, the asset is valued again, and a downward valuation of $500 is required.

How is the downward revaluation accounted for?

In this example, the downward valuation of $500 can first be set against the revaluation surplus of $400. The revaluation surplus will be reduced to $0 and a charge of $100 made as an expense in 20X9.

When the revaluation model is used, and an intangible asset is revalued upwards, the cumulative revaluation **surplus may be transferred to retained earnings** when the surplus is eventually realised. The surplus would be realised when the asset is disposed of. However, the surplus may also be realised over time as the **asset is used** by the entity. The amount of the surplus realised each year is the difference between the amortisation charge for the asset based on the revalued amount of the asset, and the amortisation that would be charged on the basis of the asset's historical cost. The realised surplus in such case should be transferred from revaluation surplus directly to retained earnings, and should not be taken through profit or loss.

Useful life

An entity should **assess** the useful life of an intangible asset, which may be **finite or indefinite**. An intangible asset has an indefinite useful life when there is **no foreseeable limit** to the period over which the asset is expected to generate net cash inflows for the entity.

Many factors are considered in determining the useful life of an intangible asset, including: expected usage; typical product life cycles; technical, technological, commercial or other types of obsolescence; the stability of the industry; expected actions by competitors; the level of maintenance expenditure required; and legal or similar limits on the use of the asset, such as the expiry dates of related leases. Computer software and many other intangible assets normally have short lives because they are susceptible to technological obsolescence. However, uncertainty does not justify choosing a life that is unrealistically short.

The useful life of an intangible asset that arises from **contractual or other legal rights** should not exceed the period of the rights, but may be shorter depending on the period over which the entity expects to use the asset.

Amortisation

An intangible asset with a finite useful life should be amortised over its **expected useful life**.

(a) Amortisation should start when the asset is **available for use**.

(b) Amortisation should cease at the earlier of the date that the asset is classified **as held for sale** in accordance with IFRS 5 *Non-current assets held for sale and discontinued operations* and the date that the asset is **derecognised**.

(c) The amortisation method used should reflect the pattern in which the asset's future economic benefits are consumed. If such a pattern cannot be predicted reliably, the straight-line method should be used.

(d) The amortisation charge for each period should normally be recognised **in profit or loss**.

The **residual value** of an intangible asset with a finite useful life is **assumed to be zero** unless a third party is committed to buying the intangible asset at the end of its useful life or unless there is an active market for that type of asset (so that its expected residual value can be measured) and it is probable that there will be a market for the asset at the end of its useful life.

The amortisation period and the amortisation method used for an intangible asset with a finite useful life should be **reviewed at each financial year-end**.

Indefinite useful lives

An intangible asset with an indefinite useful life **should not be amortised**. (IAS 36 requires that such an asset is tested for impairment at least annually.)

The useful life of an intangible asset that is not being amortised should be **reviewed each year** to determine whether it is still appropriate to assess its useful life as indefinite. Reassessing the useful life of an intangible asset as finite rather than indefinite is an indicator that the asset may be impaired and therefore it should be tested for impairment.

Disposals/retirements of intangible assets

An intangible asset should be eliminated from the statement of financial position when it is disposed of or when there is no further expected economic benefit from its future use. On disposal the gain or loss arising from the **difference between the net disposal proceeds and the carrying amount** of the asset should be taken to profit or loss as a gain or loss on disposal (ie treated as income or expense).

Disclosure requirements

The standard has fairly extensive disclosure requirements for intangible assets. The financial statements should disclose the **accounting policies** for intangible assets that have been adopted.

For **each class of intangible assets**, disclosure is required of the following.

- Whether the useful life is indefinite or finite

- The **method of amortisation** used

- The **useful life** of the assets or the amortisation rate used

- The **gross carrying amount**, the **accumulated amortisation** and the **accumulated impairment losses** as at the beginning and the end of the period

- The line in the statement of profit or loss in which any amortisation of intangible assets is included

- A **reconciliation of the carrying amount** as at the beginning and at the end of the period (additions, retirements/disposals, revaluations, impairment losses, impairment losses reversed, amortisation charge for the period, net exchange differences, other movements)

- The carrying amount of **internally-generated intangible assets**

The financial statements should also disclose the amount of research and development expenditure that have been charged as expenses of the period.

2 Goodwill (IFRS 3)

'Inherent' goodwill may exist in a business but it is not recognised as an asset because no value can be assigned to it. This is not the case for purchased goodwill which is dealt with by IFRS 3.

IFRS 3: Business combinations

IFRS 3 covers the accounting treatment of goodwill acquired in a business combination.

> **Goodwill.** Future economic benefits arising from assets that are not capable of being individually identified and separately recognised. *(IFRS 3: Appendix A)*

Goodwill acquired in a business combination is **recognised as an asset** and is initially measured at **cost**. Cost of goodwill is the excess of the cost of the combination over the acquirer's interest in the net fair value of the acquiree's identifiable assets, liabilities and contingent liabilities.

After initial recognition goodwill acquired in a business combination is measured **at cost less any accumulated impairment losses**. It is **not amortised**. Instead it is tested for impairment at least annually, in accordance with IAS 36 *Impairment of assets*.

Negative goodwill arises when the acquirer's interest in the net fair value of the acquiree's identifiable assets, liabilities and contingent liabilities exceeds the cost of the business combination. IFRS 3 refers to negative goodwill as the 'excess of acquirer's interest in the net fair value of acquiree's identifiable assets, liabilities and contingent liabilities over cost'.

Negative goodwill can arise as the result of **errors** in measuring the fair value of either the cost of the combination or the acquiree's identifiable net assets. It can also arise as the result of a **bargain purchase**.

Where there is negative goodwill, an entity should first **reassess** the amounts at which it has measured both the cost of the combination and the acquiree's identifiable net assets. This exercise should identify any errors.

Any negative goodwill remaining should be **recognised immediately in profit or loss**.

IFRS 3 requires extensive **disclosures**. These include a **reconciliation** of the carrying amount of goodwill at the beginning and end of the period, showing separately:

(a)   The gross amount and accumulated impairment losses at the beginning of the period

(b)   Additional goodwill recognised during the period

(c)   Impairment losses recognised during the period

(d)   Net exchange differences arising during the period, and

(e)   The gross amount and accumulated impairment losses at the end of the period

What are the main characteristics of goodwill which distinguish it from other intangible non-current assets?

Goodwill may be distinguished from other intangible non-current assets by reference to the following characteristics.

(a)   It is incapable of realisation separately from the business as a whole

(b)   Its value has no reliable or predictable relationship to any costs which may have been incurred

(c) Its value arises from various intangible factors such as skilled employees, effective advertising or a strategic location. These indirect factors cannot be valued

(d) The value of goodwill may fluctuate widely according to internal and external circumstances over relatively short periods of time

(e) The assessment of the value of goodwill is highly subjective

It could be argued that, because goodwill is so different from other intangible non-current assets it does not make sense to account for it in the same way. Thus the capitalisation and amortisation treatment would not be acceptable. Furthermore, because goodwill is so difficult to value, any valuation may be misleading, and it is best eliminated from the statement of financial position altogether. However, there are strong arguments for treating it like any other intangible non-current asset. This issue remains controversial.

Reporting financial performance

6

1 IAS 10: Events after the reporting period

The financial statements are significant indicators of a company's success or failure. It is important, therefore, that they include all the information necessary for an understanding of the company's position.

IAS 10 *Events after the reporting period* requires the provision of additional information in order to facilitate such an understanding. IAS 10 deals with events **after** the reporting date which may affect the position **at** the reporting date.

The standard gives the following definition.

> Events after the reporting period are those events, both favourable and unfavourable, that occur between the reporting date and the date on which the financial statements are authorised for issue. Two types of events can be identified:
>
> - Those that provide evidence of conditions that existed at the end of the reporting period; and
>
> - Those that are indicative of conditions that arose subsequent to the reporting period. *(IAS 10: para. 3)*

Between the end of the reporting period and the date on which the financial statements are authorised (ie for issue outside the organisation), events may occur which show that assets and liabilities at the end of the reporting period should be adjusted, or that disclosure of such events should be given.

Events requiring adjustment

The standard requires adjustment of assets and liabilities in certain circumstances.

An example of additional evidence which becomes available after the reporting period is where a **customer goes bankrupt, thus confirming that the trade account receivable balance at the year end is uncollectable.**

In relation to going concern, the standard states that, where operating results and the financial position have deteriorated after the reporting period, it may be necessary to reconsider whether the going concern assumption is appropriate in the preparation of the financial statements.

For instance, a warehouse fire destroying inventory after the year end would be non-adjusting, because the inventory did exist at the year end. **But** if the loss of inventory means the entity can no longer continue to trade, then the going concern assumption is no longer valid and the basis of preparing the financial statements must change.

Events not requiring adjustment

The standard then looks at events which do **not** require adjustment.

One example of such an event is where the **value of an investment falls between the end of reporting period and the date the financial statements are authorised** for issue. The fall in value represents circumstances during the current period, not conditions existing at the end of the previous reporting period, so it is not appropriate to adjust the value of the investment in the financial statements. Disclosure is an aid to users, however, indicating 'unusual changes' in the state of assets and liabilities after the reporting date.

The rule for **disclosure** of events occurring after the reporting period which relate to conditions that arose after that date, is that disclosure should be made if non-disclosure would hinder the user's ability to made **proper evaluations** and decision based on the financial statements. An example might be the acquisition of another business.

The distinction between an **adjusting event** and a **non-adjusting event** can be shown by the following diagram.

Dividends

Dividends declared by the entity after the reporting period are a special case. Even if they are stated to be in respect of the period covered by the financial statements, they should **not** be **provided for**. They should simply be disclosed in the notes.

Disclosures

The following **disclosure requirements** are given **for events** which occur after the reporting period which do **not** require adjustment. If disclosure of events occurring after the reporting period is required by this standard, the following information should be provided:

(a)   The nature of the event

(b)   An estimate of the financial effect, or a statement that such an estimate cannot be made

2 IAS 8: Accounting policies, changes in accounting estimates and errors

IAS 8 deals with the treatment of changes in accounting estimates, changes in accounting policies and errors, as defined below.

Definitions

Accounting policies are the specific principles, bases, conventions, rules and practices adopted by an entity in preparing and presenting financial statements.

A **change in accounting estimate** is an adjustment of the carrying amount of an asset or a liability or the amount of the periodic consumption of an asset, that results from the assessment of the present status of, and expected future benefits and obligations associated with, assets and liabilities. Changes in accounting estimates result from new information or new developments and, accordingly, are not corrections of errors.

Material. As defined in IAS 1.

Prior period errors are omissions from, and misstatements in, the entity's financial statements for one or more prior periods arising from a failure to use, or misuse of, reliable information that:

(a)   Was available when financial statements for those periods were authorised for issue, and

(b)   Could reasonably be expected to have been obtained and taken into account in the preparation and presentation of those financial statements.

Such errors include the effects of mathematical mistakes, mistakes in applying accounting policies, oversights or misinterpretations of facts, and fraud.

Retrospective application is applying a new accounting policy to transactions, other events and conditions as if that policy had always been applied.

Retrospective restatement is correcting the recognition, measurement and disclosure of amounts of elements of financial statements as if a prior period error had never occurred.

Prospective application of a change in accounting policy and of recognising the effect of a change in an accounting estimate, respectively, are:

(a)   Applying the new accounting policy to transactions, other events and conditions occurring after the date as at which the policy is changes; and

(b)   Recognising the effect of the change in the accounting estimate in the current and future periods affected by the change.

> **Impracticable.** Applying a requirement is impracticable when the entity cannot apply it after making every reasonable effort to do so. It is impracticable to apply a change in an accounting policy retrospectively or to make a retrospective restatement to correct an error if one of the following apply.
>
> (a) The effects or the retrospective application or retrospective restatement are not determinable.
>
> (b) The retrospective application or retrospective restatement requires assumptions about what management's intent would have been in that period.
>
> (c) The retrospective application or retrospective restatement requires significant estimates of amounts and it is impossible to distinguish objectively information about those estimates that: provides evidence of circumstances that existed on the date(s) at which those amounts are to be recognised, measured or disclosed; and would have been available when the financial statements for that prior period were authorised for issue from other information. *(IAS 8: para. 5)*

3 Accounting policies

Accounting policies are determined by **applying the relevant IFRS or IAS** and considering any relevant Implementation Guidance issued by the IASB for that IFRS/IAS.

Where there is no applicable IFRS management should use its **judgement** in developing and applying an accounting policy that results in information that is **relevant** and **reliable**. Management should refer to:

(a) The requirements and guidance in IFRSs dealing with **similar** and **related issues**

(b) The definitions, recognition criteria and measurement concepts for assets, liabilities and expenses in the **Conceptual Framework**

Management may also consider the most recent pronouncements of **other standard setting bodies** that use a similar conceptual framework to develop standards, other accounting literature and accepted industry practices if these do not conflict with the sources above.

An entity must select and apply its accounting policies for a period **consistently** for similar transactions, other events and conditions, unless an IFRS specifically requires or permits categorisation of items for which different policies may be appropriate. If an IFRS requires or permits categorisation of items, an appropriate accounting policy must be selected and applied consistently to each category.

4 Changes in accounting policies

The same accounting policies are usually adopted from period to period, to allow users to analyse trends over time in profit, cash flows and financial position. **Changes in accounting policy will therefore be rare** and should be made only if required by one of three things.

(a) By **statute**

(b) By an **accounting standard setting body**

(c) If the change will result in a **more appropriate presentation** of events or transactions in the financial statements of the entity

The standard highlights two types of event **which do not constitute changes in accounting policy**.

(a) Adopting an accounting policy for a **new type of transaction** or event not dealt with previously by the entity

(b) Adopting a **new accounting policy** for a transaction or event which has not occurred in the past or which was not material

In the case of tangible non-current assets, if a policy of revaluation is adopted for the first time then this is treated, not as a change of accounting policy under IAS 8, but as a revaluation under IAS 16 *Property, plant and equipment*. The following paragraphs do not therefore apply to a changes in policy to adopt revaluations.

A change in accounting policy **must be applied retrospectively. Retrospective application** means that the new accounting policy is applied to transactions and events as if it had always been in use. In other words, at the earliest date such transactions or events occurred, the policy is applied from that date.

Prospective application is **no longer allowed** under the revised IAS 8 unless it is **impracticable** to determine the cumulative amount of change.

What would constitute a change in accounting policy? Examples are:

- A change from inventory valuation using FIFO to weighted average, or vice versa

- A change in presentation, such as depreciation transferred from cost of sales to expenses

Adoption of an IFRS/IAS

Where a new IFRS or IAS is adopted, IAS 8 requires any transitional provisions in the new IFRS itself to be followed. If none are given in the IFRS which is being adopted, then the general principles of IAS 8 should be followed.

Other changes in accounting policy

IAS 8 requires **retrospective application, unless** it is **impracticable** to determine the cumulative amount of charge. Any resulting adjustment should be reported as an adjustment to the opening balance of retained earnings. Comparative information should be restated unless it is impracticable to do so.

This means that all comparative information must be restated **as if the new policy had always been in force**, with amounts relating to earlier periods reflected in an adjustment to opening reserves of the earliest period presented.

Prospective application is allowed only when it is impracticable to determine the cumulative effect of the change.

Certain **disclosures** are required when a change in accounting policy has a material effect on the current period or any prior period presented, or when it may have a material effect in subsequent periods.

(a)   Reasons for the change

(b)   Amount of the adjustment for the current period and for each period presented

(c)   Amount of the adjustment relating to periods prior to those included in the comparative information

(d)   The fact that comparative information has been restated or that it is impracticable to do so

An entity should also disclose information relevant to assessing the **impact of new IFRS** on the financial statements where these **have not yet come into force**.

5 Changes in accounting estimates

Estimates arise in relation to business activities because of the **uncertainties inherent within them**. Judgements are made based on the most up to date information and the use of such estimates is a necessary part of the preparation of financial statements. It does not undermine their reliability. Here are some examples of accounting estimates.

- A necessary **bad debt allowance**
- **Useful lives** of depreciable assets
- Allowance for **obsolescence of inventory**

The rule here is that the **effect of a change in an accounting estimate** should be included in the determination of net profit or loss in one of:

(a)   The period of the change, if the change affects that period only

(b)   The period of the change and future periods, if the change affects both

Changes may occur in the circumstances which were in force at the time the estimate was calculated, or perhaps additional information or subsequent developments have come to light.

An example of a change in accounting estimate which affects only the **current period** is the bad debt estimate. However, a revision in the life over which an asset is depreciated would affect both the **current and future periods,** in the amount of the depreciation expense.

The effect of a change in an accounting estimate should be included in the **same profit or loss classification** as was used previously for the estimate. This rule helps to ensure **consistency** between the financial statements of different periods. Similarly, where an accounting estimate was previously reported as an extraordinary item, so the change of estimate should be too.

The **materiality** of the change is also relevant. The nature and amount of a change in an accounting estimate that has a material effect in the current period (or which is expected to have a material effect in subsequent periods) should be disclosed. If it is not possible to quantify the amount, this impracticability should be disclosed.

6 Errors

Errors discovered during a current period may have arisen through mathematical mistakes, incorrect application of accounting policies, misinterpretation of facts, oversights or fraud.

A more formal definition was given above.

Most of the time these errors can be **corrected through net profit or loss for the current period**. Where they fulfil the definition of prior period errors (given earlier), however, this is not appropriate.

Accounting treatment

Prior period errors are corrected retrospectively.

This involves either:

(a) Restating the comparative amounts for the prior period(s) in which the error occurred; or

(b) When the error occurred before the earliest prior period presented, restating the opening balances of assets, liabilities and equity for that period so that the financial statements are presented **as if the error had never occurred**.

Only where it is **impracticable** to determine the cumulative effect of an error on prior periods can an entity correct an error **prospectively**.

Various **disclosures** are required.

(a) Nature of the prior period error

(b) For each prior period, to the extent practicable, the **amount** of the correction

    (i) For each financial statement line item affected

    (ii) If IAS 33 applies, for basic and diluted earnings per share

(c) The amount of the correction at the **beginning of the earliest prior** period presented

(d) If **retrospective restatement is impracticable** for a particular prior period, the **circumstances** that led to the existence of that condition and a description of how and from when the error has been corrected. Subsequent periods need not repeat these disclosures

Example

During 20X7 P Co discovered that certain items had been included in inventory at 31 December 20X6, valued at $4.2m, which had in fact been sold before the year end. The following figures for 20X6 (as reported) and 20X7 (draft) are available.

	20X6	20X7 (draft)
	$'000	$'000
Revenue	47,400	67,200
Cost of goods sold	(34,570)	(55,800)
Profit before taxation	12,830	11,400
Income taxes	(3,880)	(3,400)
Net profit	8,950	8,000

Reserves at 1 January 20X6 were $13m. The cost of goods sold for 20X7 includes the $4.2m error in opening inventory. The income tax rate was 30% for 20X6 and 20X7.

How will this be shown in the statement of profit or loss and the retained earnings of P Co for 20X7?

P CO

STATEMENT OF PROFIT OR LOSS

	20X6	20X7
	$'000	$'000
Revenue	47,400	67,200
Cost of goods sold	(38,770)	(51,600)
Profit before taxation	8,630	15,600
Income taxes	(2,620)	(4,660)
Net profit	6,010	10,940

RETAINED EARNINGS

	20X6	20X7
Opening retained earnings		
As previously reported	13,000	21,950
Correction of prior period error	–	(2,940)
As restated	13,000	19,010
Net profit for year	6,010	10,940
Closing retained earnings	19,010	29,950

Workings

1 Cost of goods sold	20X6 $'000	20X7 $'000
As stated in question	34,570	55,800
Inventory adjustment	4,200	(4,200)
	38,770	51,600

2 Income tax	20X6 $'000	20X7 $'000
As stated in question	3,880	3,400
Inventory adjustment (4,200 × 30%)	(1,260)	1,260
	2,620	4,660

7 IFRS 5: Non-current assets held for sale and discontinued operations

IFRS 5 is the result of a short-term convergence project with the US Financial Accounting Standards Board (FASB). It replaced IAS 35 *Discontinuing operations*.

IFRS 5 requires assets and groups of assets that are 'held for sale' to be **presented separately** on the face of the statement of financial position and the results of discontinued operations to be presented separately in profit or loss. This is required so that users of financial statements will be better able to make **projections** about the financial position, profits and cash flows of the entity.

> **Disposal group.** A group of assets to be disposed of, by sale or otherwise, together as a group in a single transaction, and liabilities directly associated with those assets that will be transferred in the transaction. (In practice a disposal group could be a subsidiary, a cash-generating unit or a single operation within an entity.) *(IFRS 5: Appendix A)*

IFRS 5 does not apply to certain assets covered by other accounting standards:

(a) Deferred tax assets (IAS 12)

(b) Assets arising from employee benefits (IAS 19)

(c) Financial assets (IFRS 9)

(d) Investment properties accounted for in accordance with the fair value model (IAS 40)

(e) Agricultural and biological assets that are measured at fair value less estimated point of sale costs (IAS 41)

(f) Insurance contracts (IFRS 4)

Classification of assets held for sale

A non-current asset (or disposal group) should be classified as **held for sale** if its carrying amount will be recovered **principally through a sale transaction** rather than **through continuing use**. A number of detailed criteria must be met:

(a) The asset must be **available for immediate sale** in its present condition.

(b) Its sale must be **highly probable** (ie, significantly more likely than not).

For the sale to be highly probable, the following must apply:

(a) Management must be **committed** to a plan to sell the asset.

(b) There must be an active programme to **locate a buyer**.

(c) The asset must be marketed for sale at a **price that is reasonable** in relation to its current fair value.

(d) The sale should be expected to take place **within one year** from the date of classification.

(e) It is unlikely that significant changes to the plan will be made or that the plan will be withdrawn.

An asset (or disposal group) can still be classified as held for sale, even if the sale has not actually taken place within one year. However, the delay must have been **caused by events or circumstances beyond the entity's control** and there must be sufficient evidence that the entity is still committed to sell the asset or disposal group. Otherwise the entity must cease to classify the asset as held for sale.

If an entity acquires a disposal group (eg a subsidiary) exclusively with a view to its subsequent disposal it can classify the asset as held for sale only if the sale is expected to take place within one year and it is highly probable that all the other criteria will be met within a short time (normally three months).

An asset that is to be **abandoned** should not be classified as held for sale. This is because its carrying amount will be recovered principally through continuing use. However, a disposal group to be abandoned may meet the definition of a discontinued operation and therefore separate disclosure may be required.

Example

On 1 December 20X8, B Co became committed to a plan to sell a manufacturing facility and has already found a potential buyer. The company does not intend to discontinue the operations currently carried out in the facility. At 31 December 20X8 there is a backlog of uncompleted customer orders. The subsidiary will not be able to transfer the facility to the buyer until after it ceases to operate the facility and has eliminated the backlog of uncompleted customer orders. This is not expected to occur until spring 20X9.

Can the manufacturing facility be classified as 'held for sale' at 31 December 20X8?

The facility will not be transferred until the backlog of orders is completed; this demonstrates that the facility is not available for immediate sale in its present condition. The facility cannot be classified as 'held for sale' at 31 December 20X8. It must be treated in the same way as other items of property, plant and equipment: it should continue to be depreciated and should not be separately disclosed.

Measurement of assets held for sale

Fair value. The amount for which an asset could be exchanged, or a liability settled, between knowledgeable, willing parties in an arm's length transaction.*

Costs to sell. The incremental costs directly attributable to the disposal of an asset (or disposal group), excluding finance costs and income tax expense.

Recoverable amount. The higher of an asset's fair value less costs to sell and its value in use.

Value in use. The present value of estimated future cash flows expected to arise from the continuing use of an asset and from its disposal at the end of its useful life.

(IFRS 5: Appendix A)

*Under **IFRS 13** this is now: The price that would be received to sell an asset or paid to transfer a liability in an orderly transaction between market participants at the measurement date.

A non-current asset (or disposal group) that is held for sale should be measured at the **lower of** its **carrying amount** and **fair value less costs to sell**. Fair value less costs to sell is equivalent to net realisable value.

An impairment loss should be recognised where fair value less costs to sell is lower than carrying amount. Note that this is an exception to the normal rule. IAS 36 *Impairment of assets* requires an entity to recognise an impairment loss only where an asset's recoverable amount is lower than its carrying value. Recoverable amount is defined as the higher of net realisable value and value in use. IAS 36 does not apply to assets held for sale.

Non-current assets held for sale **should not be depreciated**, even if they are still being used by the entity.

A non-current asset (or disposal group) that is **no longer classified as held for sale** (for example, because the sale has not taken place within one year) is measured at the **lower of**:

(a)   Its **carrying amount** before it was classified as held for sale, adjusted for any depreciation that would have been charged had the asset not been held for sale

(b)   Its **recoverable amount** at the date of the decision not to sell

Presenting discontinued operations

Discontinued operation: a component of an entity that has either been disposed of, or is classified as held for sale, and:

- Represents a separate major line of business or geographical area of operations

- Is part of a single co-ordinated plan to dispose of a separate major line of business or geographical area of operations; or

- Is a subsidiary acquired exclusively with a view to resale.

Component of an entity: operations and cash flows that can be clearly distinguished, operationally and for financial reporting purposes, from the rest of the entity.

(IFRS 5: Appendix A)

An entity should **present and disclose information** that enables users of the financial statements to evaluate the financial effects of **discontinued operations** and disposals of non-current assets or disposal groups.

An entity should disclose a **single amount** on the **face of the statement of profit or loss** comprising the total of:

(a)   The **post-tax profit or loss** of discontinued operations and

(b)   The post-tax gain or loss recognised on the **measurement to fair value less costs to sell** or on the disposal of the assets or disposal group(s) constituting the discontinued operation.

An entity should also disclose an **analysis** of the single amount into:

(a)   The revenue, expenses and pre-tax profit or loss of discontinued operations

(b)   The related income tax expense

(c)   The gain or loss recognised on the measurement to fair value less costs to sell or on the disposal of the assets or the discontinued operation

(d)   The related income tax expense

This may be presented either on the face of the statement of profit or loss or in the notes. If it is presented on the face of the statement of profit or loss it should be presented in a section identified as relating to discontinued operations, ie separately from continuing operations. This analysis is not required where the discontinued operation is a newly acquired subsidiary that has been classified as held for sale.

An entity should disclose the **net cash flows** attributable to the operating, investing and financing activities of discontinued operations. These disclosures may be presented either on the face of the statement of cash flows or in the notes.

Gains and losses on the remeasurement of a disposal group that is not a discontinued operation but is held for sale should be included in profit or loss from continuing operations.

Illustration

The following illustration is taken from the implementation guidance (amended) to IFRS 5. Profit from discontinued operations would be analysed in the notes.

XYZ GROUP

STATEMENT OF PROFIT OR LOSS AND OTHER COMPREHENSIVE INCOME FOR THE YEAR ENDED 31 DECEMBER

	20X9 $'000	20X8 $'000
Continuing operations		
Revenue	X	X
Cost of sales	(X)	(X)
Gross profit	X	X
Other income	X	X
Distribution costs	(X)	(X)
Administrative expenses	(X)	(X)
Other expenses	(X)	(X)
Finance costs	(X)	(X)
Share of profit of associates	X	X
Profit before tax	X	X
Income tax expense	(X)	(X)
Profit for the year from continuing operations	X	X
Discontinued operations		
Profit for the year from discontinued operations	X	X
Profit for the year	X	X
Profit attributable to		
Owners of the parent		
Profit for the year from continuing operations	X	X
Profit for the year from discontinued operations	X	X
Profit for the year attributable to owners of the parent	X	X
Non-controlling interests		
Profit for the year from continuing operations	X	X
Profit for the year from discontinued operations	X	X
Profit for the year attributable to non-controlling interest	X	X

An alternative to this presentation would be to analyse the profit from discontinued operations in a separate column on the face of the statement of profit or loss.

Presentation of a non-current asset or disposal group classified as held for sale

Non-current assets and disposal groups classified as held for sale should be **presented separately** from other assets in the statement of financial position. The liabilities of a disposal group should be presented separately from other liabilities in the statement of financial position.

(a)   Assets and liabilities held for sale **should not be offset**

(b)   The **major classes** of assets and liabilities held for sale should be **separately disclosed** either on the face of the statement of financial position or in the notes

Additional disclosures

In the period in which a non-current asset (or disposal group) has been either classified as held for sale or sold the following should be disclosed.

(a)   A description of the non-current asset (or disposal group)

(b)   A description of the facts and circumstances of the disposal

(c)   Any gain or loss recognised when the item was classified as held for sale

(d)   If applicable, the segment in which the non-current asset (or disposal group) is presented in accordance with IFRS 8 *Operating segments*

Where an asset previously classified as held for sale is **no longer held for sale**, the entity should disclose a description of the facts and circumstances leading to the decision and its effect on results.

1 Introduction

Accruals accounting is based on the **matching of costs with the revenue they
generate**. It is crucially important under this convention that we can establish the
point at which revenue may be recognised so that the correct treatment can be
applied to the related costs. For example, the costs of producing an item of finished
goods should be carried as an asset in the statement of financial position until such
time as it is sold; they should then be written off as a charge to profit or loss. Which
of these two treatments should be applied cannot be decided until it is clear at what
moment the sale of the item takes place.

This decision has a **direct impact on profit**. It would be unacceptable to recognise
the profit on sale until a sale had taken place in accordance with the **criteria of
revenue recognition**.

Revenue is of course open to manipulation. A good example was at Satayam
Computer Services in India where the Chairman admitted that profits were massively
inflated for years and that in the quarter to 30 September 2008 revenue was
overstated by 78%. How this got past the auditors is hard to understand, but it does
illustrate why rules on revenue recognition are needed.

The latest standard in this area is IFRS 15 *Revenue from contracts with customers*.
This replaces IAS 18 *Revenue* and IAS 11 *Construction contracts* and related
interpretations.

2 IFRS 15 Revenue from contracts with customers

IFRS 15 *Revenue from contracts with customers* is the result of a joint IASB and
FASB project on revenue recognition. It seeks to strike a balance between the IASB
rules in IAS 18, which were considered to be too general, leading to a lot of diversity
in practice, and the FASB regulations, which were too numerous.

IFRS 15 is effective for reporting periods beginning on or after 1 January 2017, with earlier application permitted. Its core principle is that revenue is recognised to depict the transfer of goods or services to a customer in an amount that reflects the consideration to which the entity expects to be entitled in exchange for those goods or services.

Under IFRS 15 the transfer of goods and services is based upon the transfer of **control**, rather than the transfer of risks and rewards as in IAS 18. For straightforward retail transactions IFRS 15 will have little, if any, effect on the amount and timing of revenue recognition. For contracts such as long-term service contracts and multi-element arrangements it could result in changes either to the amount or to the timing of revenue recognised.

Scope

IFRS 15 applies to all contracts with customers except:

- Leases within the scope of IFRS 17

- Insurance contracts within the scope of IFRS 4

- Financial instruments and other contractual rights and obligations within the scope of IFRS 9, IFRS 10, IFRS 11, IAS 27 or IAS 28

- Non-monetary exchanges between entities in the same line of business

Definitions

The following definitions are given in the standard.

Income. Increases in economic benefits during the accounting period in the form of inflows or enhancements of assets or decreases of liabilities that result in an increase in equity, other than those relating to contributions from equity participants.

Revenue. Income arising in the course of an entity's ordinary activities.

Contract. An agreement between two or more parties that creates enforceable rights and obligations.

Contract asset. An entity's right to consideration in exchange for goods or services that the entity has transferred to a customer when that right is conditioned on something other than the passage of time (for example the entity's future performance).

Receivable. An entity's right to consideration that is unconditional – ie only the passage of time is required before payment is due.

Contract liability. An entity's obligation to transfer goods or services to a customer for which the entity has received consideration (or the amount is due) from the customer.

Customer. A party that has contracted with an entity to obtain goods or services that are an output of the entity's ordinary activities in exchange for consideration.

Performance obligation. A promise in a contract with a customer to transfer to the customer either:

(a)   A good or service (or a bundle of goods or services) that is distinct; or

(b)   A series of distinct goods or services that are substantially the same ad that have the same pattern of transfer to the customer.

Stand-alone selling price. The price at which an entity would sell a promised good or service separately to a customer.

Transaction price. The amount of consideration to which an entity expects to be entitled in exchange for transferring promised goods or services to a customer, excluding amounts collected on behalf of third parties.

(IFRS 15: Appendix)

Revenue **does not include** sales taxes, value added taxes or goods and service taxes which are only collected for third parties, because these do not represent an economic benefit flowing to the entity.

Recognition and measurement of revenue

Under IFRS 15 revenue is recognised and measured using a five step model.

step 1

Identify the contract with the customer.

A contract with a customer is within the scope of IFRS 15 only when:

(a)   The parties have approved the contract and are committed to carrying out their respective obligations

(b)   Each party's rights regarding the goods and services to be transferred can be identified

(c)   The payment terms for the goods and services can be identified

(d)   The contract has commercial substance

(e)   It is probable that the entity will collect the consideration to which it will be entitled

The contract can be written, verbal or implied.

Identify the separate performance obligations.

The key point is distinct goods or services. A contract includes promises to provide goods or services to a customer. Those promises are called performance obligations. A company would account for a performance obligation separately only if the promised good or service is distinct. A good or service is distinct if it is sold separately within the context of the contract or if it could be sold separately because it has a distinct function and a distinct profit margin. It must also be distinct to the customer ie the customer can benefit from the good or service on its own or in combination with other resources it has access to. This point is important when we consider goods and services which can be sold as a package or unbundled.

Determine the transaction price.

The transaction price is the amount of consideration a company expects to be entitled to from the customer in exchange for transferring goods or services. The transaction price would reflect the company's probability-weighted estimate of variable consideration (including reasonable estimates of contingent amounts) in addition to the effects of the customer's credit risk and the time value of money (if material). Variable contingent amounts are only included where it is highly probable that there will not be a reversal of revenue when any uncertainty associated with the variable consideration is resolved.

Allocate the transaction price to the performance obligations.

Where a contract contains more than one distinct performance obligation a company allocates the transaction price to all separate performance obligations in proportion to the stand-alone selling price of the good or service underlying each performance obligation. If the good or service is not sold separately, the company would estimate its stand-alone selling price.

So, if any entity sells a bundle of goods and/or services which it also supplies unbundled, the separate performance obligations in the contract should be priced in the same proportion as the unbundled prices. This would apply to mobile phone contracts where the handset is supplied 'free'. The entity must look at the stand-alone price of such a handset and some of the consideration for the contract should be allocated to it.

Recognise revenue when (or as) a performance obligation is satisfied.

An entity satisfies a performance obligation by transferring **control** of a promised good or service to the customer. A performance obligation can be satisfied **at a point in time**, such as when goods are delivered to the customer, or **over time**. An obligation satisfied **over time** will meet one of the following criteria:

- The customer simultaneously receives and consumes the benefits as the performance takes place.

- The entity's performance creates or enhances an asset that the customer controls as the asset is created or enhanced.

- The entity's performance does not create an asset with an alternative use to the entity and the entity has an enforceable right to payment for performance completed to date.

The amount of revenue recognised is the amount allocated to that performance obligation in Step 4.

Control of an asset is defined as the ability to direct the use of and obtain substantially all of the remaining benefits from the asset. This includes the ability to prevent others from directing the use of and obtaining the benefits from the asset. The benefits related to the asset are the potential cash flows that may be obtained. These include:

- Using the asset to produce goods or provide services
- Using the asset to enhance the value of other assets
- Using the asset to settle liabilities or to reduce expenses
- Selling or exchanging the asset
- Pledging the asset to secure a loan
- Holding the asset

An entity must be able to **reasonably measure** the outcome of a performance obligation before the related revenue can be recognised. In some circumstances, such as in the early stages of a contract, it may not be possible to reasonably measure the outcome of a performance obligation, but the entity expects to recover the costs incurred. In these circumstances, revenue is recognised only to the extent of costs incurred.

Part B 7: Revenue and inventories

Other issues

Contract costs

The incremental costs of **obtaining** a contract (such as sales commission) are **recognised as an asset** if the entity expects to recover those costs.

Costs that would have been incurred regardless of whether the contract was obtained are recognised as an expense as incurred.

Costs incurred in **fulfilling** a contract, unless within the scope of another standard (such as IAS 2 *Inventories*, IAS 16 *Property, plant and equipment* or IAS 38 *Intangible assets*) are recognised as an asset if they meet all the following criteria:

(a)   The costs relate directly to an identifiable contract (costs such as labour, materials, contract management costs)

(b)   The costs generate or enhance resources of the entity that will be used in satisfying (or continuing to satisfy) performance obligations in the future; and

(c)   The costs are expected to be recovered

Costs recognised as assets are amortised on a systematic basis consistent with the transfer to the customer of the goods or services to which the asset relates.

Performance obligations satisfied over time

A performance obligation satisfied over time meets the criteria in Step 5 above and, if it entered into more than one accounting period, would previously have been described as a long-term contract.

In this type of contract an entity may have an enforceable right to payment for performance completed to date. The standard describes this as an amount that approximates the selling price of the goods or services transferred to date (for example recovery of the costs incurred by the entity in satisfying the performance plus a reasonable profit margin).

Methods of measuring the amount of performance completed to date encompass **output methods** and **input methods**.

Output methods recognise revenue on the basis of the value to the **customer** of the goods or services transferred. They include surveys of performance completed and appraisal of units produced or delivered.

Input methods recognise revenue on the basis of the **entity's** inputs, such as labour hours, resources consumed, costs incurred. If using a cost-based method, the costs incurred must contribute to the entity's progress in satisfying the performance obligation.

Performance obligations satisfied at a point in time

A performance obligation not satisfied over time will be satisfied at a point in time. This will be the point in time at which the customer obtains control of the promised asset and the entity satisfies a performance obligation.

Some indicators of the transfer of control are:

(a)   The entity has a present right to payment for the asset

(b)   The customer has legal title to the asset

(c)   The entity has transferred physical possession of the asset

(d)   The significant risks and rewards of ownership have been transferred to the customer

(e)   The customer has accepted the asset

Sale with a right of return

Where goods are sold with a right of return, an entity should not recognise revenue for goods that it expects to be returned. It can calculate the level of returns using the expected value method (the probability-weighted sum of amounts) or simply estimate the most likely amount. This will be shown as a refund liability and a deduction from revenue.

The entity also recognises an asset (adjusted against cost of sales) for its right to recover products from customers on settlement of the refund liability.

Warranties

If a customer has the option to purchase a warranty separately from the product to which it relates, it constitutes a distinct service and is accounted for as a separate performance obligation. This would apply to a warranty which provides the customer with a service in addition to the assurance that the product complies with agreed-upon specifications.

If the customer does not have the option to purchase the warranty separately, for instance if the warranty is required by law, that does not give rise to a performance obligation and the warranty is accounted for in accordance with IAS 37.

Principal versus agent

An entity must establish in any transaction whether it is acting as principal or agent.

It is a principal if it **controls** the promised good or service before it is transferred to the customer. When the performance obligation is satisfied, the entity recognises revenue in the gross amount of the consideration to which it expects to be entitled for those goods or services.

It is acting as an agent if its performance obligation is to arrange for the provision of goods or services by another party. Satisfaction of this performance obligation will give rise to the recognition of revenue in the amount of any fee or commission to which it expects to be entitled in exchange for arranging for the other party to provide its goods or services.

Indicators that an entity is an agent rather than a principal include the following:

(a)   Another party is primarily responsible for fulfilling the contract.

(b)   The entity does not have inventory risk before or after the goods have been ordered by a customer, during shipping or on return.

(c)   The entity does not have discretion in establishing prices for the other party's goods or services and, therefore, the benefit that the entity can receive from those goods or services is limited.

(d)   The entity's consideration is in the form of a commission.

(e)   The entity is not exposed to credit risk for the amount receivable from a customer in exchange for the other party's goods or services.

Options for additional goods or services

If an option in the contract grants the customer the right to acquire additional goods or services at a discount which can only be obtained by entering into the contract, that option gives rise to a performance obligation.

The customer in effect pays the entity in advance for future goods or services and revenue is recognised when the additional future goods or services are transferred, or when the option expires. Revenue will be based on the stand-alone selling price of the goods or services, taking account of the discount.

If the option granted to the customer does not offer a discount, it is treated as a marketing offer and no contract exists until the customer exercises the option to purchase.

Customers' unexercised rights

When a customer pays in advance for goods or services the prepayment gives rise to a contract liability, which is derecognised when the performance obligation is satisfied.

If, having made a non-refundable prepayment, the customer does not exercise their right to receive the good or service, the unexercised right is often referred to as breakage. A expected breakage amount can be recognised as revenue if the pattern of rights exercised by the customer gives rise to the expectation that the entity will be entitled to a breakage amount. If this does not apply, it can be recognised as revenue when the likelihood of the customer exercising its rights becomes remote.

Unclaimed loyalty points are a typical example.

Non-refundable upfront fees

A non-refundable upfront fee is often charged at the beginning of a contract, such as joining fees in health club membership contracts.

In many cases upfront fees do not relate to the transfer of any promised good or service but are simply advance payments for **future** goods or services. In this case revenue is recognised when the future goods or services are provided.

If the fee relates to a good or service the entity should evaluate whether or not it amounts to a separate performance obligation. This depends on whether it results in the transfer of an asset to the customer. The fee may relate to costs incurred in setting up a contract, but these setup activities may not result in the transfer of goods or services to the customer.

Licensing

A licence establishes a customer's rights to the intellectual property of an entity. Intellectual property can include software, music, franchises, patents, trademarks and copyrights.

The promise to grant a licence may be accompanied by the promise to transfer other goods or services to the customer. If the promise to grant the licence is **not** distinct from the promised goods or services, this is treated as a single performance obligation.

If the promise to grant the licence **is** distinct, it will constitute a separate performance obligation. The entity must establish whether the performance obligation is satisfied 'at a point in time' or 'over time'.

In this respect the entity should consider whether the nature of the entity's promise in granting the licence to a customer is to provide the customer with either:

(a)   A **right to access** the entity's intellectual property as it exists throughout the licence period; or

(b)   A **right to use** the entity's intellectual property as it exists at the point in time at which the licence is granted.

A **right to access** exists where the entity can make changes to the intellectual property throughout the licence period, the customer is exposed to the effects of these changes and the changes do not constitute the transfer of a good or service to the customer. In this case the promise to grant a licence is treated as a performance obligation satisfied over time, where control transfers over time, and the entity recognises revenue over time by measuring the progress towards complete satisfaction of that performance obligation.

Where this does not apply, the nature of the entity's promise is the **right to use** its intellectual property as it exists at the point in time at which the licence is granted. This means that the customer can direct the use of, and obtain substantially all of the remaining benefits from, the licence at the point at which it is transferred, ie control is transferred at that point in time. The point at which revenue can be recognised may be later than the date on which the licence is granted if the customer does not have immediate access to the intellectual property, for instance if it has to wait to be granted an access code.

When **royalties**, based on sales or on usage, are promised by the customer in exchange for a licence of intellectual property, revenue can be recognised at the later of the following occurrences:

(a)   The sale or usage occurs; and

(b)   The performance obligation to which the royalty has been allocated has been satisfied.

Repurchase agreements

Under a repurchase agreement an entity sells an asset and promises, or has the option, to repurchase it. Repurchase agreements generally come in three forms:

(a)   An entity has an obligation to repurchase the asset (a forward contract)

(b)   An entity has the right to repurchase the asset (a call option)

(c)   An entity must repurchase the asset if requested to do so by the customer (a put option)

In the case of a forward or a call option the customer does not obtain control of the asset, even if it has physical possession. The entity will account for the contract as:

(a)   A lease in accordance with IFRS 16, if the repurchase price is below the original selling price; or

(b)   A financing arrangement if the repurchase price is equal to or greater than the original selling price. In this case the entity will recognise both the asset and a corresponding liability.

If the entity is obliged to repurchase at the request of the customer (a put option), it must consider whether or not the customer is likely to exercise that option.

If the repurchase price is lower than the original selling price and it is considered that the customer does not therefore have significant economic incentive to exercise the option, the contract should be accounted for as an outright sale, with a right of return. If the customer is considered to have a significant economic incentive to exercise its right, the entity shall account for the agreement as a lease in accordance with IFRS 16.

If the repurchase price is greater than or equal to the original selling price and is above the expected market value of the option, the contract is treated as a financing arrangement.

Consignment arrangements

When a product is delivered to a customer under a consignment arrangement, the customer (dealer/distributor) does not obtain control of the product at that point in time, so no revenue is recognised upon delivery.

Indicators of a consignment arrangement include the following:

(a) The product is controlled by the entity until a specified event occurs, such as the product is sold on, or a specified period expires.

(b) The entity can require the return of the product, or transfer it to another party.

(c) The customer (dealer/distributor) does not have an unconditional obligation to pay for the product.

Bill-and-hold arrangements

Under a bill-and-hold arrangement goods are sold but remain in the possession of the seller for a specified period, perhaps because the customer lacks storage facilities.

An entity will need to determine at what point the customer obtains control of the product. For some contracts, control will not be transferred until the goods are delivered to the customer. For others, a customer may obtain control even though the goods remain in the entity's physical possession. In this case the entity would be providing custodial services (which may constitute a separate performance obligation) to the customer over the customer's asset.

For a customer to have obtained control of a product in a bill-and-hold arrangement, the following criteria must all be met:

(a) The reason for the bill-and-hold must be substantive (for example, requested by the customer).

(b) The product must be separately identified as belonging to the customer.

(c) The product must be ready for physical transfer to the customer.

(d) The entity cannot have the ability to use the product or to transfer it to another customer.

Presentation

Contracts with customers will be presented in an entity's statement of financial position as a contract liability, a contract asset or a receivable, depending on the relationship between the entity's performance and the customer's payment.

A **contract liability** is recognised and presented in the statement of financial position where a customer has paid an amount of consideration prior to the entity performing by transferring control of the related good or service to the customer.

When the entity has performed but the customer has not yet paid the related consideration, this will give rise to either a **contract asset** or a **receivable**. A contract asset is recognised when the entity's right to consideration is conditional on something other than the passage of time, for instance future performance. A receivable is recognised when the entity's right to consideration is unconditional except for the passage of time.

In practice, this aligns with the previous IAS 11 treatment. Where revenue has been invoiced a receivable is recognised. Where revenue has been earned but not invoiced, it is recognised as a contract asset.

Disclosure

The objective is for an entity to disclose sufficient information to enable users of financial statements to understand the nature, amount, timing and uncertainty of revenue and cash flows arising from contracts with customers.

The following amounts should be disclosed unless they have been presented separately in the financial statements in accordance with other standards:

(a) Revenue recognised from contracts with customers, disclosed separately from other sources of revenue.

(b) Any impairment losses recognised (in accordance with IFRS 9) on any receivables or contract assets arising from an entity's contracts with customers, disclosed separately from other impairment losses.

(c) The opening and closing balances of receivables, contract assets and contract liabilities from contracts with customers.

(d) Revenue recognised in the reporting period that was included in the contract liability balance at the beginning of the period; and

(e) Revenue recognised in the reporting period from performance obligations satisfied in previous periods (such as changes in transaction price).

Other information that should be provided:

(a) An explanation of significant changes in the contract asset and liability balances during the reporting period.

(b) Information regarding the entity's performance obligations, including when they are typically satisfied (upon delivery, upon shipment, as services are rendered etc), significant payment terms(such as when payment is typically due) and details of any agency transactions, obligations for returns or refunds and warranties granted.

(c) The aggregate amount of the transaction price allocated to the performance obligations that are not fully satisfied at the end of the reporting period and an explanation of when the entity expects to recognise these amounts as revenue.

(d) Judgements, and changes in judgements, made in applying the standard that significantly affect the determination of the amount and timing of revenue from contracts with customers.

(e) Assets recognised from the costs to obtain or fulfil a contract with a customer. This would include pre-contract costs and set-up costs. The method of amortisation should also be disclosed.

3 Long-term contracts

A company is building a large tower block that will house offices, under a contract with an investment company. It will take two years to build the block and over that time it will obviously have to pay for building materials, wages of workers on the building, architects' fees and so on. It will receive periodic payments from the investment company at various predetermined stages of the construction. How does it decide, in each of the three years, **what to include as income and expenditure** for the contract in profit or loss?

Example

Suppose that a contract is started on 1 January 20X5, with an estimated completion date of 31 December 20X6. The final contract price is $1,500,000. In the first year, to 31 December 20X5:

(a) Costs incurred amounted to $600,000

(b) Half the work on the contract was completed

(c) Certificates of work completed have been issued, to the value of $750,000

(d) It is estimated with reasonable certainty that further costs to completion in 20X6 will be $600,000

What is the contract profit in 20X5, and what entries would be made for the contract at 31 December 20X5?

Solution

This is a contract in which the performance obligation is satisfied **over time**. The entity is carrying out the work for the benefit of the customer rather than creating an asset for its own use and it has an enforceable right to payment for work completed to date. We can see this from the fact that certificates of work completed have been issued.

IFRS 15 states that the amount of payment that the entity is entitled to corresponds to the amount of performance completed to date, which approximates to the costs incurred in satisfying the performance obligation plus a reasonable profit margin.

In this case the contract is certified as 50% complete. At 31 December 20X5 the entity will recognise revenue of $750,000 and cost of sales of $600,000, leaving profit of $150,000. The **contract asset** will be the costs to date plus the profit - $750,000. We are not told that any of this amount has yet been invoiced, so no amount is classified as receivables.

Summary of accounting treatment

Statement of profit or loss

(a) **Revenue and costs**

    (i)   Sales revenue and associated costs should be recorded in profit or loss as the contract activity progresses.

    (ii)   Include an appropriate proportion of total contract value as sales revenue in profit or loss.

    (iii)   The costs incurred in completing that amount of the performance obligation are matched with this sales revenue, resulting in the reporting of results which can be attributed to the proportion of work completed.

    (iv)   Sales revenue is the value of work carried out to date.

(b) **Profit recognised in the contract**

    (i)   It must reflect the proportion of work carried out.

    (ii)   It should take into account any known inequalities in profitability in the various stages of a contract.

Statement of financial position

(a) **Contract asset** (presented separately under current assets)

	$
Costs to date	X
Plus recognised profits	X
	X
Less any recognised losses	(X)
	X
Less receivables (amounts invoiced)	(X)
Contract asset (amount due from the customer)	X

(b) **Receivables**
Unpaid invoices   X

(c) **Contract liability.** Where (a) gives a net amount due **to** the customer this amount should be included as a contract liability, presented separately under current liabilities.

Example

P Co has the following contract in progress:

	$m
Total contract price	750
Costs incurred to date	225
Estimated costs to completion	340
Progress payments invoiced and received	290

Now we will calculate the amounts to be recognised for the contract in the statement of profit or loss and statement of financial position assuming the amount of performance obligation satisfied is calculated using the proportion of costs incurred method.

1   *Estimated profit*

	$m
Total contract price	750
Less costs incurred to date	(225)
Less estimated costs to completion	(340)
Estimated profit	185

2   *Percentage complete*

Costs to date / total estimated costs: 225 / (225 + 340) = 40%

3   *Statement of profit or loss*

	$m
Revenue (40% × $750)	300
Cost of sales (40% × (225 + 340))	(226)
Profit (40% × 185)	74

4   *Statement of financial position*

	$m
Costs incurred to date	225
Recognised profits	74
Less receivables	(290)
Contract asset	9

How would we account for this if it was a loss-making contract? We will reduce P Co's contract price to $550m.

1   *Estimated loss*

	$m
Total contract price	550
Less costs incurred to date	(225)
Less estimated costs to completion	(340)
Estimated loss	(15)

2   *Percentage complete*

Costs to date / total estimated costs: 225 / (225 + 340) = 40%

3   Statement of profit or loss

	$m
Revenue (40% x $550)	220
Cost of sales (balancing figure)	(235)
Loss	(15)

4   Statement of financial position

	$m
Costs incurred to date	225
Recognised loss	(15)
Less receivables	(290)
Contract liability	(80)

4 Inventories and short-term WIP (IAS 2)

IAS 2 was revised in December 2003. It lays out the required accounting treatment for inventories (sometimes called stocks).

The following items are **excluded** from the scope of the standard.

- Work in progress under **long-term contracts** (covered by IFRS 15 *Revenue from contracts with customers*, see Section 3)

- **Financial instruments** (ie shares, bonds)

- **Biological assets**

Certain inventories are exempt from the **measurement rules,** ie those held by:

- Producers of **agricultural and forest products and minerals**
- **Commodity-broker traders**

Definitions

These are the important definitions:

> Inventories are assets:
> - Held for sale in the ordinary course of business;
> - In the process of production for such sale; or
> - In the form of materials or supplies to be consumed in the production process or in the rendering of services.
>
> Net realisable value is the estimated selling price in the ordinary course of business less the estimated costs of completion and the estimated costs necessary to make the sale. *(IAS 2: para. 6)*
>
> Fair value is the price that would be received to sell an asset or paid to transfer a liability in an orderly transaction between market participants at the measurement date. *(IFRS 13: para. 9)*

Inventories can **include** any of the following.

- **Goods purchased and held for resale**, eg goods held for sale by a retailer, or land and buildings held for resale

- **Finished goods** produced

- **Work in progress** being produced

- Materials and supplies awaiting use in the production process (**raw materials**)

The standard states that '**Inventories should be measured at the lower of cost and net realisable value.**' *(IAS 2, para. 9)*

Cost of inventories

The cost of inventories will consist of all costs of:

- **Purchase**

- **Costs of conversion**

- **Other costs** incurred in bringing the inventories to their **present location and condition**

The standard lists the following as comprising the costs of purchase of inventories:

- **Purchase price** *plus*

- **Import duties** and other taxes *plus*

- Transport, handling and any other cost **directly attributable** to the acquisition of finished goods, services and materials less

- **Trade discounts**, rebates and other similar amounts

Costs of conversion of inventories consist of two main parts:

(a) Costs **directly related** to the units of production, eg direct materials, direct labour

(b) Fixed and variable **production overheads** that are incurred in converting materials into finished goods, allocated on a systematic basis

Fixed production overheads are those indirect costs of production that remain relatively constant regardless of the volume of production, eg the cost of factory management and administration.

Variable production overheads are those indirect costs of production that vary directly, or nearly directly, with the volume of production, eg indirect materials and indirect labour. *(IAS 2: para.12)*

The standard emphasises that fixed production overheads must be allocated to items of inventory on the basis of the **normal capacity of the production facilities**. This is an important point.

(a)   **Normal capacity** is the expected achievable production based on the average over several periods/seasons, under normal circumstances.

(b)   The above figure should take account of the capacity lost through **planned maintenance**.

(c)   If it approximates to the normal level of activity then the **actual level of production** can be used.

(d)   **Low production** or **idle plant** will **not** result in a higher fixed overhead allocation to each unit.

(e)   **Unallocated overheads** must be recognised as an expense in the period in which they are incurred.

(f)   When production is **abnormally high**, the fixed production overhead allocated to each unit will be reduced, so avoiding inventories being stated at more than cost.

(g)   The allocation of variable production overheads to each unit is based on the **actual use** of production facilities.

Any other costs should only be recognised if they are incurred in bringing the inventories to **their present location and condition**.

Certain types of cost **would not be included** in cost of inventories and should be recognised as an **expense** in the period in which they are incurred.

(a)   **Abnormal amounts** of wasted materials, labour or other production costs

(b)   **Storage costs** (except costs which are necessary in the production process before a further production stage)

(c)   **Administrative overheads** not incurred to bring inventories to their present location and condition

(d)   **Selling costs**

Net realisable value (NRV)

As a general rule assets should not be carried at amounts greater than those expected to be realised from their sale or use. In the case of inventories this amount could fall below cost when items are **damaged or become obsolete,** or where the **costs to completion have increased** in order to make the sale.

In fact we can identify the principal situations in which NRV is likely to be less than cost, ie where there has been:

(a)   An **increase in costs** or a **fall in selling price**

(b)   A **physical deterioratio**n in the condition of inventory

(c)   **Obsolescence** of products

(d)   A decision as part of the entity's marketing strategy to manufacture and sell products at a **loss**

(e)   **Errors in production or purchasing**

A write down of inventories would normally take place on an item by item basis, but similar or related items may be **grouped together**. This grouping together is acceptable for, say, items in the same product line, but it is not acceptable to write down inventories based on a whole classification (eg finished goods) or a whole operating segment.

The assessment of NRV should take place using the most reliable information available. Fluctuations of price or cost should be taken into account if they relate directly to **events after the reporting period**, which confirm conditions existing at the end of the period. Any write down to NRV should be recorded as an expense in profit or loss in the period in which it occurs.

The reasons why inventory is held must also be taken into account. Some inventory, for example, may be held to satisfy a firm contract and its NRV will therefore be the **contract price**. Any additional inventory of the same type held at the period end will, in contrast, be assessed according to general sales prices when NRV is estimated.

Net realisable value must be reassessed at the end of each period and compared again with cost. If the NRV has risen for inventories held over the end of more than one period, then the previous write down must be **reversed** to the extent that the inventory is then valued at the lower of cost and the new NRV. This may be possible when selling prices have fallen in the past and then risen again.

On occasion a write down to NRV may be of such size, incidence or nature that it must be **disclosed separately**.

Cost formulae for inventories

IAS 2 allows two cost formulae (FIFO or weighted average cost) for inventories that are ordinarily interchangeable or are not produced and segregated for specific projects. The issue is whether an entity may use different cost formulae for different types of inventories.

IAS 2 provides that an entity should use **the same cost formula for all inventories having similar nature and use to the entity**. For inventories with different nature or use (for example, certain commodities used in one operating segment and the same type of commodities used in another operating segment), different cost formulae may be justified. A difference in geographical location of inventories (and in the respective tax rules), by itself, is not sufficient to justify the use of different cost formulae.

1 IAS 37: Provisions, contingent liabilities and contingent assets

Financial statements must include **all the information necessary for an understanding of the company's financial position**. Provisions, contingent liabilities and contingent assets are 'uncertainties' that must be accounted for consistently if we are to achieve this understanding.

IAS 37 *Provisions, contingent liabilities and contingent assets* aims to ensure that appropriate **recognition criteria** and **measurement bases** are applied to provisions, contingent liabilities and contingent assets and that **sufficient information** is disclosed in the **notes** to the financial statements to enable users to understand their nature, timing and amount.

Before IAS 37, there was no accounting standard dealing with provisions. Companies wanting to show their results in the most favourable light used to make large 'one off' provisions in years where a high level of underlying profits was generated. These provisions, often known as 'big bath' provisions, were then available to shield expenditure in future years when perhaps the underlying profits were not so good. In other words, provisions were used for profit smoothing.

Just as an example, Worldcom had set aside $3.3bn reserves in order to be able to dip into them to boost profits in the future. These were brought into current year earnings in 2002. The key aim of IAS 37 is to ensure that **provisions are made only** where there are valid grounds for them.

IAS 37 views a provision as a liability.

A **provision** is a liability of uncertain timing or amount.

A **liability** is an obligation of an entity to transfer economic benefits as a result of past transactions or events. *(IAS 37: para. 10)*

The IAS distinguishes provisions from other liabilities such as trade payables and accruals. This is on the basis that for a provision there is uncertainty about the timing or amount of the future expenditure. Whilst **uncertainty** is clearly present in the case of certain accruals the uncertainty is generally much less than for provisions.

IAS 37 states that a provision should be **recognised** as a liability in the financial statements when:

- An entity has a **present obligation** (legal or constructive) as a result of a past event

- It is probable that a **transfer of economic benefits** will be required to settle the obligation

- A **reliable estimate** can be made of the obligation

Meaning of obligation

It is fairly clear what a legal obligation is. However, there can also be a constructive obligation.

> IAS 37 defines a **constructive obligation** as
>
> 'An obligation that derives from an entity's actions where:
>
> - By an established pattern of past practice, published policies or a sufficiently specific current statement the entity has indicated to other parties that it will accept certain responsibilities; and
>
> - As a result, the entity has created a valid expectation on the part of those other parties that it will discharge those responsibilities.' *(IAS 37: para. 10)*

In which circumstances might a provision be recognised?

(a)   On 13 December 20X9 the board of an entity decided to close down a division. The accounting date of the company is 31 December. Before 31 December 20X9 the decision was not communicated to any of those affected and no other steps were taken to implement the decision.

No provision would be recognised as the decision has not been communicated and so could still be avoided.

(b)   The board agreed a detailed closure plan on 20 December 20X9 and details were given to customers and employees.

A provision would be made in the 20X9 financial statements.

(c)   A company is obliged to incur clean up costs for environmental damage (that has already been caused).

A provision for such costs is appropriate, because the obligation arises from a past event.

(d) A company intends to carry out future expenditure to operate in a particular way in the future.

No present obligation exists and under IAS 37 no provision would be appropriate. This is because the entity could avoid the future expenditure by its future actions, maybe by changing its method of operation.

Transfer of economic benefits

For the purpose of the IAS, a transfer of resources embodying economic benefits is regarded as '**probable**' if the event is **more likely than not** to occur. This appears to indicate a probability of more than 50%. However, the standard makes it clear that where there is a number of similar obligations the probability should be based on considering the population as a whole, rather than one single item.

If a company has entered into a warranty obligation then the probability of transfer of resources embodying economic benefits may well be extremely small in respect of one specific item. However, when considering the population as a whole the probability of some transfer of resources is quite likely to be much higher. If there is a **greater than 50% probability** of some transfer of economic benefits then a provision should be made for the **expected amount**.

Measurement of provisions

The amount recognised as a provision should be the best estimate of the expenditure required to settle the present obligation at the end of the reporting period.

The estimates will be determined by the **judgement** of the entity's management supplemented by the experience of similar transactions.

Allowance is made for **uncertainty**. Where the provision being measured involves a large population of items, the obligation is estimated by weighting all possible outcomes by their associated probabilities, ie expected value.

Example

A company sells goods with a warranty under which customers are covered for the cost of repairs of any manufacturing defect that becomes apparent within the first six months of purchase. The company's past experience and future expectations indicate the following pattern of likely repairs.

% of goods sold	Defects	Cost of repairs if all items suffered from these defects $m
75	None	–
20	Minor	1.0
5	Major	4.0

The cost is found using 'expected values' (75% × $nil) + (20% × $1.0m) + (5% × $4.0m) = $400,000.

Where the effect of the **time value of money** is material, the amount of a provision should be the **present value** of the expenditure required to settle the obligation. An appropriate **discount** rate should be used.

The discount rate should be a pre-tax rate that reflects current market assessments of the time value of money. The discount rate(s) should not reflect risks for which future cash flow estimates have been adjusted.

Example

A company knows that when it ceases a certain operation in five years time it will have to pay environmental cleanup costs of $5m.

The provision to be made now will be the present value of $5m in five years time.

The relevant discount rate in this case is 10%.

Therefore a provision will be made for:

	$
$5m × 0.62092*	3,104,600
The following year the provision will be:	
$5m × 0.68301**	3,415,050
Increase	310,450

* The discount rate for five years at 10%.

**The discount rate for four years at 10%

The increase in the liability in the second year of $310,450 will be charged to profit or loss. It is referred to as the **unwinding** of the discount. This is accounted for as a finance cost.

Future events which are reasonably expected to occur (eg new legislation, changes in technology) may affect the amount required to settle the entity's obligation and should be taken into account.

Gains from the expected disposal of assets should not be taken into account in measuring a provision.

Reimbursements

Some or all of the expenditure needed to settle a provision may be expected to be recovered from a third party. If so, **the reimbursement should be recognised only when it is virtually certain that reimbursement will be received if the entity settles the obligation**.

- The reimbursement should be treated as a separate asset, and the amount recognised should not be greater than the provision itself.

- The provision and the amount recognised for reimbursement may be netted off in profit or loss.

Changes in provisions

Provisions should be **reviewed at the end of each reporting period** and adjusted to reflect the current best estimate. If it is no longer probable that a transfer of resources will be required to settle the obligation, the provision should be reversed.

Use of provisions

A provision should be used only for expenditures for which the provision was originally recognised. Setting expenditures against a provision that was originally recognised for another purpose would conceal the impact of two different events.

Future operating losses

Provisions should not be recognised for future operating losses. They do not meet the definition of a liability and the general recognition criteria set out in the standard.

Onerous contracts

If an entity has a contract that is onerous, the present obligation under the contract **should be recognised and measured** as a provision. An example might be vacant leasehold property. The entity is under an obligation to maintain the property but is receiving no income from it.

> An **onerous contract** is a contract entered into with another party under which the unavoidable costs of fulfilling the terms of the contract exceed any revenues expected to be received from the goods or services supplied or purchased directly or indirectly under the contract and where the entity would have to compensate the other party if it did not fulfil the terms of the contract. *(IAS 37: para. 10)*

Examples of possible provisions

(a) **Warranties**. These are argued to be genuine provisions as on past experience it is probable, ie more likely than not, that some claims will emerge. The provision must be estimated, however, on the basis of the class as a whole and not on individual claims. There is a clear legal obligation in this case.

(b) **Major repairs**. In the past it has been quite popular for companies to provide for expenditure on a major overhaul to be accrued gradually over the intervening years between overhauls. Under IAS 37 this is no longer possible as IAS 37 would argue that this is a mere intention to carry out repairs, not an obligation. The entity can always sell the asset in the meantime. The only solution is to treat major assets such as aircraft, ships, furnaces etc as a series of smaller assets where each part is depreciated over shorter lives. Thus any major overhaul may be argued to be replacement and therefore capital rather than revenue expenditure.

(c) **Self insurance**. A number of companies have created a provision for self insurance based on the expected cost of making good fire damage etc instead of paying premiums to an insurance company. Under IAS 37 this provision is no longer justifiable as the entity has no obligation until a fire or accident occurs. No obligation exists until that time.

(d) **Environmental contamination**. If the company has an environmental policy such that other parties would expect the company to clean up any contamination or if the company has broken current environmental legislation then a provision for environmental damage must be made.

(e) **Decommissioning or abandonment costs**. When an oil company initially purchases an oilfield it is put under a legal obligation to decommission the site at the end of its life. Prior to IAS 37 most oil companies set up the provision gradually over the life of the field so that no one year would be unduly burdened with the cost.

IAS 37, however, insists that a legal obligation exists on the initial expenditure on the field and therefore a liability exists immediately. This would appear to result in a large charge to profit and loss in the first year of operation of the field. However, the IAS takes the view that the cost of purchasing the field in the first place is not only the cost of the field itself but also the costs of putting it right again. Thus all the costs of decommissioning may be capitalised.

(f) **Restructuring**. This is considered in detail below.

2 Provisions for restructuring

IAS 37 defines a **restructuring** as:

A programme that is planned and is controlled by management and materially changes one of two things.

- The scope of a business undertaken by an entity
- The manner in which that business is conducted *(IAS 37: para. 10)*

The IAS gives the following **examples** of events that may fall under the definition of restructuring.

- The **sale or termination** of a line of business

- The **closure of business locations** in a country or region or the **relocation** of business activities from one country region to another

- **Changes in management structure**, for example, the elimination of a layer of management

- **Fundamental reorganisations** that have a material effect on the **nature and focus** of the entity's operations

The question is whether or not an entity has an obligation – legal or constructive – at the end of the reporting period. For this to be the case:

- An entity must have a **detailed formal plan** for the restructuring

- It must have **raised a valid expectation** in those affected that it will carry out the restructuring by starting to implement that plan or announcing its main features to those affected by it

> A mere management decision is not normally sufficient. Management decisions may sometimes trigger off recognition, but only if earlier events such as negotiations with employee representatives and other interested parties have been concluded subject only to management approval. *(IAS 37: para. 75)*

Where the restructuring involves the **sale of an operation** then IAS 37 states that no obligation arises until the entity has entered into a **binding sale agreement**. This is because until this has occurred the entity will be able to change its mind and withdraw from the sale even if its intentions have been announced publicly.

Costs to be included within a restructuring provision

The IAS states that a restructuring provision should include only the direct expenditures arising from the restructuring, which are those that are both:

- **Necessarily entailed** by the restructuring; and
- Not associated with the **ongoing activities** of the entity.

The following costs should specifically **not** be included within a restructuring provision.

- **Retraining** or relocating continuing staff
- **Marketing**
- **Investment in new systems** and distribution networks

Disclosure

Disclosures for provisions fall into two parts.

- Disclosure of details of the **change in carrying value** of a provision from the beginning to the end of the year

- Disclosure of the **background** to the making of the provision and the uncertainties affecting its outcome

3 Contingent liabilities and contingent assets

IAS 37 defines a **contingent liability** as:

- A possible obligation that arises from past events and whose existence will be confirmed only by the occurrence or non-occurrence of one or more uncertain future events not wholly within the control of the entity; or

- A present obligation that arises from past events but is not recognised because:

  - It is not probable that an outflow of resources embodying economic benefits will be required to settle the obligation; or
  - The amount of the obligation cannot be measured with sufficient reliability. *(IAS 37: para. 10)*

As a rule of thumb, probable means more than 50% likely. If an obligation is probable, it is not a contingent liability – instead, a provision is needed.

Treatment of contingent liabilities

Contingent liabilities **should not be recognised in financial statements** but they **should be disclosed**. The required disclosures are:

- A brief description of the nature of the contingent liability
- An estimate of its financial effect
- An indication of the uncertainties that exist
- The possibility of any reimbursement

Contingent assets

IAS 37 defines a **contingent asset** as:

A possible asset that arises from past events and whose existence will be confirmed by the occurrence or non-occurrence of one or more uncertain future events not wholly within control of the entity. *(IAS 37: para. 10)*

A contingent asset must not be recognised. Only when the realisation of the related economic benefits is virtually certain should recognition take place. At that point, **the asset is no longer a contingent asset!**

Disclosure

Contingent assets must only be disclosed in the notes if they are **probable**. In that case a brief description of the contingent asset should be provided along with an estimate of its likely financial effect.

'Let out'

IAS 37 permits reporting entities to avoid disclosure requirements relating to provisions, contingent liabilities and contingent assets if they would be expected to **seriously prejudice** the position of the entity in dispute with other parties. However, this should only be employed in **extremely rare** cases. Details of the general nature of the provision/contingencies must still be provided, together with an explanation of why it has not been disclosed.

Accounting for leases

9

[IAS 17 was replaced on 13 January 2016 by IFRS 16 *Leases*, which is effective from 1 January 2019, with earlier adoption permitted if IFRS 15 has been applied. IFRS 16 does not change the IAS 17 accounting rules for lessors. As IAS 17 will be in use for some time yet and the rules for lessors will not change, we start by looking at IAS 17.]

1 IAS 17: Leases

IAS 17 *Leases* standardises the accounting treatment and disclosure of assets held under lease.

In a leasing transaction there is a **contract** between the lessor and the lessee for the hire of an asset. The lessor retains legal ownership but conveys to the lessee the right to use the asset for an agreed period of time in return for specified rentals. IAS 17 defines a lease and recognises two types.

> **Lease.** An agreement whereby the lessor conveys to the lessee in return for rent the right to use an asset for an agreed period of time.
>
> **Finance lease.** A lease that transfers substantially all the risks and rewards incident to ownership of an asset. Title may or may not eventually be transferred.
>
> **Operating lease.** A lease other than a finance lease.   (*IAS 17: para. 4*)

A **finance lease** may be a **hire purchase agreement**. (The difference is that under a hire purchase agreement the customer eventually, after paying an agreed number of instalments, becomes entitled to exercise an option to purchase the asset. Under other leasing agreements, ownership remains forever with the lessor.)

To expand on the definition above, a finance lease should be presumed if at the inception of a lease the **present value of the minimum lease payments** is approximately equal to the **fair value of the leased asset**.

The present value should be calculated by using the **interest rate implicit in the lease**.

Minimum lease payments. The payments over the lease term that the lessee is or can be required to make, excluding contingent rent, costs for services and taxes to be paid by and be reimbursed to the lessor, together with:

(a) For a lessee, any amounts guaranteed by the lessee or by a party related to the lessee

(b) For a lessor, any residual value guaranteed to the lessor by one of the following.

    (i) The lessee

    (ii) A party related to the lessee

    (iii) An independent third party financially capable of meeting this guarantee

However, if the lessee has the option to purchase the asset at a price which is expected to be sufficiently lower than fair value at the date the option becomes exercisable for it to be reasonably certain, at the inception of the lease, that the option will be exercised, the minimum lease payments comprise the minimum payments payable over the lease term to the expected date of exercise of this purchase option and the payment required to exercise it.

Interest rate implicit in the lease.

The discount rate that, at the inception of the lease, causes the aggregate present value of

(a) The minimum lease payments; and

(b) The unguaranteed residual value.

to be equal to the sum of

(a) The fair value of the leased asset; and

(b) Any initial direct costs.

Initial direct costs are incremental costs that are directly attributable to negotiating and arranging a lease, except for such costs incurred by manufacturer or dealer lessors. Examples of initial direct costs include amounts such as commissions, legal fees and relevant internal costs.

Lease term. The non-cancellable period for which the lessee has contracted to lease the asset together with any further terms for which the lessee has the option to continue to lease the asset, with or without further payment, when at the inception of the lease it is reasonably certain that the lessee will exercise the option.

A non-cancellable lease is a lease that is cancellable only in one of the following situations.

(a)   Upon the occurrence of some remote contingency

(b)   With the permission of the lessor

(c)   If the lessee enters into a new lease for the same or an equivalent asset with the same lessor

(d)   Upon payment by the lessee of an additional amount such that, at inception, continuation of the lease is reasonably certain

The inception of the lease is the earlier of the date of the lease agreement and the date of commitment by the parties to the principal provisions of the lease. As at this date:

(a)   A lease is classified as either an operating lease or a finance lease; and

(b)   In the case of a finance lease, the amounts to be recognised at the start of lease term are determined

Economic life is either:

(a)   The period over which an asset is expected to be economically usable by one or more users, or

(b)   The number of production or similar units expected to be obtained from the asset by one or more users

Useful life is the estimated remaining period, from the beginning of the lease term, without limitation by the lease term, over which the economic benefits embodied in the asset are expected to be consumed by the entity.

Guaranteed residual value is:

(a)   For a lessee, that part of the residual value which is guaranteed by the lessee or by a party related to the lessee (the amount of the guarantee being the maximum amount that could, in any event, become payable).

(b)   For a lessor, that part of the residual value which is guaranteed by the lessee or by a third party unrelated to the lessor who is financially capable of discharging the obligations under the guarantee.

Unguaranteed residual value is that portion of the residual value of the leased asset, the realisation of which by the lessor is not assured or is guaranteed solely by a party related to the lessor.

Gross investment in the lease is the aggregate of:

(a)   The minimum lease payments receivable by the lessor under a finance lease, and

(b)   Any unguaranteed residual value accruing to the lessor

Net investment in the lease is the gross investment in the lease discounted at the interest rate implicit in the lease.

Unearned finance income is the difference between:

(a) The gross investment in the lease, and

(b) The net investment in the lease.

The **lessee's incremental borrowing rate of interest** is the rate of interest the lessee would have to pay on a similar lease or, if that is not determinable, the rate that, at the inception of the lease, the lessee would incur to borrow over a similar term, and with a similar security, the funds necessary to purchase the asset.

Contingent rent is that portion of the lease payments that is not fixed in amount but is based on a factor other than just the passage of time (eg percentage of sales, amount of usage, price indices, market rates of interest).   *(IAS 17: para. 4)*

Accounting for operating leases

Operating leases do not really pose an accounting problem. The lessee pays amounts periodically to the lessor and these are **charged to profit or loss**. The lessor treats the leased asset as a non-current asset and depreciates it in the normal way. Rentals received from the lessee are credited to the profit or loss in the lessor's books.

Where the lessee is offered an incentive such as a **rent-free period** or **cashback incentive**, this is effectively a discount, which will be spread over the period of the operating lease in accordance with the accruals principle. For instance, if a company entered into a 4-year operating lease but was not required to make any payments until year 2, the total payments to be made over years 2-4 should be charged evenly over years 1-4.

Where a cashback incentive is received, the total amount payable over the lease term, less the cashback, should be charged evenly over the term of the lease. This can be done by crediting the cashback received to deferred income and releasing it to profit or loss over the lease term.

Accounting for finance leases

For assets held under **finance leases** (including hire purchase) this accounting treatment would not disclose the reality of the situation. For the lessor, in reality, what he owns is a stream of cash flows receivable from the lessee. **The asset is an amount receivable rather than a non-current asset.**

For the lessee the **substance of the transaction is that he has acquired a non-current asset**, and this is reflected in the accounting treatment prescribed by IAS 17, even though in law the lessee may never become the owner of the asset.

The following summary diagram shows the points of distinction between an operating lease and a finance lease.

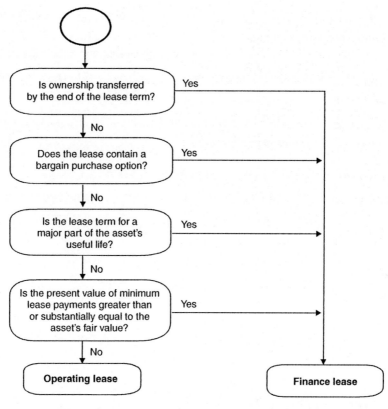

IAS 17 originally stated that when classifying a lease of **land and buildings** the **land** element is normally classified as an **operating lease unless title passes to the lessee** at the end of the contract.

This has now been amended. Effective from January 2010, entities now have the option to treat a long lease of land as a finance lease where it meets the requirements to be classified as a finance lease. This would be the case where substantially all risks and rewards are transferred to the lessee and the present value of the residual value is considered negligible.

2 Lessees

Accounting treatment for finance leases

IAS 17 requires that, when an asset changes hands under a **finance lease, lessor and lessee should account for the transaction as though it were a credit sale**. In the lessee's books therefore the lease asset is capitalised:

DEBIT   Asset account
CREDIT   Lessor (liability) account

The amount to be recorded in this way is the **lower** of the **fair value** and the **present value** of the minimum lease payments.

IAS 17 states that it is not appropriate to show liabilities for leased assets as deductions from the leased assets. A distinction should be made between **current and non-current** lease liabilities, if the entity makes this distinction for other liabilities.

The asset should be **depreciated** (on the bases set out in IASs 16 and 38) over the shorter of the lease term and the useful life of the asset.

If there is reasonable certainty of eventual ownership of the asset, then it should be depreciated over its useful life.

Apportionment of rental payments

When the lessee makes a rental payment it will comprise two elements.

(a) An **interest charge** on the finance provided by the lessor. This proportion of each payment is interest payable and interest receivable in the statements of profit or loss of the lessee and lessor respectively.

(b) A repayment of part of the **capital cost** of the asset. In the lessee's books this proportion of each rental payment must be debited to the lessor's account to reduce the outstanding liability. In the lessor's books, it must be credited to the lessee's account to reduce the amount owing (the debit of course is to cash).

The accounting problem is to decide what proportion of each instalment paid by the lessee represents interest, and what proportion represents a repayment of the capital advanced by the lessor.

The **actuarial method** is the best and most scientific method of doing this. It derives from the common-sense assumption that the interest charged by a lessor company will equal the rate of return desired by the company, multiplied by the amount of capital it has invested. This required rate of return is described as the **effective interest rate**.

(a) At the beginning of the lease the capital invested is equal to the fair value of the asset (less any initial deposit paid by the lessee).

(b) This amount reduces as each instalment is paid. It follows that the interest accruing is greatest in the early part of the lease term, and gradually reduces as capital is repaid.

Example

On 1 January 20X5 a company bought a machine under a finance lease. The cash price of the machine was $7,710 while the amount to be paid was $10,000. The agreement required the immediate payment of a $2,000 deposit with the balance being settled in four equal annual instalments commencing on 31 December 20X5. The charge of $2,290 represents interest of 15% per annum (the effective interest rate), calculated on the remaining balance of the liability during each accounting period. Depreciation on the plant is to be provided for at the rate of 20% per annum on a straight line basis assuming a residual value of nil.

Interest is calculated as 15% of the outstanding **capital** balance at the beginning of each year. The outstanding capital balance reduces each year by the capital element comprised in each instalment. This will appear as follows over the term of the lease:

	$
Cash price	7,710
Deposit	(2,000)
	5,710
Interest 15%	856
31 December 20X5 instalment	(2,000)
Balance at 31 December 20X5	4,566
Interest 15%	685
31 December 20X6 instalment	(2,000)
Balance at 31 December 20X6	3,251
Interest 15%	488
31 December 20X7 instalment	(2,000)
Balance at 31 December 20X7	1,739
Interest 15%	261
31 December 20X8 instalment	(2,000)
	–

Thus, at each year end the balance on the liability account will represent the outstanding capital liability. Future interest/finance charges are not a true liability as the capital could be paid off at any time, thus avoiding these charges.

Disclosure requirements for lessees

IAS 17 requires the following disclosures by lessees in respect of finance leases:

- The **net carrying amount** at the reporting date for each class of asset

- A **reconciliation** between the total of minimum lease payments at the reporting date, and their present value. In addition, an entity should disclose the total of minimum lease payments at the reporting date, and their present value, for each of the following periods:

    – Not later than one year
    – Later than one year and not later than five years
    – Later than five years

- **Contingent rents** recognised as income in the period

- Total of **future minimum sublease payments** expected to be received under non-cancellable subleases at the reporting date

- A **general description** of the lessee's material leasing arrangements

IAS 17 encourages (but does not require) further disclosures, as appropriate.

Example

In the case above, the company's financial statements for the first year of the lease, the year ended 31 December 20X5, would include the information given below.

STATEMENT OF FINANCIAL POSITION AS AT 31 DECEMBER 20X5 (EXTRACTS)

	$	$
Non-current assets		
Assets held under finance leases		
Plant and machinery at cost	7,710	
Less accumulated depreciation (20% × $7,710)	(1,542)	
		6,168
Non-current liabilities		
Obligations under finance leases		3,251
Current liabilities		
Obligations under finance leases (4,566 – 3,251)		1,315

(Notice that only the outstanding **capital** element is disclosed under liabilities, ie the total of the minimum lease payments with future finance charges separately deducted.)

STATEMENT OF PROFIT OR LOSS
FOR THE YEAR ENDED 31 DECEMBER 20X5 (EXTRACT)

	$
Interest payable and similar charges	
Interest on finance leases	856

Operating leases: disclosure requirements for lessees

For operating leases the disclosures are as follows.

(a)   The total of future minimum lease payments under non-cancellable operating leases for each of the following periods:

   (i)   Not later than one year
   (ii) Later than one year and not later than five years
   (iii) Later than five years

(b)   The total of any future minimum sublease payments expected to be received at the end of the reporting period

(c)   Lease and sublease payments recognised as an expense in the period

(d)   A general description of the lessees significant leasing arrangements

3 Lessors

To a certain extent at least, the accounting treatment of leases adopted by lessors will be a **mirror image** of that used by lessees.

Finance leases

Several of the definitions given earlier in this chapter are relevant to lessor accounting in particular:

- Unguaranteed residual value
- Gross investment in the lease
- Unearned finance income
- Net investment in the lease

Accounting treatment

IAS 17 requires the **amount due from the lessee** under a finance lease to be recorded in the statement of financial position of a lessor as a receivable at the amount of the **net investment in the lease**.

The **recognition of finance income** under a finance lease should normally be based on a pattern to give a **constant periodic rate of return** on the lessor's net investment outstanding in respect of the finance lease in each period. In arriving at the constant periodic rate of return, a reasonable approximation may be made.

The lease payments (excluding costs for services) relating to the accounting period should be applied against the gross investment in the lease, so as to **reduce both the principal and the unearned finance income**.

The **estimated unguaranteed residual values** used to calculate the lessor's gross investment in a lease should be reviewed regularly. If there has been a reduction in the value, then the income allocation over the lease term must be revised. Any reduction in respect of amounts already accrued should be recognised immediately.

Initial direct costs incurred by lessors (eg commissions, legal fees and other costs that are directly attributable to negotiating and arranging a lease) are included in the initial measurement of the finance lease receivable.

Manufacturer/dealer lessors

IAS 17 (revised) looks at the situation where manufacturers or dealers offer customers the choice of either buying or leasing an asset. There will be two types of income under such a lease.

(a) Profit/loss equal to that from an **outright sale** (normal selling price less any discount)

(b) **Finance income** over the lease term

IAS 17 requires the following treatment.

(a)   Recognise the **selling profit/loss** in income for the period as if it was an outright sale.

(b)   If **interest rates are artificially low**, restrict the selling profit to that which would apply had a commercial rate been applied.

(c)   Recognise **costs** incurred in connection with negotiating and arranging a lease as an **expense** when the **selling profit** is recognised (at the start of the lease term).

Lessors' disclosures for finance leases

The following should be disclosed.

- A **reconciliation** between the total gross investment in the lease at the year end, and the present value of minimum lease payments receivable at the year end. In addition, an entity should disclose the total gross investment in the lease and the present value of minimum lease payments receivable at the year end, for each of the following periods:

    - Not later than one year
    - Later than one year and not later than five years
    - Later than five years

- Unearned finance income

- The unguaranteed residual values accruing to the benefit of the lessor

- The accumulated allowance for uncollectible minimum lease payments receivable

- Contingent rents recognised in income

- A general description of the lessor's material leasing arrangements

Operating leases

Accounting treatment

An **asset** held for use in operating leases by a lessor should be recorded as a long-term asset and depreciated over its useful life. The basis for depreciation should be consistent with the lessor's policy on similar non-lease assets and follow the guidance in IAS 16.

Income from an operating lease, excluding charges for services such as insurance and maintenance, should be recognised on **a straight-line basis** over the period of the lease (even if the receipts are not on such a basis), unless another systematic and rational basis is more representative of the time pattern in which the benefit from the leased asset is receivable.

Initial direct costs incurred by lessors in negotiating and arranging an operating lease should be **added to the carrying amount** of the leased asset and recognised as an expense over the lease term on the same basis as lease income, ie capitalised and amortised over the lease term.

Lessors should refer to IAS 36 in order to determine whether a leased asset has become impaired.

A lessor who is a **manufacturer or dealer** should not recognise any selling profit on entering into an operating lease because it is not the equivalent of a sale.

Lessors' disclosures for operating leases

The following should be disclosed.

- For each class of asset, the **gross carrying amount**, the accumulated depreciation and accumulated impairment losses at the year end:

    - Depreciation recognised in income for the period
    - Impairment losses recognised in income for the period
    - Impairment losses reversed in income for the period

- The **future minimum lease payments** under non-cancellable operating leases in the aggregate and for each of the following periods:

    - Not later than one year
    - Later than one year and not later than five years
    - Later than five years

- Total **contingent rents** recognised in income

- A **general description** of the lessor's leasing arrangements

Sale and leaseback transactions

In a sale and leaseback transaction, an asset is sold by a vendor and then the same asset is **leased back** to the same vendor. The lease payment and sale price are normally interdependent because they are negotiated as part of the same package. The accounting treatment for the lessee or seller should be as follows, depending on the type of lease involved.

(a)   In a sale and leaseback transaction which results in a **finance lease**, any apparent profit or loss (that is, the difference between the sale price and the previous carrying value) should be deferred and amortised in the financial statements of the seller/lessee over the lease term. It should not be recognised as income immediately.

(b)   If the leaseback is an **operating lease**:

(i)   Any profit or loss should be recognised immediately, provided it is clear that the transaction is established at a **fair value**.

(ii)   Where the **sale price is below fair value**, any profit or loss should be recognised immediately except that if the apparent loss is compensated by future lease payments at below market price it should to that extent be deferred and amortised over the period for which the asset is expected to be used.

(iii) If the **sale price is above fair value**, the excess over fair value should be deferred and amortised over the period over which the asset is expected to be used.

In addition, for an operating lease where the fair value of the asset at the time of the sale is less than the **carrying amount**, the loss (carrying value less fair value) should be recognised immediately.

The buyer or lessor should account for a sale and leaseback in the **same way as other leases**.

The **disclosure requirements** for both lessees and lessors should force disclosure of sale and leaseback transactions.

4 IFRS 16

IFRS 16 *Leases* is the result of a joint IASB/FASB project to improve accounting for leases, following concerns expressed by the SEC in 2005 concerning lack of transparency of information about lease obligations.

Under IAS 17, leases classified as operating leases are not reported on company balance sheets, only disclosed in the notes. In 2014, according to Hans Hoogervorst, listed companies using IFRS or US GAAP disclosed almost US$3 trillion of off balance sheet lease commitments.

Lessees

For lessees, IFRS 16 eliminates the distinction made in IAS 17 between finance and operating leases, for all leases except:

- Leases with a lease term of 12 months or less and containing no purchase options

- Lease of low-value assets (such as personal computers)

In the case of short-term leases and leases of low value assets, lease payments are recognised as an expense in profit or loss over the lease term.

A contract that is, or contains, a lease if it conveys to the lessee the right to control the use of an identified asset for a period of time in exchange for consideration.

Control is conveyed where the lessee has the right to direct the use of the asset and to obtain substantially all of the economic benefits from that use.

Upon lease commencement a lessee recognises a right-of-use asset and a lease liability.

The right-of-use asset is initially measured at the amount of the lease liability plus any initial direct costs incurred by the lessee. After lease commencement it is measured using the cost model and depreciated over the shorter of the lease term and the useful life of the underlying asset, unless it is an investment property or belongs to a class of assets to which the IAS 16 revaluation model is applied.

The lease liability is initially measured at the present value of the lease payments payable over the lease term. If the rate implicit in the lease cannot be readily determined, the amounts can be discounted using the lessee's incremental borrowing rate.

> **Lessee's incremental borrowing rate.** The rate of interest that a lessee would have to pay to borrow over a similar term, and with a similar security, the funds necessary to obtain an asset of a similar value to the right-of-use asset in a similar economic environment.
>
> **Interest rate implicit in the lease.** The interest rate that yields a present value of (a) the lease payments and (b) the unguaranteed residual value equal to the sum of (i) the fair value of the underlying asset and (ii) any initial direct costs of the lessor.
>
> **Lease term.** The non-cancellable period for which a lessee has the right to use an underlying asset, plus;
>
> (a)   Periods covered by an extension option, if the exercise of that option by the lessee is reasonably certain; and
>
> (b)   Periods covered by a termination option if the lessee is reasonably certain not to exercise that option.
>
> The right-of-use asset and the lease liability are subsequently remeasured to reflect any changes in the lease term, the purchase option or the amounts payable under residual value guarantees or to reflect any changes to an index or rate used to determine payments.   *(IFRS 16: Appendix A)*

Example

[This is based on IFRS 16 Illustrative example 13]

A lessee enters into a five-year lease of a building which has a remaining useful life of 10 years. Lease payments are $50,000 per annum, payable at the beginning of each year.

The lessee incurs initial direct costs of $20,000 and receives lease incentives of $5,000. There is no transfer of the asset at the end of the lease and no purchase option.

The interest rate implicit in the lease is not immediately determinable but the lessee's incremental borrowing rate is 5%.

At the commencement date the lessee pays the initial $50,000, incurs the direct costs and receives the lease incentives.

The lease liability is measured at the present value of the remaining four payments:

	$
$50,000/1.05	47,619
$50,000/1.05^2	45,351
$50,000/1.05^3	43,192
$50,000/1.05^4	41,135
	177,297

Assets and liabilities will initially be recognised as follows:

		Debit $	Credit $
Right-of-use asset:			
Initial payment	50,000		
Discounted liability	177,297		
Initial direct costs	20,000		
Incentives received	(5,000)		
		242,297	
Lease liability			177,297
Cash	(50,000 + 20,000 – 5,000)		65,000
		242,297	242,297

At the end of year 1 the liability will be measured as:

	$
Opening balance	177,297
Interest 5%	8,865
	186,162

	$
Current liability	50,000
Non-current liability	136,162
	186,162

The right of use asset will be depreciated over five years, being the shorter of the lease term and the useful life of the underlying asset.

Lessors

Lessors continue to classify leases as operating and finance leases as they did under IAS 17. IFRS 16 carries forward the same accounting requirements for lessors.

Sale and leaseback transactions

To determine whether the transfer of an asset is accounted for as a sale an entity applies the requirements of IFRS 15 for determining when a performance obligation is satisfied.

If the fair value of the sale consideration does not equal the asset's fair value, or if the lease payments are not market rates, the sale proceeds are adjusted to fair value, either by accounting for prepayments or additional financing. (IFRS 15, para. 101)

If the transfer satisfies the IFRS 15 requirement to be accounted for as a sale:

- the seller/lessee measures the right-of-use asset arising from the leaseback at the proportion of the previous carrying amount of the asset that relates to the **right-of use retained** by the seller/lessee.

- The seller/lessee only recognises the amount of any gain or loss on the sale that relates to the **rights transferred** to the buyer (IFRS 16: para. 100)

If the fair value of the consideration for the sale does not equal the fair value of the asset, or if the lease payments are not at market rates, the following adjustments should be made:

- Any below-market terms should be accounted for as a prepayment of lease payments (the shortfall in consideration received from the lessor is treated as a lease payment made by the lessee)

- Any above-market terms are accounted for as additional financing provided by the buyer/lessor (the additional amount paid by the lessor is treated as additional liability, **not** as gain on the sale) (IFRS 16: para.101)

If the transfer does **not** satisfy the IFRS 15 requirements to be accounted for as a sale, the seller continues to recognise the transferred asset and the transfer proceeds are treated as a financial liability, accounted for in accordance with IFRS 9. The transaction is more in the nature of a secured loan.

Example

[Adapted from IFRS 16 Illustrated example 24]

The seller/lessee sells a building to the buyer/lessor for $800,000 cash. The carrying amount of the building prior to the sale was $600,000. The seller/lessee arranges to lease the building back for five years at $120,000 per annum, payable in arrears. The remaining useful life is 15 years.

The transaction satisfies the performance obligations in IFRS 15, so will be accounted for as a sale and leaseback.

At the date of sale the fair value of the building was $750,000, so the excess $50,000 paid by the buyer is recognised as additional financing provided by the buyer/lessor.

The interest rate implicit in the lease is 4.5% and the present value of the annual payments is:

	$
$120,000/1.045$	114,833
$120,000/1.045^2$	109,888
$120,000/1.045^3$	105,155
$120,000/1.045^4$	100,627
$120,000/1.045^5$	95,836
	526,339

Of this, $476,339 relates to the lease and $50,000 relates to the additional financing.

At the commencement date, the seller/lessee measures the right-of-use asset arising from the leaseback of the building at the proportion of the previous carrying amount of the building that relates to the right-of-use retained. This is calculated as carrying amount × discounted lease payments / fair value.

In our example: $600,000 × 476,339/750,000 = $381,071

The seller/lessee only recognises the amount of gain that relates to the rights transferred. The gain on sale of the building is $150,000 (750,000 – 600,000), of which:

(a)   150,000 × 476,339/750,000 = $95,268 – relates to the rights retained

(a)   The balance -150,000 – 95,268 = $54,732 – relates to the rights transferred to the buyer.

At the commencement date the lessee accounts for the transaction as follows:

	Debit $	Credit $
Cash	800,000	
Right-of-use asset	381,071	
Building		600,000
Financial liability		526,339
Gain on rights transferred		54,732
	1,181,071	1,181,071

The right-of-use asset will be depreciated over five years, the gain will be recognised in profit or loss and the financial liability will be increased each year by the interest charge and reduced by the lease payments.

Disclosure

IFRS 16 sets out detailed disclosure requirements for both lessees and lessors.

The objective of the disclosure requirements is to allow users to assess the effect that leases have on the financial position, financial performance and cash flows of the lessee (IFRS 16: para. 51).

Amounts to be disclosed include:

- Depreciation charge for right-of-use assets

- Interest expense on lease liabilities

- Expenses relating to short-term and low-value leases

- Details of sale and leaseback transactions

- The carrying amount of right-of-use assets at the end of the reporting period, by class of underlying asset

- Additions to right-of-use assets

Accounting for taxation

10

1 IAS 12: Income taxes

IAS 12 does not deal with the detailed computation of corporate or personal tax. This will be done under a specific tax regime and is not the subject of any accounting standard. IAS 12 deals with current and deferred tax. The parts relating to current tax are fairly brief, because this is the simple and uncontroversial area of tax.

Definitions

These are some of the definitions given in IAS 12.

> **Accounting profit.** Net profit or loss for a period before deducting tax expense.
>
> **Taxable profit (tax loss).** The profit (loss) for a period, determined in accordance with the rules established by the taxation authorities, upon which income taxes are payable (recoverable).
>
> **Tax expense (tax income).** The aggregate amount included in the determination of net profit or loss for the period in respect of current tax and deferred tax.
>
> **Current tax.** The amount of income taxes payable (recoverable) in respect of the taxable profit (tax loss) for a period.　　　　　　　　　　　　　(*IAS 12: para. 5*)

It is important to distinguish between current and deferred tax.

(a)　**Current tax** is the amount **actually payable** to the tax authorities in relation to the trading activities of the entity during the period.

(b)　**Deferred tax** is an **accounting measure**, used to match the tax effects of transactions with their accounting impact and thereby produce less distorted results.

Recognition of current tax liabilities and assets

IAS 12 requires any **unpaid tax** in respect of the current or prior periods to be recognised as a liability.

Conversely, any **excess tax** paid in respect of current or prior periods over what is due should be recognised as an asset.

Example

In 20X8 D Co had taxable profits of $120,000. In the previous year (20X7) income tax on 20X7 profits had been estimated as $30,000.

Any under or over payments are not settled until the following year's tax payment is due.

What would be the tax payable and the charge for 20X8 if the tax due on 20X7 profits was subsequently agreed with the tax authorities as:

(a) $35,000?
(b) $25,000?

The calculations are as follows:

(a)

	$
Tax due on 20X8 profits ($120,000 × 30%)	36,000
Underpayment for 20X7	5,000
Tax charge and liability	41,000

(b)

	$
Tax due on 20X8 profits (as above))	36,000
Overpayment for 20X7	(5,000)
Tax charge and liability	31,000

Alternatively, the rebate due could be shown separately as income in the statement of profit or loss and as an asset in the statement of financial position. An offset approach like this is, however, most likely.

Taking this a stage further, IAS 12 also requires recognition as an asset of the benefit relating to any tax loss that can be **carried back** to recover current tax of a previous period. This is acceptable because it is probable that the benefit will flow to the entity and it can be reliably measured.

Measurement

Measurement of current tax liabilities (assets) for the current and prior periods is very simple. They are measured at the amount expected to be paid to (recovered from) the tax authorities. The tax rates (and tax laws) used should be those enacted (or substantively enacted) by the end of the reporting period.

Recognition of current tax

Normally, current tax is recognised as income or expense and included in the net profit or loss for the period, except in two cases.

(a)   Tax arising from a **business combination** which is an acquisition is treated differently

(b)   Tax arising from a **transaction or event** which is recognised in other comprehensive income (in the same or a different period)

The rule in (b) is logical. If a transaction or event is charged or credited directly to equity, rather than to profit or loss, then the related tax should be also. An example of such a situation is where, under IAS 8, an adjustment is made to the **opening balance of retained earnings** due to either a change in accounting policy that is applied retrospectively, or to the correction of a material prior period error.

Presentation

In the statement of financial position, **tax assets and liabilities** should be shown separately from other assets and liabilities.

Current tax assets and liabilities can be **offset**, but this should happen only when certain conditions apply.

(a)   The entity has a **legally enforceable right** to set off the recognised amounts

(b)   The entity intends to settle the amounts on a **net basis**, or to realise the asset and settle the liability at the same time

The **tax expense (income)** related to the profit or loss from ordinary activities should be shown in the statement of profit or loss.

The **disclosure requirements** of IAS 12 are extensive and we will look at these later in the chapter.

2 Deferred tax

Deferred tax gives rise to an accounting adjustment which allows for the fact that tax will be payable or reclaimable in the future.

When a company recognises an asset or liability, it expects to **recover or settle the carrying amount** of that asset or liability. In other words, it expects to sell or use up assets, and to pay off liabilities. What happens if that recovery or settlement is likely to make future tax payments larger (or smaller) than they would otherwise have been if the recovery or settlement had no tax consequences? In these circumstances, IAS 12 requires companies to recognise a **deferred tax liability** (or **deferred tax asset**).

Definitions

Deferred tax liabilities are the amounts of income taxes payable in future periods in respect of taxable temporary differences.

Deferred tax assets are the amounts of income taxes recoverable in future periods in respect of:

- Deductible temporary differences
- The carry forward of unused tax losses
- The carry forward of unused tax credits

Temporary differences are differences between the carrying amount of an asset or liability in the statement of financial position and its tax base. Temporary differences may be either:

- **Taxable temporary differences**, which are temporary differences that will result in taxable amounts in determining taxable profit (tax loss) of future periods when the carrying amount of the asset or liability is recovered or settled

- **Deductible temporary differences**, which are temporary differences that will result in amounts that are deductible in determining taxable profit (tax loss) of future periods when the carrying amount of the asset or liability is recovered or settled

The **tax base** of an asset or liability is the amount attributed to that asset or liability for tax purposes.   (*IAS 12: para. 5*)

Tax base

We can expand on the definition given above by stating that the **tax base of an asset** is the amount that will be deductible for tax purposes against any taxable economic benefits that will flow to the entity when it recovers the carrying value of the asset. Where those economic benefits are not taxable, the tax base of the asset is the same as its carrying amount.

We can illustrate this with some examples:

(a)   A machine cost $10,000. For tax purposes, depreciation of $3,000 has already been deducted in the current and prior periods and the remaining cost will be deductible in future periods, either as tax-allowable depreciation or through a deduction on disposal. Revenue generated by using the machine is taxable, any gain on disposal of the machine will be taxable and any loss on disposal will be deductible for tax purposes.

The tax base of the machine is $7,000.

(b)   Interest receivable has a carrying amount of $1,000. The related interest revenue will be taxed on a cash basis.

The tax base of the interest receivable is nil.

(c)   Trade receivables have a carrying amount of $10,000. The related revenue has already been included in taxable profit (tax loss).

The tax base of the trade receivables is $10,000.

(d)   A loan receivable has a carrying amount of $1m. The repayment of the loan will have no tax consequences.

The tax base of the loan is $1m.

In the case of a **liability**, the tax base will be its carrying amount, less any amount that will be deducted for tax purposes in relation to the liability in future periods. For revenue received in advance, the tax base of the resulting liability is its carrying amount, less any amount of the revenue that will not be taxable in future periods.

Temporary differences

Accounting profits form the basis for computing **taxable profits**, on which the tax liability for the year is calculated; however, accounting profits and taxable profits are different. There are two reasons for the differences.

(a)   **Permanent differences**. These occur when certain items of revenue or expense are excluded from the computation of taxable profits (for example, entertainment expenses may not be allowable for tax purposes).

(b)   **Temporary differences**. These occur when items of revenue or expense are included in both accounting profits and taxable profits, but not for the same accounting period. For example, an expense which is allowable as a deduction in arriving at taxable profits for 20X7 might not be included in the financial accounts until 20X8 or later. In the long run, the total taxable profits and total accounting profits will be the same (except for permanent differences) so that temporary differences originate in one period and are capable of reversal in one or more subsequent periods. Deferred tax is the tax attributable to **temporary differences**.

The distinction made in the definition between **taxable temporary differences** and **deductible temporary differences** can be made clearer by looking at the explanations and examples given in the standard and its appendices.

3 Taxable temporary differences

All taxable temporary differences give rise to a deferred tax liability. The following are examples of circumstances that give rise to taxable temporary differences.

Transactions that affect profit or loss

(a) **Interest revenue** received in arrears and included in accounting profit on the basis of time apportionment. It is included in taxable profit, however, on a cash basis.

(b) **Sale of goods revenue** is included in accounting profit when the goods are delivered, but only included in taxable profit when cash is received.

(c) **Depreciation** of an asset is accelerated for tax purposes. When new assets are purchased, allowances may be available against taxable profits which exceed the amount of depreciation chargeable on the assets in the financial accounts for the year of purchase.

(d) **Development costs** which have been capitalised will be amortised in profit or loss, but they were deducted in full from taxable profit in the period in which they were incurred.

(e) **Prepaid expenses** have already been deducted on a cash basis in determining the taxable profit of the current or previous periods.

Transactions that affect the statement of financial position

(a) **Depreciation of an asset** is not deductible for tax purposes. No deduction will be available for tax purposes when the asset is sold/scrapped.

(b) A borrower records a **loan** at proceeds received (amount due at maturity) less transaction costs. The carrying amount of the loan is subsequently increased by amortisation of the transaction costs against accounting profit. The transaction costs were, however, deducted for tax purposes in the period when the loan was first recognised.

Fair value adjustments and revaluations

(a) **Current investments** or financial instruments are carried at fair value. This exceeds cost, but no equivalent adjustment is made for tax purposes.

(b) Property, plant and equipment is **revalued** by an entity (under IAS 16), but no equivalent adjustment is made for tax purposes. This also applies to long-term investments. As the tax base remains at the original value, there will be a difference between the carrying value and the tax base, leading to an increase in the deferred tax provision.

The reasoning behind this is as follows:

(a) **When an asset is recognised**, it is expected that its carrying amount will be recovered in the form of economic benefits that flow to the entity in future periods.

(b) If the carrying amount of the asset is greater than its tax base, then taxable economic benefits will also be **greater than** the amount that will be allowed as a deduction for tax purposes.

(c) The difference is therefore a **taxable temporary difference** and the obligation to pay the resulting income taxes in future periods is a **deferred tax liability**.

(d) As the entity recovers the carrying amount of the asset, the taxable temporary difference will **reverse** and the entity will have taxable profit.

(e) It is then probable that economic benefits will flow from the entity in the form of **tax payments**, and so the recognition of all deferred tax liabilities is required by IAS 12.

Example: taxable temporary differences

A company purchased an asset costing $1,500. At the end of 20X8 the carrying amount is $1,000. The cumulative depreciation for tax purposes is $900 and the current tax rate is 25%.

What is the deferred tax liability for the asset?

Firstly, what is the tax base of the asset? It is $1,500 – $900 = $600.

In order to recover the carrying value of $1,000, the entity must earn taxable income of $1,000, but it will only be able to deduct $600 as a taxable expense. The entity must therefore pay income tax of $400 × 25% = $100 when the carrying value of the asset is recovered.

The entity must therefore recognise a deferred tax liability of $400 × 25% = $100, recognising the difference between the carrying amount of $1,000 and the tax base of $600 as a taxable temporary difference.

Timing differences

Some temporary differences are often called **timing differences**, when income or expense is included in accounting profit in one period, but is included in taxable profit in a different period. The main types of taxable temporary differences which are timing differences and which result in deferred tax liabilities are:

- **Interest received** which is accounted for on an accruals basis, but which for tax purposes is included on a cash basis

- **Accelerated depreciation** for tax purposes

- Capitalised and amortised **development costs**

Revalued assets

Under IAS 16 assets may be revalued. If this affects the taxable profit for the current period, the tax base of the asset changes and **no temporary difference** arises.

If, however (as in some countries), the revaluation does not affect current taxable profits, the tax base of the asset is not adjusted. Consequently, the taxable flow of economic benefits to the entity as the carrying value of the asset is recovered will differ from the amount that will be deductible for tax purposes.

The difference between the carrying amount of a revalued asset and its tax base is a temporary difference and gives rise to a **deferred tax liability or asset**.

Initial recognition of an asset or liability

A temporary difference can arise on initial recognition of an asset or liability, eg if part or all of the cost of an asset will not be deductible for tax purposes. The **nature of the transaction** which led to the initial recognition of the asset is important in determining the method of accounting for such temporary differences.

If the transaction affects either accounting profit or taxable profit, an entity will **recognise any deferred tax liability** or asset. The resulting deferred tax expense or income will be recognised in profit or loss.

Where a transaction affects **neither accounting profit nor taxable profit** IAS 12 does not permit the recognition of a deferred tax asset or liability as it would make the financial statements less transparent. This will be the case both on initial recognition and subsequently.

Example: initial recognition

Suppose a company intends to use an asset which cost $10,000 in 20X1 through its useful life of five years. Its residual value will then be nil. The tax rate is 40%. Any capital gain on disposal would not be taxable (and any capital loss not deductible). Depreciation of the asset is not deductible for tax purposes.

What are the deferred tax consequences in each of years 20X1 and 20X2?

As at 20X1, as it recovers the carrying amount of the asset, the company will earn taxable income of $10,000 and pay tax of $4,000. The resulting deferred tax liability of $4,000 would not be recognised because it results from the initial recognition of the asset.

As at 20X2, the carrying value of the asset is now $8,000. In earning taxable income of $8,000, the entity will pay tax of $3,200. Again, the resulting deferred tax liability of $3,200 is not recognised, because it results from the initial recognition of the asset.

4 Deductible temporary differences

The rule to remember here is that all **deductible temporary differences give rise to a deferred tax asse**t. There is a proviso, however. The deferred tax asset must also satisfy the **recognition criteria** given in IAS 12. This is that a deferred tax asset should be recognised for all deductible temporary differences to the extent that it is **probable that taxable profit will be available** against which it can be utilised. Before we look at this issue in more detail, let us consider the examples of deductible temporary differences given in the standard.

Transactions that affect profit or loss

(a)   **Retirement benefit costs** (pension costs) are deducted from accounting profit as service is provided by the employee. They are not deducted in determining taxable profit until the entity pays either retirement benefits or contributions to a fund. (This may also apply to similar expenses.)

(b)   **Accumulated depreciation** of an asset in the financial statements is greater than the accumulated depreciation allowed for tax purposes up to the end of the reporting period.

(c)   The **cost of inventories** sold before the end of the reporting period is deducted from accounting profit when goods/services are delivered, but is deducted from taxable profit when the cash is received. (**Note.** There is also a taxable temporary difference associated with the related trade receivable, as noted in Section 3 above.)

(d) The carrying amount of inventory, or the **recoverable amount** of an item of property, plant and equipment falls and the carrying value is therefore **reduced**, but that reduction is ignored for tax purposes until the asset is sold.

(e) **Research costs** (or organisation/other start-up costs) are recognised as an expense for accounting purposes but are not deductible against taxable profits until a later period.

(f) Income is **deferred** in the statement of financial position, but has already been included in taxable profit in current/prior periods.

(g) A **government grant** is included in the statement of financial position as deferred income, but it will not be taxable in future periods. (Note. A deferred tax asset may not be recognised here according to the standard.)

Fair value adjustments and revaluations

Current investments or **financial instruments** may be carried at fair value which is less than cost, but no equivalent adjustment is made for tax purposes.

Recognition of deductible temporary differences

We looked at the important recognition criteria above. As with temporary taxable differences, there are also circumstances where the overall rule for recognition of deferred tax asset is not allowed.

(a) Where the deferred tax asset arises from **negative goodwill** which is treated as deferred income.

(b) Where the deferred tax asset arises from **initial recognition** of an asset or liability in a transaction which:

(i) Is not a business combination; and

(ii) At the time of the transaction, affects neither accounting nor taxable profit/tax loss.

Let us lay out the reasoning behind the recognition of deferred tax assets arising from deductible temporary differences.

(a) When a **liability is recognised**, it is assumed that its carrying amount will be settled in the form of outflows of economic benefits from the entity in future periods.

(b) When these resources flow from the entity, part or all may be deductible in determining taxable profits of a **period later** than that in which the liability is recognised.

(c) A **temporary tax difference** then exists between the carrying amount of the liability and its tax base.

(d)   A **deferred tax asset** therefore arises, representing the income taxes that will be recoverable in future periods when that part of the liability is allowed as a deduction from taxable profit.

(e)   Similarly, when the carrying amount of an asset is **less than its tax base**, the difference gives rise to a deferred tax asset in respect of the income taxes that will be recoverable in future periods.

Example: deductible temporary differences

X Co recognises a liability of $10,000 for accrued product warranty costs on 31 December 20X7. These product warranty costs will not be deductible for tax purposes until the entity pays claims. The tax rate is 25%.

What are the deferred tax implications of this situation?

What is the tax base of the liability? It is nil (carrying amount of $10,000 less the amount that will be deductible for tax purposes in respect of the liability in future periods).

When the liability is settled for its carrying amount, the entity's future taxable profit will be reduced by $10,000 and so its future tax payments by $10,000 × 25% = $2,500.

The difference of $10,000 between the carrying amount ($10,000) and the tax base (nil) is a deductible temporary difference. The entity should therefore recognise a deferred tax asset of $10,000 × 25% = $2,500 **provided that** it is probable that the entity will earn sufficient taxable profits in future periods to benefit from a reduction in tax payments.

Taxable profits in future periods

When can we be sure that sufficient taxable profit will be available against which a deductible temporary difference can be utilised? IAS 12 states that this will be assumed when sufficient **taxable temporary differences** exist which relate to the same taxation authority and the same taxable entity. These should be expected to reverse:

(a)   In the same period as the expected reversal of the deductible temporary difference; or

(b)   In periods into which a tax loss arising from the deferred tax asset can be carried back or forward.

Only in these circumstances is the deferred tax asset **recognised**, in the period in which the deductible temporary differences arise.

Unused tax losses and unused tax credits

An entity may have unused tax losses or credits (ie which it can offset against taxable profits) at the end of a period. Should a deferred tax asset be recognised in relation to such amounts? IAS 12 states that a deferred tax asset may be recognised in such circumstances **to the extent that it is probable future taxable profit will be available against which the unused tax losses/credits can be utilised**.

Reassessment of unrecognised deferred tax assets

For **all** unrecognised deferred tax assets, at the end of each reporting period an entity should **reassess the availability of future taxable profits** and whether part or all of any unrecognised deferred tax assets should now be recognised. This may be due to an improvement in trading conditions which is expected to continue.

5 Measurement and recognition of deferred tax

The full provision method as used in IAS 12 has the advantage that it recognises that each timing difference at the end of the reporting period has an effect on future tax payments. If a company claims an accelerated tax allowance on an item of plant, future tax assessments will be bigger than they would have been otherwise. Future transactions may well affect those assessments still further, but that is not relevant in assessing the position at the end of the reporting period.

Example

Suppose that V Co begins trading on 1 January 20X7. In its first year it makes profits of $5m, the depreciation charge is $1m and the tax allowances on those assets is $1.5m. The rate of income tax is 30%.

The tax liability is $1.35m (30% × $m(5.0 + 1.0 – 1.5), but the debit to profit or loss is increased by the deferred tax liability of 30% × $0.5m = $150,000. The total charge to profit or loss is therefore $1.5m which is an effective tax rate of 30% on accounting profits (ie 30% × $5.0m).

Changes in tax rates

Where the corporate rate of income tax **fluctuates from one year to another**, a problem arises in respect of the amount of deferred tax to be credited (debited) to profit or loss in later years.

IAS 12 requires deferred tax assets and liabilities to be measured at the tax rates expected to apply in the period **when the asset is realised or liability settled**, based on tax rates and laws enacted (or substantively enacted) at the end of the reporting period.

Discounting

Discounting is used to allow for the effect of the time value of money.

IAS 12 states that deferred tax assets and liabilities **should not be discounted** because of the complexities and difficulties involved. Discounting is applied to other non-current liabilities such as provisions and deferred payments.

Carrying amount of deferred tax assets

The carrying amount of deferred tax assets should be **reviewed at the end of each reporting period** and reduced where appropriate (insufficient future taxable profits). Such a reduction may be reversed in future years.

Recognition

As with current tax, deferred tax should normally be recognised as income or an expense and included in the net profit or loss for the period. The exception is where the tax arises from a transaction or event which is recognised (in the same or a different period) **directly in equity**.

The figures shown for deferred tax in profit or loss will consist of **two components**.

(a)   Deferred tax relating to **timing differences**

(b)   Adjustments relating to **changes in the carrying amount of deferred tax assets/liabilities** (where there is no change in timing differences), eg changes in tax rates/laws, reassessment of the recoverability of deferred tax assets, or a change in the expected recovery of an asset

Items in (b) will be recognised in profit or loss, unless they relate to items previously charged/credited to equity.

Deferred tax (and current tax) should be charged/credited directly to equity if the tax relates to items also charged/credited directly to equity (in the same or a different period).

Examples of IASs which allow certain items to be credited/charged directly to equity include:

(a)   **Revaluations** of property, plant and equipment (IAS 16)

(b)   The effect of a **change in accounting policy** (applied retrospectively) or correction of a **material error** (IAS 8)

Example

Z Co owns a property which has a carrying value at the beginning of 20X9 of $1,500,000. At the year end it has entered into a contract to sell the property for $1,800,000. The tax rate is 30%. How will this be shown in the financial statements?

STATEMENT OF PROFIT OR LOSS AND OTHER COMPREHENSIVE INCOME (EXTRACT)

	$'000
Profit for the year	X
Other comprehensive income: items not reclassified to profit or loss	
Gains on property revaluation	300
Income tax relating to components of other comprehensive income (300 × 30%)	(90)
Other comprehensive income for the year net of tax	210

The amounts will be posted as follows:

	Debit $'000	Credit $'000
Property, plant and equipment	300	
Deferred tax		90
Revaluation surplus		210

Why do we recognise deferred tax?

(a) Adjustments for deferred tax are made in accordance with the **accruals concept** and in accordance with the definition of a **liability** in the *Conceptual Framework*, ie a past event has given rise to an obligation in the form of increased taxation which will be payable in the future. The amount can be reliably estimated. A deferred tax asset similarly meets the definition of an **asset**.

(b) If the future tax consequences of transactions are not recognised, profit can be overstated, leading to overpayment of dividends and distortion of share price and EPS.

6 Taxation in financial statements

Taxation in the statement of profit or loss

The tax on profit on ordinary activities is calculated by aggregating:

(a) **Income tax** on taxable profits

(b) **Transfers to or from deferred taxation**

(c) Any **under-provision or over-provision** of income tax on profits of previous years

BPP
LEARNING MEDIA

When income tax on profits is calculated, **the calculation is only an estimate of what the company thinks its tax liability will be. In subsequent dealings with the tax authorities, a different income tax charge might eventually be agreed**.

The difference between the estimated tax on profits for one year and the actual tax charge finally agreed for the year is made as an adjustment to taxation on profits in the following year, **resulting in the disclosure of either an under-provision or an over-provision of tax**.

Example

In the accounting year to 31 December 20X3, S Co made an operating profit before taxation of $110,000.

Income tax on the operating profit has been estimated as $45,000. In the previous year (20X2) income tax on 20X2 profits had been estimated as $38,000 but it was subsequently agreed at $40,500.

A transfer to the credit of the deferred taxation account of $16,000 will be made in 20X3.

What will be:

(a)   The tax on profits for 20X3 for disclosure in the accounts?
(b)   The amount of tax payable?

The calculations are as follows:

(a)

	$
Income tax on profits (liability in the statement of FP)	45,000
Deferred taxation	16,000
Under-provision of tax in previous year $(40,500 – 38,000)	2,500
Tax on profits for 20X3 (profit or loss charge)	63,500

(b)

	$
Tax payable on 20X3 profits (liability)	45,000

Taxation in the statement of financial position

It should already be apparent from the previous examples that the income tax charge in profit or loss will not be the same as income tax liabilities in the statement of financial position.

In the statement of financial position, there are several items which we might expect to find.

(a)   **Income tax may be payable** in respect of (say) interest payments paid in the last accounting return period of the year, or accrued.

(b)   If no tax is payable (or very little), then there might be an **income tax recoverable asset** disclosed in current assets (income tax is normally recovered by offset against the tax liability for the year).

(c)   There will usually be a **liability for tax**, possibly including the amounts due in respect of previous years but not yet paid.

(d)   We may also find a **liability on the deferred taxation account**. Deferred taxation is shown under 'non-current liabilities' in the statement of financial position.

Presentation of tax assets and liabilities

These should be **presented separately** from other assets and liabilities in the statement of financial position. Deferred tax assets and liabilities should be distinguished from current tax assets and liabilities.

In addition, deferred tax assets/liabilities should not be classified as current assets/liabilities, where an entity makes such a distinction.

There are only limited circumstances where **current tax assets** and liabilities may be **offset**. This should only occur if two things apply:

(a)   The entity has a legally enforceable right to set off the recognised amounts

(b)   The entity intends either to settle on a net basis, or to realise the asset and settle the liability simultaneously

Similar criteria apply to the **offset of deferred tax assets and liabilities.**

Financial instruments

11

1 Financial assets and liabilities

If you read the financial press you will probably be aware of **rapid international expansion** in the use of financial instruments. These vary from straightforward, traditional instruments, eg bonds, through to various forms of so-called 'derivative instruments'.

We can perhaps summarise the reasons why accounting standards on financial instruments were considered necessary as follows.

(a)   The **significant growth of financial instruments** over recent years has outstripped the development of guidance for their accounting.

(b)   The topic is of **international concern**, various national standard-setters are involved as well as the IASB.

(c)   There have been a number of **high-profile disasters** involving derivatives (eg Barings) which, while not caused by accounting failures, have raised questions about accounting and disclosure practices.

There are four standards on financial instruments:

(a)   IAS 32 *Financial instruments: presentation*, which deals with:

    (i)   The classification of financial instruments between liabilities and equity from the perspective of the issuer

    (ii)   Presentation of certain compound instruments

(b)   IFRS 7 *Financial instruments: disclosures*, which revised, simplified and incorporated disclosure requirements previously in IAS 32.

(c)   IAS 39 *Financial instruments: recognition and measurement*, which includes hedge accounting guidelines that are still allowable under the provisions of IFRS 9

(d) IFRS 9 *Financial instruments*, which is effective from 1 January 2018 and deals with:

    (i) Recognition and derecognition

    (ii) Measurement

    (iii) Impairment

    (iv) Hedging

The most important definitions are relevant to all four standards.

Financial instrument. Any contract that gives rise to both a financial asset of one entity and a financial liability or equity instrument of another entity.

Financial asset. Any asset that is:

(a) Cash

(b) An equity instrument of another entity

(c) A contractual right to receive cash or another financial asset from another entity; or to exchange financial instruments with another entity under conditions that are potentially favourable to the entity

(d) A contract that will or may be settled in the entity's own equity instruments and is:

    (i) A non-derivative for which the entity is or may be obliged to receive a variable number of the entity's own equity instruments; or

    (ii) A derivative that will or may be settled other than by the exchange of a fixed amount of cash or another financial asset for a fixed number of the entity's own equity instruments.

Financial liability. Any liability that is:

(a) A contractual obligation:

    (i) To deliver cash or another financial asset to another entity, or

    (ii) To exchange financial instruments with another entity under conditions that are potentially unfavourable to the entity; or

(b) A contract that will or may be settled in the entity's own equity instruments and is:

    (i) A non-derivative for which the entity is or may be obliged to deliver a variable number of the entity's own equity instruments; or

    (ii) A derivative that will or may be settled other than by the exchange of a fixed amount of cash or another financial asset for a fixed number of the entity's own equity instruments.

Equity instrument. Any contract that evidences a residual interest in the assets of an entity after deducting all of its liabilities.

Fair value is the price that would be received to sell an asset or paid to transfer a liability in an orderly transaction between market participants at the measurement date.

> **Derivative.** A financial instrument or other contract with all three of the following characteristics:
>
> (a) Its value changes in response to the change in a specified interest rate, financial instrument price, commodity price, foreign exchange rate, index of prices or rates, credit rating or credit index, or other variable (sometimes called the 'underlying')
>
> (b) It requires no initial net investment or an initial net investment that is smaller than would be required for other types of contracts that would be expected to have a similar response to changes in market factors; and
>
> (c) It is settled at a future date. *(IFRS 9: Appendix A)*

We should clarify some points arising from these definitions. Firstly, one or two terms above should themselves be defined.

(a) A **'contract'** need not be in writing, but it must comprise an agreement that has 'clear economic consequences' and which the parties to it cannot avoid, usually because the agreement is enforceable in law.

(b) An **'entity'** here could be an individual, partnership, incorporated body or government agency.

The definitions of **financial assets and financial liabilities** may seem rather circular, referring as they do to the terms financial asset and financial instrument. The point is that there may be a chain of contractual rights and obligations, but it will lead ultimately to the receipt or payment of cash or the acquisition or issue of an equity instrument.

Examples of **financial assets** include:

(a) Trade receivables
(b) Options
(c) Shares (when used as an investment).

Examples of **financial liabilities** include:

(a) Trade payables
(b) Debenture loans payable
(c) Redeemable preference (non-equity) shares
(d) Forward contracts standing at a loss

As we have already noted, financial instruments include both of the following.

(a) **Primary instruments**: eg receivables, payables and equity securities

(b) **Derivative (or secondary) instruments**: eg financial options, futures and forwards, interest rate swaps and currency swaps, **whether recognised or unrecognised**

Part B 11: Financial instruments

IAS 32 makes it clear that the following items are not financial instruments.

- **Physical assets**, eg inventories, property, plant and equipment, leased assets and intangible assets (patents, trademarks etc). where a contract is expected to be satisfied by **physical** delivery it is **not** a financial instrument. This is known as the normal purchase/sale exemption

- **Prepaid expenses**, deferred revenue and most warranty obligations

- Liabilities or assets that are **not contractual** in nature

- Contractual rights/obligations that **do not involve transfer of a financial asset**, eg commodity futures contracts, short-term leases

Contingent rights and obligations meet the definition of financial assets and financial liabilities respectively, even though many do not qualify for recognition in financial statements. This is because the contractual rights or obligations exist because of a past transaction or event (eg assumption of a guarantee).

Derivatives

A **derivative** is a financial instrument that **derives** its value from the price or rate of an underlying item. Common **examples** of derivatives include:

(a) **Forward contracts**: agreements to buy or sell an asset at a fixed price at a fixed future date

(b) **Futures contracts**: similar to forward contracts except that contracts are standardised and traded on an exchange

(c) **Options**: rights (but not obligations) for the option holder to exercise at a pre-determined price; the option writer loses out if the option is exercised

(d) **Swaps**: agreements to swap one set of cash flows for another (normally interest rate or currency swaps)

The nature of derivatives often gives rise to **particular problems**. The **value** of a derivative (and the amount at which it is eventually settled) depends on **movements** in an underlying item (such as an exchange rate). This means that settlement of a derivative can lead to a very different result from the one originally envisaged. A company which has derivatives is exposed to **uncertainty and risk** (potential for gain or loss) and this can have a very material effect on its financial performance, financial position and cash flows.

Yet because a derivative contract normally has **little or no initial cost**, under traditional accounting it **may not be recognised** in the financial statements at all. Alternatively it may be recognised at an amount which bears no relation to its current value. This is clearly **misleading** and leaves users of the financial statements unaware of the **level of risk** that the company faces. IAS 32, IAS 39 and subsequently IFRS 9 were developed in order to correct this situation.

2 IAS 32: Financial instruments: Presentation

The objective of IAS 32 is:

> 'to establish principles for presenting financial instruments as liabilities or equity and for offsetting financial assets and financial liabilities. It applies to the classification of financial instruments, from the perspective of the issuer, into financial assets, financial liabilities and equity instruments; the classification of related interest, dividends, losses and gains; and the circumstances in which financial assets and financial liabilities should be offset'. (IAS 32: para. 1)

IAS 32 should be applied in the presentation of all types of financial instruments, whether recognised or unrecognised.

Certain items are **excluded**.

- Interests in subsidiaries (IFRS 10)

- Interests in associates (IAS 28)

- Interests in joint ventures (IFRS 11)

- Pensions and other post-retirement benefits (IAS 19)

- Insurance contracts (IFRS 4)

- Financial instruments, contracts and obligations under share-based payment transactions (IFRS 2)

Liabilities and equity

The principle of IAS 32 is that financial instruments should be presented according to their **substance, not merely their legal form**. In particular, entities which issue financial instruments should classify them (or their component parts) as **either financial liabilities, or equity**.

The classification of a financial instrument as a liability or as equity depends on the following.

- The substance of the contractual arrangement on initial recognition
- The definitions of a financial liability and an equity instrument

How should a **financial liability be distinguished from an equity instrument**? The critical feature of a **liability** is an **obligation** to transfer economic benefit. Therefore a financial instrument is a financial liability if there is a **contractual obligation** on the issuer either to deliver cash or another financial asset to the holder or to exchange another financial instrument with the holder under potentially unfavourable conditions to the issuer.

The financial liability exists **regardless of the way in which the contractual obligation will be settled**. The issuer's ability to satisfy an obligation may be restricted, eg by lack of access to foreign currency, but this is irrelevant as it does not remove the issuer's obligation or the holder's right under the instrument.

Where the above critical feature is **not** met, then the financial instrument is an **equity instrument**. IAS 32 explains that although the holder of an equity instrument may be entitled to a pro rata share of any distributions out of equity, the issuer does *not* have a contractual obligation to make such a distribution.

Although substance and legal form are often **consistent with each other**, this is not always the case. In particular, a financial instrument may have the legal form of equity, but in substance it is in fact a liability. Other instruments may combine features of both equity instruments and financial liabilities.

For example, many entities issue **preference shares** which must be **redeemed** by the issuer for a fixed (or determinable) amount at a fixed (or determinable) future date. Alternatively, the holder may have the right to require the issuer to redeem the shares at or after a certain date for a fixed amount. In such cases, the issuer has an **obligation**. Therefore the instrument is a **financial liability** and should be classified as such.

The classification of the financial instrument is made when it is **first recognised** and this classification will continue until the financial instrument is removed from the entity's statement of financial position.

Contingent settlement provisions

An entity may issue a financial instrument where the way in which it is settled depends on:

(a)   The occurrence or non-occurrence of uncertain future events; or
(b)   The outcome of uncertain circumstances.

that are beyond the control of both the holder and the issuer of the instrument. For example, an entity might have to deliver cash instead of issuing equity shares. In this situation it is not immediately clear whether the entity has an equity instrument or a financial liability.

Such financial instruments should be classified as **financial liabilities** because the issuer does not have an unconditional right to avoid settlement by delivery of cash or another financial asset, unless the possibility of settlement is remote.

Settlement options

When a derivative financial instrument gives one party a **choice** over how it is settled (eg the issuer can choose whether to settle in cash or by issuing shares) the instrument is a **financial asset** or a **financial liability** unless **all the alternative choices** would result in it being an equity instrument.

Compound financial instruments

Some financial instruments contain both a liability and an equity element. In such cases, IAS 32 requires the component parts of the instrument to be **classified separately**, according to the substance of the contractual arrangement and the definitions of a financial liability and an equity instrument.

One of the most common types of compound instrument is **convertible debt**. This creates a primary financial liability of the issuer and grants an option to the holder of the instrument to convert it into an equity instrument (usually ordinary shares) of the issuer. This is the economic equivalent of the issue of conventional debt plus a warrant to acquire shares in the future.

Although in theory there are several possible ways of calculating the split, the following method is recommended by IAS 32:

(a)   Calculate the value for the liability component

(b)   Deduct this from the instrument' carrying amount as a whole to leave a residual value for the equity component

The reasoning behind this approach is that an entity's equity is its residual interest in its assets amount after deducting all its liabilities.

The **sum of the carrying amounts** assigned to liability and equity will always be equal to the carrying amount that would be ascribed to the instrument **as a whole**.

Example: valuation of compound instruments

Z Co issues 2,000 convertible bonds at the start of 20X2. The bonds have a three year term, and are issued at par with a face value of $1,000 per bond, giving total proceeds of $2,000,000. Interest is payable annually in arrears at a nominal annual interest rate of 6%. Each bond is convertible at any time up to maturity into 250 common shares.

When the bonds are issued, the prevailing market interest rate for similar debt without conversion options is 9%. At the issue date, the market price of one common share is $3. The dividends expected over the three year term of the bonds amount to 14c per share at the end of each year. The risk-free annual interest rate for a three year term is 5%.

What is the value of the equity component in the bond?

The liability component is valued first, and the difference between the proceeds of the bond issue and the fair value of the liability is assigned to the equity component. The present value of the liability component is calculated using a discount rate of 9%, the market interest rate for similar bonds having no conversion rights, as shown.

	$
Present value of the principal: $2,000,000 payable at the end of three years ($2m × 0.772)*	1,544,000
Present value of the interest: $120,000 payable annually in arrears for three years ($120,000 × 2.531)*	303,720
Total liability component	1,847,720
Equity component (balancing figure)	152,280
Proceeds of the bond issue	2,000,000

* These figures can be obtained from discount and annuity tables.

The split between the liability and equity components remains the same throughout the term of the instrument, even if there are changes in the **likelihood of the option being exercised**. This is because it is not always possible to predict how a holder will behave. The issuer continues to have an obligation to make future payments until conversion, maturity of the instrument or some other relevant transaction takes place.

Treasury shares

If an entity reacquires its own equity instruments, those instruments ('treasury shares') shall be deducted from equity. No gain or loss shall be recognised in profit or loss on the purchase, sale, issue or cancellation of an entity's own equity instruments. Consideration paid or received shall be recognised directly in equity.

Interest, dividends, losses and gains

As well as looking at statement of financial position presentation, IAS 32 considers how financial instruments affect the profit or loss (and movements in equity). The treatment varies according to whether interest, dividends, losses or gains relate to a financial liability or an equity instrument.

(a)   Interest, dividends, losses and gains relating to a financial instrument (or component part) classified as a **financial liability** should be recognised as **income** or **expense** in profit or loss.

(b)   Distributions to holders of a financial instrument classified as an **equity instrument** should be **debited directly to equity** by the issuer.

(c)   **Transaction costs** of an equity transaction (when an entity issues or acquires its own equity) shall be accounted for as a **deduction from equity** unless they are directly attributable to the acquisition of a business, in which case they are accounted for under IFRS 3.

Offsetting a financial asset and a financial liability

A financial asset and financial liability should **only** be **offset**, with the net amount reported in the statement of financial position, when an entity:

(a)   Has a legally enforceable right of set off; and

(b)   Intends to settle on a net basis, or to realise the asset and settle the liability simultaneously, ie at the same moment.

This will reflect the expected **future cash flows** of the entity in these specific circumstances. In all other cases, financial assets and financial liabilities are presented separately.

Puttable financial instruments and obligations arising on liquidation

IAS 32 requires that if the holder of a financial instrument can require the issuer to redeem it for cash or another financial asset ('puttable' instrument) it should be classified as a liability. Some ordinary shares and partnership interests allow the holder to 'put' the instrument (that is to require the issuer to redeem it in cash). Such shares might more usually be considered as equity, but application of IAS 32 results in their being classified as liabilities.

IAS 32 allows entities to classify such instruments as equity, so long as they meet certain conditions, ie because they represent a residual interest in the net assets of the entity. IAS 32 further requires that instruments imposing an obligation on an entity to deliver to another party a pro rata share of the net assets only on liquidation should be classified as equity.

3 Recognition of financial instruments

IFRS 9 applies to **all entities** and to **all types of financial instruments except** those specifically excluded, as listed below.

(a)   Investments in **subsidiaries, associates, and joint ventures** that are accounted for under IFRS 10, IAS 27 or IAS 28

(b)   **Leases** covered in IAS 17 (now IFRS 16)

(c)   **Employee benefit plans** covered in IAS 19

(d)   **Insurance contracts**

(e)   Equity instruments **issued by the entity,** eg ordinary shares issued, or options and warrants

(f)   **Contracts for contingent consideration** in a business combination, covered in IFRS 3

(g)   **Loan commitments** that cannot be settled net in cash or another financial instrument

(h)   Financial instruments, contracts and obligations under **share based payment transactions**, covered in IFRS 2

(i)   Rights to reimbursement under IAS 37

(j)   Rights and obligations within the scope of IFRS 15 *Revenue from contracts with customers*

Initial recognition

Financial instruments should be recognised in the statement of financial position when the entity becomes a party to the **contractual provisions of the instrument.**

Notice that this is **different** from the recognition criteria in the *Conceptual Framework* and in most other standards. Items are normally recognised when there is a probable inflow or outflow of resources and the item has a cost or value that can be measured reliably.

Example: initial recognition

An entity has entered into two separate contracts.

(a)   A firm commitment (an order) to buy a specific quantity of iron

(b)   A forward contract to buy a specific quantity of iron at a specified price on a specified date, provided delivery of the iron is not taken

Contract (a) is a normal trading contract. The entity does not recognise a liability for the iron until the goods have actually been delivered. (Note that this contract is not a financial instrument because it involves a physical asset, rather than a financial asset.)

Contract (b) is a financial instrument. Under IFRS 9, the entity recognises a financial liability (an obligation to deliver cash) on the commitment date, rather than waiting for the closing date on which the exchange takes place.

Note that planned future transactions, no matter how likely, are not assets and liabilities of an entity – the entity has not yet become a party to the contract.

Derecognition

Derecognition is the removal of a previously recognised financial instrument from an entity's statement of financial position.

An entity should derecognise a **financial asset** when:

(a)   The contractual rights to the cash flows from the financial asset expire; or

(b)   The entity transfers the financial asset or substantially all the risks and rewards of ownership of the financial asset to another party.

It is possible for only **part** of a financial asset or liability to be derecognised. This is allowed if the part comprises:

(a)   Only specifically identified cash flows; or
(b)   Only a fully proportionate (pro rata) share of the total cash flows.

For example, if an entity holds a bond it has the right to two separate sets of cash inflows: those relating to the principal and those relating to the interest. It could sell the right to receive the interest to another party while retaining the right to receive the principal.

On derecognition, the amount to be included in net profit or loss for the period is calculated as follows:

	$
Carrying amount (measured at the date of derecognition) allocated to the part derecognised	X
Less: consideration received for the part derecognised (including any new asset obtained less any new liability assumed)	(X)
Difference to profit or loss	X

Derecognition of financial liabilities

A financial liability is derecognised when it is extinguished – ie when the obligation specified in the contract is discharged or cancelled or expires.

(a)   Where an existing borrower and lender of debt instruments exchange one financial instrument for another with substantially different terms, this is accounted for as an extinguishment of the original financial liability and the recognition of a new financial liability.

(b)   Similarly, a substantial modification of the terms of an existing financial liability or a part of it should be accounted for as an extinguishment of the original financial liability and the recognition of a new financial liability.

(c)   For this purpose, a modification is 'substantial' where the discounted present value of cash flows under the new terms, discounted using the original effective interest rate, is at least 10% different from the discounted present value of the cash flows of the original financial liability.

(d)   The difference between the carrying amount of a financial liability (or part of a financial liability) extinguished or transferred to another party and the consideration paid, including any non-cash assets transferred or liabilities assumed, shall be recognised in profit or loss.

Classification of financial assets

On **recognition,** IFRS 9 requires that financial assets are **classified as measured** at any of the following:

- **Amortised cost**
- **Fair value through other comprehensive income**
- **Fair value through profit or loss**

The IFRS 9 classification is made on the basis of both:

(a) The **entity's business model** for managing the financial assets

(b) The **contractual cash flow** characteristics of the financial asset

A financial asset is classified as measured at **amortised cost** where:

(a) The objective of the business model within which the asset is held is to hold assets in order to collect contractual cash flows and

(b) The contractual terms of the financial asset give rise on specified dates to cash flows that are solely payments of principal and interest on the principal outstanding.

A financial asset must be classified and measured at **fair value through other comprehensive income** (unless designated at inception as at fair value through profit or loss) if it meets both of the following criteria:

(a) The financial asset is held within a business model whose objective is achieved by **both** collecting contractual cash flows and selling financial assets.

(b) The contractual terms of the financial asset give rise on specified dates to cash flows that are solely payments of principal and interest.

For these instruments, fair value changes will go through other comprehensive income, interest charges will be measured at amortised cost and go through **profit or loss**.

All other debt instruments must be measured at **fair value through profit or loss**.

The classification of fair value through profit or loss can be used to avoid an **accounting mismatch**.

Even if an instrument meets the criteria for measurement at amortised cost or fair value through other comprehensive income, IFRS 9 allows such financial assets to be designated, at initial recognition, as being measured at fair value through profit or loss if a **recognition or measurement inconsistency (an 'accounting mismatch')** **would otherwise arise** from measuring assets or liabilities or recognising the gains and losses on them on **different bases**.

Equity instruments may not be classified as measured at amortised cost and must be measured at fair value. This is because contractual cash flows on specified dates are not a characteristic of equity instruments. However, if an equity investment is **not held for trading**, an entity can make an irrevocable election at initial recognition to measure it at **fair value through other comprehensive income** with only dividend income recognised in profit or loss.

Business model test in more detail

IFRS 9 introduces a business model test that requires an entity to assess **whether its business objective for a debt instrument is to collect the contractual cash flows of the instrument as opposed to realising its fair value change from sale prior to its contractual maturity.** Note the following key points:

(a)   The assessment of a 'business model' is not made at an individual financial instrument level.

(b)   The assessment is based on how key management personnel actually manage the business (eg how performance is reported, risk is managed, managers are compensated), rather than management's intentions for specific financial assets.

(c)   An entity may have more than one business model for managing its financial assets and the classification need not be determined at the reporting entity level. For example, it may have one portfolio of investments that it manages with the objective of collecting contractual cash flows and another portfolio of investments held with the objective of trading to realise changes in fair value. It would be appropriate for entities like these to carry out the assessment for classification purposes at portfolio level, rather than at entity level.

(d)   Although the objective of an entity's business model may be to hold financial assets in order to collect contractual cash flows, the entity need not hold all of those assets until maturity. Thus an entity's business model can be to hold financial assets to collect contractual cash flows even when sales of financial assets occur.

Business model test: Examples

The following examples, from the Application Guidance to IFRS 9, are of situations where the objective of an entity's business model may be to hold financial assets to collect the contractual cash flows.

Example 1
An entity holds investments to collect their contractual cash flows but would sell an investment in particular circumstances, perhaps to fund capital expenditure, or because the credit rating of the instrument falls below that required by the entity's investment policy.

Analysis

Although an entity may consider, among other information, the financial assets' fair values from a liquidity perspective (ie the cash amount that would be realised if the entity needs to sell assets), the entity's objective is to hold the financial assets and collect the contractual cash flows. Some sales would not contradict that objective. If sales became frequent, the entity might be required to reconsider whether the sales were consistent with an objective of collecting contractual cash flows.

Example 2

An entity's business model is to purchase portfolios of financial assets, such as loans. Those portfolios may or may not include financial assets that are credit impaired. If payment on the loans is not made on a timely basis, the entity attempts to extract the contractual cash flows through various means – for example, by contacting the debtor through mail, telephone, etc.

In some cases, the entity enters into interest rate swaps to change the interest rate on particular financial assets in a portfolio from a floating interest rate to a fixed interest rate.

Analysis

The objective of the entity's business model is to hold the financial assets and collect the contractual cash flows. The entity does not purchase the portfolio to make a profit by selling them.

The same analysis would apply even if the entity does not expect to receive all of the contractual cash flows (eg some of the financial assets are credit impaired at initial recognition).

Moreover, the fact that the entity has entered into derivatives to modify the cash flows of the portfolio does not in itself change the entity's business model.

Example 3

An entity has a business model with the objective of originating loans to customers and subsequently to sell those loans to a securitisation vehicle. The securitisation vehicle issues instruments to investors.

The originating entity controls the securitisation vehicle and thus consolidates it. The securitisation vehicle collects the contractual cash flows from the loans and passes them on to its investors in the vehicle.

It is assumed for the purposes of this example that the loans continue to be recognised in the consolidated statement of financial position because they are not derecognised by the securitisation vehicle.

Analysis

The consolidated group originated the loans with the objective of holding them to collect the contractual cash flows.

However, the originating entity has an objective of realising cash flows on the loan portfolio by selling the loans to the securitisation vehicle, so for the purposes of its separate financial statements it would not be considered to be managing this portfolio in order to collect the contractual cash flows.

Contractual cash flow test in more detail

The requirement in IFRS 9 to assess the contractual cash flow characteristics of a financial asset is based on the concept that **only instruments with contractual cash flows of principal and interest on the principal may qualify for amortised cost measurement.**

By interest, IFRS 9 means consideration for the time value of money and the credit risk associated with the principal outstanding during a particular period of time.

Amortised cost measurement is permitted when the cash flows on a loan are entirely fixed (eg a fixed interest rate loan or zero coupon bond), or where interest is floating (eg a GBP loan where interest is contractually linked to GBP LIBOR), or a combination of fixed and floating (eg where interest is LIBOR plus a fixed spread).

Examples of instruments that pass the contractual cash flows test

The following instruments satisfy the IFRS 9 criteria:

(a) A fixed term bond where the payments of principal and interest are linked to an unleveraged inflation index of the currency in which the instrument is issued

(b) A variable rate instrument with a stated maturity date that permits the borrower to choose to pay three-month LIBOR for a three-month term or one-month LIBOR for a one-month term

(c) A fixed term variable market interest rate bond where the variable interest rate is capped

Examples of instruments that do not pass the contractual cash flows test

The following instruments do not satisfy the IFRS 9 criteria:

(a) A bond that is convertible into equity instruments of the issuer (see Section 2 example above)

(b) A loan that pays an inverse floating interest rate (eg 8% minus LIBOR)

Classification of financial liabilities

On **recognition,** IFRS 9 requires that financial liabilities are **classified as measured** at either:

(a) **Fair value through profit or loss**; or

(b) **Amortised cost.**

Where the liability is measured at amortised cost, transaction costs are deducted from the initial measurement.

A financial liability is classified at fair value through profit or loss if:

(a) It is **held for trading**; or

(b) Upon initial recognition it is **irrevocably designated as at fair value through profit or loss.**

Derivatives are always measured at fair value through profit or loss.

Re-classification of financial assets

Although on initial recognition assets must be classified in accordance with IFRS 9, in some cases they may be subsequently reclassified.

IFRS 9 requires that **when an entity changes its business model for managing financial assets, it should reclassify all affected financial assets.** This reclassification applies only to debt instruments, as equity instruments must be classified as measured at fair value. Reclassification is expected to be a rare event.

The Application Guidance to IFRS 9 includes examples of circumstances when a reclassification is required or is not permitted.

Examples: Reclassification permitted

Reclassification is permitted in the following circumstances, because a **change in the business model** has taken place:

(a) An entity has a portfolio of commercial loans that it holds to sell in the short term. The entity acquires a company that manages commercial loans and has a business model that holds the loans in order to collect the contractual cash flows. The portfolio of commercial loans is no longer for sale, and the portfolio is now managed together with the acquired commercial loans and all are held to collect the contractual cash flows.

(b) A financial services firm decides to shut down its retail mortgage business. That business no longer accepts new business and the financial services firm is actively marketing its mortgage loan portfolio for sale.

Examples: Reclassification not permitted

Reclassification is **not permitted** in the following circumstances, because a **change in the business model has not taken place.**

(a) A change in intention related to particular financial assets (even in circumstances of significant changes in market conditions)

(b) A temporary disappearance of a particular market for financial assets

(c) A transfer of financial assets between parts of the entity with different business models

Reclassification of financial liabilities or equity instruments is prohibited.

When financial instruments are reclassified, disclosures are required under IFRS 7 (See Section 7).

4 Measurement of financial instruments

Initial measurement: financial assets

Financial assets are initially measured at the transaction price, that is the **fair value** of the consideration given.

An **exception** is where part of the consideration given is for something other than the financial asset. In this case the financial asset is initially measured at fair value as evidenced by a quoted price in an active market for an identical asset (ie an IFRS 13 level 1 input) or based on a valuation technique that uses only data from observable markets The difference between the fair value at initial recognition and the transaction price is recognised as a gain or loss.

In the case of financial assets classified as measured at **amortised cost**, **transaction costs** directly attributable to the acquisition of the financial asset are **added** to this amount.

Initial measurement: financial liabilities

IFRS 9 requires that financial liabilities are initially measured at transaction price, ie the fair value of consideration received except where part of the consideration received is for something other than the financial liability. In this case the financial liability is initially measured at fair value determined as for financial assets (see above). Transaction costs are **deducted** from this amount for financial liabilities classified as measured at amortised cost.

Subsequent measurement of financial assets

Under IFRS 9, financial assets are measured subsequent to recognition at:

- **Fair value** with changes in value normally recognised in **profit or loss**; or

- **Fair value** with changes in value recognised in **other comprehensive income** for debt instruments meeting the criteria; or

- **Fair value** with changes in value recognised in other comprehensive income for equity instruments where the election has been made; or

- **Amortised cost** with interest recognised in profit or loss.

Financial assets measured at amortised cost

Amortised cost. The amount at which the financial asset or financial liability is measured at initial recognition minus the principal repayments, plus or minus the cumulative amortisation using the **effective interest method** of any difference between that initial amount and the maturity amount, and, for financial assets, adjusted for any **loss allowance**.

Effective interest method. The method that is used in the calculation of the **amortised cost of a financial asset or a financial liability** and in the allocation and recognition of the interest revenue or interest expense in profit or loss over the relevant period.

Effective interest rate. The rate that exactly discounts estimated future cash payments or receipts through the expected life of the financial asset or financial liability to the **gross carrying amount of a financial asset** or to the **amortised cost of a financial liability.** *(IFRS 9: Appendix)*

Example: financial asset at amortised cost

On 1 January 20X1 Abacus Co purchases a debt instrument for its fair value of $1,000. The debt instrument is due to mature on 31 December 20X5. The instrument has a principal amount of $1,250 and the instrument carries fixed interest at 4.72% that is paid annually. (The effective interest rate is 10%.)

How should Abacus Co account for the debt instrument over its five year term?

Solution

Abacus Co will receive interest of $59 ($1,250 × 4.72%) each year and $1,250 when the instrument matures.

Abacus must allocate the discount of $250 and the interest receivable over the five year term at a constant rate on the carrying amount of the debt. To do this, it must apply the effective interest rate of 10%.

The following table shows the allocation over the years:

Year	Amortised cost at beginning of year	Profit or loss: Interest income for year @10%	Interest received during year (cash inflow)	Amortised cost at end of year
	$	$	$	$
20X1	1,000	100	(59)	1,041
20X2	1,041	104	(59)	1,086
20X3	1,086	109	(59)	1,136
20X4	1,136	113	(59)	1,190
20X5	1,190	119	(1,250+59)	–

Each year the carrying amount of the financial asset is increased by the interest income for the year and reduced by the interest actually received during the year.

Financial assets measured at fair value

Where a financial asset is classified as measured at fair value, fair value is established at each period end in accordance with IFRS 13 *Fair value measurement.* That standard requires that a fair value hierarchy is applied with three levels of input:

Level 1 inputs. Unadjusted quoted prices in active markets for identical assets or liabilities that the entity can access at the measurement date.

Level 2 inputs. Inputs other than quoted prices included within Level 1 that are observable for the asset or liability, either directly or indirectly. These may include quoted prices for similar assets or liabilities in active markets or quoted prices for identical or similar assets and liabilities in markets that are not active.

Level 3 inputs. Unobservable inputs for the asset or liability.

Any changes in fair value are normally recognised in profit or loss.

There are three **exceptions** to this rule:

(a)   The asset is part of a **hedging relationship**

(b)   The asset is an investment in an **equity instrument not held for trading.** In this case the entity can make an **irrevocable election** to recognise changes in the fair value in **other comprehensive income.**

(c)   It is a financial asset measured at **fair value through other comprehensive income** because it is held within a business model whose objective is achieved by **both collecting contractual cash flows and selling financial assets.**

Note that direct costs of acquisition are capitalised only in the case of a financial asset or liability **not** held at fair value through profit or loss. Where an asset or liability is held at fair value through profit or loss, acquisition costs are expensed.

For an asset held at fair value through other comprehensive income or assets and liabilities held at amortised cost, acquisition costs are added to the asset amount and deducted from the liability amount.

Part B 11: Financial instruments

Example: Financial asset at fair value

On 8 February 20X8 Orange Co acquires a quoted investment in the shares of Lemon Co with the intention of holding it in the long term. The investment cost $850,000. At Orange Co's year end of 31 March 20X8, the market price of an identical investment is $900,000. How is the asset initially and subsequently measured?

Orange Co has elected to recognise changes in the fair value of the equity investment in other comprehensive income.

Solution

- The asset is initially recognised at the fair value of the consideration, being $850,000
- At the period end its fair value is remeasured to $900,000
- This results in the recognition of a $50,000 gain in other comprehensive income

Subsequent measurement of financial liabilities

After initial recognition, all financial liabilities should be measured at **amortised cost**, with the exception of financial liabilities at fair value through profit or loss (including most derivatives). These should be measured at **fair value**, but where the fair value **is not capable of reliable measurement**, they should be measured at **cost**.

Financial liabilities measured at amortised cost

The definitions of amortised cost, effective interest method and effective interest rate that are used for the measurement of financial assets are also used for financial liabilities.

Example: financial liability at amortised cost

B Co issues a bond for $503,778 on 1 January 20X2. No interest is payable on the bond, but it will be redeemed on 31 December 20X4 for $600,000. The effective interest rate of the bond is 6%.

Calculate the charge to profit or loss of B Co for the year ended 31 December 20X2 and the balance outstanding at 31 December 20X2.

Solution

The bond is a 'deep discount' bond and is a financial liability measured at amortised cost. Although there is no interest as such, the difference between the initial cost of the bond and the price at which it will be redeemed is a finance cost. This must be allocated over the term of the bond at a constant rate on the carrying amount.

The charge to profit or loss for the year is $30,226 ($503,778 × 6%).

The balance outstanding at 31 December 20X2 is $534,004 ($503,778 + $30,226).

Financial liabilities measured at fair value through profit or loss

Financial liabilities which are held for trading are remeasured to fair value each year in accordance with IFRS 13 *Fair value measurement* with any gain or loss recognised in profit or loss.

Exceptions

The exceptions to the above treatment of financial liabilities are:

(a)   It is part of a hedging arrangement (see Section 6)

(b)   It is a financial liability designated as at fair value through profit or loss and the entity is required to present the effects of changes in the liability's credit risk in other comprehensive income.

Credit risk

IFRS 9 requires that financial liabilities which are **designated as measured at fair value through profit or loss are treated differently**. In this case the gain or loss in a period must be classified into:

- Gain or loss **resulting from that liability's credit risk**; and
- **Other** gain or loss.

This change to IFRS 9 was made in 2010 in response to an anomaly regarding changes in an entity's own credit risk on a financial liability.

Changes in a financial liability's credit risk affect the fair value of that financial liability. This means that when an entity's creditworthiness deteriorates, the fair value of its issued debt will decrease (and vice versa). For financial liabilities measured using the fair value option, this causes **a gain (or loss) to be recognised in profit or loss.** For example:

STATEMENT OF PROFIT OR LOSS AND OTHER COMPREHENSIVE INCOME (EXTRACT)

	$'000
Profit or loss for the year:	
Liabilities at fair value (except derivatives and liabilities held for trading):	
Change in fair value	100
Profit (loss) for the year	100

Many users of financial statements found this result to be **counter-intuitive** and confusing. Accordingly, IFRS 9 requires the gain or loss as a result of own credit risk to be recognised in other comprehensive income, unless it creates or enlarges an **accounting mismatch** (see below), in which case it is recognised in profit or loss. The other gain or loss (not the result of credit risk) is recognised in profit or loss.

On derecognition any gains or losses recognised in other comprehensive income are not transferred to **profit or loss**, although the cumulative gain or loss may be transferred within equity.

Example of IFRS 9 presentation

STATEMENT OF PROFIT OR LOSS AND OTHER COMPREHENSIVE INCOME (EXTRACT)

	$'000
Profit or loss for the year:	
Liabilities at fair value (except derivatives and liabilities held for trading):	
Change in fair value not attributable to change in credit risk	90
Profit (loss) for the year	90
Other comprehensive income (not reclassified to profit or loss):	
Fair value gain on financial liability attributable to change in credit risk	10
Total comprehensive income	100

Accounting mismatch

The guidance allows the recognition of the full change in fair value in profit or loss **only** if the recognition of changes in the financial liability's **credit risk** in other comprehensive income would **create** or **enlarge** an **accounting mismatch** in profit or loss. That determination is made at initial recognition and is not reassessed.

Impairment of financial assets

IAS 39 used an 'incurred loss' model in accounting for impairment of financial assets. This model assumed that all loans would be repaid unless there was evidence to the contrary. Only at the point when such evidence arose was the loan written down. As a result of the financial crisis, it became clear that this model provided scope for an entity to postpone losses.

The impairment model in IFRS 9 is based on providing for **expected** losses. The financial statements should reflect the general pattern of deterioration or improvement in the credit quality of financial instruments.

> **Credit loss.** The expected shortfall in contractual cash flows.
>
> **Expected credit losses.** The weighted average of credit losses with the respective risks of a default occurring as the weights.
>
> **Lifetime expected credit losses.** The expected credit losses that result from all possible default events over the expected life of a financial instrument.
>
> **Past due.** A financial asset is past due when a counterparty has failed to make a payment when that payment was contractually due.
>
> **Purchased or originated credit-impaired financial asset.** Purchased or originated financial asset(s) that are credit impaired on initial recognition.
>
> *(IFRS 9: Appendix)*

On initial recognition

The entity creates a credit loss allowance/provision equal to **twelve months' expected credit losses**. This is calculated by multiplying the probability of a default occurring in the next twelve months by the total lifetime expected credit losses that would result from that default. (This is not the same as the expected cash shortfalls over the next twelve months.)

The intention is that the amount recognised on initial recognition acts as a proxy for the initial expectation of credit losses which have not been recognised because they were factored into the initial pricing of the instrument.

Subsequent years

If the credit risk increases significantly subsequent to initial recognition, the allowance recorded to represent twelve months' expected credit losses will be replaced by **lifetime expected credit losses**. If the credit quality subsequently improves and the lifetime expected credit losses criterion is no longer met, the twelve month expected credit loss basis is reinstated. The movement in the allowance is recognised as an impairment gain or loss in profit or loss.

Certain financial institutions have a low credit risk and would not, therefore, meet the lifetime expected credit losses criterion. Entities do not recognise lifetime expected credit losses for financial instruments that are equivalent to 'investment grade', which means that the asset has a low risk of default. The model requires that there is a rebuttable presumption that lifetime expected losses should be provided for if contractual cash flows are 30 days overdue.

Amount of impairment

The amount of impairment to be recognised depends on whether or not the financial instruments in question have **significantly deteriorated** since their initial recognition.

Stage 1 – Financial instruments whose credit quality has not significantly deteriorated since their initial recognition.

Stage 2 – Financial instruments whose credit quality has significantly deteriorated since their initial recognition.

Stage 3 – Financial instruments for which there is objective evidence of an impairment as at the reporting date.

For stage 1 financial instruments, the impairment represents the present value of expected credit losses that will result if a default occurs in the 12 months after the reporting date (12 months expected credit losses).

For financial instruments classified as stage 2 or 3, an impairment is recognised at the present value of expected credit shortfalls over their remaining life (lifetime expected credit loss). Entities are required to reduce the gross carrying amount of a financial asset in the period in which they no longer have a reasonable expectation of recovery.

Interest

For stage 1 and 2 instruments interest revenue will be calculated on their gross carrying amounts, whereas interest revenue for stage 3 financial instruments would be recognised on a net basis (ie after deducting expected credit losses from the carrying amount).

Measuring expected credit losses

Credit losses are the present value of all cash shortfalls. Expected credit losses are an estimate of credit losses over the life of the financial instrument. An entity should consider the following when measuring expected credit losses:

(a) The **probability-weighted outcome**. Expected losses should reflect the possibility that a credit loss will occur, and the possibility that it will not.

(b) The **time value of money** – so expected losses should be discounted.

(c) **Reasonable and supportable information** about past events, current conditions and expected future conditions.

Possible effects

Possible effects of the new model include the following:

(a) It is likely that this model will result in **earlier recognition** of credit losses than under the incurred loss model, because it requires the recognition of not only credit losses that have already occurred but also losses that are expected in the future. However, in the case of shorter term and higher-quality financial instruments the effects may not be significant.

(b) The IFRS 9 model will require significantly more **judgement** to be applied when considering information related to the past, present and future, particularly as it relies on more forward-looking information.

(c) Costs of implementing the new model are likely to be material.

(d) There are differences between the IASB and the FASB approach, which may lead to significant differences in reported figures.

5 Embedded derivatives

Certain contracts that are not themselves derivatives (and may not be financial instruments) include derivative contracts that are 'embedded' within them. These non-derivatives are called **host contracts**.

An **embedded derivative** is a component of a hybrid contract that also includes a non-derivative host – with the effect that some of the cash flows of the combined instrument vary in a way similar to a stand-alone derivative.   *(IFRS 9: para. 4.3.1)*

An embedded derivative causes some or all of the cash flows that otherwise would be required by the host contract to be modified according to a variable.

Examples of host contracts

Possible examples include:

(a)   A lease
(b)   A debt or equity instrument
(c)   An insurance contract
(d)   A sale or purchase contract
(e)   A construction contract

Examples of embedded derivatives

Possible examples include:

(a)   A term in a lease of retail premises that provides for contingent rentals based on sales:

(b)   A bond which is redeemable in five years' time with part of the redemption price being based on the increase in the FTSE 100 index.

(c)   Construction contract priced in a foreign currency. The construction contract is a non-derivative contract, but the change in foreign exchange rate is the embedded derivative.

Accounting treatment of embedded derivatives

Financial asset host contract

Where the host contract is a financial asset within the scope of IFRS 9, the classification and **measurement rules of the standard are applied to the entire hybrid contract**.

This is a simplification of the IAS 39 rules, which required that an embedded derivative be **separated from its host contract** and accounted for as a derivative under certain conditions. These rules applied to financial assets as well as other host contracts.

Other host contracts

Where the host contract is not a financial asset within the scope of IFRS 9, the standard requires that an embedded derivative be **separated from its host contract** and accounted for as a derivative when the following conditions are met.

(a)   The economic characteristics and risks of the embedded derivative are not closely related to the economic characteristics and risks of the host.

(b)   A separate instrument with the same terms as the embedded derivative would meet the definition of a derivative.

(c)   The hybrid (combined) instrument is not measured at fair value with changes in fair value recognised in the profit or loss (a derivative embedded in a financial liability need not be separated out if the entity holds the combined instrument at fair value through profit or loss).

6 Hedging

Under IFRS 9 **hedge accounting is required** where there is a **designated hedging relationship** between a hedging instrument and a hedged item. It is prohibited otherwise.

Hedging, for accounting purposes, means designating one or more hedging instruments so that their change in fair value is an offset, in whole or in part, to the change in fair value or cash flows of a hedged item.

A **hedged item** is an asset, liability, firm commitment, or highly probable forecast transaction that:

(a)   Exposes the entity to risk of changes in fair value or future cash flows; and
(b)   Is designated as being hedged.

A **hedging instrument** is a designated derivative or (in limited circumstances) another financial asset or liability whose fair value or cash flows are expected to offset changes in the fair value or cash flows of a designated hedged item. (A non-derivative financial asset or liability may be designated as a hedging instrument for hedge accounting purposes only if it hedges the risk of changes in foreign currency exchange rates.)

Hedge effectiveness is the degree to which changes in the fair value or cash flows of the hedged item that are attributable to a hedged risk are offset by changes in the fair value or cash flows of the hedging instrument.

(IFRS 9: para. 6.2–6.3)

Option to use IAS 39 rules

Note that the IASB will allow an accounting policy choice to apply either the IFRS 9 hedging model or the IAS 39 model, with an additional option to use IAS 39 for macro hedging (currently a separate project) if using IFRS 9 for general hedge accounting.

Hedge accounting

In simple terms, entities hedge to reduce their exposure to risk and uncertainty, such as changes in prices, interest rates or foreign exchange rates. The objective of hedge accounting is to represent the effects of such risk management activities by recognising hedging relationships and allowing (for example) losses on a hedged item to be offset against gains on a hedging instrument.

Generally only assets, liabilities etc that involve external parties can be designated as hedged items. The foreign currency risk of an intragroup monetary item (eg payable/receivable between two subsidiaries) may qualify as a hedged item in the group financial statements if it results in an exposure to foreign exchange rate gains or losses that are not fully eliminated on consolidation. This can happen (per IAS 21) when the transaction is between entities with different functional currencies.

In addition the foreign currency risk of a highly probable group transaction may qualify as a hedged item if it is in a currency other than the functional currency of the entity entering into the transaction and the foreign currency risk will affect profit or loss.

Conditions for hedge accounting

Before a hedging relationship qualifies for hedge accounting, **all** of the following **conditions** must be met.

(a) The hedging relationship consists **only of eligible hedging instruments and eligible hedged items**.

(b) There must be **formal documentation** (including identification of the hedged item, the hedging instrument, the nature of the risk that is to be hedged and how the entity will assess the hedging instrument's effectiveness in offsetting the exposure to changes in the hedged item's fair value or cash flows attributable to the hedged risk).

(c) The hedging relationship meets all of the following hedge effectiveness criteria:

   (i) There is an **economic relationship** between the hedged item and the hedging instrument, ie the hedging instrument and the hedged item have values that generally move in the opposite direction because of the same risk, which is the hedged risk;

   (ii) The **effect of credit risk does not dominate the value** changes that result from that economic relationship, ie the gain or loss from credit risk does not frustrate the effect of changes in the underlyings on the value of the hedging instrument or the hedged item, even if those changes were significant; and

Part B 11: Financial instruments

(iii)   The **hedge ratio of the hedging relationship** (quantity of hedging instrument vs quantity of hedged item) is the same as that resulting from the quantity of the hedged item that the entity **actually hedges** and the quantity of the hedging instrument that the entity **actually uses** to hedge that quantity of hedged item.

Example: Hedging

A company owns inventories of 20,000 gallons of oil which cost $400,000 on 1 December 20X3.

In order to hedge the fluctuation in the market value of the oil the company signs a futures contract to deliver 20,000 gallons of oil on 31 March 20X4 at the futures price of $22 per gallon.

The market price of oil on 31 December 20X3 is $23 per gallon and the futures price for delivery on 31 March 20X4 is $24 per gallon.

What is the impact of these transactions on the financial statements of the company at 31 December 20X3:

(a)   Without hedge accounting?
(b)   With hedge accounting?

The futures contract was intended to protect the company from a fall in oil prices (which would have reduced the profit when the oil was eventually sold). However, oil prices have actually risen, so that the company has made a loss on the contract.

Without hedge accounting:

The futures contract is a derivative and therefore must be remeasured to fair value under IFRS 9. The loss on the futures contract is recognised in profit or loss:

DEBIT	Profit or loss (20,000 × 24 – 22)	$40,000	
CREDIT	Financial liability		$40,000

With hedge accounting:

The loss on the futures contract is recognised in profit or loss as before.
The inventories are revalued to fair value:

	$
Fair value at 31 December 20X4 (20,000 × 23)	460,000
Cost	(400,000)
Gain	60,000

The gain is also recognised in profit or loss:

DEBIT	Inventory	$60,000	
CREDIT	Profit or loss		$60,000

The net effect on profit or loss is a gain of $20,000 compared with a loss of $40,000 without hedging.

Types of hedge

IFRS 9 identifies three types of **hedging relationship**.

Fair value hedge. A hedge of the exposure to changes in the fair value of a recognised asset or liability, or an unrecognised firm commitment, or a component of any such item, that is attributable to a particular risk and could affect profit or loss.

Cash flow hedge. A hedge of the exposure to variability in cash flows that is attributable to a particular risk associated with all, or a component of, a recognised asset or liability (such as all or some future interest payments on variable rate debt) or a highly probable forecast transaction, and could affect profit or loss.

Hedge of a net investment in a foreign operation. IAS 21 defines a net investment in a foreign operation as the amount of the reporting entity's interest in the net assets of that operation. *(IFRS 9: para. 6.5.2)*

The hedge in the example above is a **fair value hedge** (it hedges exposure to changes in the fair value of a recognised asset: the oil).

Accounting treatment

Fair value hedges

The **gain or loss** resulting from **re-measuring** the hedging instrument at fair value is **recognised in profit or loss**.

The gain or loss on the hedged item attributable to the **hedged risk** should **adjust the carrying amount** of the hedged item and be **recognised in profit or loss**.

However, if the hedged item is an **investment in an equity instrument held at fair value through other comprehensive income**, the **gains and losses on both** the hedged investment and the hedging instrument will be **recognised in other comprehensive income**.

This ensures that hedges of investments of equity instruments held at fair value through other comprehensive income can be accounted for as hedges.

Example: Fair value hedge

On 1 July 20X6 J Co acquired 10,000 ounces of a material which it held in its inventory. This cost $200 per ounce, so a total of $2 million. J Co was concerned that the price of this inventory would fall, so on 1 July 20X6 they sold 10,000 ounces in the futures market for $210 per ounce for delivery on 30 June 20X7. On 1 July 20X6 the conditions for hedge accounting were all met.

At 31 December 20X6, the end of J Co's reporting period, the fair value of the inventory was $220 per ounce while the futures price for 30 June 20X7 delivery was $227 per ounce. On 30 June 20X7 J Co both sold the inventory and closed out the futures position at the then spot price of $230 per ounce.

The hedge was considered highly effective at both 31 December 20X6 and 30 June 20X7.

How would we set out the accounting entries in respect of the above transactions?

Solution

At 31 December 20X6 the increase in the fair value of the inventory was $200,000 (10,000 × ($220 – $200)) and the increase in the forward contract liability was $170,000 (10,000 × ($227 – $210)).

	Debit $	Credit $
31 December 20X6		
Profit or loss	170,000	
Financial liability		170,000
(To record the loss on the forward contract)		
Inventories	200,000	
Profit or loss		200,000
(To record the increase in the FV of the inventories)		

At 30 June 20X7 the increase in the fair value of the inventory was another $100,000 (10,000 × ($230 – $220)) and the increase in the forward contract liability was another $30,000 (10,000 × ($230 – $227)).

	Debit $	Credit $
30 June 20X7		
Profit or loss	30,000	
Financial liability		30,000
(To record the loss on the forward contract)		
Inventories	100,000	
Profit or loss		100,000
(To record the increase in the FV of the inventories)		
Profit or loss	2,300,000	
Inventories		2,300,000
(To record the inventories now sold)		
Cash	2,300,000	
Profit or loss – revenue		2,300,000
(To record the revenue from the sale of inventories, excluding any trading profit)		
Financial liability	200,000	
Cash		200,000
(To record the settlement of the net balance due on closing the financial liability)		

Note that because the fair value of the material rose, J Co made a profit of only $100,000 on the sale of inventories. Without the forward contract, the profit would have been $300,000 ($2,300,000 – $2,000,000). In the light of the rising fair value they might in practice have closed out the futures position earlier, rather than waiting until the settlement date.

Cash flow hedges

The portion of the gain or loss on the hedging instrument that is determined to be an **effective** hedge should be **recognised in other comprehensive income** and directly in equity through the statement of changes in equity.

The **ineffective portion** of the gain or loss on the hedging instrument should be **recognised in profit or loss**.

When a hedging transaction results in the recognition of an asset or liability, changes in the value of the hedging instrument recognised in equity either:

(a)   Are adjusted against the carrying value of the asset or liability; or

(b)   Affect the profit or loss at the same time as the hedged item (for example, through depreciation or sale).

Example: Cash flow hedge

W Co signs a contract on 1 November 20X1 to purchase an asset on 1 November 20X2 for €60,000,000. W Co reports in US$ and hedges this transaction by entering into a forward contract to buy €60,000,000 on 1 November 20X2 at US$1: €1.50.

Spot and forward exchange rates at the following dates are:

	Spot	*Forward (for delivery on 1.11.X2)*
1.11.X1	US$1: €1.45	US$1: €1.50
31.12.X1	US$1: €1.20	US$1: €1.24
1.11.X2	US$1: €1.00	US$1: €1.00 (actual)

What are the double entries relating to these transactions at 1 November 20X1, 31 December 20X1 and 1 November 20X2?

Solution

Entries at 1 November 20X1
The value of the forward contract at inception is zero so no entries are recorded (other than any transaction costs), but risk disclosures will be made.

The contractual commitment to buy the asset would be disclosed if material (IAS 16).

Entries at 31 December 20X1
Gain on forward contract liability:

	$
Value of contract at 31.12.X1 (€60,000,000/1.24)	48,387,097
Value of contract at 1.11.X1 (€60,000,000/1.5)	40,000,000
Gain on contract	8,387,097

Compare to movement in value of asset (unrecognised):

Increase in $ cost of asset

(€60,000,000/1.20 – €60,000,000/1.45)	$8,620,690

As this is higher, the hedge is fully effective at this point:

DEBIT	Financial asset (Forward a/c)	$8,387,097	
CREDIT	Equity		$8,387,097

Entries at 1 November 20X2
Additional gain on forward contract liability

	$
Value of contract at 1.11.X2 (€60,000,000/1.00)	60,000,000
Value of contract at 31.12.X1 (€60,000,000/1.24)	48,387,097
Gain on contract	11,612,903

Compare to movement in value of asset (unrecognised):

	$
Increase in $ cost of asset	
(€60,000,000/1.00 – €60,000,000/1.20)	$10,000,000

Therefore, the hedge is not fully effective during this period, but is still highly effective

DEBIT	Financial asset (Forward a/c)	$11,612,903	
CREDIT	Equity		$10,000,000
CREDIT	Profit or loss		$1,612,903

Purchase of asset at market price

DEBIT	Asset (€60,000,000/1.00)	$60,000,000	
CREDIT	Cash		$60,000,000

Settlement of forward contract liability

DEBIT	Cash	$20,000,000	
CREDIT	Financial asset (Forward a/c)		$20,000,000

Realisation of gain on hedging instrument

The cumulative gain of $18,387,097 recognised in equity is removed from equity (the cash flow hedge reserve) and included directly in the initial cost of the asset.

In this way the cash flow hedge achieves the objective of deferring the gain or loss on the hedging instrument to the periods in which the hedged expected future cash flows affect profit or loss.

Rebalancing hedging relationships

Rebalancing denotes adjustments to the designated quantities of the hedged item or the hedging instrument of an already existing hedging relationship for the purpose of maintaining a hedge ratio that complies with the hedge.

IFRS 9 requires rebalancing to be undertaken if the risk management objective remains the same, but the hedge effectiveness requirements are no longer met. Where the risk management objective for a hedging relationship has changed, rebalancing does not apply and the hedging relationship must be discontinued.

Discontinuing

An entity cannot voluntarily discontinue hedge accounting as it could under IAS 39. Using IFRS 9, an entity is **not allowed to discontinue hedge accounting where the hedging relationship still meets the risk management objective and continues to meet all other qualifying criteria.**

Hedge accounting should be discontinued only when the hedging relationship ceases to meet the qualifying criteria. This includes instances when the hedging instrument expires or is sold, terminated or exercised.

Discontinuing hedge accounting can either affect a hedging relationship in its entirety or only a part of it. If only part of the hedging relationship is affected, hedge accounting continues for the remainder of the hedging relationship.

Premium paid for options

Under IFRS 9, **the part of an option that reflects time value premium should be treated as a cost of hedging**, which will be presented in other comprehensive income. This is intended to decrease inappropriate volatility in profit or loss and it should be more consistent with risk management practices.

Under IAS 39 the time value premium was treated as if it was a derivative held for trading purposes. This created volatility in profit or loss. It did not reflect the way risk managers saw it: when hedging, risk managers viewed the time value premium paid as a cost of hedging rather than a speculative trading position.

Forward element of forward contracts and foreign currency basis spreads

When an entity separates the forward element and the spot element of a forward contract and designates as the hedging instrument only the change in the value of the spot element, or when an entity excludes the foreign currency basis spread from a hedge the entity may recognise the change in value of the excluded portion in other comprehensive income. The change in value of the excluded portion will later be removed or reclassified from equity as a single amount or on an amortised basis (depending on the nature of the hedged item) and ultimately **recognised in profit or loss**.

Part B 11: Financial instruments

Hedges of a group of items

IFRS 9 **permits** the designation of a group of assets as a hedged item provided that the following **two conditions** are met.

(a)   It consists of items that are eligible individually for hedging

(b)   The items in the group are managed together on a group basis for the purposes of risk management

Accounting for hedges of credit risk using credit derivatives

IFRS 9 **permits certain credit exposures to be designated at fair value through profit or loss** if a credit derivative that is measured at fair value through profit or loss is used to manage the credit risk of all, or a part of, the exposure on a fair value basis.

A credit exposure may be a financial instrument within or outside the scope of IFRS 9, for example, a loan commitment, that is managed for credit risk. The designation would be permitted if both of the following apply.

(a)   The name of the credit exposure matches the reference entity of the credit derivative.

(b)   The seniority of the financial instrument matches that of the instruments that can be delivered in accordance with the credit derivative.

If the qualifying criteria are no longer met and the instrument is not otherwise required to be measured at fair value through profit or loss, the entity must discontinue measuring the financial instrument that gave rise to the credit risk at fair value through profit or loss.

7 IFRS 7: Financial instruments: Disclosures

The IASB maintains that users of financial instruments need information about an entity's exposures to risks and how those risks are managed, as this information can **influence a user's assessment of the financial position and financial performance of an entity** or of the amount, timing and uncertainty of its **future cash flows**.

There have been new techniques and approaches to measuring risk management, which highlighted the need for guidance.

This was addressed in IFRS 7 *Financial instruments: disclosures* which has since been updated for the issue of IFRS 9.

General requirements

The extent of disclosure required depends on the extent of the entity's use of financial instruments and on its exposure to risk. IFRS 7 **adds to the requirements previously in IAS 32** by requiring:

- Enhanced statement of financial position and statement of profit or loss and other comprehensive income disclosures

- Disclosures about an allowance account when one is used to reduce the carrying amount of impaired financial instruments

The standard requires **qualitative and quantitative disclosures about exposure to risks** arising from financial instruments, and specifies minimum disclosures about **credit risk, liquidity risk** and **market risk**.

The objective of the IFRS is to require entities to provide disclosures in their financial statements that enable users to evaluate:

(a) The significance of financial instruments for the entity's financial position and performance

(b) The nature and extent of risks arising from financial instruments to which the entity is exposed during the period and at the reporting date, and how the entity manages those risks

Classes of financial instruments and levels of disclosure

The entity must group financial instruments into classes **appropriate to the nature of the information disclosed**. An entity must decide in the light of its circumstances how much detail it provides. Sufficient information must be provided to permit reconciliation to the line items presented in the statement of financial position.

Statement of financial position

The following must be disclosed.

(a) **Carrying amount** of financial assets and liabilities by IFRS 9 category

(b) **Reason for any reclassification of a financial asset** between fair value and amortised cost (and vice versa)

(c) The **carrying amount** of financial assets the entity has **pledged as collateral** for liabilities or contingent liabilities and the associated terms and conditions

(d) When financial assets are impaired by credit losses and the entity records the impairment in a separate account (eg an **allowance account** used to record individual impairments or a similar account used to record a collective impairment of assets) rather than directly reducing the carrying amount of the asset, it must disclose a **reconciliation** of changes in that account during the period for each class of financial assets

(e)   The **existence of multiple embedded derivatives**, where compound instruments contain these

(f)   Defaults and breaches

(g)   **Details** of the assets and exposure to risk where the entity has made a **transfer** such that part or all of the financial assets do not qualify for derecognition

Statement of profit or loss and other comprehensive income

The entity must disclose the following **items of income, expense, gains or losses,** either on the face of the financial statements or in the notes.

(a)   Net gains/losses by IFRS 9 category (broken down as appropriate: eg interest, fair value changes, dividend income)

(b)   Interest income/expense

(c)   Impairments losses by class of financial asset

Other disclosures

Entities must disclose in the summary of **significant accounting policies** the measurement basis used in preparing the financial statements and the other accounting policies that are relevant to an understanding of the financial statements.

Disclosures must be made relating to **hedge accounting,** as follows:

(a)   An entity's risk management strategy and how it is applied to manage risk;

(b)   How the entity's hedging activities may affect the amount, timing and uncertainty of its future cash flows; and

(c)   The effect that hedge accounting has had on the entity's statement of financial position, statement of comprehensive income and statement of changes in equity.

Disclosures relating to hedging must be presented in a **single note** or **separate section** of the financial statements.

Disclosures must be made relating to **fair value:**

IFRS 7 retains the following general requirements in relation to the disclosure of fair value for those financial instruments **measured at amortised cost:**

(a)   For each class of financial assets and financial liabilities an entity should disclose the **fair value of that class of assets and liabilities** in a way that permits it to be compared with its carrying amount.

(b)   In disclosing fair values, an entity should group financial assets and financial liabilities into classes, but should **offset them only to the extent that their carrying amounts are offset in the statement of financial position**

It also states that **disclosure of fair value is not required** where carrying amount is a reasonable approximation of fair value.

IFRS 13 provides disclosure requirements in respect of the fair value of financial instruments **measured at fair value**. It requires that information is disclosed to help users assess:

(a)   For assets and liabilities measured at **fair value after initial recognition, the valuation techniques and inputs used to develop those measurements.**

(b)   For **recurring fair value measurements** (ie those measured at each period end) using significant unobservable (level 3) inputs, the **effect of the measurements on profit or loss** or other comprehensive income for the period.

In order to achieve this, the following should be **disclosed as a minimum** for each class of financial assets and liabilities measured at fair value (asterisked disclosures are also required for financial assets and liabilities measured at amortised cost but for which fair value is disclosed).

(a)   The fair value measurement at the end of the reporting period.

(b)   The level of the fair value hierarchy within which the fair value measurements are categorised in their entirety.*

(c)   For assets and liabilities measured at fair value at each reporting date (recurring fair value measurements), the amounts of any transfers between level 1 and level 2 of the fair value hierarchy and reasons for the transfers.

(d)   For fair value measurements categorised within level 2 and 3 of the hierarchy, a description of the valuation techniques and inputs used in the fair value measurement, plus details of any changes in valuation techniques.*

(e)   For recurring fair value measurements categorised within level 3 of the fair value hierarchy:

- A reconciliation from the opening to closing balances.

- The amount of unrealised gains or losses recognised in profit or loss in the period and the line item in which they are recognised.

- A narrative description of the sensitivity of the fair value measurement to changes in unobservable inputs.

(f)   For recurring and non-recurring fair value measurements categorised within level 3 of the fair value hierarchy, a description of the valuation processes used by the entity.

(g)   If the highest and best use of a non-financial asset differs from its current use, an entity shall disclose that fact and why the non-financial asset is being used in a manner that differs from its highest and best use.

An entity should also disclose its policy for determining when transfers between levels of the fair value hierarchy are deemed to have occurred.

Example: Fair value disclosures

For assets and liabilities measured at fair value at the end of the reporting period, the IFRS requires quantitative disclosures about the fair value measurements for each class of assets and liabilities. An entity might disclose the following for assets:

Description	$'000 31.12.X9	*Fair value measurements at the end of the reporting period using*		
		Level 1 inputs	*Level 2 inputs*	*Level 3 inputs*
Trading equity securities	45	45		
Non-trading equity securities	32			32
Corporate securities	90	9	81	
Derivatives – Interest rate contracts	78	—	78	—
Total recurring fair value measurements	245	54	159	32

Nature and extent of risks arising from financial instruments

In undertaking transactions in financial instruments, an entity may assume or transfer to another party one or more of **different types of financial risk** as shown in the list of IFRS 7 defined terms below. The disclosures required by the standard show the extent to which an entity is exposed to these different types of risk, relating to both recognised and unrecognised financial instruments.

Credit risk	The risk that one party to a financial instrument will cause a financial loss for the other party by failing to discharge an obligation.
Currency risk	The risk that the fair value or future cash flows of a financial instrument will fluctuate because of changes in foreign exchange rates.
Interest rate risk	The risk that the fair value or future cash flows of a financial instrument will fluctuate because of changes in market interest rates.
Liquidity risk	The risk that an entity will encounter difficulty in meeting obligations associated with financial liabilities.
Loans payable	Loans payable are financial liabilities, other than short-term trade payables on normal credit terms.

Market risk	The risk that the fair value or future cash flows of a financial instrument will fluctuate because of changes in market prices. Market risk comprises three types of risk: currency risk, interest rate risk and other price risk.
Other price risk	The risk that the fair value or future cash flows of a financial instrument will fluctuate because of changes in market prices (other than those arising from interest rate risk or currency risk), whether those changes are caused by factors specific to the individual financial instrument or its issuer, or factors affecting all similar financial instruments traded in the market.
Past due	A financial asset is past due when a counterparty has failed to make a payment when contractually due. (IFRS 7: Appendix A)

Qualitative disclosures

For each type of risk arising from financial instruments, an entity must disclose:

(a)   The **exposures to risk** and how they arise

(b)   Its objectives, policies and processes for managing the risk and the methods used to measure the risk

(c)   Any **changes** in (a) or (b) from the previous period

Quantitative disclosures

For each financial instrument risk, **summary quantitative data** about risk exposure must be disclosed. This should be based on the information provided internally to key management personnel. More information should be provided if this is unrepresentative.

Credit risk is the risk that one party to a financial instrument will cause a loss for the other party by failing to pay for its obligation.

Disclosures about **credit risk** include:

- Maximum amount of exposure (before deducting the value of collateral)

- Description of collateral

- Information about credit quality of financial assets that are neither past due nor impaired

- Information about credit quality of financial assets whose terms have been renegotiated

- For financial assets that are past due or impaired, analytical disclosures are required

- Information about collateral or other credit enhancements obtained or called

For **liquidity risk** entities must disclose:

(a) A maturity analysis of financial liabilities

(b) A description of the way risk is managed

Disclosures required in connection with **market risk** are:

(a) Sensitivity analysis, showing the effects on profit or loss and equity of changes in each market risk and the method and assumptions used

(b) If the sensitivity analysis reflects interdependencies between risk variables, such as interest rates and exchange rates, an explanation of the method used, its objectives and its limitations must also be disclosed

Capital disclosures

Certain disclosures about managing **capital** are required. An entity's capital does not relate solely to financial instruments, but has more general relevance. Accordingly, those disclosures are included in IAS 1, rather than in IFRS 7.

Earnings per share

12

1 IAS 33: Earnings per share

The objective of IAS 33 is to improve the **comparability** of the performance of different entities in the same period and of the same entity in different accounting periods by prescribing methods for determining the number of shares to be included in the calculation of earnings per share and other amounts per share and by specifying their presentation.

The following definitions are given in IAS 33, some of which are given in other IASs.

> **Ordinary share.** An equity instrument that is subordinate to all other classes of equity instruments.
>
> **Potential ordinary share.** A financial instrument or other contract that may entitle its holder to ordinary shares.
>
> **Warrants or options.** Financial instruments that give the holder the right to purchase ordinary shares.
>
> **Financial instrument.** Any contract that gives rise to both a financial asset of one entity and a financial liability or equity instrument of another entity.
>
> **Equity instrument.** Any contract that evidences a residual interest in the assets of an entity after deducting all of its liabilities. *(IAS 33: para. 5)*

There may be more than one class of ordinary shares, but ordinary shares of the same class will have the same rights to receive dividends. Ordinary shares participate in the net profit for the year **only after other types of shares**, eg preference shares.

Potential ordinary shares

IAS 33 identifies the following examples of financial instruments and other contracts generating potential ordinary shares.

(a)   **Debt or equity instruments**, including preference shares, that are convertible into ordinary shares

(b)   **Share warrants and options**

(c)   **Employee plans** that allow employees to receive ordinary shares as part of their remuneration and other share purchase plans

(d)   Shares that would be issued upon the satisfaction of **certain conditions** resulting from contractual arrangements, such as the purchase of a business or other assets

IAS 33 has the following scope restrictions.

(a)   Only companies with (potential) ordinary shares which are **publicly traded** need to present EPS (including companies in the process of being listed)

(b)   EPS need only be presented on the basis of **consolidated results** where the parent's results are shown as well

(c)   Where companies **choose** to present EPS, even when they have no (potential) ordinary shares which are traded, they must do so in accordance with IAS 33

2 Basic EPS

Measurement

Basic EPS should be calculated by dividing the **net profit** or loss for the period attributable to ordinary shareholders by the **weighted average number of ordinary shares** outstanding during the period.

$$\text{Basic EPS} = \frac{\text{Net profit/(loss) attributable to ordianry shareholders}}{\text{Weighted average number of ordinary shares outstanding during the period}}$$

Earnings

Earnings includes **all items of income and expense** (including deductions for tax and non-controlling interests) less net profit attributable to **preference shareholders,** including preference dividends.

Preference dividends deducted from net profit consist of:

(a) Preference dividends on non-cumulative preference shares declared in respect of the period

(b) The full amount of the required preference dividends for cumulative preference shares for the period, whether or not they have been declared (excluding those paid/declared during the period in respect of previous periods)

Per share

The number of ordinary shares used should be the weighted average number of ordinary shares during the period. This figure (for all periods presented) should be **adjusted for events**, other than the conversion of potential ordinary shares, that have changed the number of shares outstanding without a corresponding change in resources.

The **time-weighting factor** is the number of days the shares were outstanding compared with the total number of days in the period; a reasonable approximation is usually adequate.

Example: Weighted average number of shares

J Co, a listed company, has the following share transactions during 20X7.

Date	Details	Shares issued	Treasury shares*	Shares outstanding
1 Jan 20X7	Balance at beginning of year	200,000	30,000	170,000
31 May 20X7	Issue of new shares for cash	80,000	–	250,000
1 Dec 20X7	Purchase of treasury shares	–	25,000	225,000
31 Dec 20X7	Balance at year end	280,000	55,000	225,000

* Treasury shares are an entity's own shares acquired. In some countries own shares cannot be held, but must be cancelled on acquisition.

What is the weighted average number of shares outstanding for 20X7?

The weighted average number of shares can be calculated in two ways.

(a) $(170,000 \times 5/12) + (250,000 \times 6/12) + (225,000 \times 1/12) = 214,583$ shares

(b) $(170,000 \times 12/12) + (80,000 \times 7/12) - (25,000 \times 1/12) = 214,583$ shares

Consideration

Shares are usually included in the weighted average number of shares from the **date consideration is receivable** which is usually the date of issue; in other cases consider the specific terms attached to their issue (consider the substance of any contract). The treatment for the issue of ordinary shares in different circumstances is as follows.

Consideration	Start date for inclusion
In exchange for cash	When cash is receivable
On the voluntary reinvestment of dividends on ordinary or preferred shares	The dividend payment date
As a result of the conversion of a debt instrument to ordinary shares	Date interest ceases accruing
In place of interest or principal on other financial instruments	Date interest ceases accruing
In exchange for the settlement of a liability of the entity	The settlement date
As consideration for the acquisition of an asset other than cash	The date on which the acquisition is recognised
For the rendering of services to the entity	As services are rendered

Ordinary shares issued as **purchase consideration** in an acquisition should be included as of the date of acquisition because the acquired entity's results will also be included from that date.

If ordinary shares are **partly paid**, they are treated as a fraction of an ordinary share to the extent they are entitled to dividends relative to fully paid ordinary shares.

Contingently issuable shares (including those subject to recall) are included in the computation when all necessary conditions for issue have been satisfied.

3 Effect on EPS of changes in capital structure

We looked at the effect of issues of new shares or buy-backs of shares on basic EPS above. In these situations, the corresponding figures for EPS for the previous year will be comparable with the current year because, as the weighted average number of shares has risen or fallen, there has been a **corresponding increase or decrease in resources.** Money has been received when shares were issued, and money has been paid out to repurchase shares. It is assumed that the sales or purchases have been made at full market price.

Example: Earnings per share with a new issue

On 30 September 20X2, B Co made an issue at full market price of 1,000,000 ordinary shares. The company's accounting year runs from 1 January to 31 December. Relevant information for 20X1 and 20X2 is as follows.

	20X2	20X1
Shares in issue as at 31 December	9,000,000	8,000,000
Profits after tax and preference dividend	$3,300,000	$3,280,000

What is the EPS for 20X2 and the corresponding figure for 20X1?

Weighted average number of shares	20X2	20X1
9 months × 8 million	6,000,000	
3 months × 9 million	2,250,000	
	8,250,000	8,000,000
Earnings	$3,300,000	$3,280,000
EPS	40 cents	41 cents

In spite of the increase in total earnings by $20,000 in 20X2, the EPS is not as good as in 20X1, because there was extra capital employed for the final 3 months of 20X2.

There are other events, however, which change the number of shares outstanding, **without a corresponding change in resources**. In these circumstances it is necessary to make adjustments so that the current and prior period EPS figures are comparable.

Four such events are considered by IAS 33.

(a) **Capitalisation or bonus issue** (sometimes called a stock dividend)
(b) Bonus element in any other issue, eg a rights issue to existing shareholders
(c) **Share split**
(d) **Reverse share split** (consolidation of shares)

Capitalisation/bonus issue and share split/reverse share split

These two types of event can be considered together as they have a similar effect. In both cases, ordinary shares are issued to existing shareholders for **no additional consideration**. The number of ordinary shares has increased without an increase in resources.

This problem is solved by **adjusting the number of ordinary shares outstanding before the event** for the proportionate change in the number of shares outstanding as if the event had occurred at the beginning of the earliest period reported.

Example: earnings per share with a bonus issue

G Co had 400,000 shares in issue, until on 30 September 20X2 it made a bonus issue of 100,000 shares. Total earnings were $80,000 in 20X2 and $75,000 in 20X1. The company's accounting year runs from 1 January to 31 December.

EPS will be:

	20X2	20X1
Earnings	$80,000	$75,000
Shares at 1 January	400,000	400,000
Bonus issue	100,000	100,000
Total shares	500,000	500,000
EPS	16c	15c

The number of shares for 20X1 must also be adjusted if the figures for EPS are to remain comparable.

Rights issue

A rights issue of shares is an issue of new shares to existing shareholders **at a price below the current market value**. The offer of new shares is made on the basis of x new shares for every y shares currently held; eg a 1 for 3 rights issue is an offer of 1 new share at the offer price for every 3 shares currently held. This means that there is a bonus element included.

To arrive at figures for EPS when a rights issue is made, we need to calculate first of all the **theoretical ex rights price**. This is a weighted average value per share, and is perhaps explained most easily with a numerical example.

Example: Theoretical ex-rights price

Suppose that E Co has 10,000,000 shares in issue. It now proposes to make a 1 for 4 rights issue at a price of $3 per share. The market value of existing shares on the final day before the issue is made is $3.50 (this is the 'with rights' value). What is the theoretical ex rights price per share?

	$
Before issue 4 shares, value $3.50 each	14.00
Rights issue 1 share, value $3	3.00
Theoretical value of 5 shares	17.00

$$\text{Theoretical ex rights price} = \frac{\$17.00}{5} = \$3.40 \text{ per share}$$

Note that this calculation can alternatively be performed using the total value and number of outstanding shares.

Procedures

The procedures for calculating the EPS for the current year and a corresponding figure for the previous year are now as follows.

(a)   The **EPS for the corresponding previous period** should be multiplied by the following fraction. (Note. The market price on the last day of quotation is taken as the fair value immediately prior to exercise of the rights, as required by the standard.)

$$\frac{\text{Theoretical ex-rights price}}{\text{Market price on last day of quotation (with rights)}}$$

(b)   To obtain the **EPS for the current year**:

       (i)   Multiply the number of shares before the rights issue by the fraction of the year before the date of issue and by the following fraction

$$\frac{\text{Market price on last day of quotation with rights}}{\text{Theoretical ex-rights price}}$$

       (ii)   Multiply the number of shares after the rights issue by the fraction of the year after the date of issue and add to the figure arrived at in (i)

The total earnings should then be divided by the total number of shares so calculated.

Example: Earnings per share with a rights issue

B Co had 100,000 shares in issue, but then makes a 1 for 5 rights issue on 1 October 20X2 at a price of $1. The market value on the last day of quotation with rights was $1.60.

Total earnings are $50,000 in 20X2 and $40,000 in 20X1.

What is the EPS for 20X2 and the corresponding figure for 20X1?

Calculation of theoretical ex rights price:

	$
	8.00
Before issue 5 shares, value × $1.60	
Rights issue 1 share, value × $1.00	1.00
Theoretical value of 6 shares	9.00

$$\text{Theoretical ex rights price} = \frac{\$9}{6} = \$1.50$$

EPS for 20X1

EPS as calculated before taking into account the rights issue = 40c ($40,000 divided by 100,000 shares).

$$\text{EPS} = \frac{1.50}{1.60} \times 40c = 37\tfrac{1}{2}c$$

(This is the corresponding value for 20X1 which will be shown in the financial statements for B Co at the end of 20X2.)

EPS for 20X2

Number of shares before the rights issue was 100,000. 20,000 shares were issued.

Stage 1:	$100,000 \times 9/12 \times \dfrac{1.60}{1.50}$	=	80,000
Stage 2:	$120,000 \times 3/12$	=	30,000
			110,000

$$\text{EPS} = \frac{\$50,000}{110,000} = 45\tfrac{1}{2}c$$

The figure for total earnings is the actual earnings for the year.

4 Diluted EPS

At the end of an accounting period, a company may have in issue some **securities** which do not (at present) have any 'claim' to a share of equity earnings, but **may give rise to such a claim in the future**. These securities include:

(a)   A **separate class of equity shares** which at present is not entitled to any dividend, but will be entitled after some future date

(b)   **Convertible loan stock** or **convertible preference shares** which give their holders the right at some future date to exchange their securities for ordinary shares of the company, at a pre determined conversion rate

(c)   **Options** or **warrants**

In such circumstances, the future number of ordinary shares in issue might increase, which in turn results in a fall in the EPS. In other words, a **future increase** in the **number of ordinary shares will cause a dilution or 'watering down' of equity**, and it is possible to calculate a **diluted earnings per share** (ie the EPS that would have been obtained during the financial period if the dilution had already taken place). This will indicate to investors the possible effects of a future dilution.

Earnings

The earnings calculated for basic EPS should be adjusted by the **post-tax** (including deferred tax) effect of:

(a) Any **dividends** on dilutive potential ordinary shares that were deducted to arrive at earnings for basic EPS

(b) **Interest recognised** in the period for the dilutive potential ordinary shares

(c) Any **other changes in income or expenses** (fees and discount, premium accounted for as yield adjustments) that would result from the conversion of the dilutive potential ordinary shares

The conversion of some potential ordinary shares may lead to changes in **other income or expenses**. For example, the reduction of interest expense related to potential ordinary shares and the resulting increase in net profit for the period may lead to an increase in the expense relating to a non-discretionary employee profit-sharing plan. When calculating diluted EPS, the net profit or loss for the period is adjusted for any such consequential changes in income or expense.

Per share

The number of ordinary shares is the weighted average number of ordinary shares calculated for basic EPS plus the weighted average number of ordinary shares that would be issued on the conversion of all the **dilutive potential ordinary shares** into ordinary shares.

It should be assumed that dilutive ordinary shares were converted into ordinary shares at the **beginning of the period** or, if later, at the actual date of issue. There are two other points.

(a) The computation assumes the most **advantageous conversion rate** or exercise rate from the standpoint of the holder of the potential ordinary shares.

(b) **Contingently issuable** (potential) ordinary shares are treated as for basic EPS; if the conditions have not been met, the number of contingently issuable shares included in the computation is based on the number of shares that would be issuable if the end of the reporting period was the end of the contingency period. Restatement is not allowed if the conditions are not met when the contingency period expires.

Example: Diluted EPS

In 20X7 F Co had a basic EPS of 105c based on earnings of $105,000 and 100,000 ordinary $1 shares. It also had in issue $40,000 15% Convertible Loan Stock which is convertible in two years' time at the rate of 4 ordinary shares for every $5 of stock. The rate of tax is 30%. In 20X7 gross profit of $200,000 and expenses of $50,000 were recorded, including interest payable of $6,000.

What is the diluted EPS?

Diluted EPS is calculated as follows.

| step 1 | **Number of shares:** the additional equity on conversion of the loan stock will be 40,000 × 4/5 = 32,000 shares |

| step 2 | **Earnings:** F Co will save interest payments of $6,000 but this increase in profits will be taxed. Hence the earnings figure may be recalculated: |

	$
Gross profit	200,000
Expenses (50,000 – 6,000)	(44,000)
Profit before tax	156,000
Tax expense (30%)	(46,800)
Earnings	109,200

| step 3 | **Calculation:** Diluted EPS = $\dfrac{\$109,200}{132,000}$ = 82.7c |

| step 4 | **Dilution:** the dilution in earnings would be 105c – 82.7c = 22.3c per share. |

Dilutive potential ordinary shares

According to IAS 33, potential ordinary shares should be treated as dilutive when, and only when, their conversion to ordinary shares would **decrease net profit per share** from continuing operations. It is important to only include in the diluted EPS calculation those potential ordinary shares which are actually dilutive.

Example

A Co has 5,000,000 ordinary shares of 25 cents each in issue, and also had in issue in 20X4:

(a) $1,000,000 of 14% convertible loan stock, convertible in three years' time at the rate of 2 shares per $10 of stock;

(b) $2,000,000 of 10% convertible loan stock, convertible in one year's time at the rate of 3 shares per $5 of stock.

The total earnings in 20X4 were $1,750,000.

The rate of income tax is 35%.

What is the basic EPS and diluted EPS?

(a)   Basic EPS = $\dfrac{\$1,750,000}{5\text{ million}}$ = 35 cents

(b)   We must decide which of the potential ordinary shares (ie the loan stocks) are dilutive (ie would decrease the EPS if converted).

For the 14% loan stock, incremental EPS $= \dfrac{0.65 \times \$140,000}{200,000 \text{ shares}} = 45.5c$

For the 10% loan stock, incremental EPS $= \dfrac{0.65 \times \$200,000}{1.2m \text{ shares}} = 10.8c$

The effect of converting the 14% loan stock is therefore to increase the EPS figure, since the incremental EPS of 45.5c is greater than the basic EPS of 35c. The 14% loan stock is not dilutive and is therefore excluded from the diluted EPS calculation.

The 10% loan stock is dilutive.

Diluted EPS $= \dfrac{\$1.75m + \$0.13m}{5m + 1.2m} = 30.3c$

Restatement

If the number of ordinary or potential ordinary shares outstanding **increases** as a result of a capitalisation, bonus issue or share split, or decreases as a result of a reverse share split, the calculation of basic and diluted EPS for all periods presented should be **adjusted retrospectively**.

If these changes occur **after the reporting date** but before the financial statements are authorised for issue, the calculations per share for the financial statements and those of any prior period should be based on the **new number of shares** (and this should be disclosed).

In addition, basic and diluted EPS of all periods presented should be adjusted for the effects of **material errors**, and adjustments resulting from **changes** in **accounting policies**, dealt with in accordance with IAS 8.

An entity **does not restate diluted EPS** of any prior period for changes in the assumptions used or for the conversion of potential ordinary shares into ordinary shares outstanding.

Entities are encouraged to disclose a description of ordinary share transactions or potential ordinary share transactions, other than capitalisation issues and share splits, which occur **after the reporting date** when they are of such importance that non-disclosure would affect the ability of the users of the financial statements to make proper evaluations and decisions (see IAS 10). Examples of such transactions include the following.

(a)   Issue of shares for cash

(b)   Issue of shares when the proceeds are used to repay debt or preferred shares outstanding at the reporting date

(c)   Redemption of ordinary shares outstanding

(d)   Conversion or exercise of potential ordinary shares, outstanding at the reporting date, into ordinary shares

(e)   Issue of warrants, options or convertible securities

(f)   Achievement of conditions that would result in the issue of contingently issuable shares

EPS amounts are not adjusted for such transactions occurring after the reporting date because such transactions **do not affect the amount of capital used** to produce the net profit or loss for the period.

5 Presentation, disclosure and other matters

Basic and diluted EPS should be presented by an entity on the **face of the statement of profit or loss and other comprehensive income** for each class of ordinary share that has a different right to share in the net profit for the period. The basic and diluted EPS should be presented with **equal prominence** for all periods presented.

Disclosure must still be made where the EPS figures (basic and/or diluted) are **negative** (ie a loss per share).

An entity should disclose the following.

(a)   The amounts used as the **numerators** in calculating basic and diluted EPS, and a reconciliation of those amounts to the net profit or loss for the period

(b)   The weighted average number of ordinary shares used as the **denominator** in calculating basic and diluted EPS, and a **reconciliation** of these denominators to each other

Significance of earnings per share

Earnings per share (EPS) is one of the most frequently quoted statistics in financial analysis. Because of the widespread use of the price earnings **(P/E) ratio** as a yardstick for investment decisions, it became increasingly important.

Reported and forecast EPS can, through the P/E ratio, have a **significant effect on a company's share price.** Thus, a share price might fall if it looks as if EPS is going to be low. This is not very rational, as EPS can depend on many, often subjective, assumptions used in preparing a historical statement such as the statement of profit or loss. It does not necessarily bear any relation to the value of a company, and of its shares. Nevertheless, the market is sensitive to EPS.

EPS has also served as a means of assessing the **stewardship and management** role performed by company directors and managers. Remuneration packages might be linked to EPS growth, thereby increasing the pressure on management to improve EPS. The danger of this, however, is that management effort may go into distorting results to produce a favourable EPS.

Statement of cash flows

13

1 IAS 7: Statement of cash flows

The aim of IAS 7 is to provide information to users of financial statements about the entity's **ability to generate cash and cash equivalents**, as well as indicating the cash needs of the entity. The statement of cash flows provides **historical** information about cash and cash equivalents, classifying cash flows between operating, investing and financing activities.

A statement of cash flows should be presented as an **integral part** of an entity's financial statements. All types of entity can provide useful information about cash flows as the need for cash is universal, whatever the nature of their revenue-producing activities. Therefore **all entities are required by the standard to produce a statement of cash flows**.

Benefits of cash flow information

The use of statements of cash flows is very much **in conjunction** with the rest of the financial statements. Users can gain further appreciation of the change in net assets, of the entity's financial position (liquidity and solvency) and the entity's ability to adapt to changing circumstances by affecting the amount and timing of cash flows. Statements of cash flows **enhance comparability** as they are not affected by differing accounting policies used for the same type of transactions or events.

Cash flow information of a historical nature can be used as an indicator of the amount, timing and certainty of future cash flows. Past forecast cash flow information can be **checked for accuracy** as actual figures emerge. The relationship between profit and cash flows can be analysed as can changes in prices over time.

Definitions

The standard gives the following definitions, the most important of which are **cash** and **cash equivalents**.

> **Cash** comprises cash on hand and demand deposits.
>
> **Cash equivalents** are short-term, highly liquid investments that are readily convertible to known amounts of cash and which are subject to an insignificant risk of changes in value.
>
> **Cash flows** are inflows and outflows of cash and cash equivalents.
>
> **Operating activities** are the principal revenue-producing activities of the entity and other activities that are not investing or financing activities.
>
> **Investing activities** are the acquisition and disposal of non-current assets and other investments not included in cash equivalents.
>
> **Financing activities** are activities that result in changes in the size and composition of the equity capital and borrowings of the entity. *(IAS 7: para. 6)*

Cash and cash equivalents

The standard expands on the definition of cash equivalents: they are not held for investment or other long-term purposes, but rather to meet short-term cash commitments. To fulfil the above definition, an investment's **maturity date should normally be within three months from its acquisition date**. It would usually be the case then that equity investments (ie shares in other companies) are **not** cash equivalents. An exception would be where preferred shares were acquired with a very close maturity date.

Loans and other borrowings from banks are classified as investing activities. In some countries, however, **bank overdrafts** are repayable on demand and are treated as part of an entity's total cash management system. In these circumstances an overdrawn balance will be included in cash and cash equivalents. Such banking arrangements are characterised by a balance which fluctuates between overdrawn and credit.

Movements between different types of cash and cash equivalent are not included in cash flows. The investment of surplus cash in cash equivalents is part of cash management, not part of operating, investing or financing activities.

The manner of presentation of cash flows between operating, investing and financing activities **depends on the nature of the entity**. By classifying cash flows between different activities in this way users can see the impact on cash and cash equivalents of each one, and their relationships with each other. We can look at each in more detail.

Operating activities

This is perhaps the key part of the statement of cash flows because it shows whether, and to what extent, companies can **generate cash from their operations**. It is these operating cash flows which must, in the end pay for all cash outflows relating to other activities, ie paying loan interest, dividends and so on.

Most of the components of cash flows from operating activities will be those items which **determine the net profit or loss of the entity**, ie they relate to the main revenue-producing activities of the entity. The standard gives the following as examples of cash flows from operating activities.

(a)   Cash receipts from the sale of goods and the rendering of services
(b)   Cash receipts from royalties, fees, commissions and other revenue
(c)   Cash payments to suppliers for goods and services
(d)   Cash payments to and on behalf of employees

Certain items may be included in the net profit or loss for the period which do not relate to operational cash flows, for example the profit or loss on the sale of a piece of plant will be included in net profit or loss, but the cash flows will be classed as **investing**.

Investing activities

The cash flows classified under this heading show the extent of new investment in **assets which will generate future profit and cash flows**. The standard gives the following examples of cash flows arising from investing activities.

(a)   Cash payments to acquire property, plant and equipment, intangibles and other non-current assets, including those relating to capitalised development costs and self-constructed property, plant and equipment

(b)   Cash receipts from sales of property, plant and equipment, intangibles and other non-current assets

(c)   Cash payments to acquire shares or debentures of other entities

(d)   Cash receipts from sales of shares or debentures of other entities

(e)   Cash advances and loans made to other parties

(f)   Cash receipts from the repayment of advances and loans made to other parties

Financing activities

This section of the statement of cash flows shows the share of cash which the entity's capital providers have claimed during the period. This is an indicator of **likely future interest and dividend payments**. The standard gives the following examples of cash flows which might arise under this heading.

(a)   Cash proceeds from issuing shares

(b)   Cash payments to owners to acquire or redeem the entity's shares

(c)   Cash proceeds from issuing debentures, loans, notes, bonds, mortgages and other short or long-term borrowings

(d)   Principal repayments of amounts borrowed under leases

Item (d) needs more explanation. Where the reporting entity uses an asset held under a lease, the amounts to go in the statement of cash flows as financing activities are repayments of the **principal (capital)** rather than the **interest**. The interest paid will be shown under operating activities.

Example: Lease rental

The notes to the financial statements of H Co show the following in respect of obligations under leases.

Year ended 30 June	20X5 $'000	20X4 $'000
Amounts payable within one year	12	8
Within two to five years	110	66
	122	74
Less finance charges allocated to future periods	(14)	(8)
	108	66

Interest paid on leases in the year to 30 June 20X5 amounted to $6m. Additions to tangible non-current assets acquired under leases were shown in the non-current asset note at $56,000.

What is the capital repayment to be shown in the statement of cash flows of H Co for the year to 30 June 20X5?

OBLIGATIONS UNDER LEASES

	$'000		$'000
Capital repayment (bal fig)	14	Bal 1.7.X4	66
Bal 30.6.X5	108	Additions	56
	122		122

Reporting cash flows from operating activities

The standard offers a choice of method for this part of the statement of cash flows.

(a)   **Direct method**: disclose major classes of gross cash receipts and gross cash payments

(b)   **Indirect method**: net profit or loss is adjusted for the effects of transactions of a non-cash nature, any deferrals or accruals of past or future operating cash receipts or payments, and items of income or expense associated with investing or financing cash flows

The **direct method is the preferred method** because it discloses information, not available elsewhere in the financial statements, which could be of use in estimating future cash flows. The example below shows both methods.

Using the direct method

The direct method requires **information about gross cash receipts and payments.** There are different ways in which this can be obtained. The most obvious way is simply to extract the information from the accounting records. This may be a laborious task, however, and the indirect method is probably more widely used.

Using the indirect method

This method is undoubtedly **easier** from the point of view of the preparer of the statement of cash flows. The net profit or loss for the period is adjusted for the following.

(a)   Changes during the period in inventories, operating receivables and payables

(b)   Non-cash items, eg depreciation, provisions, profits/losses on the sales of assets

(c)   Other items, the cash flows from which should be classified under investing or financing activities

A **proforma** of such a calculation, taken from the IAS, is as follows. (The proforma has been amended to reflect changes to IFRS.)

	$
Cash flows from operating activities	
Profit before taxation	X
Adjustments for:	
Depreciation	X
Foreign exchange loss	X
Investment income	(X)
Interest expense	X
	X
Increase in trade and other receivables	(X)
Decrease in inventories	X
Decrease in trade payables	(X)
Cash generated from operations	X
Interest paid	(X)
Income taxes paid	(X)
Net cash from operating activities	X

It is important to understand why **certain items are added and others subtracted.** Note the following points.

(a)   Depreciation is not a cash expense, but is deducted in arriving at profit. It makes sense, therefore, to eliminate it by adding it back.

(b) By the same logic, a loss on a disposal of a non-current asset (arising through under allowance of depreciation) needs to be added back and a profit deducted.

(c) An increase in inventories means less cash – you have spent cash on buying inventory.

(d) An increase in receivables means the company's debtors have not paid as much, and therefore there is less cash.

(e) If we pay off payables, causing the figure to decrease, again we have less cash.

The direct method is encouraged where the necessary information is not too costly to obtain, but IAS 7 does not require it. In practice the indirect method is more commonly used, since it is quicker and easier.

Interest and dividends

Cash flows from interest and dividends received and paid should each be **disclosed separately**. Each should be classified in a consistent manner from period to period as either operating, investing or financing activities.

Dividends paid by the entity can be classified in **one of two ways**.

(a) As a **financing cash flow**, showing the cost of obtaining financial resources.

(b) As a component of **cash flows from operating activities** so that users can assess the entity's ability to pay dividends out of operating cash flows.

Taxes on income

Cash flows arising from taxes on income should be **separately disclosed** and should be classified as cash flows from operating activities unless they can be specifically identified with financing and investing activities.

Taxation cash flows are often **difficult to match** to the originating underlying transaction, so most of the time all tax cash flows are classified as arising from operating activities.

Components of cash and cash equivalents

The components of cash and cash equivalents should be disclosed and a **reconciliation** should be presented, showing the amounts in the statement of cash flows reconciled with the equivalent items reported in the statement of financial position.

It is also necessary to disclose the **accounting policy** used in deciding the items included in cash and cash equivalents, in accordance with IAS 1 *Presentation of financial statements*, but also because of the wide range of cash management practices worldwide.

Other disclosures

All entities should disclose, together with a **commentary by management**, any other information likely to be of importance, for example:

(a)   Restrictions on the use of or access to any part of cash equivalents

(b)   The amount of undrawn borrowing facilities which are available

(c)   Cash flows which increased operating capacity compared to cash flows which merely maintained operating capacity

(d)   Cash flows arising from each reported industry and geographical segment

Example of a statement of cash flows

This example is adapted from the example given in the standard. Note that 'net cash from operating activities' is the same under both methods.

Direct method

STATEMENT OF CASH FLOWS YEAR ENDED 31 DECEMBER 20X7

	$m	$m
Cash flows from operating activities		
Cash receipts from customers	30,330	
Cash paid to suppliers and employees	(27,600)	
Cash generated from operations	2,730	
Interest paid	(270)	
Income taxes paid	(900)	
Net cash from operating activities		1,560
Cash flows from investing activities		
Purchase of property, plant and equipment	(900)	
Proceeds from sale of equipment	20	
Interest received	200	
Dividends received	200	
Net cash used in investing activities		(480)
Cash flows from financing activities		
Proceeds from issue of share capital	250	
Proceeds from long-term borrowings	250	
Dividends paid*	(1,290)	
Net cash used in financing activities		(790)
Net increase in cash and cash equivalents		290
Cash and cash equivalents at beginning of period		120
Cash and cash equivalents at end of period		410

* This could also be shown as an operating cash flow

'Net cash from operating activities' can also be calculated using the **indirect method**.

Indirect method

STATEMENT OF CASH FLOWS (extract) YEAR ENDED 31 DECEMBER 20X7

	$m
Cash flows from operating activities	
Profit before taxation	3,570
Adjustments for:	
Depreciation	450
Investment income	(500)
Interest expense	400
	3,920
Increase in trade and other receivables	(500)
Decrease in inventories	1,050
Decrease in trade payables	(1,740)
Cash generated from operations	2,730
Interest paid	(270)
Income taxes paid	(900)
Net cash from operating activities	1,560

2 Preparing a statement of cash flows

In essence, preparing a statement of cash flows under IAS 7 is very straightforward.

We will now go through a full example.

D CO
STATEMENT OF PROFIT OR LOSS AND OTHER COMPREHENSIVE INCOME FOR
THE YEAR ENDED 31 DECEMBER 20X2

	$'000
Revenue	2,553
Cost of sales	(1,814)
Gross profit	739
Other income: interest received	25
Distribution costs	(125)
Administrative expenses	(264)
Finance costs	(75)
Profit before tax	300
Income tax expense	(140)
Profit for the year	160
Other comprehensive income:	
Revaluation gain on property	9
Total comprehensive income for the year	169

D CO
STATEMENTS OF FINANCIAL POSITION AS AT 31 DECEMBER

	20X2	20X1
Assets	$'000	$'000
Non-current assets		
Property, plant and equipment	380	305
Intangible assets	250	200
Investments	–	25
Current assets		
Inventories	150	102
Receivables	390	315
Short-term investments	50	–
Cash in hand	2	1
Total assets	1,222	948
Equity and liabilities		
Equity		
Share capital ($1 ordinary shares)	200	150
Share premium account	160	150
Revaluation surplus	100	91
Retained earnings	260	180
Non-current liabilities		
Long-term loan	170	50
Current liabilities		
Trade payables	127	119
Bank overdraft	85	98
Taxation	120	110
Total equity and liabilities	1,222	948

The following information is available.

(a)   The proceeds of the sale of non-current asset investments amounted to $30,000.

(b)   Fixtures and fittings, with an original cost of $85,000 and a carrying amount of $45,000, were sold for $32,000 during the year.

(c)   The following information relates to property, plant and equipment.

	31.12.20X2	31.12.20X1
	$'000	$'000
Cost	720	595
Accumulated depreciation	(340)	(290)
Net book value	380	305

(d)   50,000 $1 ordinary shares were issued during the year at a premium of 20c per share.

(e)   The short-term investments are highly liquid and are close to maturity.

(f)   Dividends of $80,000 were paid during the year.

BPP
LEARNING MEDIA

The statement of cash flows will be as follows:

D CO

STATEMENT OF CASH FLOWS FOR THE YEAR ENDED 31 DECEMBER 20X2

	$'000	$'000
Cash flows from operating activities		
Profit before tax	300	
Depreciation charge (W1)	90	
Loss on sale of property, plant and equipment (45 – 32)	13	
Profit on sale of non-current asset investments	(5)	
Interest expense (net)	50	
(Increase)/decrease in inventories	(48)	
(Increase)/decrease in receivables	(75)	
Increase/(decrease) in payables	8	
	333	
Interest paid	(75)	
Dividends paid	(80)	
Tax paid (110 + 140 – 120)	(130)	
Net cash from operating activities		48
Cash flows from investing activities		
Payments to acquire property, plant and equipment (W2)	(201)	
Payments to acquire intangible non-current assets	(50)	
Receipts from sales of property, plant and equipment	32	
Receipts from sale of non-current asset investments	30	
Interest received	25	
Net cash flows from investing activities		(164)
Cash flows from financing activities		
Issue of share capital	60	
Long-term loan	120	
Net cash flows from financing		180
Increase in cash and cash equivalents		64
Cash and cash equivalents at 1.1.X2 (1 – 98)		(97)
Cash and cash equivalents at 31.12.X2 (50 + 2 – 85)		(33)

Workings

1   *Depreciation charge*

	$'000	$'000
Depreciation at 31 December 20X2		340
Depreciation 31 December 20X1	290	
Depreciation on assets sold (85 – 45)	40	
		250
Charge for the year		90

PROPERTY, PLANT AND EQUIPMENT (COST)

	$'000		$'000
1.1.X2 Balance b/d	595	Disposals	85
Revaluation (100 – 91)	9		
Purchases (bal fig)	201	31.12.X2 Balance c/d	720
	805		805

Examples of other items that may arise are:

- Share capital issues: the proceeds will be split between share capital and share premium.

- Bonus issues: these do not involve cash.

- Revaluation of non-current assets: this must be taken into account in calculating acquisitions and disposals.

- Movement on deferred tax: this must be taken into account in calculating tax paid.

- Leases: assets acquired under leases must be adjusted for in non-current asset calculations and the amount paid under the lease must appear as a cash flow.

3 Interpretation of statements of cash flows

So what kind of information does the statement of cash flows, along with its notes, provide?

Some of the main areas where IAS 7 should provide information not found elsewhere in the financial statements are as follows.

(a)   The **relationships between profit and cash** can be seen clearly and analysed accordingly.

(b)   **Cash equivalents** are highlighted, giving a better picture of the liquidity of the company.

(c)   **Financing inflows and outflows must be shown, rather than simply passed through reserves.**

One of the most important things to realise at this point is that it is wrong to try to assess the health or predict the death of a reporting entity solely on the basis of a single indicator. When analysing cash flow data, **the comparison should not just be between cash flows and profit, but also between cash flows over a period of time** (say three to five years).

Part B 13: Statement of cash flows

The **relationship between profit and cash flows will vary constantly**. Healthy companies do not always have reported profits exceeding operating cash flows. Similarly, unhealthy companies can have operating cash flows well in excess of reported profit. The value of comparing them is in determining the extent to which earned profits are being converted into the necessary cash flows.

Profit is not as important as the extent to which a company can **convert its profits into cash on a continuing basis**. This process should be judged over a period longer than one year. The cash flows should be compared with profits over the same periods to decide how successfully the reporting entity has converted earnings into cash.

Cash flow figures should also be considered in terms of their specific relationships with each other over time. A form of 'cash flow gearing' can be determined by comparing operating cash flows and financing flows, particularly borrowing, to establish the extent of dependence of the reporting entity on external funding.

Other relationships can be examined.

(a)   Operating cash flows and investment flows can be related to match cash recovery from investment to investment.

(b)   Investment can be compared to distribution to indicate the proportion of total cash outflow designated specifically to investor return and reinvestment.

(c)   A comparison of tax outflow to operating cash flow minus investment flow will establish a 'cash basis tax rate'.

The 'ratios' mentioned above can be monitored **inter– and intra-firm** and the analyses can be undertaken in monetary, general price-level adjusted, or percentage terms.

Criticisms of IAS 7

The inclusion of **cash equivalents** has been criticised because it does not reflect the way in which businesses are managed: in particular, the requirement that to be a cash equivalent an investment has to be within three months of maturity is considered **unrealistic**.

The management of assets similar to cash (ie 'cash equivalents') is not distinguished from other investment decisions.

14

1 IAS 24: Related party disclosures

In the absence of information to the contrary, it is assumed that a reporting entity has **independent discretionary power** over its resources and transactions and pursues its activities independently of the interests of its individual owners, managers and others. Transactions are presumed to have been undertaken on an **arm's length basis**, ie on terms such as could have obtained in a transaction with an external party, in which each side bargained knowledgeably and freely, unaffected by any relationship between them.

These assumptions may not be justified when **related party relationships** exist, because the requisite conditions for competitive, free market dealings may not be present. Whilst the parties may endeavour to achieve arm's length bargaining the very nature of the relationship may preclude this occurring.

This is the related parties issue and IAS 24 tackles it by ensuring that financial statements contain the disclosures necessary to draw attention to the possibility that the reported financial position and results may have been affected by the existence of related parties and by material transactions with them. In other words, this is a standard which is primarily concerned with **disclosure**.

Scope

The standard requires disclosure of related party transactions and outstanding balances in the **separate financial statements** of a parent, venturer or investor presented in accordance with IAS 27 as well as in consolidated financial statements.

This is a **change** from the previous version of IAS 24, which did not require disclosure in the separate financial statements of a parent or wholly-owned subsidiary that are made available or published with consolidated financial statements for the group.

An entity's financial statements disclose related party transactions and outstanding balances with other entities in a group. **Intragroup** transactions and balances are **eliminated** in the preparation of consolidated financial statements.

Definitions

The following important definitions are given by the standard which was subjected to minor amendment in November 2009. Note that the definitions of **control** and **significant influence** are now the same as those given in IASs 27, 28 and 31.

Related party. A party is related to an entity if:

(a) Directly, or indirectly through one or more intermediaries, it:

    (i) Controls, is controlled by, or is under common control with, the entity (this includes parents, subsidiaries and fellow subsidiaries);

    (ii) Has an interest in the entity that gives it significant influence over the entity; or

    (iii) Has joint control over the entity.

(b) It is an associate

(c) It is a joint venture in which the entity is a venturer

(d) It is a member of the key management personnel of the entity or its parent

(e) It is a close member of the family of any individual referred to in (a) or (d)

(f) It is an entity that is controlled, jointly controlled or significantly influenced by; or for which significant voting power in such entity resides with, directly or indirectly, any individual referred to in (d) or (e); or

(g) Both entities are joint ventures of the same third party

(h) One is a joint venture and the other an associate of the same third party

(i) It is a post-employment benefit plan for the benefit of employees of the entity, or of any entity that is a related party of the entity

Related party transaction. A transfer of resources, services or obligations between related parties, regardless of whether a price is charged.

Control is the power to govern the financial and operating policies of an entity so as to obtain benefits from its activities.

Significant influence is the power to participate in the financial and operating policy decisions of an entity, but is not control over these policies. Significant ownership may be gained by share ownership, statute or agreement.

Joint control is the contractually agreed sharing of control over an economic activity.

> **Key management personnel** are those persons having authority and responsibility for planning, directing and controlling the activities of the entity, directly or indirectly, including any director (whether executive or otherwise) of that entity.
>
> **Close members of the family of an individual** are those family members who may be expected to influence, or be influenced by, that individual in their dealings with the entity. They may include:
>
> (a)   The individual's domestic partner and children
> (b)   Children of the domestic partner; and
> (c)   Dependants of the individual or the domestic partner.
>
> *(IAS 24: para. 9)*

The most important point to remember here is that, when considering each possible related party relationship, attention must be paid to the **substance of the relationship, not merely the legal form**.

IAS 24 lists the following which are **not necessarily related parties**.

(a)   Two entities simply because they have a director or other key management in common (notwithstanding the definition of related party above, although it is necessary to consider how that director would affect both entities).

(b)   **Two venturers, simply because they share joint control over a joint venture.**

(c)   Certain other bodies, simply as a result of their **role in normal business dealings** with the entity

    (i)   Providers of finance
    (ii)   Trade unions
    (iii)   Public utilities
    (iv)   Government departments and agencies

(d)   **Any single customer, supplier, franchisor, distributor, or general agent** with whom the entity transacts a significant amount of business, simply by virtue of the resulting economic dependence.

Disclosure

As noted above, IAS 24 is almost entirely concerned with disclosure and its provisions are meant to **supplement** those disclosure requirements required by national company legislation and other IASs (particularly IASs 1, 22, 27 and 28).

The standard lists some **examples** of transactions that are disclosed if they are with a related party:

- Purchases or sales of goods (finished or unfinished)

- Purchases or sales of property and other assets

- Rendering or receiving of services

- Leases

- Transfer of research and development

- Transfers under licence agreements

- Provision of finance (including loans and equity contributions in cash or in kind)

- Provision of guarantees and collateral security

- Settlement of liabilities on behalf of the entity or by the entity on behalf of another party

Parents and subsidiaries

Relationships between **parents and subsidiaries** must be **disclosed irrespective** of **whether** any **transactions** have **taken place between** the related parties. An entity must disclose the **name** of its **parent** and, if different, the **ultimate controlling party**. This will enable a reader of the financial statements to be able to form a view about the effects of a related party relationship on the reporting entity.

If neither the parent nor the ultimate controlling party produces financial statements available for public use, the name of the next most senior parent that does so shall also be disclosed.

If there are transactions between a parent and subsidiary then they may benefit one of the parties in a way that would not occur in an arms-length transaction. For example, the subsidiary may sell goods to the parent at lower than market price which means that the subsidiary's profits will be lower than if it were a stand alone entity.

If the parent is putting the subsidiary up for sale then a potential purchaser will have to assess the subsidiary's financial statements and understand the impact that related party transactions have had. It is more likely in this circumstance that the parent will wish to make the subsidiary's financial statements as attractive as possible in order to ensure a sale.

There are a number of areas that the purchaser may need to consider:

- The terms of trading between the entities to assess how much of the subsidiary's trade is recurring and whether it is on fair market terms. In a sale situation the parent may sell goods to the subsidiary at below market price to make the subsidiary look more attractive.

- The existence of debt between the parties. Possible the parent could loan money to the subsidiary at below the market interest rate which may not be possible to maintain once the subsidiary is sold.

- The level of dividends payable as the subsidiary may have paid large dividends to the parent which may not be sustainable post sale.

Management personnel

An entity should disclose **key management personnel compensation** in **total** and for **each** of the following **categories**:

(a)   **Short-term employee benefits** (eg wages, salaries, social security contributions, paid annual leave and paid sick-leave, profit sharing and bonuses and non-monetary benefits such as medical care, housing, cars and free or subsidised goods or services)

(b)   **Post-employment benefits** (eg pensions, other retirement benefits, life insurance and medical care)

(c)   **Other long-term benefits** (eg long-service leave, sabbatical leave, long-term disability benefits and, if they are not payable within twelve months after the end of the period, profit sharing, bonuses and deferred compensation)

(d)   **Termination benefits**

(e)   **Equity compensation benefits**

Compensation includes amounts paid on behalf of a parent of the entity in respect of the entity.

Disclosures

Where **transactions have taken place** between related parties, the entity should disclose the **nature** of the related party relationships, as well as information about the **transactions and outstanding balances** necessary for an understanding of the potential effect of the relationship on the financial statements. As a minimum, disclosures must include:

(a)   The **amount of the transactions**

(b)   The **amount of outstanding balances** and:

    (i)   Their terms and conditions, including whether they are secured, and the nature of the consideration to be provided in settlement

    (ii)   Details of any guarantees given or received

(c)   Allowances for **doubtful debts** related to the amount of outstanding balances

(d)   The **expense** recognised during the period in respect of **irrecoverable debts** due from related parties

The above disclosures shall be made separately for **each** of the following categories:

(a)   The parent
(b)   Entities with joint control or significant influence over the entity
(c)   Subsidiaries
(d)   Associates

(e)   Joint ventures in which the entity is a venturer

(f)   Key management personnel of the entity or its parent

(g)   Other related parties

Items of a similar nature may be **disclosed in aggregate unless** separate disclosure is necessary for an understanding of the effect on the financial statements.

Disclosures that related party transactions were made on terms equivalent to those that prevail in arm's length transactions are made only if such disclosures can be substantiated.

2 IFRS 8: Operating segments

Large entities produce a wide range of products and services, often in several different countries. Further information on how the overall results of entities are made up from each of these product or geographical areas will help the users of the financial statements. This is the reason for **segment reporting**.

- The entity's **past performance** will be better understood
- The entity's **risks and returns** may be better assessed
- More **informed judgements** may be made about the entity as a whole

Risks and returns of a **diversified, multi-national company** can only be assessed by looking at the individual risks and rewards attached to groups of products or services or in different groups of products or services or in different geographical areas. These are subject to differing rates of profitability, opportunities for growth, future prospects and risks.

Segment reporting is covered by IFRS 8 *Operating segments*.

An entity must disclose information to enable users of its financial statements to evaluate the nature and financial effects of the business activities in which it engages and the economic environments in which it operates.

Only entities whose **equity or debt securities are publicly traded** (ie on a stock exchange) need disclose segment information. In group accounts, only **consolidated** segmental information needs to be shown. (The statement also applies to entities filing or in the process of filing financial statements for the purpose of issuing instruments.)

Definition of operating segment

Operating segment: This is a component of an entity:

(a) That engages in business activities from which it may earn revenues and incur expenses (including revenues and expenses relating to transactions with other components of the same entity)

(b) Whose operating results are regularly reviewed by the entity's chief operating decision maker to make decisions about resources to be allocated to the segment and assess its performance, and

(c) For which discrete financial information is available.   *(IFRS 8: para. 5)*

The term 'chief operating decision maker' identifies a function, not necessarily a manager with a specific title. That function is to allocate resources and to assess the performance of the entity's operating segments.

Aggregation

Two or more operating segments may be **aggregated** if the segments have **similar economic characteristics**, and the segments are similar in each of the following respects:

- The **nature of the products or services**
- The **nature of the production process**
- The **type or class of customer for their products or services**
- The **methods used to distribute their products or provide their services**
- If applicable, the **nature of the regulatory environment** *(IFRS 8: para. 12)*

Determining reportable segments

An entity must report separate information about **each operating segment** that:

(a) Has been identified as meeting the **definition of an operating segment**; and

(b) Segment total is **10% or more of total:**

    (i) **Revenue** (internal and external); or

    (ii) **Profit** of **all segments not reporting a loss** (or all segments in loss if greater); or

    (iii) **Assets.**

At least **75% of the entity's total external revenue** must be reported by the operating segments identified. Where this is not the case, additional segments must be identified (even if they do not meet the 10% thresholds).

Two or more operating segments **below** the thresholds may be aggregated to produce a reportable segment if the segments have similar economic characteristics, and the segments are similar in a **majority** of the aggregation criteria above.

Operating segments that do not meet **any of the quantitative thresholds** may be reported separately if management believes that information about the segment would be useful to users of the financial statements.

The following decision tree will assist in identifying reportable segments.

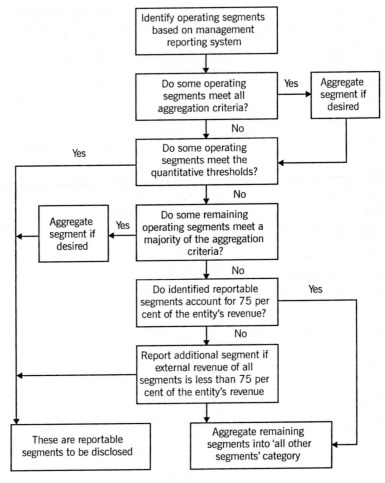

IFRS 8 disclosures are of:

- Operating segment profit or loss
- Segment assets
- Segment liabilities
- Certain income and expense items

Disclosures are also required about the revenues derived from products and services and about the countries in which revenues are earned or assets held, even if that information is not used by management in making decisions.

Here is an example taken from the *Implementation Guidance* to IFRS 8, which is presented for illustration purposes only.

	Car parts $	Vessel $	Software $	Electronics $	Finance $	All other $	Totals $
Revenues from external customers	3,000	5,000	9,500	12,000	5,000	(a) 1,000	35,500
Inter-segment revenues	–	–	3,000	1,500	–	–	4,500
Interest revenue	450	800	1,000	1,500	–	–	3,750
Interest expense	350	600	700	1,100	–	–	2,750
Net interest revenue (b)	–	–	–	–	1,000	–	1,000
Depreciation and amortisation	200	100	50	1,500	1,100	–	2,950
Reportable segment profit	200	70	900	2,300	500	100	4,070
Other material non-cash items: Impairment of assets	–	200	–	–	–	–	200
Reportable segment assets	2,000	5,000	3,000	12,000	57,000	2,000	81,000
Expenditure for reportable segment non-current assets	300	700	500	800	600	–	2,900
Reportable segment liabilities	1,050	3,000	1,800	8,000	30,000	–	43,850

(a) Revenues from segments below the quantitative thresholds are attributable to four operating segments of the company. Those segments include a small property business, an electronics equipment rental business, a software consulting practice and a warehouse leasing operation. None of those segments has ever met any of the quantitative thresholds for determining reportable segments.

(b) The finance segment derives a majority of its revenue from interest. Management primarily relies on net interest revenue, not the gross revenue and expense amounts, in managing that segment. Therefore, as permitted by IFRS 8, only the net amount is disclosed.

Part B 14: Related party disclosures and segment reporting

In April 2009 under the annual IFRS Improvements, IFRS 8 was amended to state that segment assets no longer have to be disclosed if they are not reported internally. This is effective from January 2010.

Part C

Group financial statements

Constitution of a group

15

1 Group accounts

There are many reasons for businesses to operate as groups; for the goodwill associated with the names of the subsidiaries, for tax or legal purposes and so forth. In many countries, company law requires that the results of a group should be presented as a whole. In traditional accounting terminology, a group of **companies** consists of a **parent company** and one or more **subsidiary companies** which are controlled by the parent company.

We will be looking at five accounting standards in this and the next three chapters.

- IAS 27 *(revised) Separate financial statements*
- IFRS 10 *Consolidated financial statements*
- IFRS 3 *Business combinations*
- IAS 28 *Investments in associates and joint ventures*
- IFRS 12 *Disclosure of interests in other entities*

These standards are all concerned with different aspects of group accounts, but there is some overlap between them, particularly between IFRS 10 and IAS 27.

In this and the next chapter we will concentrate on IAS 27 and IFRS 10, which cover the basic group definitions and consolidation procedures of a parent-subsidiary relationship. First of all, however, we will look at all the important definitions involved in group accounts, which **determine how to treat each particular type of investment** in group accounts.

Definitions

Control. An investor controls and investee when the investor is exposed, or has rights, to variable returns from its involvement with the investee and has the ability to affect those returns through its power over the investee.

(IFRS 10: para. 6)

Power. Existing rights that give the current ability to direct the relevant activities.

(IFRS 10: Appendix)

Subsidiary. An entity that is controlled by another entity.   *(IFRS 10: Appendix)*

Parent. An entity that controls one or more entities.   *(IFRS 10: Appendix)*

Group. A parent and its subsidiaries.   *(IFRS 10: Appendix)*

Associate. An entity over which an investor has significant influence.

(IAS 28: para. 3)

Significant influence. The power to participate in the financial and operating policy decisions of an investee but it is not control or joint control over those policies.

(IAS 28: para. 3)

We can summarise the different types of investment and the required accounting for them as follows.

Investment	Criteria	Required treatment in group accounts
Subsidiary	Control	Full consolidation
Associate	Significant influence	Equity accounting
Investment which is none of the above	Asset held for accretion of wealth	As for single company accounts per IFRS 9

Investments in subsidiaries

The important point here is **control**. In most cases, this will involve the holding company or parent owning a majority of the ordinary shares in the subsidiary (to which normal voting rights are attached). There are circumstances, however, when the parent may own only a minority of the voting power in the subsidiary, **but** the parent still has control.

IFRS 10 provides a definition of control and identifies three separate elements of control.

An investor controls an investee if, and only if, it has all of the following:

(a) Power over the investee

(b) Exposure to, or rights to, variable returns from its involvement with the investee

(c) The ability to use its power over the investee to affect the amount of the investor's returns *(IFRS 10: para. 7)*

If there are changes to one or more of these three elements of control, then an investor should reassess whether it controls an investee.

Power (as defined above) can be obtained directly from ownership of the majority of voting rights or can be derived from other rights, such as:

- Rights to appoint, reassign or remove key management personnel who can direct the relevant activities

- Rights to appoint or remove another entity that directs the relevant activities

- Rights to direct the investee to enter into, or veto changes to, transactions for the benefit of the investor

- Other rights, such as those specified in a management contract

IFRS 10 requires a parent to present consolidated financial statements, in which the accounts of the parent and subsidiary (or subsidiaries) are combined and presented as **a single entity**.

Investments in associates

This type of investment is something less than a subsidiary, but more than a simple investment. The key criterion here is **significant influence**. This is defined as the 'power to participate', but not to 'control' (which would make the investment a subsidiary).

Significant influence can be determined by the holding of voting rights (usually attached to shares) in the entity. IAS 28 states that if an investor holds **20% or more** of the voting power of the investee, it can be presumed that the investor has significant influence over the investee, unless it can be clearly shown that this is not the case.

Significant influence can be presumed not to exist if the investor holds **less than 20%** of the voting power of the investee, unless it can be demonstrated otherwise.

The **existence of significant influence** is evidenced in one or more of the following ways.

(a) Representation on the **board of directors** (or equivalent) of the investee
(b) Participation in the **policy making process**
(c) **Material transactions** between investor and investee
(d) Interchange of management personnel
(e) Provision of essential technical information

2 Consolidated and separate financial statements

> **Consolidated financial statements.** The financial statements of a group in which the assets, liabilities, equity, income, expenses and cash flows of the parent and its subsidiaries are presented as those of a single economic entity.
>
> *(IFRS 10: Appendix)*

When a parent issues consolidated financial statements, it should consolidate **all subsidiaries**, both foreign and domestic.

Exemption from preparing group accounts

A parent **need not present** consolidated financial statements if and only if **all** of the following hold:

(a)   The parent is itself a **wholly-owned subsidiary** or it is a **partially owned subsidiary** of another entity and its other owners, including those not otherwise entitled to vote, have been informed about, and do not object to, the parent not presenting consolidated financial statements

(b)   Its securities are **not publicly traded**

(c)   It is **not in the process of issuing securities** in public securities markets

(d)   The **ultimate or intermediate parent** publishes consolidated financial statements that comply with International Financial Reporting Standards

A parent that does not present consolidated financial statements must comply with the IAS 27 rules on separate financial statements (discussed later in this section).

Potential voting rights

An entity may own share warrants, share call options, or other similar instruments that are **convertible into ordinary shares** in another entity. If these are exercised or converted they may give the entity voting power or reduce another party's voting power over the financial and operating policies of the other entity (potential voting rights). The **existence and effect** of potential voting rights, including potential voting rights held by another entity, should be considered when assessing whether an entity has control over another entity (and therefore has a subsidiary).

Exclusion of a subsidiary from consolidation

The rules on exclusion of subsidiaries from consolidation are necessarily strict, because this is a common method used by entities to manipulate their results. If a subsidiary which carries a large amount of debt can be excluded, then the gearing of the group as a whole will be improved. In other words, this is a way of taking debt **out of the statement of financial position**.

IAS 27 did originally allow a subsidiary to be excluded from consolidation where **control is intended to be temporary**. This exclusion was then removed by IFRS 5.

Subsidiaries held for sale are accounted for in accordance with IFRS 5 *Non-current assets held for sale and discontinued operations*.

It has been argued in the past that subsidiaries should be excluded from consolidation on the grounds of **dissimilar activities,** ie the activities of the subsidiary are so different to the activities of the other companies within the group that to include its results in the consolidation would be misleading. IAS 27and IFRS 10 both reject this argument: exclusion on these grounds is not justified because better (relevant) information can be provided about such subsidiaries by consolidating their results and then giving additional information about the different business activities of the subsidiary.

The previous version of IAS 27 permitted exclusion where the subsidiary operates under **severe long-term restrictions** and these significantly impair its ability to transfer funds to the parent. This exclusion has now been **removed**. Control must actually be lost for exclusion to occur.

Different reporting dates

In most cases, all group companies will prepare accounts to the same reporting date. One or more subsidiaries may, however, prepare accounts to a different reporting date from the parent and the bulk of other subsidiaries in the group.

In such cases the subsidiary may prepare additional statements to the reporting date of the rest of the group, for consolidation purposes. If this is not possible, the subsidiary's accounts may still be used for the consolidation, provided that the gap between the reporting dates is **three months or less**.

Where a subsidiary's accounts are drawn up to a different accounting date, **adjustments should be made** for the effects of significant transactions or other events that occur between that date and the parent's reporting date.

Uniform accounting policies

Consolidated financial statements should be prepared using **the same accounting policies** for like transactions and other events in similar circumstances.

Adjustments must be made where members of a group use different accounting policies, so that their financial statements are suitable for consolidation.

Date of inclusion/exclusion

The results of subsidiary undertakings are included in the consolidated financial statements from:

(a)   The date of 'acquisition', ie the **date control passes to the parent**, to
(b)   The date of 'disposal', ie the **date control passes from the parent**.

Once an investment is no longer a subsidiary, it should be treated as an associate under IAS 28 (if applicable) or as an investment under IFRS 9.

Accounting for subsidiaries and associates in the parent's separate financial statements

A parent company will usually produce its own single company financial statements. In these statements, investments in subsidiaries and associates included in the consolidated financial statements should be *either*:

(a)   Accounted for at **cost**; or
(b)   In accordance with **IFRS 9**; or
(c)   Using the **equity method** as described in IAS 28.

Where subsidiaries are **classified as held for sale** in accordance with IFRS 5 they should be accounted for in accordance with IFRS 5.

3 Content of group accounts and group structure

In simple terms a set of consolidated accounts is prepared by **adding together** the assets and liabilities of the parent company and each subsidiary. The **whole** of the assets and liabilities of each company are included, even though some subsidiaries may be only partly owned. The 'equity and liabilities' section of the statement of financial position will indicate how much of the net assets are attributable to the group and how much to outside investors in partly owned subsidiaries. These **outside investors** are known as the **non-controlling interest**.

> **Non-controlling interest.** The equity in a subsidiary not attributable, directly or indirectly, to a parent.   *(IFRS 10: Appendix)*

Non-controlling interest should be presented in the consolidated statement of financial position **within equity, separately from the parent shareholders' equity**.

Most parent companies present their own individual accounts and their group accounts in a single **package**. The package typically comprises the following.

- **Parent company financial statements**, which will include 'investments in subsidiary undertakings' as an asset in the statement of financial position, and income from subsidiaries (dividends) in the statement of profit or loss and other comprehensive income
- **Consolidated statement of financial position**
- **Consolidated statement of profit or loss and other comprehensive income**
- **Consolidated statement of cash flows**

It may not be necessary to publish all of the parent company's financial statements, depending on local or national regulations.

Group structure

With the difficulties of definition and disclosure dealt with, let us now look at group structures. The simplest are those in which a parent company has only a **direct interest** in the shares of its subsidiary companies. For example:

S1 Co is a wholly owned subsidiary of P Co. S2 Co, S3 Co and S4 Co are partly owned subsidiaries; a proportion of the shares in these companies is held by outside investors.

Often a parent will have **indirect holdings** in its subsidiary companies. This can lead to more complex group structures.

(a)

P Co owns 51% of the equity shares in S Co, which is therefore its subsidiary. S Co in its turn owns 51% of the equity shares in SS Co. SS Co is therefore a subsidiary of S Co and consequently a subsidiary of P Co. SS Co would describe S Co as its parent (or holding) company and P Co as its ultimate parent company.

Note that although P Co can control the assets and business of SS Co by virtue of the chain of control, its interest in the assets of SS Co is only 26%. This can be seen by considering a dividend of $100 paid by SS Co: as a 51% shareholder, S Co would receive $51; P Co would have an interest in 51% of this $51 = $26.01.

(b)

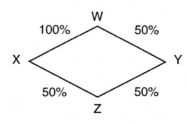

Part C 15: Constitution of a group

W Co owns 100% of the equity of X Co and 50% of the equity of Y Co. X Co and Y Co each own 50% of the equity of Z Co. Assume that:

(i)   W Co does not control the composition of Y Co's board, nor can it cast a majority of votes on the board

(ii) W Co does not hold or control more than 50% of the **voting rights** in Y Co, either directly or by agreement with other investors

(iii) W Co does not have the power to govern the financial or operating policies of Y Co by virtue of statute or an agreement

(iv) None of the above apply to either X Co's or Y Co's holdings in Z Co

In other words, because W Co is not in co operation with the holder(s) of the other 50% of the shares in Y Co, neither Y nor Z can be considered subsidiaries.

In that case:

(i)   X Co is a subsidiary of W Co

(ii) Y Co is not a subsidiary of W Co

(iii) Z Co is not a subsidiary of either X Co or Y Co. Consequently, it is not a subsidiary of W Co

If Z Co pays a dividend of $100, X Co and Y Co will each receive $50. The interest of W Co in this dividend is as follows.

	$
Through X Co (100% × $50)	50
Through Y Co (50% × $50)	25
	75

Although W Co has an interest in 75% of Z Co's assets, Z Co is not a subsidiary of W Co.

(c)

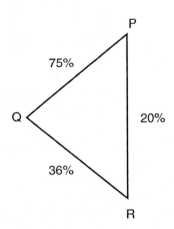

Q Co is a subsidiary of P Co. P Co therefore has indirect control over 36% of R Co's equity. P Co also has direct control over 20% of R Co's equity. R Co is therefore a subsidiary of P Co, although P Co's interest in R Co's assets is only 20% + (75% × 36%) = 47%.

Examples (b) and (c) illustrate an important point: in deciding whether a company A holds more than 50% of the equity (or equivalent) of an entity B it is necessary to aggregate:

- Shares (or equivalent) in B held directly by A
- Shares (or equivalent) in B held by entities which are subsidiaries of A

4 Group accounts: the related parties issue

IAS 24 draws attention to the significance of related party relationships and transactions – that transactions between the parties may not be 'at arm's length' and that users of the accounts must be made aware of this, as it may affect their view of the financial statements.

Individual company financial statements

The relationship between a parent and a subsidiary is the most obvious example of a related party relationship and it offers a number of opportunities for manipulating results. Some of these may be aimed at improving the parent's individual financial statements.

Any of the following could take place:

- The subsidiary sells goods to the parent company at an artificially low price. This increases parent company profit while reducing profit in the subsidiary, thus increasing profit available for distribution to parent company shareholders at the expense of the non-controlling interest.

- The parent sells goods to the subsidiary at an artificially high price. This has the same result as above.

- The subsidiary makes a loan to the parent at an artificially low rate of interest or the parent makes a loan to the subsidiary at an artificially high rate of interest. The loans will be cancelled on consolidation but the interest payments will transfer profits from the subsidiary to the parent.

- The parent can sell an asset to the subsidiary at an amount in excess of its carrying amount. This again serves to transfer profit (and cash) to the parent.

Consolidated financial statements

The transactions above seek to improve the **individual** parent company accounts at the expense of the individual subsidiary accounts. Dividends are paid to shareholders on the basis of these individual company financial statements, not the consolidated financial statements.

The tightening up of the opportunities for excluding a subsidiary from consolidation under IFRS have reduced the opportunities for improving the appearance of the **consolidated** financial statements. Prior to this, a number of possibilities could be exploited:

- A group could obtain loans via a subsidiary, which was not then consolidated. The loan would not appear in the consolidated statement of financial position and group gearing (% of capital provided by loans) would appear lower than it actually was.

- Sale and leaseback transactions could be carried out in which assets were sold to a non-consolidated subsidiary and leased back under a short-term lease. This enabled the asset and its associated borrowings to be removed from the statement of financial position.

Disposal of subsidiaries

While the situations above are all concerned with improving the appearance of the parent company or group financial statements at the expense of those of the subsidiary, there may be occasions where the **opposite** is the intention.

For instance, when a parent company has decided to dispose of its shares in a poorly-performing subsidiary, it may seek to enhance the results of that subsidiary for the purpose of selling at a profit. In this case, transactions such as those above may be undertaken in the other direction – to transfer profit from the parent to the subsidiary.

Effect on trading

Even where no related party transactions have taken place, the parent/subsidiary relationship can still affect how the parties do business. For instance if, prior to acquisition by the parent, the subsidiary had a major customer or supplier who was a competitor of the parent, that trading arrangement can be expected to cease. The subsidiary may itself have been a competitor of the parent, in which case it may now have had to withdraw from certain markets in favour of the parent.

5 Disclosure

IFRS 12 *Disclosure of interests in other entities* was issued in May 2011.

The objective of IFRS 12 is to require the disclosure of information that enables users of the financial statements of an entity to evaluate:

- The nature of, and risks associated with, its interests in other entities

- The effect of those interests on its financial position, financial performance and cash flows

The standard requires disclosure of:

- The significant judgements and assumptions made in determining the nature of an interest in another entity

- Information about interests in subsidiaries and associates

Disclosures regarding subsidiaries

In respect of subsidiaries an entity should disclose information regarding:

(a) The interest held by non-controlling interests in the groups relevant activities and cash flows

(b) The nature and extent of any significant restrictions on the investor's ability to use group assets and liabilities

(c) The consequences of any change in ownership in a subsidiary (whether or not control is lost)

Disclosures regarding associates and joint arrangements

In respect of associates an entity should disclose information regarding:

(a) The nature, extent and financial effects of the entity's interests in associates, including the nature and effects of its contractual relationship with other investors having significant influence over associates

(b) The nature of, and changes in, the risks associated with its interests in associates

Separate financial statements – IAS 27

Where a parent chooses to take advantage of the exemptions from preparing consolidated financial statements under IAS 27 the **separate financial statements** must disclose:

(a) The fact that the financial statements are separate financial statements; that the exemption from consolidation has been used; the name and country of incorporation of the entity whose consolidated financial statements that comply with IFRSs have been published; and the address where those consolidated financial statements are obtainable

(b) A list of significant investments in subsidiaries, jointly controlled entities and associates, including the name, country of incorporation, proportion of ownership interest and, if different, proportion of voting power held

(c) A description of the method used to account for the investments listed under (b)

When a parent prepares separate financial statements in addition to consolidated financial statements, the separate financial statements must disclose:

(a) The fact that the statements are separate financial statements and the reasons why they have been prepared if not required by law

(b) Information about investments and the method used to account for them, as above

The consolidated statement of financial position

16

1 IFRS 10: Summary of consolidation procedures

The financial statements of a parent and its subsidiaries are **combined on a line-by-line basis** by adding together like items of assets, liabilities, equity, income and expenses.

The following steps are then taken, in order that the consolidated financial statements should **show financial information about the group as if it was a single entity**.

(a) The carrying amount of the parent's **investment in each subsidiary** and the parent's **portion of equity** of each subsidiary are eliminated or cancelled.

(b) **Non-controlling interests in the net income of consolidated subsidiaries** are adjusted against group income, to arrive at the net income attributable to the owners of the parent.

(c) **Non-controlling interests in the net assets of consolidated subsidiaries** should be presented separately in the consolidated statement of financial position.

Other matters to be dealt with include the following.

(a) **Goodwill on consolidation** should be dealt with according to IFRS 3

(b) **Dividends paid** by a subsidiary must be accounted for

IFRS 10 states that all intra group balances and transactions, and the resulting **unrealised profits**, should be **eliminated in full**. **Unrealised losses** resulting from intragroup transactions should also be eliminated unless cost can be recovered.

Cancellation and part cancellation

The preparation of a consolidated statement of financial position, in a very simple form, consists of two procedures.

(a) Take the individual accounts of the parent company and each subsidiary and **cancel out items** which appear as an asset in one company and a liability in another.

(b) Add together all the uncancelled assets and liabilities throughout the group.

Items requiring cancellation may include the following.

(a)   The asset **'shares in subsidiary companies'** which appears in the parent company's accounts will be matched with the liability 'share capital' in the subsidiaries' accounts.

(b)   There may be **intra group trading** within the group. For example, S Co may sell goods on credit to P Co. P Co would then be a receivable in the accounts of S Co, while S Co would be a payable in the accounts of P Co.

Part cancellation

An item may appear in the statements of financial position of a parent company and its subsidiary, but not at the same amounts.

(a)   The parent company may have acquired **shares in the subsidiary** at a price **greater or less than their par value**. The asset will appear in the parent company's accounts at cost, while the liability will appear in the subsidiary's accounts at par value. This raises the issue of **goodwill**, which is dealt with later in this chapter.

(b)   Even if the parent company acquired shares at par value, it **may not** have **acquired all the shares of the subsidiary** (so the subsidiary may be only partly owned). This raises the issue of **non-controlling interests**, which are also dealt with later in this chapter.

(c)   The inter company trading balances may be out of step because of **goods or cash in transit**.

(d)   One company may have **issued loan stock** of which a **proportion only** is taken up by the other company.

The procedure for items (c) and (d) is to **cancel as far as possible**. The remaining uncancelled amounts will appear in the consolidated statement of financial position.

(a)   **Uncancelled loan stock** will appear as a **liability of the group**.

(b)   **Uncancelled balances on intra group accounts** represent **goods or cash in transit**, which will appear in the consolidated statement of financial position.

2 Non-controlling interests – IFRS 3

It was mentioned earlier that the total assets and liabilities of subsidiary companies are included in the consolidated statement of financial position, even in the case of subsidiaries which are only partly owned. A proportion of the net assets of such subsidiaries in fact belongs to investors from outside the group **(non-controlling interests)**.

IFRS 3 allows two alternative ways of calculating non-controlling interest in the group statement of financial position. Non-controlling interest can be valued at:

(a)   Its proportionate share of the fair value of the subsidiary's net assets; or

(b)   Full (or fair) value (usually based on the market value of the shares held by the non-controlling interest).

The following example shows non-controlling interest calculated at its proportionate share of the subsidiary's net assets.

Example: Non-controlling interest

P Co has owned 75% of the share capital of S Co since the date of S Co's incorporation. Their latest statements of financial position are given below.

P CO
STATEMENT OF FINANCIAL POSITION

	$	$
Assets		
Non-current assets		
Property, plant and equipment	50,000	
30,000 $1 ordinary shares in S Co at cost	30,000	
		80,000
Current assets		45,000
Total assets		125,000
Equity and liabilities		
Equity		
80,000 $1 ordinary shares	80,000	
Retained earnings	25,000	
		105,000
Current liabilities		20,000
Total equity and liabilities		125,000

S CO
STATEMENT OF FINANCIAL POSITION

	$	$
Assets		
Property, plant and equipment		35,000
Current assets		35,000
Total assets		70,000
Equity and liabilities		
Equity		
40,000 $1 ordinary shares	40,000	
Retained earnings	10,000	
		50,000
Current liabilities		20,000
Total equity and liabilities		70,000

The consolidated statement of financial position will be as follows.

P GROUP
CONSOLIDATED STATEMENT OF FINANCIAL POSITION

	$	$
Assets		
Property, plant and equipment		85,000
Current assets		80,000
Total assets		165,000
Equity and liabilities		
Equity attributable to owners of the parent		
Share capital	80,000	
Retained earnings $(25,000 + (75\% \times \$10,000))$	32,500	
		112,500
Non-controlling interest		12,500
		125,000
Current liabilities		40,000
Total equity and liabilities		165,000

3 Dividends paid by a subsidiary

When a subsidiary company pays a **dividend** during the year the accounting treatment is not difficult. Suppose S Co, a 60% subsidiary of P Co, pays a dividend of $1,000 on the last day of its accounting period. Its total reserves before paying the dividend stood at $5,000.

(a) $400 of the dividend is paid to non-controlling shareholders. The cash leaves the group and will not appear anywhere in the consolidated statement of financial position.

(b) The parent company receives $600 of the dividend, debiting cash and crediting profit or loss. This will be cancelled on consolidation.

(c) The remaining balance of retained earnings in S Co's statement of financial position ($4,000) will be consolidated in the normal way. The group's share (60% × $4,000 = $2,400) will be included in group retained earnings in the statement of financial position; the non-controlling interest share (40% × $4,000 = $1,600) is credited to the non-controlling interest account in the statement of financial position.

4 Goodwill arising on consolidation

When a company P Co wishes to **purchase shares** in a company S Co it must pay the previous owners of those shares. The most obvious form of payment would be in **cash**.

However, the previous shareholders might be prepared to accept some other form of consideration. For example, they might accept an agreed number of **shares** in P Co. P Co would then issue new shares in the agreed number and allot them to the former shareholders of S Co. This kind of deal might be attractive to P Co since it avoids the need for a heavy cash outlay. The former shareholders of S Co would retain an indirect interest in that company's profitability via their new holding in its parent company.

Suppose P Co. wishes to purchase all of the $40,000 shares in S Co. The shareholders of S Co agreed to accept one $1 ordinary share in P Co for every two $1 ordinary shares in S Co. P Co would then need to issue and allot 20,000 new $1 shares. How would this transaction be recorded in the books of P Co?

The 40,000 $1 shares acquired in S Co are thought to have a value of $60,000. The former shareholders of S Co have presumably agreed to accept 20,000 shares in P Co because they consider each of those shares to have a value of $3. The transaction is recorded as follows:

DEBIT	Investment in S Co	$60,000	
CREDIT	Share capital		$20,000
	Share premium account		$40,000

The amount which P Co records in its books as the cost of its investment in S Co may be more or less than the book value of the assets it acquires. Suppose that S Co in the previous example has nil reserves and nil liabilities, so that its share capital of $40,000 is balanced by tangible assets with a book value of $40,000. For simplicity, assume that the book value of S Co's assets is the same as their market or fair value.

Now when the directors of P Co agree to pay $60,000 for a 100% investment in S Co they must believe that, in addition to its tangible assets of $40,000, S Co must also have intangible assets worth $20,000. This amount of $20,000 paid over and above the value of the tangible assets acquired is **goodwill arising on consolidation**.

Following the normal cancellation procedure the $40,000 share capital in S Co's statement of financial position could be cancelled against $40,000 of the 'investment in S Co' in the statement of financial position of P Co. This would leave a $20,000 debit uncancelled in the parent company's accounts and this $20,000 would appear in the consolidated statement of financial position under the caption 'Intangible non-current assets: goodwill arising on consolidation'.

Goodwill and pre acquisition profits

Up to now we have assumed that S Co had nil retained earnings when its shares were purchased by P Co. Assuming instead that S Co had earned profits of $8,000 in the period before acquisition, its statement of financial position just before the purchase would look as follows.

	$
Total assets	48,000
Share capital	40,000
Retained earnings	8,000
	48,000

If P Co now purchases all the shares in S Co it will acquire total assets worth $48,000 at a cost of $60,000. Clearly in this case S Co's intangible assets (goodwill) are being valued at $12,000. It should be apparent that any earnings retained by the subsidiary **prior to its acquisition** by the parent company must be **incorporated in the cancellation** process so as to arrive at a figure for goodwill arising on consolidation. In other words, not only S Co's share capital, but also its **pre acquisition** retained earnings, must be cancelled against the asset 'investment in S Co' in the accounts of the parent company. The uncancelled balance of $12,000 appears in the consolidated statement of financial position.

The consequence of this is that any **pre acquisition retained earnings of a subsidiary company are not aggregated with the parent company's retained earnings** in the consolidated statement of financial position. The figure of consolidated retained earnings comprises the retained earnings of the parent company plus the **post acquisition retained earnings only of subsidiary companies**. The post-acquisition retained earnings are simply retained earnings now less retained earnings at acquisition.

Example: goodwill and pre acquisition profits

P Co acquired all of the ordinary shares of S Co for $80,000 on 31 March when its draft statement of financial position was as follows:

	$
Current assets	60,000
Equity	
50,000 ordinary shares of $1 each	50,000
Retained earnings	10,000
	60,000

The goodwill is calculated as:

	$	$
Consideration transferred		80,000
Net assets acquired as represented by:		
Ordinary share capital	50,000	
Retained earnings on acquisition	10,000	
		(60,000)
Goodwill		20,000

Goodwill and non-controlling interest

Not let us look at what would happen if P Co had obtained less than 100% of the shares of S Co.

If P Co had paid $80,000 for 40,000 shares in S Co, the goodwill working would be as follows:

	$
Consideration transferred	80,000
Non-controlling interest (60,000 × 20%)	12,000
Net assets acquired	(60,000)
Goodwill	32,000

The goodwill has been increased by the non-controlling interest – P Co has paid the same amount but acquired a smaller shareholding.

Non-controlling interest at fair value

IFRS 3 gives entities the option of valuing non-controlling interest at fair value. The thinking behind this is that the non-controlling interest, in purchasing their shares, also purchased goodwill in the subsidiary, and that the traditional method of consolidation does not show this goodwill.

IFRS 3 suggests that the closest approximation to fair value will be the market price of the shares held by non-controlling shareholders just before acquisition by the parent.

Continuing our example above, we will assume that the market price of the shares was $1.25. The goodwill calculation will then be as follows:

	$
Consideration transferred	80,000
Non-controlling interest (10,000 × $1.25)	12,500
Net assets at acquisition	(60,000)
Goodwill	32,500

Goodwill is $500 higher than goodwill calculated measuring non-controlling interest at its share of the net assets of the subsidiary. This $500 represents the **goodwill attributable to the non-controlling interest.**

Non-controlling interest at year end

Where the option is used to value non-controlling interest at fair value, this applies only to **non-controlling interest at acquisition**. At the year end, the non-controlling interest is measured at its share of the subsidiary's year end net assets, subject to adjustments for intra-group trading which we will cover later. However, **where the fair value option has been used**, goodwill at the year end will include the additional goodwill attributable to the non-controlling interest, in the example above $500. The other side of the entry is to **add the goodwill onto the non-controlling interest at the year end.**

Example: non-controlling interest at fair value

P acquired 75% of the shares in S on 1 January 2007 when S had retained earnings of $15,000. The market price of S's shares just before the date of acquisition was $1.60. P values non-controlling interest at fair value. Goodwill is not impaired.

The statements of financial position of P and S at 31 December 20X7 were as follows:

	P $	S $
Property, plant and equipment	60,000	50,000
Shares in S	68,000	–
	128,000	50,000
Current assets	52,000	35,000
	180,000	85,000
Share capital – $1 shares	100,000	50,000
Retained earnings	70,000	25,000
	170,000	75,000
Current liabilities	10,000	10,000
	180,000	85,000

Now we will prepare the consolidated statement of financial position of the P Group.

CONSOLIDATED STATEMENT OF FINANCIAL POSITION

	$
Assets	
Non-current assets	
Property plant and equipment (60,000 + 50,000)	110,000
Goodwill (W1)	23,000
Current assets (52,000 + 35,000)	87,000
Total assets	220,000
Equity and liabilities	
Equity attributable to the owners of P	
Share capital	100,000
Retained earnings (W2)	77,500
	177,500
Non-controlling interest (W3)	22,500
Total equity	200,000
Current liabilities (10,000 + 10,000)	20,000
Total equity and liabilities	220,000

Workings

1   *Goodwill*

		$
Consideration transferred		68,000
Non-controlling interest at acquisition (12,500 shares @ $1.60)		20,000
Net assets of S at acquisition (50,000 + 15,000)		(65,000)
Goodwill (parent and non-controlling interest)		23,000
Non-controlling interest at fair value (as above)		20,000
Non-controlling share of net assets at acquisition (65,000 × 25%)		(16,250)
Goodwill attributable to non-controlling interest		3,750

2   *Retained earnings*

	P	S
	$	$
Per statement of financial position	70,000	25,000
Less pre- acquisition		(15,000)
		10,000
Group share of S (10,000 × 75%)	7,500	
Group retained earnings	77,500	

3   *Non-controlling interest at year end*

	$
Share of net assets of S (75,000 × 25%)	18,750
Goodwill (W1)	3,750
	22,500

Note that non-controlling interest at the year end can also be calculated as follows:

	$
Non-controlling interest at acquisition	20,000
Share of post-acquisition retained earnings (10,000 × 25%)	2,500
	22,500

Effect of non-controlling interest at fair value

You can see from the above example that the use of the fair value option increases goodwill and non-controlling interest by the same amount. That amount represents goodwill attributable to the shares held by non-controlling shareholders. It is not necessarily proportionate to the goodwill attributed to the parent. The parent may have paid more to acquire a controlling interest.

Part C 16: The consolidated statement of financial position

Impairment of goodwill

Goodwill arising on consolidation is subjected to an annual impairment review and impairment may be expressed as an amount or as a percentage.

However, when non-controlling interest is valued at **fair value** the goodwill in the statement of financial position includes goodwill attributable to the non-controlling interest. In this case the double entry will reflect the non-controlling interest proportion based on their shareholding.

In our solution above the non-controlling interest holds 25%. If the goodwill of $23,000 was impaired by 20% the double entry for this would be:

	$		$
DEBIT Retained earnings	3,450	CREDIT Goodwill	4,600
DEBIT Non-controlling interest	1,150		

Non-controlling interest at the year end would then be $21,350.

Gain on a bargain purchase

Goodwill arising on consolidation is one form of **purchased goodwill**, and is governed by IFRS 3. As explained in an earlier chapter IFRS 3 requires that goodwill arising on consolidation should be **capitalised in the consolidated statement of financial position** and **reviewed for impairment every year**.

Goodwill arising on consolidation is the difference between the cost of an acquisition and the value of the subsidiary's net assets acquired. This difference can be negative: the aggregate of the fair values of the separable net assets acquired may **exceed** what the parent company paid for them. IFRS 3 refers to this as a 'bargain purchase'. In this situation:

(a)   An entity should first **re-assess** the amounts at which it has measured both the cost of the combination and the acquiree's identifiable net assets. This exercise should identify any errors.

(b)   Any **excess remaining** should be **recognised immediately in profit or loss**.

Forms of consideration

The consideration paid by the parent for the shares in the subsidiary can take different forms and this will affect the calculation of goodwill. Here are some examples:

Contingent consideration

The parent acquired 60% of the subsidiary's $100m share capital on 1 January 20X6 for a cash payment of $150m and a further payment of $50m on 31 March 20X7 if the subsidiary's post acquisition profits have exceeded an agreed figure by that date.

In the financial statements for the year to 31 December 20X6 $50m will be added to the cost of the combination, discounted as appropriate.

IFRS 3 requires the acquisition-date **fair value** of contingent consideration to be recognised as part of the consideration for the acquiree. The acquirer may be required to pay contingent consideration in the form of equity or of a debt instrument or cash. A debt instrument should be presented as under IAS 32. Contingent consideration can also be an asset, if the consideration has already been transferred and the acquirer has the right to return of some of it, if certain considerations are met.

Note. The previous version of IFRS 3 only required contingent consideration to be recognised if it was **probable** that it would become payable. IFRS 3 dispenses with this requirement – **all contingent consideration is now recognised.**

Deferred consideration

The parent acquired 75% of the subsidiary's 80m $1 shares on 1 January 20X6. It paid $3.50 per share and agreed to pay a further $108m on 1 January 20X7.

The parent company's cost of capital is 8%.

At the acquisition date the cost of the combination will be as follows:

	$m
80m shares × 75% × $3.50	210
Deferred consideration:	
$108m × 1/1.08	100
Total consideration	310

At 31 December 20X6, the cost of the combination will be unchanged but $8m will be charged to finance costs, being the unwinding of the discount on the deferred consideration.

Share exchange

The parent has acquired 12,000 $1 shares in the subsidiary by issuing 5 of its own $1 shares for every 4 shares in the subsidiary. The market value of the parent company's shares is $6.

Cost of the combination:

	$m
12,000 × 5/4 × $6	90,000

Note that this is credited to the share capital and share premium of the parent company as follows:

	Debit	Credit
Investment in subsidiary	90,000	
Share capital ($12,000 × 5/4)		15,000
Share premium ($12,000 × 5/4 × 5)		75,000

Expenses and issue costs

Expenses of the combination, such as lawyers and accountants fees are written off as incurred. However, IFRS 3 requires that the costs of issuing equity are treated as a deduction from the proceeds of the equity issue. Share issue costs will therefore be debited to the share premium account. Issue costs of financial instruments are deducted from the proceeds of the financial instrument.

5 Intra-group trading

Unrealised profit

Any receivable/payable balances outstanding between the companies are cancelled on consolidation. No further problem arises if all such intra group transactions are **undertaken at cost**, without any mark up for profit.

However, each company in a group is a separate trading entity and may wish to treat other group companies in the same way as any other customer. In this case, a company (say A Co) may buy goods at one price and sell them at a higher price to another group company (B Co). The accounts of A Co will quite properly include the profit earned on sales to B Co; and similarly B Co's statement of financial position will include inventories at their cost to B Co, ie at the amount at which they were purchased from A Co.

This gives rise to two problems.

(a)   Although A Co makes a profit as soon as it sells goods to B Co, the group does not make a sale or achieve a profit until an outside customer buys the goods from B Co.

(b)   Any purchases from A Co which remain unsold by B Co at the year end will be included in B Co's inventory. Their value in the statement of financial position will be their cost to B Co, which is not the same as their cost to the group.

The objective of consolidated accounts is to present the financial position of several connected companies as that of a single entity, the group. This means that **in a consolidated statement of financial position the only profits recognised should be those earned by the group** in providing goods or services to outsiders; and similarly, inventory in the consolidated statement of financial position should be valued at cost to the group.

Suppose that a holding company P Co buys goods for $1,600 and sells them to a wholly owned subsidiary S Co for $2,000. The goods are in S Co's inventory at the year end and appear in S Co's statement of financial position at $2,000. In this case, P Co will record a profit of $400 in its individual accounts, but from the group's point of view the figures are:

Cost	$1,600
External sales	nil
Closing inventory at cost	$1,600
Profit/loss	nil

If we add together the figures for retained earnings and inventory in the individual statements of financial position of P Co and S Co the resulting figures for consolidated retained earnings and consolidated inventory will each be overstated by $400. A consolidation adjustment is therefore necessary as follows.

DEBIT   Group retained earnings

CREDIT   Group inventory (statement of financial position)

with the amount of profit **unrealised by the group.**

Non-controlling interests in unrealised intra-group profits

A further problem occurs where a subsidiary company which is not wholly owned is involved in **intra-group trading** within the group. If a subsidiary S Co is 75% owned and sells goods to the parent company for $16,000 cost plus $4,000 profit, ie for $20,000 and if these items are unsold by P Co at the end of the reporting period, the 'unrealised' profit of $4,000 earned by S Co and charged to P Co will be partly owned by the non-controlling interest of S Co. As far as the non-controlling interest of S Co is concerned, their share (25% of $4,000) amounting to $1,000 of profit on the sale of goods would appear to have been fully realised. It is only the group that has not yet made a profit on the sale.

However, best practice is to debit the non-controlling interest with its share, so the entries are:

DEBIT   Group retained earnings

DEBIT   Non-controlling interest

CREDIT   Group inventory (statement of financial position)

6 Intra group sales of non-current assets

Accounting treatment

In their individual accounts the companies concerned will treat the transfer just like a sale between unconnected parties: the selling company will record a profit or loss on sale, while the purchasing company will record the asset at the amount paid to acquire it, and will use that amount as the basis for calculating depreciation.

On consolidation, the usual **'group entity' principle applies**. The consolidated statement of financial position must show assets at their cost to the group, and any depreciation charged must be based on that cost. Two consolidation adjustments will usually be needed to achieve this.

(a) An adjustment to alter retained earnings and non-current assets cost so as to remove any element of unrealised profit or loss. This is similar to the adjustment required in respect of unrealised profit in inventory.

(b) An adjustment to alter retained earnings and accumulated depreciation is made so that consolidated depreciation is based on the asset's cost to the group.

In practice, these steps are combined so that the retained earnings of the entity making the unrealised profit are debited with the unrealised profit less the additional depreciation.

The double entry is as follows.

(a) Sale by parent

DEBIT   Group retained earnings
CREDIT   Non-current assets

with the profit on disposal, less the additional depreciation.

(b) Sale by subsidiary

DEBIT   Group retained earnings (P's share of S)
DEBIT   Non-controlling interest (NCI's share of S)
CREDIT   Non-current assets

with the profit on disposal, less additional depreciation

Example: Intra group sale of non-current assets

P Co owns 60% of S Co and on 1 January 20X1 S Co sells plant costing $10,000 to P Co for $12,500. The companies make up accounts to 31 December 20X1 and the balances on their retained earnings at that date are:

P Co	after charging depreciation of 10% on plant	$27,000
S Co	including profit on sale of plant	$18,000

The working for consolidated retained earnings will be as follows:

	P Co $	S Co $
	27,000	18,000
Disposal of plant:		
Profit		(2,500)
Depreciation: 10% × $2,500		250
		15,750
Share of S Ltd: $15,750 × 60%	9,450	
Group retained earnings	36,450	

7 Acquisition of a subsidiary during its accounting period

The subsidiary company's accounts to be consolidated will show the subsidiary's profit or loss for the whole year. For consolidation purposes, however, it will be necessary to distinguish between:

(a)   Profits earned before acquisition
(b)   Profits earned after acquisition

In practice, a subsidiary company's profit may not accrue evenly over the year. Nevertheless, the assumption can be made that **profits accrue evenly** whenever it is impracticable to arrive at an accurate split of pre and post acquisition profits.

Once the amount of pre acquisition profit has been established the appropriate consolidation workings (goodwill, retained earnings) can be produced.

Bear in mind that in calculating **non-controlling interests** at the year end, the distinction between pre and post acquisition profits is irrelevant. The non-controlling shareholders are simply credited with their share of the subsidiary's total net assets at the end of the reporting period.

It is worthwhile to summarise what happens on consolidation to the retained earnings figures extracted from a subsidiary's statement of financial position. Suppose the accounts of S Co, a 60% subsidiary of P Co, show retained earnings of $20,000 at the end of the reporting period, of which $14,000 were earned prior to acquisition. The figure of $20,000 will appear in the consolidated statement of financial position as follows.

	$
Non-controlling interests working: their share of total retained earnings at the end of the reporting period (40% × $20,000)	8,000
Goodwill working: group share of pre-acquisition retained earnings (60% × $14,000)	8,400
Consolidated retained earnings working: group share of post-acquisition retained earnings (60% × $6,000)	3,600
	20,000

Example: pre acquisition losses of a subsidiary

As an illustration of the entries arising when a subsidiary has pre acquisition losses, suppose P Co acquired all 50,000 $1 ordinary shares in S Co for $20,000 on 1 January 20X1 when there was a debit balance of $35,000 on S Co's retained earnings. In the years 20X1 to 20X4 S Co makes profits of $40,000 in total, leaving a credit balance of $5,000 on retained earnings at 31 December 20X4. P Co's retained earnings at the same date are $70,000.

The consolidation workings would appear as follows.

1. *Goodwill*

	$	$
Consideration transferred		20,000
Net assets acquired as represented by		
Ordinary share capital	50,000	
Retained earnings	(35,000)	
		(15,000)
Goodwill		5,000

2. *Retained earnings*

	P Co	S Co
	$	$
At the end of the reporting period	70,000	5,000
Pre-acquisition loss		35,000
		40,000
S Co – share of post-acquisition retained earnings (40,000 × 100%)	40,000	
	110,000	

8 Fair values in acquisition accounting

To understand the importance of fair values in the acquisition of a subsidiary consider again what we mean by goodwill.

> **Goodwill.** An asset representing the future economic benefits arising from other assets acquired in a business combination that are not individually identified and separately recognised.
> *(IFRS 3: Appendix A)*

The **statement of financial position of a subsidiary company** at the date it is acquired may not be a guide to the fair value of its net assets. For example, the market value of a freehold building may have risen greatly since it was acquired, but it may appear in the statement of financial position at historical cost less accumulated depreciation.

Fair value is defined as follows by IFRS 13 – it is an important definition.

> **Fair value.** The price that would be received to sell an asset or paid to transfer a liability in an orderly transaction between market participants at the measurement date.
> *(IFRS 13: Appendix)*

We will look at the requirements of IFRS 13 regarding fair value in more detail below. First let us look at some practical matters.

Fair value adjustment calculations

Until now we have calculated goodwill as the difference between the consideration transferred and the **carrying value** of net assets acquired by the group. If this calculation is to comply with the definition above we must ensure that the carrying value of the subsidiary's net assets is the same as their **fair value**.

There are two possible ways of achieving this.

(a)   The **subsidiary company** might **incorporate any necessary revaluations** in its own books of account. In this case, we can proceed directly to the consolidation, taking asset values and reserves figures straight from the subsidiary company's statement of financial position.

(b)   The **revaluations** may be made as a **consolidation adjustment without being incorporated** in the subsidiary company's books. In this case, we must make the necessary adjustments to the subsidiary's statement of financial position as a working. Only then can we proceed to the consolidation.

Note. Remember that when depreciating assets are revalued there may be a corresponding alteration in the amount of depreciation charged and accumulated.

IFRS 3 and IFRS 13

IFRS 3 *Business combinations* sets out **general principles** for arriving at the fair values of a subsidiary's assets and liabilities. The acquirer should recognise the acquiree's identifiable assets, liabilities and contingent liabilities at the acquisition date only if they satisfy the following criteria.

(a) In the case of an **asset** other than an intangible asset, it is **probable** that any associated **future economic benefits** will flow to the acquirer, and its fair value can be **measured reliably**.

(b) In the case of a liability other than a contingent liability, it is probable that an outflow of resources embodying economic benefits will be required to settle the obligation, and its fair value can be measured reliably.

(c) In the case of an **intangible asset** or a **contingent liability**, its fair value can be **measured reliably**.

The acquiree's identifiable assets and liabilities might include assets and liabilities **not previously recognised** in the acquiree's financial statements. For example, a tax benefit arising from the acquiree's tax losses that was not recognised by the acquiree may be recognised by the group if the acquirer has future taxable profits against which the unrecognised tax benefit can be applied.

IFRS 13 *Fair value measurement* provides extensive guidance on how the fair value of assets and liabilities should be established.

The standard requires that the following are considered in determining fair value:

(a) The asset or liability being measured

(b) The principal market (ie that where the most activity takes place) or where there is no principal market, the most advantageous market (ie that in which the best price could be achieved) in which an orderly transaction would take place for the asset or liability

(c) The highest and best use of the asset or liability and whether it is used on a standalone basis or in conjunction with other assets or liabilities

(d) Assumptions that market participants would use when pricing the asset or liability

Having considered these factors, IFRS 13 provides a hierarchy of inputs for arriving at fair value. It requires that level 1 inputs are used where possible:

Level 1   Quoted prices in active markets for identical assets that the entity can access at the measurement date.

Level 2   Inputs other than quoted prices that are directly or indirectly observable for the asset.

Level 3   Unobservable inputs for the asset.

Examples of fair value and business combinations

For non-financial assets, fair value is decided based on the **highest and best** use of the asset as determined by a market participant. The following example, adapted from the illustrative examples to IFRS 13, demonstrates what is meant by this.

Example: Land

A Co has acquired land in a business combination. The land is currently developed for industrial use as a site for a factory. The current use of land is presumed to be its highest and best use unless market or other factors suggest a different use. Nearby sites have recently been developed for residential use as sites for high-rise apartment buildings. On the basis of that development and recent zoning and other changes to facilitate that development, A Co determines that the land currently used as a site for a factory could be developed as a site for residential use (ie for high-rise apartment buildings) because market participants would take into account the potential to develop the site for residential use when pricing the land.

How would the highest and best use of the land be determined?

The highest and best use of the land would be determined by comparing both of the following:

(a)   The value of the land as currently developed for industrial use (ie the land would be used in combination with other assets, such as the factory, or with other assets and liabilities)

(b)   The value of the land as a vacant site for residential use, taking into account the costs of demolishing the factory and other costs (including the uncertainty about whether the entity would be able to convert the asset to the alternative use) necessary to convert the land to a vacant site (ie the land is to be used by market participants on a stand-alone basis)

The highest and best use of the land would be determined on the basis of the higher of those values.

Restructuring and future losses

An acquirer **should not recognise liabilities for future losses** or other costs expected to be incurred as a result of the business combination.

IFRS 3 explains that a plan to restructure a subsidiary following an acquisition is not a present obligation of the acquiree at the acquisition date. Neither does it meet the definition of a contingent liability. Therefore an acquirer **should not recognise a liability for** such a **restructuring plan** as part of allocating the cost of the combination unless the subsidiary was already committed to the plan before the acquisition.

Part C 16: The consolidated statement of financial position

This **prevents creative accounting**. An acquirer cannot set up a provision for restructuring or future losses of a subsidiary and then release this to profit or loss in subsequent periods in order to reduce losses or smooth profits.

Intangible assets

The acquiree may have **intangible assets**, such as development expenditure. These can be recognised separately from goodwill only if they are **identifiable**. An intangible asset is identifiable only if it:

(a) Is **separable**, ie capable of being separated or divided from the entity and sold, transferred, or exchanged, either individually or together with a related contract, asset or liability; or

(b) Arises from contractual or other legal rights.

Contingent liabilities

Contingent liabilities of the acquirer are **recognised** if their **fair value can be measured reliably**. This is a departure from the normal rules in IAS 37; contingent liabilities are not normally recognised, but only disclosed.

After their initial recognition, the acquirer should measure contingent liabilities that are recognised separately at the higher of:

(a) The amount that would be recognised in accordance with IAS 37
(b) The amount initially recognised

Cost of a business combination

The general principle is that the acquirer should measure the cost of a business combination as the total of the **fair values**, at the date of exchange, **of assets given**, liabilities incurred or assumed, and equity instruments issued by the acquirer, in exchange for control of the acquiree.

Sometimes all or part of the cost of an acquisition is deferred (ie, does not become payable immediately). The fair value of any deferred consideration is determined by **discounting** the amounts payable to their **present value** at the date of exchange.

Where equity instruments (eg, ordinary shares) of a quoted entity form part of the cost of a combination, the **published price** at the date of exchange normally provides the best evidence of the instrument's fair value and except in rare circumstances this should be used.

Future losses or other costs expected to be incurred as a result of a combination should not be included in the cost of the combination.

Costs **attributable** to the combination, for example professional fees and administrative costs, should not be included: they are recognised as an expense when incurred. **Costs of issuing debt instruments and equity shares** are covered by IAS 32 *Financial instruments: presentation*, which states that such costs should **reduce the proceeds from the debt issue or the equity issue.**

17

The consolidated statement of profit or loss and other comprehensive income and statement of cash flows

1 The consolidated statement of profit or loss

The consolidated statement of profit or loss and other comprehensive income is the consolidated statement of profit or loss with the addition of 'other comprehensive income' attributable to either the parent or one or more subsidiaries. The consolidation work is done in the statement of profit or loss, so that is where we begin.

Simple example: consolidated statement of profit or loss

P Co acquired 75% of the ordinary shares of S Co on that company's incorporation in 20X3. The summarised statements of profit or loss and movement on retained earnings of the two companies for the year ending 31 December 20X9 are set out below.

	P Co	S Co
	$	$
Sales revenue	75,000	38,000
Cost of sales	(30,000)	(20,000)
Gross profit	45,000	18,000
Administrative expenses	(14,000)	(8,000)
Profit before tax	31,000	10,000
Income tax expense	(10,000)	(2,000)
Profit for the year	21,000	8,000

Note. Movement on retained earnings

	P Co	S Co
Retained earnings brought forward	87,000	17,000
Profit for the year	21,000	8,000
Retained earnings carried forward	108,000	25,000

We will prepare the consolidated statement of profit or loss and extract from the statement of changes in equity showing retained earnings and non-controlling interest.

P CO CONSOLIDATED STATEMENT OF PROFIT OR LOSS FOR THE YEAR ENDED 31 DECEMBER 20X9

	$
Sales revenue (75 + 38)	113,000
Cost of sales (30 + 20)	50,000
Gross profit	63,000
Administrative expenses (14 + 8)	22,000
Profit before tax	41,000
Income tax expense	12,000
Profit for the year	29,000
Profit attributable to:	
Owners of the parent	27,000
Non-controlling interest ($8,000 × 25%)	2,000
	29,000

STATEMENT OF CHANGES IN EQUITY (EXTRACT)

	Retained earnings $	Non-controlling interest $	Total equity $
Balance b/f	99,750	4,250	104,000
Profit for the year	27,000	2,000	29,000
	126,750	6,250	133,000

Notice how the non-controlling interest is dealt with.

(a) Down to the line **'profit for the year'** the **whole** of S Co's results is included without reference to group share or non-controlling share. A **one-line adjustment** is then inserted to deduct the non-controlling share of S Co's profit.

(b) The non-controlling share ($4,250) of S Co's retained earnings brought forward (17,000 × 25%) is **excluded** from group retained earnings. This means that the carried forward figure of $126,750 is the figure which would appear in the statement of financial position for group retained earnings.

Intra-group trading

Like the consolidated statement of financial position, the consolidated statement of profit or loss should deal with the results of the group as those of a single entity. When one company in a group sells goods to another an identical amount is added to the sales revenue of the first company and to the cost of sales of the second. Yet as far as the entity's dealings with outsiders are concerned no sale has taken place.

The consolidated figures for sales revenue and cost of sales should represent **sales to**, and **purchases from, outsiders**. An adjustment is therefore necessary to reduce the sales revenue and cost of sales figures by the value of intra-group sales during the year.

Any unrealised profits on intra group trading should be excluded from the figure for group profits. This will occur whenever goods sold at a profit within the group remain in the inventory of the purchasing company at the year end. The best way to deal with this is to **calculate the unrealised profit on unsold inventories at the year end** and add this amount back to cost of sales, thereby reducing gross profit.

Example: Intra-group trading

Suppose in our earlier example that S Co had recorded sales of $5,000 to P Co during 20X9. S Co had purchased these goods from outside suppliers at a cost of $3,000. One half of the goods remained in P Co's inventory at 31 December 20X9.

The consolidated statement of profit or loss for the year ended 31 December 20X9 would now be as follows.

	$
Sales revenue (75 + 38 – 5)	108,000
Cost of sales (30 + 20 – 5 + 1*)	(46,000)
Gross profit	62,000
Administrative expenses	(22,000)
Profit before taxation	40,000
Income tax expense	(12,000)
Profit for the year	28,000
Profit attributable to:	
Owners of the parent	26,250
Non-controlling interest	1,750
	28,000

Note.

	$
Retained earnings brought forward	99,750
Profit for the year	26,250
Retained earnings carried forward	126,000

* Unrealised profit: ½ × ($5,000 – $3,000)

An adjustment will be made for the unrealised profit against the inventory figure in the consolidated statement of financial position.

Intra-group dividends

In our example so far we have assumed that S Co retains all of its after tax profit. It may be, however, that S Co distributes some of its profits as dividends. As before, the non-controlling interest in the subsidiary's profit should be calculated immediately after the figure of after tax profit. For this purpose, no account need be taken of how much of profit due to the **non-controlling interest** is to be distributed by S Co as dividend.

Note that group retained earnings are only adjusted for dividends paid to the parent company shareholders. Dividends paid by the subsidiary to the parent are cancelled on consolidation and dividends paid to the non-controlling interest are replaced by the allocation to the non-controlling interest of their share of the profit for the year of the subsidiary.

Pre acquisition profits

As explained above, the figure for retained earnings carried forward must be the same as the figure for retained earnings in the consolidated statement of financial position. We have seen in previous chapters that retained earnings in the consolidated statement of financial position comprise:

(a)   The **whole of the parent company's** retained earnings

(b)   A **proportion of the subsidiary company's** retained earnings. The proportion is the **group's share of post acquisition retained earnings** in the subsidiary. From the total retained earnings of the subsidiary we must therefore **exclude** both the **non-controlling share** of total retained earnings and the **group's share of pre acquisition** retained earnings

A **similar procedure is necessary in the consolidated profit or loss** if it is to link up with the consolidated statement of financial position. Previous examples have shown how the non-controlling share of profits is excluded in the statement of profit or loss. Their share of profits for the year is deducted from profit after tax, while the figure for profits brought forward in the consolidation schedule includes only the group's proportion of the subsidiary's profits.

In the same way, when considering examples which include pre acquisition profits in a subsidiary, the figure for profits brought forward should include only the group's share of the post acquisition retained profits. If the subsidiary is **acquired during the accounting year**, it is therefore necessary to apportion its profit for the year between pre acquisition and post acquisition elements. The part-year method is used.

With the part-year method, the entire statement of profit or loss of the subsidiary is split between pre acquisition and post acquisition proportions. Only the post acquisition figures are included in the consolidated statement of profit or loss.

Example

P Co acquired 60% of the equity of S Co on 1 April 20X5. The statements of profit or loss of the two companies for the year ended 31 December 20X5 are set out below.

	P Co $	S Co $	S Co ($^9/_{12}$) $
Sales revenue	170,000	80,000	60,000
Cost of sales	65,000	36,000	27,000
Gross profit	105,000	44,000	33,000
Other income – dividend received S Co	3,600		
Administrative expenses	43,000	12,000	9,000
Profit before tax	65,600	32,000	24,000
Income tax expense	23,000	8,000	6,000
Profit for the year	42,600	24,000	18,000

Note.

Dividends (paid 31 December)	12,000	6,000
Profit retained	30,600	18,000
Retained earnings brought forward	81,000	40,000
Retained earnings carried forward	111,600	58,000

Now we will prepare the consolidated statement of profit or loss and the retained earnings extract from the statement of changes in equity.

The shares in S Co were acquired three months into the year. Only the post acquisition proportion (9/12ths) of S Co's statement of profit or loss is included in the consolidated statement of profit or loss. This is shown above for convenience.

P CO CONSOLIDATED STATEMENT OF PROFIT OR LOSS
FOR THE YEAR ENDED 31 DECEMBER 20X5

	$
Sales revenue (170 + 60)	230,000
Cost of sales (65 + 27)	(92,000)
Gross profit	138,000
Administrative expenses (43 + 9)	(52,000)
Profit before tax	86,000
Income tax expense (23 + 6)	(29,000)
Profit for the year	57,000
Profit attributable to:	
Owners of the parent	49,800
Non-controlling interest (18 × 40%)	7,200
	57,000

STATEMENT OF CHANGES IN EQUITY

	Retained earnings $
Balance brought forward*	81,000
Dividend paid (P)	(12,000)
Total comprehensive income for the year	49,800
Balance carried forward	118,800

* All of S Co's profits brought forward are pre acquisition.

2 The consolidated statement of profit or loss and other comprehensive income

A consolidated statement of profit or loss and other comprehensive income is simple to produce once the statement of profit or loss has been prepared. Any item of 'other comprehensive income' is attributable to either the parent or a subsidiary. If it is attributable to a subsidiary, part of it is allocated to the non-controlling interest.

Here is an example where an 80% subsidiary has 'other comprehensive income'.

CONSOLIDATED STATEMENT OF PROFIT OR LOSS AND OTHER COMPREHENSIVE INCOME FOR THE YEAR TO 30 APRIL 20X7

	$'000
Sales revenue	1,600
Cost of sales	(930)
Gross profit	670
Administrative expenses	(255)
Profit before tax	415
Income tax expense	(75)
Profit for the year	340
Other comprehensive income:	
Gain on property revaluation	200
Total comprehensive income for the year	540
Profit attributable to:	
Owners of the parent	332
Non-controlling interest	8
	340
Total comprehensive income attributable to:	
Owners of the parent (332 + (200 × 80%))	492
Non-controlling interest (8 + (200 × 20%))	48
	540

Consolidated statement of changes in equity

These amounts would appear in the consolidated statement of changes in equity as follows:

	Retained earnings $'000	Revaluation surplus $'000	Total $'000	Non-controlling interest $'000	Total $'000
Total comprehensive income for the year	332	160	492	48	540

3 The consolidated statement of cash flows

The method of preparing the group statement of cash flows is the same as for the individual entity statement. The aim is to show the cash flows of the group with third parties. As the statement is based on the consolidated financial statements, any intra-group transactions will already have been eliminated.

However there are a number of additional issues to be considered.

Non-controlling interest

The non-controlling interest is not part of the group, so dividends paid to the non-controlling interest should be shown as a cash outflow under 'financing activities'.

Associates

We will be dealing with associates in the next chapter. For the statement of cash flows, it is important just to remember that an associate is also not part of the group.

Group 'profit before tax' in the consolidated statement of profit or loss and other comprehensive income will include 'share of profit of associate'. This must be removed as part of the reconciliation to arrive at 'cash generated from operations'.

Dividends received from the associate are disclosed as a separate cash flow under 'cash flows from investing activities'.

Acquisition of a subsidiary

If a subsidiary is acquired during the reporting period, the net cash effect of the acquisition is shown separately under 'cash flows from investing activities'. The net cash flow will be the cash amount paid less any cash and cash equivalents acquired.

Example: P Co acquires 65% of S Co by issuing 200,000 $1 shares at $1.60 and paying $500,000.

S Co's statement of financial position at acquisition shows cash and cash equivalents of $75,000.

BPP
LEARNING MEDIA

In the statement of cash flows this will appear as follows:

	$'000
Cash flows from investing activities	
Acquisition of S Co, net of cash acquired (500 – 75)	(425)

Note. Because the cash balance of the acquired subsidiary has been taken into account as a one-line entry, the assets and liabilities of the subsidiary should be excluded when calculating movement on PPE, inventories, receivables etc. Otherwise the cash effect of the acquisition would be double-counted.

Disposal of a subsidiary

The same principle applies when a subsidiary is disposed of during the year. If P Co disposes of its interest in S Co a few years later for $700,000 when S Co has an overdraft of $30,000, the statement of cash flows will show:

	$'000
Cash flows from investing activities	
Disposal of S Co, net of cash disposed of (700 + 30)	730

Again, the assets and liabilities of S Co will be added back in for the purposes of calculating movements over the year, as the effect of the disposal has already been taken into account.

Where dividend paid to the NCI has to be calculated as a balancing figure using the equity balances and the attributable profit, these equity balances must also be adjusted for acquisitions and disposals, before the calculation is done. The NCI added on acquisition of a subsidiary acquired during the year should be deducted and the NCI deducted on disposal of a subsidiary should be added back. The correct amount of dividend paid will then be the balancing figure.

In a reporting period where both an acquisition and a disposal took place, the working would be as follows:

NON-CONTROLLING INTEREST

	$m		$m
NCI deducted on disposal	4	NCI b/f (consolidated SFP)	15
Dividend paid to NCI (bal figure)	3	NCI added on acquisition	5
NCI c/f (consolidated SFP)	20	Profit attributable to NCI	7
	27		27

Accounting for associates and joint arrangements

18

1 IAS 28: Investments in associates and joint ventures

Here are the main definitions relating to associates:

> **Associate.** An entity over which an investor has significant influence.
>
> **Significant influence** is the power to participate in the financial and operating policy decisions of the investee but is not control or joint control over those policies.
>
> **Equity method.** A method of accounting whereby the investment is initially recognised at cost and adjusted thereafter for the post-acquisition change in the investor's share of the investee's net assets. The investor's profit or loss includes its share of the investee's profit or loss and the investor's other comprehensive income includes its share of the investee's other comprehensive income. *(IAS 28: para. 3)*

IAS 28 requires all investments in associates to be accounted for in the consolidated accounts using the equity method, unless the investment is classified as 'held for sale' in accordance with IFRS 5 in which case it should be accounted for under IFRS 5 or the exemption below applies.

An investor is exempt from applying the equity method if:

(a)   It is a parent exempt from preparing consolidated financial statements under IAS 27; or

(b)   All of the following apply:

    (i)   The investor is a **wholly-owned subsidiary** or it is a **partially owned subsidiary** of another entity and its other owners, including those not otherwise entitled to vote, have been informed about, and do not object to, the investor not applying the equity method

    (ii)   The investor's securities are **not publicly traded**

(iii)   It is **not in the process of issuing securities** in public securities markets

(iv)   The **ultimate or intermediate parent** publishes consolidated financial statements that comply with IFRS   *(IAS 28, para.17)*

The revised version of IAS 28 **no longer allows** an investment in an associate to be excluded from equity accounting when an investee operates under severe long-term restrictions that significantly impair its ability to transfer funds to the investor. Significant influence must be lost before the equity method ceases to be applicable.

The use of the equity method should be **discontinued** from the date that the investor **ceases to have significant influence,** or if the associate becomes a subsidiary.

From that date, the investor shall account for the investment in accordance with IFRS 9 *Financial instruments*. The carrying amount of the investment at the date that it ceases to be an associate shall be regarded as its cost on initial measurement as a financial asset under IFRS 9.

Separate financial statements of the investor

If an investor **issues consolidated financial statements** (because it has subsidiaries), an investment in an associate should be **either** of the following:

(a)   Accounted for at cost
(b)   In accordance with IFRS 9
(c)   Using the **equity method** as described in **IAS 28.**in its separate financial statements

If an investor that does **not issue consolidated financial statements** (ie it has no subsidiaries) has an investment in an associate this should similarly be included in the financial statements of the investor either at cost, or in accordance with IFRS 9.

2 The equity method

Many of the procedures required to apply the equity method are the same as are required for full consolidation. In particular, **intra-group unrealised profits** must be excluded.

Consolidated statement of profit or loss and other comprehensive income

The basic principle is that the investing company (X Co) should take account of its **share of the earnings** of the associate, Y Co, whether or not Y Co distributes the earnings as dividends. X Co achieves this by adding to consolidated profit the group's share of Y Co's profit after tax.

Notice the difference between this treatment and the **consolidation** of a subsidiary company's results. If Y Co were a subsidiary X Co would take credit for the whole of its sales revenue, cost of sales etc and would then make a one line adjustment to remove any non-controlling share.

Under equity accounting, the associate's sales revenue, cost of sales and so on are **not amalgamated** with those of the group. Instead the group share only of the associate's profit after tax and other comprehensive income for the year is included in the relevant sections of the consolidated statement of profit or loss and other comprehensive income.

Consolidated statement of financial position

A figure for **investment in associates** is shown which at the time of the acquisition must be stated at cost. This amount will increase (decrease) each year by the amount of the group's share of the associated company's profit (loss) for the year.

Example: Associate

P Co, a company with subsidiaries, acquires 25,000 of the 100,000 $1 ordinary shares in A Co for $60,000 on 1 January 20X8. In the year to 31 December 20X8, A Co earns profits after tax of $24,000, from which it pays a dividend of $6,000.

How will A Co's results be accounted for in the individual and consolidated accounts of P Co for the year ended 31 December 20X8?

In the individual accounts of P Co, the investment will be recorded on 1 January 20X8 at cost. Unless there is an impairment in the value of the investment (see below), this amount will remain in the individual statement of financial position of P Co permanently. The only entry in P Co's individual statement of profit or loss will be to record dividends received. For the year ended 31 December 20X8, P Co will:

DEBIT	Cash	$1,500	
CREDIT	Income from shares in associates		$1,500

In the **consolidated accounts** of P Co equity accounting principles will be used to account for the investment in A Co. Consolidated profit after tax will include the group's share of A Co's profit after tax (25% × $24,000 = $6,000). To the extent that this has been distributed as dividend, it is already included in P Co's individual accounts and will automatically be brought into the consolidated results. That part of the group's share of profit in the associate which has not been distributed as dividend ($4,500) will be brought into consolidation by the following adjustment.

DEBIT	Investment in associates	$4,500	
CREDIT	Income from associates		$4,500

The asset 'Investment in associates' is then stated at $64,500, being cost plus the group share of post acquisition retained profits.

3 Presentation of associates

Consolidated statement of profit or loss

The following is a **suggested layout** for the consolidated statement of profit or loss for a company having subsidiaries as well as associated companies.

	$'000
Revenue	1,400
Cost of sales	(770)
Gross profit	630
Other income: interest receivable	30
Administrative expenses	290)
Finance costs	(20)
Share of profit of associate (30 – 13)*	17
Profit before taxation	367
Income tax expense	(145)
Profit for the year	222
Profit attributable to:	
Owners of the parent	200
Non-controlling interest	22
	222

* Profit for the year less tax

Consolidated statement of financial position

The consolidated statement of financial position will contain an **asset 'Investment in associates'**. The amount at which this asset is stated will be its original cost plus the group's share of any **profits earned since acquisition** which have not been distributed as dividends.

Example: Consolidated statement of financial position

On 1 January 20X6 the net tangible assets of A Co amount to $220,000, financed by 100,000 $1 ordinary shares and revenue reserves of $120,000. P Co, a company with subsidiaries, acquires 30,000 of the shares in A Co for $75,000. During the year ended 31 December 20X6 A Co's profit after tax is $30,000, from which dividends of $12,000 are paid.

How will P Co's investment in A Co would appear in the consolidated statement of financial position at 31 December 20X6?

CONSOLIDATED STATEMENT OF FINANCIAL POSITION AS AT 31 DECEMBER 20X6 (extract)

	$
Non-current assets	
Investment in associate	
Cost	75,000
Group share of post-acquisition retained profits	
(30% × $18,000)	5,400
	80,400

The following points are also relevant and are similar to a parent-subsidiary consolidation situation.

(a) Use financial statements drawn up to the **same reporting date**.

(b) If this is impracticable, adjust the financial statements for **significant transactions/ events** in the intervening period. The difference between the reporting date of the associate and that of the investor must be no more than three months.

(c) Use **uniform accounting policies** for like transactions and events in similar circumstances, adjusting the associate's statements to reflect group policies if necessary.

'Upstream' and 'downstream' transactions

'Upstream' transactions are, for example, sales from an associate to the investor. 'Downstream' transactions are, for example, sales from the investor to an associate.

Unrealised profits resulting from 'upstream' and 'downstream' transactions between an investor (including its consolidated subsidiaries) and an associate are eliminated to the extent of the investor's interest in the associate. This is very similar to the procedure for eliminating unrealised profit between a parent and a subsidiary. The important thing to remember is that **only the group's share is eliminated**.

Example: Downstream transaction

A Co, a parent with subsidiaries, holds 25% of the equity shares in B Co. During the year, A Co makes sales of $1,000,000 to B Co at cost plus a 25% mark-up. At the year-end, B Co has all these goods still in inventories.

A Co has made an unrealised profit of $200,000 (1,000,000 × 25/125) on its sales to the associate. The group's share (25%) of this must be eliminated:

DEBIT	Cost of sales (consolidated profit or loss)	$50,000	
CREDIT	Investment in associate (consolidated statement of financial position)		$50,000

Because the sale was made to the associate, the group's share of the unsold inventory forms part of the investment in the associate at the year-end. If the associate had made the sale to the parent, the adjustment would have been:

DEBIT	Cost of sales (consolidated profit or loss)	$50,000	
CREDIT	Inventories (consolidated statement of financial position)		$50,000

Associate's losses

When the equity method is being used and the investor's share of losses of the associate equals or exceeds its interest in the associate, the investor should discontinue including its share of further losses. The investment is reported at nil value. The interest in the associate is normally the carrying amount of the investment in the associate, but it also includes any other long-term interests, for example, long term receivables or loans.

After the investor's interest is reduced to nil, additional losses should only be recognised where the investor has incurred obligations or made payments on behalf of the associate (for example, if it has guaranteed amounts owed to third parties by the associate).

Impairment losses

IFRS 9 sets out a list of indications that a financial asset (including an associate) may have become impaired. Any impairment loss is recognised in accordance with IAS 36 *Impairment of assets* for each associate individually.

In the case of an associate, any impairment loss will be deducted from the carrying amount in the statement of financial position.

The working would be as follows.

	$
Cost of investment	X
Share of post-acquisition retained earnings	X
	X
Impairment loss	(X)
Interest in associate	X

4 IFRS 11: Joint arrangements

IFRS 11 classes joint arrangements as either joint operations or joint ventures.

The classification of a joint arrangement as a joint operation or a joint venture depends upon the **rights and obligations** of the parties to the arrangement.

Joint arrangements are often found when each party can **contribute in different ways** to the activity. For example, one party may provide finance, another purchases or manufactures goods, while a third offers his marketing skills.

IFRS 11 *Joint arrangements* covers all types of joint arrangements. It is not concerned with the accounts of the joint arrangement itself (if separate accounts are maintained), but rather **how the interest in a joint venture is accounted for by each party**.

Definitions

The IFRS begins by listing some important definitions.

> **Joint arrangement.** An arrangement of which two or more parties have joint control.
> *(IFRS 11: para. 4)*
>
> **Joint control.** The contractually agreed sharing of control of an arrangement, which exists only when decisions about the relevant activities require the unanimous consent of the parties sharing control.
> *(IFRS 11: para. 7)*
>
> **Joint operation.** A joint arrangement whereby the parties that have joint control of the arrangement have rights to the assets and obligations for the liabilities relating to the arrangement.
> *(IFRS 11: para. 15)*
>
> **Joint venture.** A joint arrangement whereby the parties that have joint control of the arrangement have rights to the net assets of the arrangement.
> *(IFRS 11: para 16)*

Forms of joint arrangement

IFRS 11 classes joint arrangements as either joint operations or joint ventures. The classification of a joint arrangement as a joint operation or a joint venture depends upon the rights and obligations of the parties to the arrangement.

A **joint operation** is a joint arrangement whereby the parties that have joint control (the joint operators) have rights to the assets, and obligations for the liabilities, of that joint arrangement. A joint arrangement that is **not structured through a separate entity** is always a joint operation.

A **joint venture** is a joint arrangement whereby the parties that have **joint control** (the joint venturers) of the arrangement have **rights to the net assets** of the arrangement.

A **joint arrangement** that is structured through a **separate entity** may be either a joint operation or a joint venture. In order to ascertain the classification, the parties to the arrangement should assess the terms of the contractual arrangement together with any other facts or circumstances to assess whether they have:

- Rights to the assets, and obligations for the liabilities, in relation to the arrangement (indicating a joint operation)

- Rights to the net assets of the arrangement (indicating a joint venture)

Detailed guidance is provided in the appendices to IFRS 11 in order to help this assessment, giving consideration to, for example, the wording contained within contractual arrangements.

IFRS 11 summarises the basic issues that underlie the classifications in the following diagram:

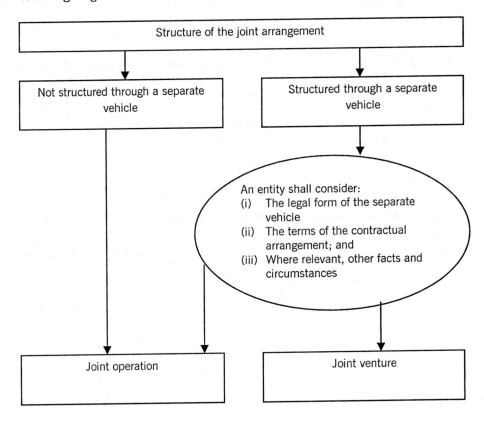

Contractual arrangement

The existence of a contractual agreement distinguishes a joint arrangement from an investment in an associate. **If there is no contractual arrangement, then a joint arrangement does not exist.**

Evidence of a contractual arrangement could be in one of several forms.

- **Contract** between the parties
- **Minutes** of discussion between the parties
- Incorporation in the **articles or by-laws** of the joint venture

The contractual arrangement is usually **in writing**, whatever its form, and it will deal with the following issues surrounding the joint venture.

- **Its activity, duration and reporting obligations**
- The appointment of its **board of directors** (or equivalent) and the **voting rights** of the parties
- **Capital contributions** to it by the parties
- How its output, income, expenses or results are **shared** between the parties

It is the contractual arrangement which establishes **joint control** over the joint venture, so that no single party can control the activity of the joint venture on its own.

The terms of the contractual arrangement are key to deciding whether the arrangement is a joint venture or joint operation. IFRS 11 includes a table of issues to consider and explains the influence of a range of points that could be included in the contract. The table is summarised below:

	Joint operation	Joint venture
The terms of the contractual arrangement	The parties to the joint arrangement have rights to the assets, and obligations for the liabilities, relating to the arrangement.	The parties to the joint arrangement have rights to the **net assets** of the arrangement (ie it is the separate vehicle, not the parties, that has rights to the assets, and obligations for the liabilities).
Rights to assets	The parties to the joint arrangement share all interests (eg rights, title or ownership) in the assets relating to the arrangement in a specified proportion (eg in proportion to the parties' ownership interest in the arrangement or in proportion to the activity carried out through the arrangement that is directly attributed to them).	The assets brought into the arrangement or subsequently acquired by the joint arrangement are the arrangement's assets. The parties have no interests (ie no rights, title or ownership) in the assets of the arrangement.

	Joint operation	Joint venture
Obligations for liabilities	The parties share all liabilities, obligations, costs and expenses in a specified proportion (eg in proportion to their ownership interest in the arrangement or in proportion to the activity carried out through the arrangement that is directly attributed to them).	The joint arrangement is liable for the debts and obligations of the arrangement.
		The parties are liable to the arrangement only to the extent of their respective: • Investments in the arrangement • Obligations to contribute any unpaid or additional capital to the arrangement
	The parties to the joint arrangement are liable for claims by third parties.	Creditors of the joint arrangement do not have rights of recourse against any party.
Revenues, expenses, profit or loss	The contractual arrangement establishes the allocation of revenues and expenses on the basis of the relative performance of each party to the joint arrangement. For example, the contractual arrangement might establish that revenues and expenses are allocated on the basis of the capacity that each party uses in a plant operated jointly.	The contractual arrangement establishes each party's share in the profit or loss relating to the activities of the arrangement.
Guarantees	The provision of guarantees to third parties, or the commitment by the parties to provide them, does not, by itself, determine that the joint arrangement is a joint operation.	

IFRS 11 contains many examples illustrating the principles of how to classify joint arrangements, you can find them at: www.iasb.org

Accounting treatment

The accounting treatment of joint arrangements depends on whether the arrangement is a joint venture or joint operation.

Accounting for joint operations

IFRS 11 requires that a joint operator recognises line-by-line the following in relation to its interest in a joint operation:

(a) Its assets, including its share of any jointly held assets

(b) Its liabilities, including its share of any jointly incurred liabilities

(c) Its revenue from the sale of its share of the output arising from the joint operation

(d) Its share of the revenue from the sale of the output by the joint operation

(e) Its expenses, including its share of any expenses incurred jointly

(IFRS 11: para. 20)

This treatment is applicable in both the separate and consolidated financial statements of the joint operator.

Accounting for joint ventures

IFRS 11 and IAS 28 require joint ventures to be accounted for using the equity method.

Prior to the new group accounting standards issued in 2011, the old standard on joint ventures (IAS 31) permitted either equity accounting or proportionate consolidation to be used for joint ventures. The choice has now been removed. (Proportionate consolidation meant including the investor's share of the assets, liabilities, income and expenses of the joint venture, line by line).

The rules for equity accounting are included in IAS 28 *Associates and joint ventures.*

Application of IAS 28 (2011) to joint ventures

The consolidated statement of financial position is prepared by:

- Including the interest in the joint venture at cost plus share of post-acquisition total comprehensive income
- Including the group share of the post-acquisition total comprehensive income in group reserves

The consolidated statement of profit or loss and other comprehensive income will include:

- The group share of the joint venture's profit or loss
- The group share of the joint venture's other comprehensive income

The use of the equity method should be **discontinued** from the date on which the joint venturer ceases to have joint control over, or have significant influence on, a joint venture.

Part C 18: Accounting for associates and joint arrangements

Transactions between a joint venturer and a joint venture

Upstream transactions

A joint venturer may **sell or contribute assets** to a joint venture so making a profit or loss. Any such gain or loss should, however, only be recognised to the extent that it reflects the substance of the transaction.

Therefore:

- Only the **gain** attributable to the interest of the other joint venturers should be recognised in the financial statements

- The full amount of any **loss** should be recognised when the transaction shows evidence that the net realisable value of current assets is less than cost, or that there is an impairment loss.

Downstream transactions

When a joint venturer purchases assets from a joint venture, the joint venturer should not recognise its share of the profit made by the joint venture on the transaction in question until it resells the assets to an independent third party, ie until the profit is realised.

Losses should be treated in the same way, **except** losses should be recognised immediately if they represent a reduction in the net realisable value of current assets, or a permanent decline in the carrying amount of non-current assets.

Accounting for acquisition of an interest in a joint operation

In May 2014, the International Accounting Standards Board published a narrow-scope amendment to IFRS 11 *Joint arrangements.*

IFRS 11 did not give explicit guidance on the accounting for acquisitions of interests in joint operations. The objective of the amendment is to add new guidance to IFRS 11 on accounting for the acquisition of an interest in a joint operation in which the activity of the joint operation constitutes a business, as defined in IFRS 3 *Business combinations.*

The amendment requires that acquirers of such interests should **apply the relevant principles of business combination accounting in IFRS 3 and other standards and other IFRSs, that do not conflict with the guidance in this IFRS and disclose the relevant information specified in these standards for business combinations.**

The guidance only applies to accounting for an interest in a joint operation when the joint operation is formed and there is an existing business that is contributed or where the acquisition of the interest is in an existing joint operation that is a business.

Changes in group structures

19

1 Disposals

Disposals can drop a subsidiary holding to associate status, long-term investment status and to zero, or a the parent might still retain a subsidiary with a reduced holding. Disposals of shares in a subsidiary may or may not result in a loss of control. If control is lost, then any remaining investment will need to be re-categorised as an associate or an investment in equity instruments.

Types of disposal

Disposals where control is lost

There are three main kinds of disposals in which control is lost:

(a)   Full disposal: all the holding is sold (say, 80% to nil)
(b)   Subsidiary to associate (say, 80% to 30%)
(c)   Subsidiary to trade investment (say, 80% to 10%)

Disposals where control is retained

There is only one kind of disposal where control is retained: **subsidiary to subsidiary**, for example an 80% holding to a 60% holding.

Disposals where control is lost are treated differently from disposals where control is retained. There is a reason for this.

General principle: 'crossing an accounting boundary'

Under the revised IFRS 3 disposal occurs only when one entity loses control over another, which is generally when its holding is decreased to less than 50%. The Deloitte guide: *Business Combinations and Changes in Ownership Interests* calls this 'crossing an accounting boundary'.

On disposal of a controlling interest, any **retained interest** (an associate or trade investment) is measured at **fair value on the date that control is lost**. This fair value is used in the calculation of the gain or loss on disposal, and also becomes the carrying amount for subsequent accounting for the retained interest.

If the **50%** boundary is **not crossed**, as when the interest in a subsidiary is reduced, the event is treated as a **transaction between owners**.

Whenever the 50% boundary is crossed, you revalue, and a gain or loss is reported in profit or loss for the year. If you do not cross the 50% boundary, no gain or loss is reported; instead there is an adjustment to the parent's equity.

Effective date of disposal

The effective date of disposal is **when control passes**: the date for accounting for an undertaking ceasing to be a subsidiary undertaking is the date on which its former parent undertaking relinquishes its control over that undertaking. The consolidated statement of profit or loss and other comprehensive income should include the results of a subsidiary undertaking up to the date of its disposal. IAS 37 on provisions and IFRS 5 on disclosure of discontinued operations will have an impact here.

Control lost: Calculation of group gain on disposal

A proforma calculation is shown below. This needs to be adapted for the circumstances of the disposal, in particular whether it is a full or partial disposal:

	$
Fair value of consideration received	X
Fair value of investment retained	X
Less: net assets × share (%) held at date control lost	(X)
goodwill less any NCI in goodwill at date control lost	(X)
Add/less gains/losses previously recognised in OCI*	X(X)
Group profit/loss	X(X)

Following IAS 1, this gain may need to be disclosed separately if it is material.

* This will only arise on items such as fair value gains and losses on investments in equity instruments held by subsidiaries.

Control lost: Calculation of gain in parent's separate financial statements

This calculation is more straightforward: the proceeds are compared with the carrying value of the investment sold. The investment will be held at cost or at fair value if held as an investment in equity instruments:

	$
Fair value of consideration received	X
Less carrying value of investment disposed	(X)
Add/(less) fair value changes previously recognised in OCI (if an IEI)	X/(X)
Profit/(loss) on disposal	X/(X)

The profit on disposal is generally taxable, and the **tax based on the parent's gain** rather than the group's will also need to be recognised in the consolidated financial statements.

Disposals where control is lost: accounting treatment

For a **full disposal**, apply the following treatment.

(a) **Statement of profit or loss and other comprehensive income**

    (i)   Consolidate results and non-controlling interest to the date of disposal.

    (ii)   Show the group profit or loss on disposal.

(b) **Statement of financial position**

    There will be no non-controlling interest and no consolidation as there is no subsidiary at the date the statement of financial position is being prepared.

For **partial disposals**, use the following treatments.

(a) **Subsidiary to associate**

    (i)   **Statement of profit or loss and other comprehensive income**

        (1)   Treat the undertaking as a subsidiary up to the date of disposal, ie consolidate for the correct number of months and show the non-controlling interest in that amount.

        (2)   Show the profit or loss on disposal.

        (3)   Treat as an associate thereafter.

    (ii)   **Statement of financial position**

        (1)   The investment remaining is at its fair value at the date of disposal (to calculate the gain).

        (2)   Equity account (as an associate) thereafter, using the fair value as the new 'cost'. (Post 'acquisition' retained earnings are added to this cost in future years to arrive at the carrying value of the investment in the associate in the statement of financial position.)

(b) **Subsidiary to trade investment/IEI**

    (i)   **Statement of profit or loss and other comprehensive income**

        (1)   Treat the undertaking as a subsidiary up to the date of disposal, ie consolidate.

        (2)   Show profit or loss on disposal.

(3)   Show dividend income only thereafter.

(ii)   **Statement of financial position**

(1)   The investment remaining is at its fair value at the date of disposal (to calculate the gain).

(2)   Thereafter, treat as an investment in equity instruments under IFRS 9.

Disposals where control is retained

Control is retained where the disposal is from **subsidiary to subsidiary.** The accounting treatment is as follows:

Statement of profit or loss and other comprehensive income

(a)   The subsidiary is **consolidated in full** for the whole period.

(b)   The **non-controlling interest in the statement of profit or loss** will be based on percentage before and after disposal, ie time apportion.

(c)   There is no profit or loss on disposal.

Statement of financial position

(a)   The non-controlling interest in the statement of financial position is based on the year end percentage.

(b)   The change (increase) in non-controlling interests is shown as an adjustment to the parent's equity.

(c)   Goodwill on acquisition is unchanged in the consolidated statement of financial position.

Adjustment to the parent's equity

This reflects the fact that the non-controlling share has increased (as the parent's share has reduced). A subsidiary to subsidiary disposal is, in effect, **a transaction between owners.** Specifically, it is a reallocation of ownership between parent and non-controlling equity holders. **The goodwill is unchanged,** because it is a historical figure, unaffected by the reallocation. The adjustment to the parent's equity is calculated as follows:

	$
Fair value of consideration received	X
Increase in NCI in net assets at disposal	(X)
Increase in NCI in goodwill at disposal *	(X)
Adjustment to parent's equity	X

* **Note.** This line is only required where non-controlling interests are measured at fair value at the date of acquisition (ie where there is an increase in the non-controlling interest share of goodwill already recognised).

IFRS 3 views **the group as an economic entity**, and views **all providers of equity**, including non-controlling interests, as **owners of the group**. Non-controlling shareholders are not outsiders, they are owners of the group just like the parent.

Gain in the parent's separate financial statements

This is calculated as for disposals where control is lost: see above.

Example: Partial disposals

Chalk Co bought 100% of the voting share capital of Cheese Co on its incorporation on 1 January 20X2 for $160,000. Cheese Co earned and retained $240,000 from that date until 31 December 20X7. At that date the statements of financial position of the company and the group were as follows.

	Chalk Co	Cheese Co	Consolidated
	$'000	$'000	$'000
Investment in Cheese	160	–	–
Other assets	1,000	500	1,500
	1,160	500	1,500
Share capital	400	160	400
Retained earnings	560	240	800
Current liabilities	200	100	300
	1,160	500	1,500

It is the group's policy to value the non-controlling interest at its proportionate share of the fair value of the subsidiary's identifiable net assets.

On 1 January 20X8 Chalk Co sold 40% of its shareholding in Cheese Co for $280,000. The profit on disposal (ignoring tax) in the financial statements of the parent company is calculated as follows.

	$'000
Fair value of consideration received	280
Carrying value of investment disposed of (40% × 160)	(64)
Profit on sale	216

We now move on to calculate the adjustment to equity for the group financial statements.

Because only 40% of the 100% subsidiary has been sold, leaving a 60% subsidiary, **control is retained**. This means that there is **no group profit on disposal in profit or loss for the year**. Instead, there is an **adjustment to the parent's equity**, which affects group retained earnings.

> Remember that, when control is retained, the disposal is just a transaction between owners. The non-controlling shareholders are owners of the group, just like the parent.

The adjustment to parent's equity is calculated as follows:

	$'000
Fair value of consideration received	280
Increase in non-controlling interest in net assets at the date of disposal (40% × 400)	(160)
Adjustment to parent's equity	120

This increases group retained earnings and does not go through group profit or loss for the year. (Note that there is no goodwill in this example, or non-controlling interest in goodwill, as the subsidiary was acquired on incorporation.)

Solution: subsidiary status

The statements of financial position immediately after the sale will appear as follows.

	Chalk Co $'000	Cheese Co $'000	Consolidated $'000
Investment in Cheese (160-64)	96		
Other assets	1,280	500	1,780
	1,376	500	1,780
Share capital	400	160	400
Retained earnings*	776	240	920
Current liabilities	200	100	300
	1,376	500	1,620
Non-controlling interest			160
			1,780

*Chalk's retained earnings are $560,000 + $216,000 profit on disposal. Group retained earnings are increased by the adjustment above: $800,000 + $120,000 = $920,000.

Solution: associate status

Using the above example, assume that Chalk Co sold 60% of its holding in Cheese Co for $440,000. The fair value of the 40% holding retained was $200,000. The gain or loss on disposal in the books of the parent company would be calculated as follows.

	Parent company $'000
Fair value of consideration received	440
Carrying value of investment disposed of (60% × 160)	(96)
Profit on sale	344

This time control is lost, so there will be a gain in group profit or loss, calculated as follows:

	$'000
Fair value of consideration received	440
Fair value of investment retained	200
Less Chalk's share of consolidated carrying	
value at date control lost 100% × 400	(400)
Group profit on sale	240

Note that there was no goodwill arising on the acquisition of Cheese, otherwise this too would be deducted in the calculation.

The statements of financial position would now appear as follows.

	Chalk Co $'000	Cheese Co $'000	Consolidated $'000
Investment in Cheese (Note 1)	64		200
Other assets	1,440	500	1,440
	1,504	500	1,640
Share capital	400	160	400
Retained earnings (Note 2)	904	240	1,040
Current liabilities	200	100	200
	1,504	500	1,640

Notes

1 The investment in Cheese is at fair value in the group SOFP. In fact it is equity accounted at fair value at date control lost plus share of post-'acquisition' retained earnings. But there are no retained earnings yet because control has only just been lost.

2 Group retained earnings are $800,000 (per question) plus group profit on the sale of $240,000, ie $1,040,000.

2 Business combinations achieved in stages

A parent company may acquire a controlling interest in the shares of a subsidiary as a result of **several successive share purchases**, rather than by purchasing the shares all on the same day. Business combinations achieved in stages may also be known as 'piecemeal acquisitions'.

> Business combinations achieved in stages are in many ways a mirror image of disposals. The same principles underlie both.

Types of business combination achieved in stages

There are three possible types of business combinations achieved in stages:

(a) A previously held **interest**, say 10%, with **no significant influence** (accounted for under IFRS 9) is **increased to a controlling interest** of 50% or more.

(b) A **previously held equity interest**, say 35%, accounted for as an **associate** under IAS 28, is increased to a controlling interest of 50% or more.

(c) A **controlling interest** in a subsidiary is **increased**, say from 60% to 80%.

The first two transactions are treated in the same way, but the third is not. There is a reason for this.

General principle: 'Crossing an accounting boundary'

Under IFRS 3 a business combination occurs only when one entity **obtains control over another**, which is generally when 50% or more has been acquired. As noted above under disposals, this principle can be referred to as **'crossing an accounting boundary'**.

When this happens, the original investment – whether an investment under IFRS 9 with no significant influence, or an associate – is treated as if it were **disposed of at fair value and re-acquired at fair value**. This **previously held interest** at fair value, together with any consideration transferred, is the **'cost' of the combination** used in calculating the goodwill.

If the 50% **boundary is not crossed**, as when the interest in a subsidiary is increased, the event is treated as a **transaction between owners**.

Whenever the 50% boundary is crossed, you revalue, and a gain or loss is reported in profit or loss for the year. If you do not cross the 50% boundary, no gain or loss is reported; instead there is an adjustment to the parent's equity.

The situation where an interest in a subsidiary is increased from, say, 60% to 80%, does not involve crossing that all-important 50% threshold. Likewise, purchases of stakes of up to 50% do not involve crossing the boundary, and therefore do not trigger a calculation of goodwill.

Investment or associate becomes a subsidiary: Calculation of goodwill

The previously held investment is re-measured to fair value, with any gain being reported in profit or loss, and the goodwill calculated as follows:

Consideration transferred	X
Non-controlling interest (at % FV of new assets or 'full' FV)	X
Fair value of acquirer's previously held equity interest	X
Less: net fair value of identifiable assets	
acquired and liabilities assumed	(X)
	X

In accordance with IFRS 9 the profit on derecognition of the associate is taken to other comprehensive income, or, in the SOFP, other components of equity.

Increase in previously held controlling interest: adjustment to parent's equity

An example of this would be where an investment goes from a 60% subsidiary to an 80% subsidiary. The 50% threshold has not been crossed, so there is no re-measurement to fair value and no gain or loss to profit or loss for the year. The increase is treated as a **transaction between owners.** As with disposals, ownership has been **reallocated** between parent and non-controlling shareholders.

Accordingly the parent's equity is adjusted. The required adjustment is calculated by comparing the consideration paid with the decrease in non-controlling interest. (As the parent's share has increased, the NCI share has decreased.) The **calculation is as follows:**

	$
Fair value of consideration paid	(X)
Decrease in NCI in net assets at date of transaction	X
Decrease in NCI in goodwill at date of transaction *	X
Adjustment to parent's equity	(X)

*Note. This line is only required where non-controlling interests are measured at fair value at the date of acquisition (ie where there is an decrease in the non-controlling interest share of goodwill already recognised).

The increase in shareholding is treated as a transaction between owners because the revised IFRS 3 views **the group as an economic entity,** and **views all providers of equity**, including non-controlling interests, as **owners of the group.**

3 Changes in direct ownership

Changes in direct ownership (ie internal group reorganisations) can take many forms. Apart from divisionalisation, all other internal reorganisations will not affect the consolidated financial statements, but they will affect the accounts of individual companies within the group.

Groups will reorganise on occasions for a variety of reasons.

(a) A group may want to float a business to **reduce the gearing** of the group. The holding company will initially transfer the business into a separate company.

(b) Companies may be transferred to another business during a **divisionalisation** process.

(c)   The group may 'reverse' into another company to obtain a **stock exchange quotation**.

(d)   Internal reorganisations may create efficiencies of group structure for **tax purposes**.

Such reorganisations involve a restructuring of the relationships within a group. Companies may be transferred to another business during a divisionalisation process. There is generally no effect on the consolidated financial statements, *provided that* no non-controlling interests are affected, because such reorganisations are only internal. The impact on the individual companies within the group, however, can be substantial. A variety of different transactions are described here, **only involving 100% subsidiaries**.

New top parent company

A new top holding company might be needed as a vehicle for flotation or to improve the co-ordination of a diverse business. The new company, P, will issue its own shares to the holders of the shares in S.

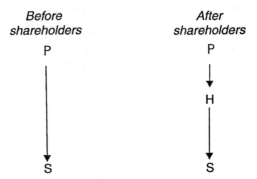

Subsidiary moved up

This transaction is shown in the diagram below. It might be carried out to allow S_1 to be **sold** while S_2 is retained, or to **split diverse businesses**.

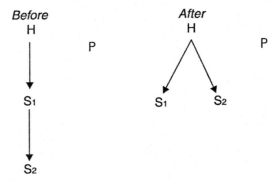

S_1 could transfer its investment in S_2 to P as a dividend *in specie* or by P paying cash. A share for share exchange is not possible because an allotment by P to S_1 is void. A **dividend in specie** is simply a dividend paid other than in cash.

S_1 must have sufficient **distributable profits** for a dividend *in specie*. If the investment in S_2 has been revalued then that can be treated as a realised profit for the purposes of determining the legality of the distribution. For example, suppose the statement of financial position of S_1 is as follows.

	$m
Investment in S_2 (cost $100m)	900
Other net assets	100
	1,000
Share capital	100
Revaluation surplus	800
Retained earnings	100
	1,000

It appears that S_1 cannot make a distribution of more than $100m. If, however, S_1 makes a distribution in kind of its investment in S_2, then the **revaluation surplus** can be treated as realised.

It is not clear how P should account for the transaction. The carrying value to S_2 might be used, but there may be **no legal rule**. P will need to write down its investment in S_1 at the same time. A transfer for cash is probably easiest, but there are still legal pitfalls as to what is distributable, depending on how the transfer is recorded.

There will be **no effect** on the group financial statements as the group has stayed the same: it has made no acquisitions or disposals.

Subsidiary moved along

This is a transaction which is treated in a very similar manner to that described above.

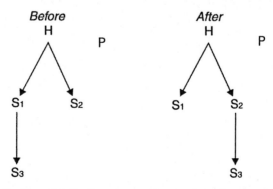

The problem of an effective distribution does not arise here because the holding company did not buy the subsidiary. There may be problems with **financial**

assistance if S_2 pays less than the fair value to purchase S_3 as a prelude to S_1 leaving the group.

Subsidiary moved down

This situation could arise if H is in one country and S_1 and S_2 are in another. A **tax group** can be formed out of such a restructuring.

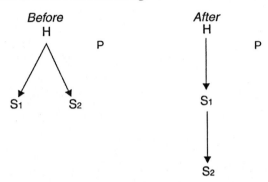

Before
H

P

S_1 S_2

After
H

P

S_1

S_2

If S_1 paid cash for S_2, the transaction would be straightforward (as described above). It is unclear whether H should recognise a gain or loss on the sale if S_2 is sold for more or less than carrying value. S_1 would only be deemed to have made a distribution (avoiding any advance tax payable) only if the **price was excessive.**

A share for share exchange accounted for as a uniting of interests may obtain partial relief against the need to create a **share premium account**. A share premium account must be set up with a 'minimum premium value'. This is the amount by which the book value of the shares (or lower cost) exceeds the nominal value of the shares issued. This preserves the book value of the investment.

Example: Minimum premium value

Hop Co has two 100% subsidiaries, Skip and Jump. The statements of financial position at 31 December 20X5 are as follows.

	Hop Co $'000	Skip Co $'000	Jump Co $'000	Group $'000
Investment in Skip Co	1,000			
Investment in Jump Co	500			
Net assets	1,500	1,375	1,500	4,375
	3,000	1,375	1,500	4,375
Share capital	2,500	1,000	500	2,500
Retained earnings	500	375	1,000	1,875
	3,000	1,375	1,500	4,375

Hop Co wants to transfer Jump Co to Skip Co.

Solution

Skip Co issues 250,000 $1 shares in exchange for Hop Co's investment in Jump Co. The minimum premium value is $500,000 (carrying value) – $250,000 = $250,000. The statements of financial position are now as follows.

	Hop Co $'000	Skip Co $'000	Jump Co $'000	Group $'000
Investment in Skip	1,500			
Investment in Jump		500		
Net assets	1,500	1,375	1,500	4,375
	3,000	1,875	1,500	4,375
Share capital	2,500	1,250	500	2,500
Share premium		250		
Retained earnings	500	375	1,000	1,875
	3,000	1,875	1,500	4,375

Divisionalisation

This type of transaction involves the **transfer of businesses** from subsidiaries into just one company. The businesses will all be similar and this is a means of rationalising and streamlining. The savings in administration costs can be quite substantial. The remaining shell company will leave the cash it was paid on an intragroup balance as it is no longer trading. The accounting treatment is generally straightforward.

Part D

Specialised standards

Share-based payment

20

1 IFRS 2: Share-based payment

Transactions whereby entities purchase goods or services from other parties, such as suppliers and employees, by **issuing shares or share options** to those other parties are **increasingly common**. Share schemes are a common feature of director and executive remuneration and in some countries the authorities may offer tax incentives to encourage more companies to offer shares to employees. Companies whose shares or share options are regarded as a valuable 'currency' commonly use share-based payment to obtain employee and professional services.

The increasing use of share-based payment has raised questions about the accounting treatment of such transactions in company financial statements.

Share options are often granted to employees at an exercise price that is equal to or higher than the market price of the shares at the date the option is granted. Consequently the options have no intrinsic value and so **no transaction is recorded in the financial statements**.

This leads to an **anomaly**: if a company pays its employees in cash, an expense is recognised in profit or loss, but if the payment is in share options, no expense is recognised.

There are a number of arguments **against** recognition. The IASB has considered and rejected the arguments below.

(a) **No cost therefore no charge**

There is no cost to the entity because the granting of shares or options does not require the entity to sacrifice cash or other assets. Therefore a charge should not be recognised.

This argument is unsound because it ignores the fact that a transaction has occurred. The employees have provided valuable services to the entity in return for valuable shares or options.

(b) **Earnings per share is hit twice**

It is argued that the charge to profit or loss for the employee services consumed reduces the entity's earnings, while at the same time there is an increase in the number of shares issued. However, the dual impact on earnings per share simply reflects the two economic events that have occurred.

(i) The entity has issued shares or options, thus increasing the denominator of the earnings per share calculation.

(ii) It has also consumed the resources it received for those shares or options, thus reducing the numerator.

(c) **Adverse economic consequences**

It could be argued that entities might be discouraged from introducing or continuing employee share plans if they were required to recognise them in the financial statements. However, if this happened, it might be because the requirement for entities to account properly for employee share plans had revealed the economic consequences of such plans.

A situation where entities are able to obtain and consume resources by issuing valuable shares or options without having to account for such transactions could be perceived as a distortion.

IFRS 2 requires an entity to **reflect the effects of share-based payment transactions** in its profit or loss and financial position.

IFRS 2 applies to all share-based payment transactions. There are three types.

(a) **Equity-settled share-based payment transactions**, in which the entity receives goods or services in exchange for equity instruments of the entity (including shares or share options)

(b) **Cash-settled share-based payment transactions**, in which the entity receives goods or services in exchange for amounts of cash that are based on the price (or value) of the entity's shares or other equity instruments of the entity

(c) Transactions in which the entity receives or acquires goods or services and either the entity or the supplier has a **choice** as to whether the entity settles the transaction in cash (or other assets) or by issuing equity instruments

Certain transactions are **outside the scope** of the IFRS:

(a) Transactions with employees and others in their capacity as a holder of equity instruments of the entity (for example, where an employee receives additional shares in a rights issue to all shareholders)

(b) The issue of equity instruments in exchange for control of another entity in a business combination

These are the main definitions used in IFRS 2.

Share-based payment transaction. A transaction in which the entity receives goods or services as consideration for equity instruments of the entity (including shares or share options), or acquires goods or services by incurring liabilities to the supplier of those goods or services for amounts that are based on the price of the entity's shares or other equity instruments of the entity.

Share-based payment arrangement. An agreement between the entity and another party (including an employee) to enter into a share-based payment transaction, which thereby entitles the other party to receive cash or other assets of the entity for amounts that are based on the price of the entity's shares or other equity instruments of the entity, or to receive equity instruments of the entity, provided the specified vesting conditions, if any, are met.

Equity instrument. A contract that evidences a residual interest in the assets of an entity after deducting all of its liabilities.

Equity instrument granted. The right (conditional or unconditional) to an equity instrument of the entity conferred by the entity on another party, under a share-based payment arrangement.

Share option. A contract that gives the holder the right, but not the obligation, to subscribe to the entity's shares at a fixed or determinable price for a specified period of time.

Fair value. The amount for which an asset could be exchanged, a liability settled, or an equity instrument granted could be exchanged, between knowledgeable, willing parties in an arm's length transaction.

Grant date. The date at which the entity and another party (including an employee) agree to a share-based payment arrangement, being when the entity and the other party have a shared understanding of the terms and conditions of the arrangement. At grant date the entity confers on the other party (the counterparty) the right to cash, other assets, or equity instruments of the entity, provided the specified vesting conditions, if any, are met. If that agreement is subject to an approval process (for example, by shareholders), grant date is the date when that approval is obtained.

Intrinsic value. The difference between the fair value of the shares to which the counterparty has the (conditional or unconditional) right to subscribe or which it has the right to receive, and the price (if any) the other party is (or will be) required to pay for those shares. For example, a share option with an exercise price of $15 on a share with a fair value of $20, has an intrinsic value of $5.

Measurement date. The date at which the fair value of the equity instruments granted is measured. For transactions with employees and others providing similar services, the measurement date is grant date. For transactions with parties other than employees (and those providing similar services), the measurement date is the date the entity obtains the goods or the counterparty renders service.

> **Vest.** To become an entitlement. Under a share-based payment arrangement, a counterparty's right to receive cash, other assets, or equity instruments of the entity vests upon satisfaction of any specified vesting conditions.
>
> **Vesting conditions.** The conditions that must be satisfied for the counterparty to become entitled to receive cash, other assets or equity instruments of the entity, under a share-based payment arrangement. Vesting conditions include service conditions, which require the other party to complete a specified period of service, and performance conditions, which require specified performance targets to be met (such as a specified increase in the entity's profit over a specified period of time).
>
> **Vesting period.** The period during which all the specified vesting conditions of a share-based payment arrangement are to be satisfied.　　　　　　　　(*IFRS 2: Appendix*)

Recognition: the basic principle

An entity should **'recognise goods or services received or acquired in a share-based payment transaction when it obtains the goods or as the services are received'** *(IFRS 2: para. 7)*. Goods or services received or acquired in a share-based payment transaction **should be recognised as expenses unless they qualify for recognition as assets**. For example, services are normally recognised as expenses (because they are normally rendered immediately), while goods are recognised as assets.

If the goods or services were received or acquired in an **equity-settled** share-based payment transaction the entity should recognise **a corresponding increase in equity** (reserves).

If the goods or services were received or acquired in a **cash-settled** share-based payment transaction the entity should recognise a **liability**.

Equity-settled share-based payment transactions

Measurement

The issue here is how to measure the 'cost' of the goods and services received and the equity instruments (eg the share options) granted in return.

The general principle in IFRS 2 is that when an entity recognises the goods or services received and the corresponding increase in equity, it should measure these at the **fair value of the goods or services received**. Where the transaction is with **parties other than employees**, there is a rebuttable presumption that the fair value of the goods or services received can be estimated reliably.

If the fair value of the goods or services received cannot be measured reliably, the entity should measure their value by reference to the **fair value of the equity instruments granted**.

Where the transaction is with a party other than an employee fair value should be measured at the date the entity obtains the goods or the counterparty renders service.

Where shares, share options or other equity instruments are granted to **employees** as part of their remuneration package, it is not normally possible to measure directly the services received. For this reason, the entity should measure the **fair value of the employee services received by reference to the fair value of the equity instruments granted**. The fair value of those equity instruments should be measured at **grant date**.

Determining the fair value of equity instruments granted

Where a transaction is measured by reference to the fair value of the equity instruments granted, fair value is based on **market prices** if available, taking into account the terms and conditions upon which those equity instruments were granted.

If market prices are not available, the entity should estimate the fair value of the equity instruments granted using a **valuation technique**, such as an option pricing model.

Transactions in which services are received

The issue here is **when** to recognise the transaction. When equity instruments are granted they may vest immediately, but often the counterparty has to meet specified conditions first. For example, an employee may have to complete a specified period of service. This means that the effect of the transaction normally has to be allocated over more than one accounting period.

If the equity instruments granted **vest immediately,** (ie the counterparty is not required to complete a specified period of service before becoming unconditionally entitled to the equity instruments) it is presumed that the services have already been received (in the absence of evidence to the contrary). The entity should **recognise the services received in full**, with a corresponding increase in equity, **on the grant date**.

If the equity instruments granted do not vest until the counterparty completes a specified period of service, the entity should account for those services **as they are rendered** by the counterparty during the vesting period. For example if an employee is granted share options on condition that he or she completes three years' service, then the services to be rendered by the employee as consideration for the share options will be received in the future, over that three-year vesting period.

The entity should recognise an amount for the goods or services received during the vesting period based on the **best available estimate** of the **number of equity instruments expected to vest**. It should **revise** that estimate if subsequent information indicates that the number of equity instruments expected to vest differs from previous estimates. On **vesting date**, the entity should revise the estimate to **equal the number of equity instruments that actually vest**.

Once the goods and services received and the corresponding increase in equity have been recognised, the entity should make no subsequent adjustment to total equity after the vesting date.

Example: Equity-settled share-based payment transaction

On 1 January 20X1 an entity grants 100 share options to each of its 400 employees. Each grant is conditional upon the employee working for the entity until 31 December 20X3. The fair value of each share option is $20.

During 20X1 20 employees leave and the entity estimates that 20% of the employees will leave during the three year period.

During 20X2 a further 25 employees leave and the entity now estimates that 25% of its employees will leave during the three year period.

During 20X3 a further 10 employees leave.

What is the remuneration expense that will be recognised in respect of the share-based payment transaction for each of the three years ended 31 December 20X3?

IFRS 2 requires the entity to recognise the remuneration expense, based on the fair value of the share options granted, as the services are received during the three year vesting period.

In 20X1 and 20X2 the entity estimates the number of options expected to vest (by estimating the number of employees likely to leave) and bases the amount that it recognises for the year on this estimate.

In 20X3 it recognises an amount based on the number of options that actually vest. A total of 55 employees left during the three year period and therefore 34,500 options $(400 - 55 \times 100)$ vested.

The amount recognised as an expense for each of the three years is calculated as follows:

	Cumulative expense at year-end $	Expense for year $
20X1 $40,000 \times 80\% \times 20 \times 1/3$	213,333	213,333
20X2 $40,000 \times 75\% \times 20 \times 2/3$	400,000	186,667
20X3 $34,500 \times 20$	690,000	290,000

Example

On 1 January 20X3 an entity grants 250 share options to each of its 200 employees. The only condition attached to the grant is that the employees should continue to work for the entity until 31 December 20X6. Five employees leave during the year.

The market price of each option was $12 at 1 January 20X3 and $15 at 31 December 20X3.

How will this transaction be reflected in the financial statements for the year ended 31 December 20X3?

The remuneration expense for the year is based on the fair value of the options granted at the grant date (1 January 20X3). As five of the 200 employees left during the year it is reasonable to assume that 20 employees will leave during the four year vesting period and that therefore 45,000 options (250 × 180) will actually vest.

Therefore the entity recognises a remuneration expense of $135,000 (45,000 × 12 × ¼) in the profit or loss and a corresponding increase in equity of the same amount.

Cash-settled share-based payment transactions

Examples of this type of transaction include:

(a) **Share appreciation rights** granted to employees: the employees become entitled to a future cash payment (rather than an equity instrument), based on the increase in the entity's share price from a specified level over a specified period of time

(b) An entity might grant to its employees a right to receive a future cash payment by granting to them a **right to shares that are redeemable**

The basic principle is that the entity measures the goods or services acquired and the liability incurred at the **fair value of the liability**.

The entity should **remeasure** the fair value of the liability **at each reporting date** until the liability is settled **and at the date of settlement**. Any **changes** in fair value are recognised in **profit or loss** for the period.

The entity should recognise the services received, and a liability to pay for those services, **as the employees render service**. For example, if share appreciation rights do not vest until the employees have completed a specified period of service, the entity should recognise the services received and the related liability, over that period.

Example: Cash-settled share-based payment transaction

On 1 January 20X1 an entity grants 100 cash share appreciation rights (SARS) to each of its 500 employees, on condition that the employees continue to work for the entity until 31 December 20X3.

During 20X1 35 employees leave. The entity estimates that a further 60 will leave during 20X2 and 20X3.

During 20X2 40 employees leave and the entity estimates that a further 25 will leave during 20X3.

During 20X3 22 employees leave.

At 31 December 20X3 150 employees exercise their SARs. Another 140 employees exercise their SARs at 31 December 20X4 and the remaining 113 employees exercise their SARs at the end of 20X5.

The fair values of the SARs for each year in which a liability exists are shown below, together with the intrinsic values at the dates of exercise.

	Fair value	Intrinsic value
	$	$
20X1	14.40	
20X2	15.50	
20X3	18.20	15.00
20X4	21.40	20.00
20X5		25.00

Now we will calculate the amount to be recognised in profit or loss for each of the five years ended 31 December 20X5 and the liability to be recognised in the statement of financial position at 31 December for each of the five years.

For the three years to the vesting date of 31 December 20X3 the expense is based on the entity's estimate of the number of SARs that will actually vest (as for an equity-settled transaction). However, the fair value of the liability is **re-measured** at each year-end.

The intrinsic value of the SARs at the date of exercise is the amount of cash actually paid.

		Liability at year-end $		Expense for year $
20X1	Expected to vest (500 – 95):			
	405 × 100 × 14.40 × 1/3	194,400		194,400
20X2	Expected to vest (500 – 100):			
	400 × 100 × 15.50 × 2/3	413,333		218,933

BPP LEARNING MEDIA

	Liability at year-end	Expense for year
20X3 Exercised:		
150 ×100 × 15.00		225,000
Not yet exercised (500 – 97 – 150):		
253 × 100 × 18.20	460,460	47,127
		272,127
20X4 Exercised:		
140 × 100 × 20.00		280,000
Not yet exercised (253 – 140):		
113 × 100 × 21.40	241,820	(218,640)
		61,360
20X5 Exercised:		
113 × 100 × 25.00		282,500
	Nil	(241,820)
		40,680
		787,500

Transactions which either the entity or the other party has a choice of settling in cash or by issuing equity instruments

If the entity has incurred a liability to settle in cash or other assets it should account for the transaction as a cash-settled share-based payment transaction.

If no such liability has been incurred the entity should account for the transaction as an equity-settled share-based payment transaction.

2 Deferred tax implications

An entity may receive a tax deduction that differs from related cumulative remuneration expense, and may arise in a later accounting period.

For instance an entity recognises an expense for share options granted under IFRS 2, but does not receive a tax deduction until the options are exercised and receives the tax deduction at the share price on the exercise date.

Measurement

The deferred tax asset temporary difference is measured as:

Carrying amount of share-based payment expense	0
Less tax base of share-based payment expense (estimated amount tax authorities will permit as a deduction in future periods, based on year end information)	(X)
Temporary difference	(X)
Deferred tax asset at X%	X

Part D 20: Share-based payment

If the amount of the tax deduction (or estimated future tax deduction) exceeds the amount of the related cumulative remuneration expense, this indicates that the tax deduction relates also to an equity item.

The excess is therefore recognised directly in equity.

Example: Deferred tax implications of share-based payment

On 1 January 20X2, a company granted 5,000 share options to an employee vesting two years later on 31 December 20X3. The fair value of each option measured at the grant date was $3.

Tax law in the jurisdiction in which the entity operates allows a tax deduction of the intrinsic value of the options on exercise. The intrinsic value of the share options was $1.20 at 31 December 20X2 and $3.40 at 31 December 20X3 on which date the options were exercised.

We will assume a tax rate of 30%.

The deferred tax accounting treatment of the above transaction at 31 December 20X2, 31 December 20X3 (before exercise), and on exercise will be:

	31/12/20X2	31/12/20X3 before exercise
	$	$
Carrying amount of share-based payment expense	0	0
Less tax base of share-based payment expense		–
(5,000 × $1.2 × ½)/(5,000 × $3.40)	(3,000)	(17,000)
Temporary difference	(3,000)	(17,000)
Deferred tax asset @ 30%	900	5,100
Deferred tax (Cr P/L) (5,100 – 900 – (Working) 600)	900	3,600
Deferred tax (Cr Equity) (Working)	0	600

On exercise, the deferred tax asset is replaced by a current tax one. The double entry is:

Debit deferred tax (P/L)   4,500
Debit deferred tax (equity)   600   } reversal
Credit deferred tax asset   5,100

Debit current tax asset   5,100
Credit current tax (P/L)   4,500
Credit current tax (equity)   600

Accounting expense recognised

(5,000 × $3 × ½)/(5,000 × $3)	7,500	15,000
Tax deduction	(3,000)	(17,000)
Excess temporary difference	0	(2,000)
Excess deferred tax asset to equity @ 30%	0	600

3 Further developments

Amendment to IFRS 2

IFRS 2 was amended in 2008 to define vesting conditions and clarify the accounting treatment of cancellations by parties other than the entity. The amendment restricts vesting conditions to service conditions and performance conditions.

The amendment additionally requires cancellations by the employee to be treated in the same way as cancellations by the employer, resulting in an **accelerated charge to profit or loss of the unamortised balance of the options granted**.

Further amendments to IFRS 2

Payment for goods or services received by an entity within a group may be made in the form of granting equity instruments of the parent company, or equity instruments of another group company.

The standard makes it clear that this type of transaction qualifies as a share-based payment transaction within the scope of IFRS 2.

The standard was not, however clear as regards the following types of arrangements:

- Where the entity's suppliers (including employees) will receive cash payments that are linked to the price of the equity instruments of the entity

- Where the entity's suppliers (including employees) will receive cash payments that are linked to the price of the equity instruments of the entity's parent

Under either arrangement, the entity's parent had an obligation to make the required cash payments to the entity's suppliers. The entity itself did not have any obligation to make such payments.

IFRS 2 was amended in June 2009 to address situations in those parts of the world where, for public policy or other reasons, companies give their shares or rights to shares to individuals, organisations or groups that have not provided goods or services to the company. An example is the issue of shares to a charitable organisation for less than fair value, where the benefits are more intangible than usual goods or services.

Part D 20: Share-based payment

The June 2009 amendment to IFRS 2 clarifies that **IFRS 2 applies to arrangements such as those described above** even if the entity that receives goods or services from its suppliers has no obligation to make the required share-based cash payments.

Employee benefits

21

1 IAS 19: Employee benefits

IAS 19 *Employee benefits* has been revised several times, most recently in November 2013. The standard covers **all employee benefit costs**, except share-based payment, not only retirement benefit (pension) costs. Before we look at IAS 19, we should consider the nature of employee benefit costs and why there is an accounting problem which must be addressed by a standard.

When a company or other entity employs a new worker, that worker will be offered a **package of pay and benefits**. Some of these will be short-term and the employee will receive the benefit at about the same time as he or she earns it, for example basic pay, overtime etc. Other employee benefits are **deferred**, however, the main example being retirement benefits (ie a pension).

The cost of these deferred employee benefits to the employer can be viewed in various ways. They could be described as **deferred salary** to the employee. Alternatively, they are a **deduction** from the employee's true gross salary, used as a tax-efficient means of saving. In some countries, tax efficiency arises on retirement benefit contributions because they are not taxed on the employee, but they are allowed as a deduction from taxable profits of the employer.

Accounting for employee benefit costs

Accounting for **short-term employee benefit costs** tends to be quite straightforward, because they are simply recognised as an expense in the employer's financial statements of the current period.

Accounting for the cost of **deferred employee benefits** is much more difficult. This is because of the large amounts involved, as well as the long time scale, complicated estimates and uncertainties. In the past, entities accounted for these benefits simply by charging the profit or loss of the employing entity on the basis of actual payments made. This led to substantial variations in reported profits of these entities and disclosure of information on these costs was usually sparse.

IAS 19 is intended to prescribe the following.

(a) **When** the cost of employee benefits should be **recognised as a liability or an expense**

(b) The **amount** of the liability or expense that should be recognised

As a basic rule, the standard states the following.

(a) A **liability** should be recognised when an employee has provided a service in exchange for benefits to be received by the employee at some time in the future.

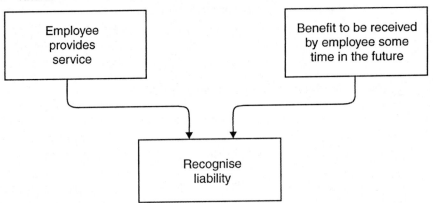

(b) An **expense** should be recognised when the entity enjoys the economic benefits from a service provided by an employee regardless of when the employee received or will receive the benefits from providing the service.

The basic problem is therefore fairly straightforward. An entity will often enjoy the **economic benefits** from the services provided by its employees in advance of the employees receiving all the employment benefits from the work they have done, for example they will not receive pension benefits until after they retire.

Categories of employee benefits

The standard recognises four categories of employee benefits, and proposes a different accounting treatment for each. These four categories are as follows.

(a) **Short-term benefits** including:

- Wages and salaries
- Social security contributions
- Paid annual leave
- Paid sick leave
- Paid maternity/paternity leave

- Profit shares and bonuses paid within 12 months of the year end
- Paid jury service
- Paid military service
- Non-monetary benefits, eg medical care, cars, free goods

(b) **Post-employment benefits**, eg pensions, post-employment medical care and post-employment insurance

(c) **Other long-term benefits**, eg profit shares, bonuses or deferred compensation payable later than 12 months after the year end, sabbatical leave, long-service benefits and long-term disability benefits

(d) **Termination benefits**, eg early retirement payments and redundancy payments. These should be accrued where the entity is demonstrably committed to the termination.

Benefits may be paid to the employees themselves, to their dependants (spouses, children, etc) or to third parties.

Definitions

Employee benefits are all forms of consideration given by an entity in exchange for service rendered by employees.

Short-term employee benefits are employee benefits (other than termination benefits) which fall due wholly within twelve months after the end of the period in which the employees render the related service.

Post-employment benefits are employee benefits (other than termination benefits) which are payable after the completion of employment.

Post-employment benefit plans are formal or informal arrangements under which an entity provides post-employment benefits for one or more employees.

Defined contribution plans are post-employment benefit plans under which an entity pays fixed contributions into a separate entity (a fund) and will have no legal or constructive obligation to pay further contributions if the fund does not hold sufficient assets to pay all employee benefits relating to employee service in the current and prior periods.

Defined benefit plans are post-employment benefit plans other than defined contribution plans.

Multi-employer plans are defined contribution plans (other than state plans) or defined benefit plans (other than state plans) that:

(a) Pool the assets contributed by various entities that are not under common control, and

(b) Use those assets to provide benefits to employees of more than one entity, on the basis that contribution and benefit levels are determined without regard to the identity of the entity that employs the employees concerned.

Other long-term employee benefits are employee benefits (other than post-employment benefits and termination benefits) which do not fall due wholly within twelve months after the end of the period in which the employees render the related service.

Termination benefits are employee benefits payable as a result of either:

(a)   An entity's decision to terminate an employee's employment before the normal retirement date; or

(b)   An employee's decision to accept voluntary redundancy in exchange for those benefits.

Vested employee benefits are employee benefits that are not conditional on future employment.

The present value of a defined benefit obligation is the present value, without deducting any plan assets, of expected future payments required to settle the obligation resulting from employee service in the current and prior periods.

Current service cost is the increase in the present value of the defined benefit obligation resulting from employee service in the current period.

Interest cost is the increase during a period in the present value of a defined benefit obligation which arises because the benefits are one period closer to settlement.

Plan assets comprise:

(a)   Assets held by a long-term employee benefit fund; and

(b)   Qualifying insurance policies.

The **return on plan assets** is interest, dividends and other revenue derived from the plan assets, together with realised and unrealised gains or losses on the plan assets, less any cost of administering the plan and loess any tax payable by the plan itself.

Actuarial gains and losses comprise:

(a)   Experience adjustments (the effects of differences between the previous actuarial assumptions and what has actually occurred); and

(b)   The effects of changes in actuarial assumptions.

Past service cost is the increase in the present value of the defined benefit obligation for employee service in prior periods, resulting in the current period from the introduction of, or changes to, post-employment benefits or other long-term employee benefits. Past service cost may be either positive (where benefits are introduced or improved) or negative (where existing benefits are reduced).

(IAS 19)

2 Short-term employee benefits

The rules for short-term benefits are essentially an application of **basic accounting principles and practice**.

(a) **Unpaid short-term employee benefits** as at the end of an accounting period should be recognised as an accrued expense. Any short-term benefits **paid in advance** should be recognised as a prepayment (to the extent that it will lead to, eg a reduction in future payments or a cash refund).

(b) The **cost of short-term employee benefits** should be recognised as an **expense** in the period when the economic benefit is given, as employment costs (except insofar as employment costs may be included within the cost of an asset, eg property, plant and equipment).

Short-term paid absences

There may be **short-term accumulating paid absences**. These are absences for which an employee is paid, and if the employee's entitlement has not been used up at the end of the period, they are carried forward to the next period. An example is paid holiday leave, where any unused holidays in one year are carried forward to the next year. The cost of the benefits of such absences should be **charged as an expense** as the employees render service that increases their entitlement to future compensated absences.

There may be **short-term non-accumulating paid absences**. These are absences for which an employee is paid when they occur, but an **entitlement to the absences does not accumulate**. The employee can be absent, and be paid, but only if and when the circumstances arise. Examples are maternity/paternity pay, (in most cases) sick pay, and paid absence for jury service.

Measurement

The cost of accumulating paid absences should be measured as the additional amount that the entity expects to pay as a result of the unused entitlement that has accumulated at the end of the reporting period.

Profit sharing or bonus plans

Profit shares or bonuses payable within 12 months after the end of the accounting period should be recognised as an expected cost when the entity has a **present obligation to pay** it, ie when the employer has no real option but to pay it. This will usually be when the employer recognises the profit or other performance achievement to which the profit share or bonus relates. The measurement of the constructive obligation reflects the possibility that some employees may leave without receiving a bonus.

3 Post-employment benefits

Many employers provide post-employment benefits for their employees after they have stopped working. **Pension schemes** are the most obvious example, but an employer might provide post-employment death benefits to the dependants of former employees, or post-employment medical care.

Post-employment benefit schemes are often referred to as '**plans**'. The 'plan' receives regular contributions from the employer (and sometimes from current employees as well) and the money is invested in assets, such as stocks and shares and other investments. The post-employment benefits are paid out of the income from the plan assets (dividends, interest) or from money from the sale of some plan assets.

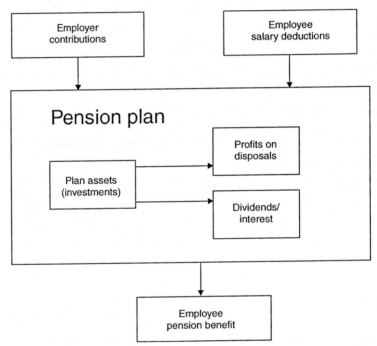

There are two types or categories of post-employment benefit plan, as given in the definitions in Section 1 above.

(a) **Defined contribution plans**. With such plans, the employer (and possibly current employees too) pay regular contributions into the plan of a given or 'defined' amount each year. The contributions are invested, and the size of the post-employment benefits paid to former employees depends on how well or how badly the plan's investments perform. If the investments perform well, the plan will be able to afford higher benefits than if the investments performed less well.

(b) **Defined benefit plans**. These are defined very simply as 'other than defined contribution plans'. But behind that simple definition is a complex and expensive arrangement from which many companies are now seeking to extricate themselves. With these plans, the size of the post-employment benefits is determined in advance, ie the benefits are 'defined'. The employer (and possibly current employees too) pay contributions into the plan, and the contributions are invested. The size of the contributions is set at an amount that is expected to earn enough investment returns to meet the obligation to pay the post-employment benefits. If, however, it becomes apparent that the assets in the fund are insufficient, the employer will be required to make additional contributions into the plan to make up the expected shortfall. On the other hand, if the fund's assets appear to be larger than they need to be, and in excess of what is required to pay the post-employment benefits, the employer may be allowed to take a 'contribution holiday' (ie stop paying in contributions for a while).

It is important to make a clear distinction between the following.

(a)   **Funding** a defined benefit plan, ie paying contributions into the plan

(b)   **Accounting** for the cost of funding a defined benefit plan

The key difference between the two types of plan is the nature of the 'promise' made by the entity to the employees in the scheme:

(a)   Under a defined contribution plan, the 'promise' is to pay the agreed amount of contributions, Once this is done, the entity has no further liability and no exposure to risks related to the performance of the assets held in the plan.

(b)   Under a defined benefit plan, the 'promise' is to pay the amount of benefits agreed under the plan. The entity is taking on a far more uncertain liability that may change in future as a result of many variables and has continuing exposure to risks related to the performance of assets held in the plan. In simple terms, of the plan assets are insufficient to meet the plan liabilities to pay pensions in future, the entity will have to make up any deficit.

Multi-employer plans

These were defined above. IAS 19 requires an entity to **classify** such a plan as a defined contribution plan or a defined benefit plan, depending on its terms (including any constructive obligation beyond those terms).

For a multi-employer plan that is a **defined benefit plan**, the entity should account for its proportionate share of the defined benefit obligation, plan assets and cost associated with the plan in the same way as for any other defined benefit plan and make full disclosure.

When there is **insufficient information** to use defined benefit accounting, then the multi-employer plan should be accounted for as a defined contribution plan and additional disclosures made (that the plan is in fact a defined benefit plan and information about any known surplus or deficit).

4 Defined contribution plans

Accounting for payments into defined contribution plans is straightforward.

(a) The **obligation** is determined by the amount paid into the plan in each period.

(b) There are no actuarial assumptions to make.

(c) If the obligation is settled in the current period (or at least no later than 12 months after the end of the current period) there is no **requirement for discounting**.

IAS 19 requires the following.

(a) **Contributions** to a defined contribution plan should be recognised as an **expense** in the period they are payable (except to the extent that labour costs may be included within the cost of assets).

(b) Any liability for **unpaid contributions** that are due as at the end of the period should be recognised as a **liability** (accrued expense).

(c) Any **excess contributions** paid should be recognised as an asset (prepaid expense), but only to the extent that the prepayment will lead to, eg a reduction in future payments or a cash refund.

In the (unusual) situation where contributions to a defined contribution plan do not fall due entirely within 12 months after the end of the period in which the employees performed the related service, then these should be **discounted**. The discount rate to be used is discussed below.

Disclosure requirements

(a) A **description** of the plan

(b) The amount recognised as an **expense** in the period

5 Defined benefit plans: recognition and measurement

Accounting for defined benefit plans is much more complex. The complexity of accounting for defined benefit plans stems largely from the following factors.

(a) The future benefits (arising from employee service in the current or prior years) cannot be estimated exactly, but whatever they are, the employer will have to pay them, and the liability should therefore be recognised now. To estimate these future obligations, it is necessary to use actuarial assumptions.

(b) The obligations payable in future years should be valued, by discounting, on a present value basis. This is because the obligations may be settled in many years' time.

(c) If actuarial assumptions change, the amount of required contributions to the fund will change, and there may be actuarial gains or losses. A contribution into a fund in any period is not necessarily the total for that period, due to actuarial gains or losses.

Most of the definitions given in the standard (shown in Section 1) are to do with defined benefit plans. These are additional important terms:

The **net defined benefit liability (asset)** is the deficit or surplus, adjusted for any effect of limiting a net defined benefit asset to the asset ceiling.

The **deficit or surplus** is:

(a) The present value of the defined benefit obligation less
(b) The fair value of plan assets (if any).

The **asset ceiling** is the present value of any economic benefits available in the form of refunds from the plan or reductions in future contributions to the plan.

The **present value of a defined benefit** obligation is the present value, without deducting any plan assets, of expected future payments required to settle the obligation resulting from employee service in the current and prior periods.

Plan assets comprise:

(a) Assets held by a long-term employee benefit fund; and
(b) Qualifying insurance policies

Assets held by a long-term employee benefit fund are assets (other than non-transferable financial instruments issued by the reporting entity) that:

(a) Are held by an entity (a fund) that is legally separate from the reporting entity and exists solely to pay or fund employee benefits; and

(b) Are available to be used only to pay or fund employee benefits, are not available to the reporting entity's own creditors (even in bankruptcy), and cannot be returned to the reporting entity, unless either:

    (i) The remaining assets of the fund are sufficient to meet all the related employee benefit obligations of the plan or the reporting entity; or

    (ii) The assets are returned to the reporting entity to reimburse it for employee benefits already paid.

A **qualifying insurance policy** is an insurance policy* issued by an insurer that is not a related party (as defined in IAS 24 *Related party disclosures*) of the reporting entity, if the proceeds of the policy:

(a) Can be used only to pay or fund employee benefits under a defined benefit plan; and

(b) Are not available to the reporting entity's own creditors (even in bankruptcy) and cannot be paid to the reporting entity, unless either:

> (i) The proceeds represent surplus assets that are not needed for the policy to meet all the related employee benefit obligations; or
>
> (ii) The proceeds are returned to the reporting entity to reimburse it for employee benefits already paid.
>
> **Fair value** is the price that would be received to sell an asset in an orderly transaction between market participants at the measurement date.

Outline of the method

step 1

Determine the deficit or surplus:

(a) An **actuarial technique** (the **Projected Unit Credit Method**), should be used to make a reliable estimate of the amount of future benefits employees have earned from service in relation to the current and prior years. The entity must determine how much benefit should be attributed to service performed by employees in the current period, and in prior periods. Assumptions include, for example, assumptions about employee turnover, mortality rates, future increases in salaries (if these will affect the eventual size of future benefits such as pension payments).

(b) The benefit should be **discounted** to arrive at the present value of the defined benefit obligation and the current service cost.

(c) The **fair value** of any **plan assets** should be deducted from the present value of the defined benefit obligation.

step 2

The surplus or deficit determined in Step 1 may have to be adjusted if a net benefit asset has to be restricted by the **asset ceiling**.

step 3

Determine the amounts to be recognised in **profit or loss:**

(a) **Current service cost**

(b) Any **past service cost** and **gain or loss on settlement**

(c) Net interest on the net defined benefit liability (asset)

step 4

Determine the **remeasurements** of the **net defined benefit liability (asset)**, to be recognised in **other comprehensive income** (items that will not be reclassified to profit or loss):

(a) **Actuarial gains and losses**

(b) **Return on plan assets** (excluding amounts included in net interst on the net defined benefit liability (asset)

(c) Any change in the effect of the **asset ceiling** (excluding amounts included in net interest on the net defined benefit liability (asset)

Constructive obligation

IAS 19 makes it very clear that it is not only its legal obligation under the formal terms of a defined benefit plan that an entity must account for, but also any constructive obligation that it may have. A **constructive obligation**, which will arise from the entity's informal practices, exists when the entity has no realistic alternative but to pay employee benefits, for example if any change in the informal practices would cause unacceptable damage to employee relationships.

The Projected Unit Credit Method

With this method, it is assumed that each period of service by an employee gives rise to an **additional unit of future benefits**. The present value of that unit of future benefits can be calculated, and attributed to the period in which the service is given. The units, each measured separately, build up to the overall obligation. The accumulated present value of (discounted) future benefits will incur interest over time as the discount unwinds, and an interest expense should be recognised.

In practice, the mathematics will be complex. Here is a simplified example, using figures rounded to whole numbers.

Example: projected unit credit method

A lump sum benefit is payable on termination of service and equal to 1% of final salary for each year of service. The salary in year 1 is $10,000 and is assumed to increase at 7% (compound) each year. The discount rate used is 10% per year. The following table shows how the obligation builds up for an employee who is expected to leave at the end of year 5, assuming that there are no changes in actuarial assumptions. [This example ignores the additional adjustment needed to reflect the probability that the employee may leave the entity at an earlier or later date.]

Year	1	2	3	4	5
	$	$	$	$	$
Benefit attributed to:					
Prior years	0	131	262	393	524
Current year (1% × final salary)	131	131	131	131	131
Current and prior years	131	262	393	524	655
Opening obligation	–	89	196	324	476
Interest at 10%	–	9	20	33	48
Current service cost	89	98	108	119	131
Closing obligation	89	196	324	476	655

Notes

1   The opening obligation is the present value of the benefit attributed to prior years

2   The current service cost is the present value of the benefit attributed to the current year

3   The closing obligation is the present value of the benefit attributed to current and prior years

Actuarial assumptions

Actuarial assumptions are needed **to estimate the size of the future (post-employment) benefits** that will be payable under a defined benefits scheme. The main categories of actuarial assumptions are as follows.

Demographic assumptions	Financial assumptions
Mortality rates before and after retirement	Discount rates to apply
Rate of employee turnover	Expected return on plan assets
Early retirement	Future salary levels (allowing for seniority and promotion as well as inflation)
Claim rates under medical plans for former employees	Future rate of increase in medical costs (not just inflationary cost rises, but also cost rises specific to medical treatments and to medical treatments required given the expectations of longer average life expectancy)

The standard requires actuarial assumptions to be neither too cautious nor too imprudent: they should be '**unbiased**'. They should also be based on '**market expectations**' at the reporting date, over the period during which the obligations will be settled. The discount rate adopted should be determined by reference to market yields (at the reporting date) on high quality fixed-rate corporate bonds.

The statement of financial position

In the statement of financial position, the amount recognised as a **defined benefit liability** (which may be a negative amount, ie an asset) should be the total of the following.

(a)   The **present value of the defined obligation** at the year end, **minus**

(b)   The **fair value of the assets of the plan** as at the year end (if there are any) out of which the future obligations to current and past employees will be directly settled

Plan assets

Plan assets are:

(a) Assets such as stocks and shares, held by a fund that is legally separate from the reporting entity, which exists solely to pay employee benefits

(b) Insurance policies, issued by an insurer that is not a related party, the proceeds of which can only be used to pay employee benefits

Investments which may be used for purposes other than to pay employee benefits are not plan assets.

The standard requires that the plan assets are measured at fair value, as 'the price that would be received to sell an asset in an orderly transaction between market participants at the measurement date. You may spot that this definition is slightly different to the revised definition in accordance with IFRS 13 *Fair value measurement*. The two standards were being updated around the same time so the definitions are currently out of step but the IFRS 13 definition will replace that in IAS 19.

IAS 19 includes the following **specific requirements:**

(a) The plan assets should exclude any contributions due from the employer but not yet paid.

(b) Plan assets are reduced by any liabilities of the fund that do not relate to employee benefits, such as trade and other payables.

The statement of profit or loss and other comprehensive income

All of the gains and losses that affect the plan obligation and plan asset must be recognised. The **components of defined benefit cost must be recognised as follows** in the statement of profit or loss and other comprehensive income:

Component	Recognised in
(a) **Service cost**	Profit or loss
(b) **Net interest on the net defined benefit liability**	Profit or loss
(c) **Remeasurements of the net defined benefit liability**	Other comprehensive income (not reclassified to P/L)

Service costs

These comprise:

(a)   **Current service cost,** this is the increase in the present value of the defined benefit obligation resulting from employee services during the period. The measurement and recognition of this cost was introduced above.

(b)   **Past service cost,** which is the change in the obligation relating to service in **prior periods.** This results from amendments or curtailments to the pension plan, and

(c)   Any **gain or loss on settlement.**

The detail relating to points (b)and (c) above will be covered in a later section. First we will continue with the basic elements of accounting for defined benefit pension costs.

Net interest on the defined benefit liability (asset)

In the outline of the method above we looked at the recognition and measurement of the defined benefit obligation. This figure is the discounted **present value** of the future benefits payable. Every year the discount must be "unwound", increasing the present value of the obligation as time passes through an interest charge.

Interest calculation

IAS 19 requires that the interest should be calculated on the **net defined benefit liability (asset).** This means that the amount recognised in profit or loss is the net of the interest charge on the obligation and the interest income recognised on the assets.

The calculation is as follows:

$$\boxed{\text{Net defined benefit liability/(asset)}} \quad \times \quad \boxed{\text{Discount rate}}$$

The **net defined benefit liability/(asset)** should be determined as at the **start** of the accounting period, taking account of changes during the period as a result of contributions paid into the scheme and benefits paid out.

Discount rate

The **discount rate** adopted should be determined by reference to **market yields** on high quality fixed-rate corporate bonds. In the absence of a 'deep' market in such bonds, the yields on comparable government bonds should be used as reference instead. The maturity of the corporate bonds that are used to determine a discount rate should have a term to maturity that is consistent with the expected maturity of the post-employment benefit obligations, although a single weighted average discount rate is sufficient.

BPP
LEARNING MEDIA

The guidelines comment that there may be some difficulty in obtaining a **reliable yield for long-term maturities**, say 30 or 40 years from now. This should not, however, be a significant problem: the present value of obligations payable in many years time will be relatively small and unlikely to be a significant proportion of the total defined benefit obligation. The total obligation is therefore unlikely to be sensitive to errors in the assumption about the discount rate for long-term maturities (beyond the maturities of long-term corporate or government bonds).

Remeasurements of the net defined benefit liability

Remeasurements of the net defined benefit liability/(asset) comprise:

(a)   Actuarial gains and losses;

(b)   The return on plan assets, (excluding amounts included in net interest on the net defined benefit liability/(asset)

(c)   Any change in the effect of the asset ceiling, (excluding amounts included in net interest on the net defined benefit liability/(asset)

The gains and losses relating to points (a) and (b) above will arise in every defined benefit scheme so we will look at these in this section. The asset ceiling is a complication that is not relevant in every case, so it is dealt with separately, later in the chapter.

Actuarial gains and losses

At the end of each accounting period, a new valuation, using updated assumption, should be carried out on the obligation. Actuarial gains or losses arise because of the following.

- **Actual events** (eg employee turnover, salary increases) differ from the actuarial assumptions that were made to estimate the defined benefit obligations

- The effect of **changes to assumptions** concerning benefit payment options

- **Estimates are revised** (eg different assumptions are made about future employee turnover, salary rises, mortality rates, and so on)

- The effect of changes to the **discount rate**

Actuarial gains and losses are recognised in other comprehensive income. They are **not reclassified to profit or loss** under the 2011 revision to IAS 1.

Return on plan assets

A new valuation of the plan assets is carried out at each period end, using current fair values. Any difference between the new value, and what has been recognised up to that date (normally the opening balance, interest, and any cash payments into or out of the plan) is treated as a 'remeasurement' and recognised in other comprehensive income.

Part D 21: Employee benefits

Example

At 1 January 20X2 the fair value of the assets of a defined benefit plan were valued at $1,100,000 and the present value of the defined benefit obligation was $1,250,000.On 31 December 20X2, the plan received contributions from the employer of $490,000 and paid out benefits of $190,000.

The current service cost for the year was $360,000 and a discount rate of 6% is to be applied to the net liability/(asset).

After these transactions, the fair value of the plan's assets at 31 December 20X2 was $1.5m. The present value of the defined benefit obligation was $1,553,600.

We want to calculate the actuarial gains or losses and the return on plan assets and illustrate how this pension plan will be treated in the statement of profit or loss and other comprehensive income and statement of financial position for the year ended 31 December 20X2.

It is always useful to set up a working reconciling the assets and obligation:

	Assets $	Obligation $
Fair value/present value at 1/1/X2	1,100,000	1,250,000
Interest (1,100,000 × 6%)/(1,250,000 × 6%)	66,000	75,000
Current service cost		360,000
Contributions received	490,000	
Benefits paid	(190,000)	(190,000)
Return on plan assets (balancing figure)	34,000	–
Actuarial loss (balancing figure)	–	58,600
	1,500,000	1,553,600

The following accounting treatment is required:

In the **statement of profit or loss and other comprehensive income**, the following amounts will be recognised in **profit or loss**:

	$
Current service cost	360,000
Net interest on net defined benefit liability (75,000 – 66,000)	9,000

The following amount will be recognised in **other comprehensive income**:

	$
Actuarial loss less return on plan assets (58,600 – 34,000)	24,600

In the **statement of financial position**, the net defined benefit liability of $53,600 (1,553,600 – 1,500,000) will be recognised.

6 Defined benefit plans: other matters

We have now covered the basics of accounting for defined benefit plans. This section looks at the special circumstances of past service costs, curtailment and settlements.

Past service cost and gains and losses on settlement

We noted above that the total service cost may comprise not only the current service costs but other items, past service cost and gains and losses on settlement. This section explain these issues and their accounting treatment.

Past service cost

Past service cost is the change in the present value of the defined benefit obligation resulting from a plan **amendment** or **curtailment**.

A plan **amendment** arises when an entity either introduces a defined benefits plan or **changes the benefits payable** under an existing plan. As a result, the entity has taken on additional obligations that it has not hitherto provided for. For example, an employer might decide to introduce a medical benefits scheme for former employees. This will create a new defined benefit obligation, that has not yet been provided for.

A **curtailment occurs when an entity significantly reduces the number of employees covered by a plan.** This could result from an isolated event, such as closing a plant, discontinuing an operation or the termination or suspension of a plan.

Past service costs can be either **positive** (if the changes increase the obligation) or **negative** (if the change reduces the obligation).

Gains and losses on settlement

A **settlement** occurs either when an employer enters into a transaction to eliminate part or all of its post-employment benefit obligations(other than a payment of benefits to or on behalf of employees under the terms of the plan and included in the actuarial assumptions).

A curtailment and settlement might **happen together**, for example when an employer brings a defined benefit plan to an end by settling the obligation with a one-off lump sum payment and then scrapping the plan.

The gain or losses on a settlement is the difference between:

(a) The **present value of the defined benefit obligation** being settled, as valued on the date of the settlement; and

(b) The **settlement price**, including any plan assts transferred and any payments made by the entity directly in connection with the settlement.

Accounting for past service cost and gains and losses on settlement

An entity should **remeasure the obligation** (and the related plan assets, if any) using current actuarial assumptions, before determining past service cost or a gain or loss on settlement.

The rules for recognition for these items are:

Past service costs are recognised at the earlier of the following dates:

(a)   When the plan amendment or curtailment occurs

(b)   When the entity recognises related restructuring costs (in accordance with IAS 37) or termination benefits

Employee and third party contributions

A November 2013 amendment to IAS 19 clarifies the treatment of employee and third party contributions to defined benefit schemes, such as fixed amounts deducted from an employees salary. The amendment sets out how such contributions should be attributed to periods of service.

If the amount of the contributions is independent of the number of years of service, the contributions are permitted to be recognised as a reduction in the service cost in the period in which the related service is rendered.

If the amount of the contribution depends on the number of years of service, the contributions must be attributed to periods of service using the same attribution method as for the gross benefit – either using the plan's contribution formula or on a straight-line basis.

This is a simplification of the 2011 requirements under which the contributions had to be attributed to periods of service in accordance with the plan's benefit formula.

Asset ceiling test

When we looked at the recognition of the net defined benefit liability/(asset) in the statement of financial position at the beginning of Section 5 the term 'asset ceiling' was mentioned. This term relates to a threshold established by IAS 19 to ensure that any defined benefit asset (ie a pension surplus) is carried at **no more than its recoverable amount**. In simple terms, this means that any net asset is restricted to the amount of cash savings that will be available to the entity in future.

Net defined benefit assets

A net defined benefit asset may arise if the plan has been overfunded or if actuarial gains have arisen. This meets the definition of an asset (as stated in the *Conceptual Framework*) because **all** of the following apply:

(a) The entity **controls a resource** (the ability to use the surplus to generate future benefits).

(b) That control is the **result of past events** (contributions paid by the entity and service rendered by the employee).

(c) **Future benefits** are available to the entity in the form of a reduction in future contributions or a cash refund, either directly or indirectly to another plan in deficit.

The **asset ceiling** is the **present value** of those future benefits. The discount rate used is the same as that used to calculate the net interest on the net defined benefit liability/(asset). The net defined benefit asset would be reduced to the asset ceiling threshold. Any related write down would be treated as a **remeasurement** and recognised in **other comprehensive income.**

If the asset ceiling adjustment was needed in a subsequent year, the changes in its value would be treated as follows:

(a) **Interest** (as it is a discounted amount) recognised in profit or loss as part of the net interest amount

(b) **Other changes** recognised in profit or loss

7 Other long term benefits

IAS 19 (para. 8) defines **other long-term employee benefits** as all employee benefits other than short-term employee benefits, post-employment benefits and termination benefits if not expected to be settled wholly before twelve months after the end of the annual reporting period in which the employees render the related service.

The types of benefits that might fall into this category include:

(a) Long-term paid absences such as long-service or sabbatical leave
(b) Jubilee or other long-service benefits
(c) Long-term disability benefits; profit-sharing and bonuses
(d) Deferred remuneration

Accounting treatment for other long-term benefits

There are many similarities between these types of benefits and defined benefit pensions. For example, in a long-term bonus scheme, the employees may provide service over a number of periods to earn their entitlement to a payment at a later date. In some case, the entity may put cash aside, or invest it in some way (perhaps by taking out an insurance policy) to meet the liabilities when they arise.

As there is normally far less uncertainty relating to the measurement of these benefits, IAS 19 requires a simpler method of accounting for them. Unlike the accounting method for post-employment benefits, this method does **not recognise remeasurements in other comprehensive income.**

The entity should recognise all of the following in **profit or loss.**

(a) **Service cost**
(b) **Net interest** on the defined benefit liability(asset)
(c) **Remeasurement** of the defined benefit liability (asset)

8 Disclosures

Principles of disclosures required by IAS 19

The outline requirements are for the entity to disclose information that:

(a) Explains the characteristics of its defined benefit plans and risks associated with them

(b) Identifies and explains the amounts in its financial statements arising from its defined benefit plans

(c) Describes how its defined benefit plans may affect the amount, timing and uncertainty of the entity's future cash flows

9 Other issues

Revisions to IAS 19

In June 2011, the IASB issued a revised version of *IAS 19 Employee benefits.* It is the revised version that has been covered in this chapter. The purpose of the revision is to improve accounting in the short-term for employee benefits in the light of criticisms of the current IAS 19 by users and preparers of financial statements, including the US SEC and the EU's European Financial Reporting Advisory Group (that approves IFRS for use in the EU). In the long term, the IASB intends to produce a common IASB-FASB standard, but recognises that this will take many years to complete.

Accounting for employee benefits, particularly retirement benefits, had been seen as **problematic** in the following respects:

(a) **Treatment in the statement of profit or loss and other comprehensive income.** It has been argued that the complexity of the presentation makes the treatment hard to understand and the splitting up of the various components is arbitrary.

(b) **Fair value and volatility.** The fair value of plan assets may be volatile, and values in the statement of financial position may fluctuate. However, not all those fluctuations are recognised in the statement of financial position.

(c) **Fair value and economic reality.** Fair value, normally market value, is used to value plan assets. This may not reflect economic reality, because fair values fluctuate in the short term, while pension scheme assets and liabilities are held for the long term. It could be argued that plan assets should be valued on an actuarial basis instead.

(d) **Problems in determining the discount rate used in measuring the defined benefit obligation.** Guidance is contradictory.

The main changes

Scope

Because the revised standard is a short-term measure, its scope is limited to the following areas.

(a) Recognition of gains and losses arising from defined benefit plans
(b) Presentation of changes in value of the defined benefit obligation and assets

However, the IASB recognises that the scope could be expanded to include items such as:

(a) **Recognition of the obligation based on the 'benefit' formula.** This current approach means that unvested benefits are recognised as a liability which is inconsistent with other IFRSs.

(b) **Measurement of the obligation.** The 'projected unit credit method' (as defined before) is used which is based on expected benefits (including salary increases). Alternative approaches include accumulated benefit, projected benefit, fair value and settlement value.

(c) **Presenting of a net defined benefit obligation.** Defined benefit plan assets and liabilities are currently presented net on the grounds that the fund is not controlled (which would require consolidation of the fund).

(d) **Multi-employer plans.** Current accounting is normally for the entity's proportionate share of the obligation, plan assets and costs as for a single-employer plan, but an exemption is currently provided where sufficient information is not available, and defined contribution accounting can be used instead. Should the exemption be removed?

(e) Accounting for **benefits that are based on contributions and a promised return.**

The main changes

(a) **Actuarial gains and losses**

    (i) The revised standard requires actuarial gains and losses to be **recognised in the period incurred.**

    (ii) The previous standard permitted a range of choices for the recognition of actuarial gains and losses:

        (1) Immediate recognition in other comprehensive income (as now) was permitted

        (2) Deferral of actuarial gains and losses was permitted through what was known as the 'corridor' method. The 'corridor' was defined as the higher of 10% of the opening plan assets or 10% of the opening plan obligation. If the accumulated actuarial gains and losses brought forward exceeded the corridor, the excess would then be divided by the average remaining service lives of employees in the scheme and this amount recognised in profit or loss. The balance of unrecognised gains and losses was carried on the statement of financial position.

        (3) Actuarial gains and losses could also be recognised in profit or loss on any other systematic basis, subject to the 'corridor' amount as a minimum.

    (iii) The changes will improve comparability between companies and will also eliminate some of the anomalies where the effect of unrecognised actuarial gains and losses (and unrecognised past service costs (see point (iii) below) could turn a deficit into a surplus on the statement of financial position.

(b) **Remeasurements**

(i) The revised standard introduced the term 'remeasurements'. This is made up of the actuarial gains and losses on the defined benefit obligation, the difference between actual investment returns and the return implied by the net interest cost and the effect of the asset ceiling. Remeasurements are recognised immediately in other comprehensive income and **not** reclassified to profit or loss.

(ii) This reduces diversity of presentation that was possible under the previous standard.

(b) **Net interest cost**

(i) The revised standard requires interest to be calculated on **both** the plan assets and plan obligation at the same rate and the **net** interest to be recognised in the statement of profit or loss and other comprehensive income. The rationale for this is the view that the **net** defined benefit liability/(asset) is equivalent to an amount owed by the company to the plan.

(ii) The difference under the previous standard was that an 'Expected return on assets' was calculated, based on assumptions about the long term rates of return on the particular classes of asset held within the plan.

(c) **Past service costs**

(i) The revised standard requires all past service costs to be recognised in the period of plan amendment.

(ii) The previous standard made a distinction between past service costs that were **vested** (all past service costs related to former employees and those that related to current employees and not subject to any condition relating to further service) and those that were **not vested** (relating to current employees and where the entitlement was subject to further service). Only **vested** past service costs were recognised in profit or loss, and unvested benefits were deferred, and spread over remaining service lives.

Foreign currency translation

22

1 Foreign currency

If a company trades overseas, it will buy or sell assets in **foreign currencies**. For example, an Indian company might buy materials from Canada, and pay for them in US dollars, and then sell its finished goods in Germany, receiving payment in Euros, or perhaps in some other currency. If the company owes money in a foreign currency at the end of the accounting year, or holds assets which were bought in a foreign currency, those liabilities or assets must be translated into the local currency (in this text $), in order to be shown in the books of account.

A company might have a subsidiary abroad (ie a foreign entity that it owns), and the subsidiary will trade in its own local currency. The subsidiary will keep books of account and prepare its annual accounts in its own currency. However, at the year end, the holding company must 'consolidate' the results of the overseas subsidiary into its group accounts, so that somehow, the assets and liabilities and the **annual profits of the subsidiary must be translated from the foreign currency into $.**

If foreign currency exchange rates remained constant, there would be no accounting problem. As you will be aware, however, foreign exchange rates are continually changing, and it is not inconceivable for example, that the rate of exchange between the Polish zloty and sterling might be Z6.2 to £1 at the start of the accounting year, and Z5.6 to £1 at the end of the year (in this example, a 10% increase in the relative strength of the zloty).

There are two distinct types of foreign currency transaction, **conversion and translation**.

Conversion gains and losses

Conversion is the process of exchanging amounts of one foreign currency for another. For example, suppose a local company buys a large consignment of goods from a supplier in Argentina. The order is placed on 1 May and the agreed price is 124,250 pesos. At the time of delivery the rate of foreign exchange was 3.50 pesos to $1. The local company would record the amount owed in its books as follows.

DEBIT	Inventory account (124,250 ÷ 3.5)	$35,500	
CREDIT	Payables account		$35,500

When the local company comes to pay the supplier, it needs to obtain some foreign currency. By this time, however, if the rate of exchange has altered to 3.55 pesos to $1, the cost of raising 124,250 pesos would be (÷ 3.55) $35,000. The company would need to spend only $35,000 to settle a debt for inventories 'costing' $35,500. Since it would be administratively difficult to alter the value of the inventories in the company's books of account, it is more appropriate to record a profit on conversion of $500.

DEBIT	Payables account	$35,500	
CREDIT	Cash		$35,000
CREDIT	Profit on conversion		$500

Profits (or losses) on conversion would be included in profit or loss for the year in which conversion (whether payment or receipt) takes place.

Suppose that another home company sells goods to a Chinese company, and it is agreed that payment should be made in Chinese Yuan at a price of Y116,000. We will further assume that the exchange rate at the time of sale is Y10.74 to $1, but when the debt is eventually paid, the rate has altered to Y10.79 to $1. The company would record the sale as follows.

DEBIT	Receivables account (116,000 ÷ 10.75)	$10,800	
CREDIT	Sales account		$10,800

When the Y116,000 are paid, the local company will convert them into $, to obtain (÷ 10.79) $10,750. In this example, there has been a loss on conversion of $50 which will be written off to profit or loss:

DEBIT	Cash	$10,750	
DEBIT	Loss on conversion	$50	
CREDIT	Receivables account		$10,800

There are **no accounting difficulties** concerned with foreign currency conversion gains or losses, and the procedures described above are uncontroversial.

BPP
LEARNING MEDIA

Translation

Foreign currency translation, as distinct from conversion, does not involve the act of exchanging one currency for another. **Translation is required at the end of an accounting period when a company still holds assets or liabilities in its statement of financial position which were obtained or incurred in a foreign currency.**

These assets or liabilities might consist of any of the following:

(a) An individual home company holding individual **assets** or **liabilities** originating in a foreign currency 'deal'

(b) An individual home company with a separate **branch** of the business operating abroad which keeps its own books of account in the local currency

(c) A home company which wishes to consolidate the **results of a foreign subsidiary**

There has been great **uncertainty** about the method which should be used to translate the following.

- Value of assets and liabilities from a foreign currency into $ for the year end statement of financial position

- Profits of an independent foreign branch or subsidiary into $ for the annual statement of profit or loss and other comprehensive income

Suppose, for example, that an Albanian subsidiary purchases a piece of property for Leks 2,100,000 on 31 December 20X7. The rate of exchange at this time was L70 to $1. During 20X8, the subsidiary charged depreciation on the building of L16,800, so that at 31 December 20X8, the subsidiary recorded the asset as follows.

	L
Property at cost	2,100,000
Less accumulated depreciation	(16,800)
Carrying amount	2,083,200

At this date, the rate of exchange has changed to L60 to $1.

The local holding company must translate the asset's value into $, but there is a choice of exchange rates.

(a) Should the rate of exchange for translation be the rate which existed at the date of purchase, which would give a net book value of 2,083,200 ÷ 70 = $29,760?

(b) Should the rate of exchange for translation be the rate existing at the end of 20X8 (the closing rate of L60 to $1)? This would give a net book value of $34,720.

Similarly, should depreciation be charged in the group statement of profit or loss at the rate of L70 to $1 (the historical rate), L60 to $1 (the closing rate), or at an average rate for the year (say, L64 to $1)?

Consolidated accounts

If a parent has a subsidiary whose accounts are presented in a foreign currency, those accounts must be translated into the local currency before they can be included in the consolidated financial statements.

- Should the subsidiary's accounts be translated as if the subsidiary is an extension of the parent?

- Or should they be translated as if the subsidiary is a separate business?

Where the affairs of a foreign operation are very closely interlinked with those of the investing company, it should be included in the consolidated financial statements as if the transactions had been entered into by the investing company in its own currency. Non-monetary assets and depreciation are translated at **historical rate** and sales, purchase and expenses at **average rate**. **Exchange differences** arising on retranslation are reported as part of **profit or loss** on ordinary activities.

Where a foreign operation is effectively a separate business, the **closing rate** is used for most items in the financial statements. **Exchange differences** are recognised **in other comprehensive income**.

2 IAS 21: The effects of changes in foreign exchange rates

The questions discussed above are addressed by IAS 21. We will examine those matters which affect single company accounts here.

These are some of the definitions given by IAS 21.

Foreign currency. A currency other than the functional currency of the entity.

Functional currency. The currency of the primary economic environment in which the entity operates.

Presentation currency. The currency in which the financial statements are presented.

Exchange rate. The ratio of exchange for two currencies.

Exchange difference. The difference resulting from translating a given number of units of one currency into another currency at different exchange rates.

Closing rate. The spot exchange rate at the reporting date.

Spot exchange rate. The exchange rate for immediate delivery.

Monetary items. Units of currency held and assets and liabilities to be received or paid in a fixed or determinable number of units of currency. *(IAS 21: para. 8)*

Each entity – whether an individual company, a parent of a group, or an operation within a group (such as a subsidiary, associate or branch) – should determine its **functional currency** and **measure its results and financial position in that currency**.

For most individual companies the functional currency will be the currency of the country in which they are located and in which they carry out most of their transactions. Determining the functional currency is much more likely to be an issue where an entity operates as part of a group. IAS 21 contains detailed guidance on how to determine an entity's functional currency and we will look at this in more detail.

An entity can present its financial statements in any currency (or currencies) it chooses. IAS 21 deals with the situation in which financial statements are presented in a currency other than the functional currency.

Again, this is unlikely to be an issue for most individual companies. Their presentation currency will normally be the same as their functional currency (the currency of the country in which they operate). A company's presentation currency may be different from its functional currency if it operates within a group and we will look at this further on.

Foreign currency transactions: Initial recognition

IAS 21 states that a foreign currency transaction should be recorded, on initial recognition in the functional currency, by applying the exchange rate between the reporting currency and the foreign currency **at the date of the transaction** to the foreign currency amount.

An **average rate** for a period may be used if exchange rates do not fluctuate significantly.

Reporting at subsequent reporting dates

The following rules apply at each subsequent reporting date.

(a) Report foreign currency **monetary items** using the **closing rate**.

(b) Report **non-monetary items** (eg non-current assets, inventories) which are carried at **historical cost** in a foreign currency using the **exchange rate at the date of the transaction** (historical rate).

(c) Report **non-monetary items** which are carried at **fair value** in a foreign currency using the exchange rates that existed **when the values were determined**.

Recognition of exchange differences

Exchange differences occur when there is a **change in the exchange rate** between the transaction date and the date of settlement of monetary items arising from a foreign currency transaction.

Exchange differences arising on the settlement of monetary items (receivables, payables, loans, cash in a foreign currency) or on translating an entity's monetary items at rates different from those at which they were translated initially, or reported in previous financial statements, should be **recognised in profit or loss** in the period in which they arise.

There are two situations to consider.

(a) The transaction is **settled in the same period** as that in which it occurred: all the exchange difference is recognised in that period.

(b) The transaction is **settled in a subsequent accounting period**: the exchange difference recognised in each intervening period up to the period of settlement is determined by the change in exchange rates during that period.

In other words, where a monetary item has not been settled at the end of a period, it should be **restated using the closing exchange rate** and any gain or loss taken to profit or loss (income statement).

BPP
LEARNING MEDIA

Example

R Co, whose year end is 31 December, buys some goods from SA of France on 30 September. The invoice value is €40,000 and is due for settlement in equal instalments on 30 November and 31 January. The exchange rate moved as follows.

	€ = $1
30 September	1.60
30 November	1.80
31 December	1.90
31 January	1.85

What are the accounting entries in the books of R Co?

The purchase will be recorded in the books of R Co using the rate of exchange ruling on 30 September.

DEBIT	Purchases	$25,000	
CREDIT	Trade payables		$25,000

Being the $ cost of goods purchased for €40,000 (€40,000 ÷ €1.60/$1)

On 30 November, R Co must pay €20,000. This will cost €20,000 ÷ €1.80/$1 = $11,111 and the company has therefore made an exchange gain of $12,500 − $11,111 = $1,389.

DEBIT	Trade payables	$12,500	
CREDIT	Exchange gains: Profit or loss		$1,389
CREDIT	Cash		$11,111

On 31 December, the reporting date, the outstanding liability will be recalculated using the rate applicable to that date: €20,000 ÷ €1.90/$1 = $10,526. A further exchange gain of $1,974 has been made and will be recorded as follows.

DEBIT	Trade payables	$1,974	
CREDIT	Exchange gains: Profit or loss		$1,974

The total exchange gain of $3,363 will be included in the operating profit for the year ending 31 December.

On 31 January, R Co must pay the second instalment of €20,000. This will cost them $10,811 (€20,000 ÷ €1.85/$1).

DEBIT	Trade payables	$10,526	
	Exchange losses: Profit or loss	$285	
CREDIT	Cash		$10,811

When a gain or loss on a non-monetary item is recognised **in other comprehensive income** (for example, where property is revalued), any **related exchange differences** should also be **recognised in other comprehensive income**.

3 IAS 21: Consolidated financial statements stage

The following definitions are relevant here.

> **Foreign operation.** A subsidiary, associate, joint venture or branch of a reporting entity, the activities of which are based or conducted in a country or currency other than those of the reporting entity.
>
> **Net investment in a foreign operation.** The amount of the reporting entity's interest in the net assets of that operation. *(IAS 21: para. 8)*

Determining functional currency

A holding or parent company with foreign operations must **translate the financial statements** of those operations into its own reporting currency before they can be consolidated into the group accounts. There are two methods: **the method used depends** upon **whether** the foreign operation has the **same functional currency as the parent.**

IAS 21 states that an entity should consider the following factors in determining its functional currency:

(a)   The currency that mainly **influences sales prices** for goods and services (often the currency in which prices are denominated and settled)

(b)   The currency of the **country whose competitive forces and regulations** mainly determine the sales prices of its goods and services

(c)   The currency that mainly **influences labour, material and other costs** of providing goods or services (often the currency in which prices are denominated and settled)

Sometimes the functional currency of an entity is not immediately obvious. Management must then exercise judgement and may also need to consider:

(a)   The currency in which **funds from financing activities** (raising loans and issuing equity) are generated

(b)   The currency in which **receipts from operating activities** are usually retained

Where a parent has a foreign operation a number of factors are considered:

(a)   Whether the activities of the foreign operation are carried out as an **extension of the parent**, rather than being carried out with a **significant degree of autonomy**

(b)   Whether **transactions with the parent** are a high or a low proportion of the foreign operation's activities

(c)   Whether cash flows from the activities of the foreign operation directly affect the cash flows of the parent and are readily available for remittance to it

(d)   Whether the activities of the foreign operation are **financed from its own cash flows** or by **borrowing from the parent**

To sum up: in order to determine the functional currency of a foreign operation it is necessary to consider the **relationship** between the foreign operation and its parent:

- If the foreign operation carries out its business as though it were an **extension of the parent's operations**, it almost certainly has the **same functional currency** as the parent.

- If the foreign operation is semi-autonomous it almost certainly has **a different functional currency** from the parent.

The translation method used has to reflect the economic reality of the relationship between the reporting entity (the parent) and the foreign operation.

Same functional currency as the reporting entity

In this situation, the foreign operation normally carries on its business as though it were an **extension of the reporting entity's operations**. For example, it may only sell goods imported from, and remit the proceeds directly to, the reporting entity.

Any **movement in the exchange rate** between the reporting currency and the foreign operation's currency will have an **immediate impact** on the reporting entity's cash flows from the foreign operations. In other words, changes in the exchange rate affect the **individual monetary items** held by the foreign operation, not the reporting entity's net investment in that operation.

Different functional currency from the reporting entity

In this situation, although the reporting entity may be able to exercise control, the foreign operation normally operates in a **semi-autonomous** way. It accumulates cash and other monetary items, generates income and incurs expenses, and may also arrange borrowings, all in its own local currency.

A change in the exchange rate will produce **little or no direct effect on the present and future cash flows** from operations of either the foreign operation or the reporting entity. Rather, the change in exchange rate affects the reporting entity's **net investment** in the foreign operation, not the individual monetary and non-monetary items held by the foreign operation.

Accounting treatment: different functional currency from the reporting entity

The financial statements of the foreign operation must be translated to the functional currency of the parent. Different procedures must be followed here, because the functional currency of the parent is the **presentation currency** of the foreign operation.

(a) The **assets and liabilities** shown in the foreign operation's statement of financial position are translated at the **closing rate** at the year end, regardless of the date on which those items originated. The balancing figure in the translated statement of financial position represents the reporting entity's net investment in the foreign operation.

(b) Amounts in the **statement of profit or loss and other comprehensive income** should be translated at the rate ruling at the date of the transaction (an **average rate** will usually be used for practical purposes).

(c) **Exchange differences** arising from the re translation at the end of each year of the parent's net investment should be **recognised in other comprehensive income**, not through the profit or loss for the year, until the disposal of the net investment. On disposal the gains or losses recognised to date will be reclassified to profit or loss.

Example: different functional currency from the reporting entity

A dollar-based company, set up a foreign subsidiary on 30 June 20X7. It subscribed €24,000 for share capital when the exchange rate was €2 = $1. The subsidiary, borrowed €72,000 and bought a non monetary asset for €96,000. The parent prepared its accounts on 31 December 20X7 and by that time the exchange rate had moved to €3 = $1. As a result of highly unusual circumstances, the subsidiary sold its asset early in 20X8 for €96,000. It repaid its loan and was liquidated. The parent's capital of €24,000 was repaid in February 20X8 when the exchange rate was €3 = $1.

From the above it can be seen that the parent will record its initial investment at $12,000 which is the starting cost of its shares. The statement of financial position of the subsidiary at 31 December 20X7 is summarised below.

	€'000
Non-monetary asset	96
Share capital	24
Loan	72
	96

This may be translated as follows.

	$'000
Non-monetary asset	
(€3 = $1)	32
Share capital and reserves (retained earnings) (balancing figure)	8
Loan (€3 = $1)	24
	32
Exchange gain/(loss) for 20X7	(4)

The exchange gain and loss are the differences between the value of the original investment ($12,000) and the total of share capital and reserves (retained earnings) as disclosed by the above statements of financial position.

On liquidation, the parent will receive $8,000 (€24,000 converted at €3 = $1). No gain or loss will arise in 20X8.

Comprehensive example

The abridged statements of financial position and statement of profit or loss and other comprehensive incomes of Darius Co and its foreign subsidiary, Xerxes Inc, appear below.

DRAFT STATEMENT OF FINANCIAL POSITION AS AT 31 DECEMBER 20X9

	Darius Co		Xerxes Inc	
	$	$	€	€
Assets				
Non-current assets				
Plant at cost	600		500	
Less depreciation	(250)		(200)	
		350		300
Investment in Xerxes				
100 €1 shares		25		–
		375		300
Current assets				
Inventories	225		200	
Receivables	150		100	
		375		300
		750		600
Equity and liabilities				
Equity				
Ordinary $1/€1 shares	300		100	
Retained earnings	300		280	
		600		380
Long-term loans		50		110
Current liabilities		100		110
		750		600

STATEMENTS OF COMPREHENSIVE INCOME
FOR THE YEAR ENDED 31 DECEMBER 20X9

	Darius Co $	Xerxes Inc €
Profit before tax	200	160
Tax	100	80
Profit after tax, retained	100	80

The following further information is given.

(a) Darius Co has had its interest in Xerxes Inc since the incorporation of the company. Neither company paid dividends during the year to 31 December 20X9 and neither company had any other comprehensive income in their separate financial statements.

(b) Depreciation is 8% per annum on cost.

(c) There have been no loan repayments or movements in non-current assets during the year. The opening inventory of Xerxes Inc was €120. Assume that inventory turnover times are very short.

(d) Exchange rates:

€4 to $1 when Xerxes Inc was incorporated

€2.5 to $1 when Xerxes Inc acquired its non-current assets

€2 to $1 on 31 December 20X8

€1.6 to $1 average rate of exchange year ending 31 December 20X9

€1 to $1 on 31 December 20X9

Now we will prepare the summarised consolidated financial statements of Darius Co.

 step 1

The statement of financial position of Xerxes Inc at 31 December 20X9, other than share capital and retained earnings, should be translated at €1 = $1.

SUMMARISED STATEMENT OF FINANCIAL POSITION AT 31 DECEMBER 20X9

	$	$
Non-current assets (NBV)		300
Current assets		
Inventories	200	
Receivables	100	
		300
		600
Non-current liabilities		110
Current liabilities		110

∴ Shareholders' funds = 600 − 110 − 110 = $380

Since Darius Co acquired the whole of the issued share capital on incorporation, the post-acquisition retained earnings including exchange differences will be the value of shareholders' funds arrived at above, less the original cost to Darius Co of $25. Post-acquisition retained earnings = $380 − $25 = $355.

SUMMARISED CONSOLIDATED STATEMENT OF FINANCIAL POSITION AS AT 31 DECEMBER 20X9

		$	$
Assets			
Non-current assets (NBV)	$(350 + 300)		650
Current assets			
Inventories	$(225 + 200)	425	
Receivables	$(150 + 100)	250	
			675
			1,325
Equity and liabilities			
Equity			
Ordinary $1 shares (Darius only)			300
Retained earnings	$(300 + 355)		655
			955
Non-current liabilities: loans	$(50 + 110)		160
Current liabilities	$(100 + 110)		210
			1,325

Note. It is quite unnecessary to know the amount of the exchange differences when preparing the consolidated statement of financial position.

step 2

The statement of profit or loss and other comprehensive income should be translated at average rate (€1.6 = $1).

SUMMARISED STATEMENT OF COMPREHENSIVE INCOME OF XERXES INC FOR THE YEAR ENDED 31 DECEMBER 20X9

	$
Profit before tax	100
Tax	50
Profit after tax	50

SUMMARISED CONSOLIDATED STATEMENT OF PROFIT OR LOSS AND OTHER COMPREHENSIVE INCOME FOR THE YEAR ENDED 31 DECEMBER 20X9

		$
Profit before tax	$(200 + 100)	300
Tax	$(100 + 50)	150
Profit after tax	$(100 + 50)	150

The statement of profit or loss and other comprehensive income cannot be completed until the exchange difference has been calculated.

step 3

The equity interest at the beginning of the year can be found as follows.

	€
Equity value at 31 December 20X9	380
Retained profit for year	80
Equity value at 31 December 20X8	300
Translated at €2 = $1, this gives	$150

step 4

The exchange difference can now be calculated and the statement of profit or loss and other comprehensive income completed.

	$
Equity interest at 31 December 20X9	380
Equity interest at 1 January 20X9	150
	230
Less retained profit	50
Exchange gain	180

SUMMARISED CONSOLIDATED STATEMENT OF PROFIT OR LOSS AND OTHER COMPREHENSIVE INCOME FOR THE YEAR ENDED 31 DECEMBER 20X9

		$
Profit before tax	$(200 + 100)	300
Tax	$(100 + 50)	150
Profit after tax	$(100 + 50)	150
Other comprehensive income (items that may be re-classified to profit or loss)		
Exchange difference on translating foreign operations		180
Total comprehensive income		330

CONSOLIDATED STATEMENT OF CHANGES IN EQUITY (EXTRACT FOR RESERVES) FOR THE YEAR ENDED 31 DECEMBER 20X9

	$
Consolidated reserves at 31 December 20X8	325
Total comprehensive income	330
Consolidated reserves at 31 December 20X9	655

Note. The post-acquisition reserves of Xerxes Inc at the beginning of the year must have been $150 − $25 = $125 and the reserves of Darius Co must have been $300 − $100 = $200. The consolidated reserves must therefore have been $325.

Analysis of exchange differences

Exchange differences could be reconciled by splitting them into their component parts.

Exchange differences consist of those exchange gains/losses arising from:

- Translating **income/expense items** at the exchange rates at the date of transactions, whereas **assets/liabilities** are translated at the closing rate.

- Translating the **opening net investment** (opening net assets) in the foreign entity at a closing rate different from the closing rate at which it was previously reported.

This can be demonstrated using the above example.

Using the opening statement of financial position and translating at €2 = $1 and €1 = $1 gives the following.

	€2 = $1	€1 = $1	Difference
	$	$	$
Non-current assets at NBV	170	340	170
Inventories	60	120	60
Net current monetary liabilities	(25)	(50)	(25)
	205	410	205
Equity	150	300	150
Loans	55	110	55
	205	410	205

Translating the statement of profit or loss and other comprehensive income using €1.60 = $1 and €1 = $1 gives the following results.

	€1.60 = $1	€1 = $1	Difference
	$	$	$
Profit before tax, depreciation and increase in inventory values	75	120	45
Increase in inventory values	50	80	30
	125	200	75
Depreciation	(25)	(40)	(15)
	100	160	60
Tax	(50)	(80)	(30)
Profit after tax, retained	50	80	30

The overall position is then:

	$	$
Gain on non-current assets ($170 − $15)		155
Loss on loan		(55)
Gain on inventories ($60 + $30)	90	
Loss on net monetary current assets/ liabilities (all other differences)		
($45 − $30 − $25)	(10)	
		80
Net exchange gain: as above		180

Further matters relating to foreign operations

Goodwill and fair value adjustments

Goodwill and fair value adjustments arising on the acquisition of a foreign operation should be treated as assets and liabilities of the acquired entity. This means that they should be expressed in the functional currency of the foreign operation and translated at the **closing rate**.

This means that goodwill is restated at the end of each reporting period and the resulting foreign exchange gain or loss is recognised.

Consolidation procedures

Follow normal consolidation procedures, except that where an exchange difference arises on **long- or short-term intra-group monetary items**, these cannot be offset against other intra-group balances. This is because these are commitments to convert one currency into another, thus exposing the reporting entity to a gain or loss through currency fluctuations.

If the foreign operation's **reporting date** is different from that of the parent, it is acceptable to use the accounts made up to that date for consolidation, as long as adjustments are made for any significant changes in rates in the interim.

Hyperinflationary economies

We will look at IAS 29 *Financial reporting in hyperinflationary economies* later in this chapter. The financial statements of a foreign operation operating in a hyperinflationary economy must be adjusted under IAS 29 before they are translated into the parent's reporting currency and then consolidated. When the economy **ceases to be hyperinflationary**, and the foreign operation ceases to apply IAS 29, the amounts restated to the price level at the date the entity ceased to restate its financial statements should be used as the historical costs for translation purposes.

Disposal of foreign entity

When a parent disposes of a foreign entity, the cumulative amount of deemed exchange differences relating to that foreign entity should be **recognised as an income or expense** in the same period in which the gain or loss on disposal is recognised. Effectively, this means that these exchange differences are recognised once by taking them to reserves and then are recognised for a second time ('reclassified') by transferring them to profit or loss on disposal of the foreign operation.

In the parent's own financial statements

In the parent company's own financial statements, exchange differences arising on a **monetary item** that is effectively part of the parent's net investment in the foreign entity should be recognised **in profit or loss** in the separate financial statements of the reporting entity or the individual financial statements of the foreign operation, as appropriate.

Change in functional currency

The functional currency of an entity can be changed only if there is a change to the underlying transactions, events and conditions that are relevant to the entity. For example, an entity's functional currency may change if there is a change in the currency that mainly influences the sales price of goods and services.

Where there is a change in an entity's functional currency, the entity translates all items into the new functional currency **prospectively** (ie from the date of the change) using the exchange rate at the date of the change.

Tax effects of exchange differences

IAS 12 *Income taxes* should be applied when there are tax effects arising from gains or losses on foreign currency transactions and exchange differences arising on the translation of the financial statements of foreign operations.

Foreign associates

Foreign associates will be companies with substantial autonomy from the group and so their **functional currency will be different** from that of the parent.

Disclosure

IAS 21 requires disclosure of the following.

(a)   Amount of exchange differences recognised in profit or loss

(b)   Net exchange differences (classified as equity) as a separate component of equity, and a reconciliation of the amount of such exchange differences at the beginning and end of the period

In addition, when the **presentation currency is different** from the functional currency, that fact should be stated and the functional currency should be disclosed. The reason for using a different presentation currency should also be disclosed.

Where there is a **change in the functional currency** of either the reporting entity or a significant foreign operation, that fact and the reason for the change in functional currency should be disclosed.

An entity may present its financial statements or other financial information in a currency that is different from either its functional currency or its presentation currency. For example, it may convert selected items only, or it may use a translation method that does not comply with IFRSs in order to deal with hyperinflation. In this situation the entity must:

(a)   Clearly identify the information as supplementary information to distinguish it from information that complies with IFRSs

(b)   Disclose the currency in which the supplementary information is displayed

(c)   Disclose the entity's functional currency and the method of translation used to determine the supplementary information

4 IAS 29: Financial reporting in hyperinflationary economies

In a hyperinflationary economy, **money loses its purchasing power very quickly.** Comparisons of transactions at different points in time, even within the same accounting period, are misleading. It is therefore considered inappropriate for entities to prepare financial statements without making adjustments for the **fall in the purchasing power of money over time**.

IAS 29 *Financial reporting in hyperinflationary economies* applies to the **primary financial statements** of entities (including consolidated accounts and statements of cash flows) whose functional currency is the currency of a hyperinflationary economy. In this section, we will identify the hyperinflationary currency as $H.

The standard does not define a **hyperinflationary economy** in exact terms, although it indicates the characteristics of such an economy, for example, where the cumulative inflation rate over three years approaches or exceeds 100%.

What other factors might indicate a hyperinflationary economy?

These are examples, but the list is not exhaustive.

(a)   The population prefers to retain its wealth in non-monetary assets or in a relatively stable foreign currency. Amounts of local currency held are immediately invested to maintain purchasing power.

(b) The population regards monetary amounts not in terms of the local currency but in terms of a relatively stable foreign currency. Prices may be quoted in that currency.

(c) Sales/purchases on credit take place at prices that compensate for the expected loss of purchasing power during the credit period, if that period is short.

(d) Interest rates, wages and prices are linked to a price index.

The reported value of **non-monetary assets**, in terms of current measuring units, increases over time. For example, if a fixed asset is purchased for $H1,000 when the price index is 100, and the price index subsequently rises to 200, the value of the asset in terms of current measuring units (ignoring accumulated depreciation) will rise to $H2,000.

In contrast, the value of **monetary assets and liabilities**, such as a debt for 300 units, is unaffected by changes in the prices index, because it is an actual money amount payable or receivable. If a debtor owes $H300 when the price index is 100, and the debt is still unpaid when the price index has risen to 150, the debtor still owes just $H300. The purchasing power of monetary assets, however, will decline over time as the general level of prices goes up.

Requirement to restate financial statements in terms of measuring units current at the year end

In most countries, financial statements are produced on the basis of either:

(a) **Historical cost**, except to the extent that some assets (eg property and investments) may be revalued; or

(b) **Current cost**, which reflects the changes in the values of specific assets held by the entity.

In a hyperinflationary economy, neither of these methods of financial reporting are meaningful unless adjustments are made for the fall in the purchasing power of money. IAS 29 therefore requires that the **primary financial statements** of entities in a hyperinflationary economy should be produced by restating the figures prepared on either a historical cost basis or a current cost basis in terms of **measuring units current at the year end**.

Measuring unit current at the year end date. This is a unit of local currency with a purchasing power as at the date of the statement of financial position, in terms of a general prices index.

Financial statements that are not restated (ie that are prepared on a historical cost basis or current cost basis without adjustments) may be presented as **additional statements** by the entity, but this is discouraged. The primary financial statements are those that have been restated.

After the assets, liabilities, equity and statement of profit or loss and other comprehensive income of the entity have been restated, there will be a **net gain or loss on monetary assets and liabilities (the 'net monetary position')** and this should be recognised separately in profit or loss for the period.

Making the adjustments

IAS 29 recognises that the resulting financial statements, after restating all items in terms of measuring units current at the year end, will **lack precise accuracy**. However, it is more important that certain procedures and judgements should be applied consistently from year to year. The implementation guidelines to the Standard suggest what these procedures should be.

Statement of financial position: Historical cost

Where the entity produces its accounts on a historical cost basis, the following procedures should be applied.

(a) Items that are not already expressed in terms of measuring units current at the year end should be restated, using a **general prices index**, so that they are valued in measuring units current at the year end.

(b) **Monetary assets and liabilities** are not restated, because they are already expressed in terms of measuring units current at the year end.

(c) Assets that are **already stated at market value or net realisable value** need not be restated, because they too are already valued in measuring units current at the year end.

(d) Any assets or liabilities **linked by agreement to changes in the general level of prices**, such as indexed-linked loans or bonds, should be adjusted in accordance with the terms of the agreement to establish the amount outstanding as at the year end.

(e) All **other non-monetary assets**, ie tangible long-term assets, intangible long-term assets (including accumulated depreciation/amortisation) investments and inventories, should be restated in terms of measuring units as at the year end, by applying a general prices index.

The **method of restating** these assets should normally be to multiply the original cost of the assets by a factor: [prices index at year end /prices index at date of acquisition of the asset]. For example, if an item of machinery was purchased for $H2,000 units when the prices index was 400 and the prices index at the year end is 1,000, the restated value of the long-term asset (before accumulated depreciation) would be:

$$\$H2,000 \times (1,000/400) = \$H5,000$$

If, in the above example, the non current asset has been held for half its useful life and has no residual value, the **accumulated depreciation** would be restated as $H2,500. (The depreciation charge for the year should be the amount of depreciation based on historical cost, multiplied by the same factor as above: 1,000/400.)

If an asset has been **revalued** since it was originally purchased (eg a property), it should be restated in measuring units at the year end date by applying a factor: (prices index at year end/prices index at revaluation date) to the revalued amount of the asset.

If the restated amount of a non-monetary asset **exceeds its recoverable value** (ie its net realisable value or market value), its value should be reduced accordingly.

The **owners' equity** (all components) as at the start of the accounting period should be restated using a general prices index from the beginning of the period.

Statement of profit or loss: Historical cost

In the statement of profit or loss, all amounts of income and expense should be **restated in terms of measuring units current at the year end**. All amounts therefore need to be restated by a factor that allows for the change in the prices index since the item of income or expense was first recorded.

Gain or loss on net monetary position

In a period of inflation, an entity that holds monetary assets (cash, receivables) will suffer a fall in the purchasing power of these assets. By the same token, in a period of inflation, the value of monetary liabilities, such as a bank overdraft or bank loan, declines in terms of current purchasing power.

(a) If an entity has an **excess of monetary assets over monetary liabilities**, it will suffer a loss over time on its net monetary position, in a period of inflation, in terms of measuring units as at 'today's date'.

(b) If an entity has an **excess of monetary liabilities over monetary assets**, it will make a gain on its net monetary position, in a period of inflation.

Example: Hyperinflationary accounts

An entity maintains an unchanged position over time. At 1 January, when the general prices index was 100, its statement of financial position was as follows.

	$H
Assets	
Non-monetary assets	2,000
Monetary assets	2,000
	4,000
Liabilities and equity	
Monetary liabilities	1,000
Equity	3,000
	4,000

Suppose that the general prices index rises to 150 at 31 December.

What are the adjustments required in the statement of financial position?

Restating this statement of financial position in terms of measuring units when the prices index is 50% higher gives the following.

	$H
Assets	
Non-monetary assets (× 150/100)	3,000
Monetary assets	2,000
	5,000
Liabilities and equity	
Monetary liabilities	1,000
Equity (× 150/100)	4,500
	5,500

The entity has suffered a loss on its net monetary position of $H500, in terms of measuring units at the current date $H(5,500 – 5,000). This is because it has held net monetary assets of $H1,000 during the period.

In the financial statements of an entity reporting in the currency of a hyperinflationary economy, the gain or loss on the net monetary position:

(a)   May be derived as the **difference between total assets and total equity and liabilities**, after restating the non-monetary assets, owners' equity, profit or loss items and index-linked items; or

(b)   May be estimated by **applying the change in the general prices index** for the period to the weighted average of the net monetary position of the entity in the period.

The gain or loss on the net monetary position should be **included in net income** and disclosed separately. (Any adjustment that was made to index-linked items can be set off against this net monetary gain or loss.)

Current cost accounts: Restating the accounts

A similar procedure is required to restate the accounts of an entity that prepares its accounts using a current cost basis.

(a) Items stated in the statement of financial position at current cost do not need to be restated. Other items should be restated in the same way as for adjusting accounts prepared on a historical cost basis.

(b) In the **statement of profit or loss,** cost of sales and depreciation are generally reported at current costs at the time of consumption and sales and other expenses at money amounts at the time they occurred. These items will need to be restated in terms of measuring units as at the year end by making a prices index adjustment.

(c) There will be a **gain or loss on the net monetary position,** which will be established in the same way as for accounts based on historical cost.

Economies ceasing to be hyperinflationary economies

When an economy ceases to be a hyperinflationary economy, entities reporting in the currency of the economy are no longer required to produce financial statements in compliance with IAS 29.

Suppose for example that in 20X4 an entity reports in compliance with IAS 29, but in 20X5 it reverts to historical cost accounting because the economy is no longer a hyperinflationary economy. As a starting point for reverting to historical cost accounts reporting, the entity should use the amounts expressed in terms of measuring units as at the end of 20X4 as the basis for its carrying amounts in 20X5 and subsequent years.

Disclosures

IAS 29 calls for the following disclosures.

- The fact that the **financial statements have been restated** for the changes in general purchasing power.

- Whether the financial statements as shown are based on **historical cost or current cost.**

- The **identity of the prices index** used to make the restatements, its level at the year end the movement in the index during the current and the previous reporting periods.

In financial statements prepared under IAS 29, corresponding figures for the previous year should be **restated using the general prices index.**

Hyperinflation and changes in foreign exchange rates

IAS 21 *The effects of changes in foreign exchange rates* was covered earlier. A parent may have a foreign operation whose functional currency is the currency of a hyperinflationary economy. When the parent prepares consolidated financial statements it should:

(1) **Restate the financial statements** of the foreign operation in accordance with IAS 29

(2) **Translate all amounts** from the foreign operation's functional currency to the presentation currency **at the closing rate**

The following example is a simple illustration of the problems that can arise where a foreign subsidiary operates in a hyperinflationary economy.

Example: 'Disappearing assets'

A company has a subsidiary in a country which suffers from hyperinflation. On 31 December 20X2 the subsidiary acquired freehold land for $H1,000,000. At that date the exchange rate was $H4 = $1 and the relevant price index was 100.

At 31 December 20X3 the exchange rate was $H10 = $1 and the price index was 300.

At what value will the freehold land be included in the consolidated financial statements of the parent at 31 December 20X3 if the subsidiary's financial statements:

(a) Are not restated to reflect current price levels;
(b) Are restated to reflect current price levels?

(a) **Without restatement**

Assuming that the subsidiary has a different functional currency ($H) from that of its parent ($) the statement of financial position is translated at the closing rate.

At 31 December 20X3 the land is included at $100,000 ($H1,000,000 @ 10).

At 31 December 20X2 (the date of purchase) its was stated at $250,000 ($H1,000,000 @ 4). Therefore there has been an exchange loss of $150,000 (which may significantly reduce equity) and the land appears to have fallen to only 40% of its original value.

(b) **With restatement**

At 31 December 20X3 the land is included at $300,000 ($H1,000,000 × 300/100 @ 10).

The value of the land is now adjusted so that it reflects the effect of inflation over the year and the 'disappearing assets' problem is overcome.

Where the financial statements of an entity whose functional currency is that of a hyperinflationary economy are translated into a different presentation currency, **comparative amounts** should be those that were presented as current year amounts in the relevant prior year financial statements (ie **not adjusted** for subsequent changes in the price level or subsequent changes in exchange rates).

Accounting for agriculture and mineral resources

23

1 IAS 41: Agriculture

IAS 41 was issued by the old IASC in 2001, and is an instance of the IASC/IASB developing standards that are specific to individual industries where the accounting issues involved are of sufficient substance and significance.

IAS 41 has contributed to the international harmonisation of accounting standards, because agriculture in particular was characterised by a **great diversity in accounting treatments**. Cows, for instance, were accounted for as 'stocks' in Ireland but as 'fixed assets' in the UK. IAS 41 has helped to foster increased comparability between accounts produced in these different regions.

Perhaps more interestingly, it is quite difficult to apply **traditional accounting methods** to agricultural activities, which explains why agriculture is excluded from many IASs.

(a)   When and how do you account for the **critical events** associated with biological transformation (growth, procreation, production and degeneration), which alter the substance of biological assets?

(b)   **Statement of financial position classification** is made difficult by the variety and characteristics of the living assets of agriculture.

(c)   The nature of the management of agricultural activities also causes problems, particularly determination of the **unit of measurement**, ie whether biological assets are a perpetual group of assets or a number of limited life assets.

The standard has improved and harmonised practice in accounting for agriculture, which demonstrates fundamental **differences in its nature and characteristics** to other business activities.

Definitions

The following definitions are used in IAS 41.

Agricultural activity is the management by an entity of the biological transformation of biological assets for sale, into agricultural produce or into additional biological assets.

Agricultural produce is the harvested product of an entity's biological assets.

A biological asset is a living animal or plant.

Biological transformation comprises the processes of growth, degeneration, production and procreation that cause qualitative and quantitative changes in a biological asset.

A group of biological assets is an aggregation of similar living animals or plants.

Harvest is the detachment of produce from a biological asset or the cessation of a biological asset's life processes   *(IAS 41: para. 5)*

Fair value is the price that would be received to sell an asset, or paid to transfer a liability in an orderly transaction between market participants.   *(IFRS 13: para. 9)*

Carrying amount is the amount at which an asset is recognised in the statement of financial position.   *(IAS 41: para. 5)*

Note the key parts of the definition of agriculture.

(a)   **Biological** agriculture relates to 'life phenomena', living animals and plants with an innate capacity of biological transformation which are dependent upon a combination of natural resources (sunlight, water, etc).

(b)   **Transformation** agriculture involves physical transformation, whereby animals and plants undergo a change in biological quantity (fat cover, density, etc) and/or quantity (progeny, live weight etc) over time, which is measured and monitored (increasingly objectively) as part of management control.

(c)   **Management**. Biological transformation is managed.

   (i)   Conditions are stabilised or enhanced

   (ii)   The transparency of the relationship between inputs and outputs is determined by the degree of control (intensive versus extensive)

   (iii)   It is different from exploitation through extraction, where no attempt is made to facilitate the transformation

   (iv)   Biological assets are managed in groups of plant or animal classes, using individual assets to ensure the sustainability of the group

   (v)   Sustainability of an agricultural activity is a function of quality and quantity

(d)   **Produce**. Agricultural produce is diverse and may require further processing before ultimate consumption.

The standard applies to the three elements that form part of, or result from, agricultural activity.

- Biological assets
- Agricultural produce at the point of harvest
- Government grants

The standard does not apply to agricultural land (IASs 16 and 40) or intangible assets related to agricultural activity (IAS 38). After harvest, IAS 2 is applied.

Biological assets

Biological assets are the core income-producing assets of agricultural activities, held for their transformative capabilities. **Biological transformation** leads to various **different outcomes**.

- **Asset changes:**
  - – Growth: increase in quantity and or quality
  - – Degeneration: decrease in quantity and/or quality

- **Creation of new assets:**
  - – Production: producing separable non-living products
  - – Procreation: producing separable living animals

We can distinguish between the importance of these by saying that asset changes are **critical to the flow of future economic benefits** both in and beyond the current period, but the relative importance of new asset creation will depend on the purpose of the agricultural activity.

The IAS distinguishes therefore between two broad categories of agricultural production system.

(a) **Consumable** animals/plants themselves are harvested
(b) **Bearer** animals/plants bear produce for harvest

A few further points are made.

(a) Biological assets are usually managed in groups of animal or plant classes, with characteristics (eg male/female ratio) which allow sustainability in perpetuity.

(b) **Land often forms an integral part** of the activity itself in pastoral and other land-based agricultural activities.

Bearer biological assets

An amendment has been issued to IAS 41 regarding plant-based bearer biological assets, which would include trees grown in plantations, such as grape vines, rubber trees and oil palms.

These plants are used solely to grow produce crops over several periods and are not in themselves consumed. When no longer productive they are usually scrapped.

It was decided that fair value was not an appropriate measurement for these assets as, once they reach maturity, the only economic benefit they produce comes from the agricultural produce they create. In this respect, they are similar to assets in a manufacturing activity.

Consequently, these assets have been removed from the scope of IAS 41 and should be accounted for under IAS 16 *Property, plant and equipment*. They are measured at accumulated costs until maturity and are then subject to depreciation and impairment charges. The IAS 16 revaluation model could also be applied. Agricultural produce from these plants continues to be recognised under IAS 41.

Recognition of biological assets

The recognition criteria are very **similar to those for other assets**, in that animals or plants should be recognised as assets in the following circumstances.

(a) The entity **controls** the asset as a result of past events

(b) It is probable that the **future economic benefits** associated with the asset will flow to the entity

(c) The fair value or cost of the asset to the entity can be **measured reliably**

The significant physical attributes of biological assets can be measured using various methods (which are used by markets to measure value) and generally indicate the source of future economic benefits. The **certainty** of the flow of rewards can be determined by formal ownership records, eg land title and branding. The availability of both cost and value for biological assets indicates the reliability aspect of the measurement criteria is fulfilled.

Measurement of biological assets

The IAS provides for a benchmark treatment and an allowed alternative treatment.

Benchmark treatment	**Allowed alternative treatment**
Fair value less estimated point of sale costs	Cost less accumulated depreciation and impairment losses

The alternative method is allowed, if a fair value cannot be determined because market-determined prices or values are not available.

This alternative basis is only allowed on **initial recognition**.

The **measurement basis** used to depict the fair value of a biological asset will differ depending on the existence of an active market, market efficiency and the use made of the asset.

In summary, it is felt that **fair value**, when compared to historical cost, has greater relevance, comparability and understandability as a measure of future economic benefits.

Determining fair value

The standard states that the primary indicator of fair value should be **net market value**. This is reasonable as efficient markets exist for most biological assets in most locations, and net market value is usually considered as providing the best evidence of fair value where an active market exists. Markets will generally differentiate between differing **qualities and quantities**. Market value is not generally predicted on management's intended use, however, but recognises alternative uses.

An active and efficient market may not be available for a class of biological assets in a specific location, or there may be imperfections in the market. The standard goes into some detail about **how fair value should be estimated** in such circumstances, but in summary, the valuation techniques should be consistent with the objectives of measuring fair value and should attain an appropriate balance between relevance and faithful representation.

Recognition

This is an important principle, whereby the change in the carrying amount for a group of biological assets should be allocated between:

(a)   The change attributable to **differences in fair value**; and
(b)   The **physical change** in biological assets held.

The total change in carrying value between the beginning and end of the period thus consists of two components. Although the separation of these two components might appear impractical, the Standard states that separate disclosure of each is **fundamental to appraising current period performance and future prospects**. This is because they will not be reported in the same way in the financial statements.

(a)   The change in carrying amount attributable to the **physical change in biological assets** must be recognised as income or expense and described as the change in biological assets. This allows management's performance to be evaluated in relation to the production from, and maintenance and renewal of, biological assets. This is the 'operating' part of the change in carrying amount.

(b)   The change in carrying amount attributable to **differences in fair value** should be recognised in the statement of non-owner movements in equity and presented in equity under the heading of surplus/(deficit) on fair valuation of biological assets. This is the 'holding' part of the change in carrying amount.

In the **statement of financial position** the biological assets must be shown at fair value, incorporating the consequences of all biological transformations. These assets, with their differing risk and return characteristics, should be identified clearly.

The recommended **method of separating the above components** is to calculate the change attributable to the differences in fair value by restating biological assets on hand at the opening reporting date using end of period fair values and comparing this with the closing carrying amount. The biological assets on hand at the beginning and end of the period will then be expressed in a common measurement unit, ie period-end fair value. This allows the relative significance of sales, disposals, purchases, additions and biological transformations to be evaluated in relation to the overall change in substance of the biological assets held during the period.

There are **exceptions to this approach** in certain situations. For example, in some agricultural systems the predominant activity has a production cycle of less than a year (eg broiler chickens, mushroom growing, cereal crops). In such cases the total change in carrying amount is reported in profit or loss as a single item of income or expense.

Any other events giving rise to a change in biological assets of such a **size, nature or incidence** that their disclosure is relevant to explain the entity's performance (as defined in IAS 8) should be included in the change in biological assets recognised as income or expense. They should, however, be shown as a separate item in the reconciliation required to determine the change attributable to biological transformation.

Presentation and disclosure

In the **statement of financial position** biological assets should be classified as a separate class of assets falling under neither current nor non-current classifications. This reflects the view of such assets as having an unlimited life on a collective basis; it is the total exposure of the entity to this type of asset that is important.

Biological assets should also be **sub-classified** (either on the face of the statement of financial position or as a note to the accounts).

(a)   Class of animal or plant
(b)   Nature of activities (consumable or bearer)
(c)   Maturity or immaturity for intended purpose

Where activities are **consumable**, the maturity criterion will be attainment of harvestable specifications, whereas in **bearer** activities, it will be attainment of sufficient maturity to sustain economic harvests.

In the **statement of profit or loss**, entities with significant agricultural activity are encouraged to provide, on the face of the statement, an analysis of the income and expenses used in determining profit from operating activities based on the nature of income and expenses (ie rather than the cost of sales method).

The IAS also lists some detailed disclosure requirements including the measurement base used for fair value, the details of the reconciliation of the change in carrying value for the year and so on.

Agricultural produce

This was defined in the key terms above. It is **recognised at the point of harvest** (eg detachment from the biological asset). Agricultural produce is either incapable of biological process or such processes remain dormant (eg stored grain). **Recognition ends** once the produce enters trading activities or production processes within integrated agribusinesses, although processing activities that are incidental to agricultural activities and that do not materially alter the form of the produce (eg drying or cleaning) are not counted as processing. Following harvest, the provisions of IAS 2 apply.

Measurement and presentation

Following the treatment of biological assets above, the IAS states that agricultural produce should be **measured at each reporting date at fair value** less estimated point-of-sale costs, to the extent that it is sourced from an entity's biological assets, which are also valued at fair value. This is logical when you consider that, until harvest, the agricultural produce was valued at fair value anyway as part of the biological asset.

The **change in the carrying amount** of the agricultural produce held at two reporting dates should be recognised as **income or expense** in profit or loss. This will be rare as such produce is usually sold or processed within a short time, so that produce held over two reporting dates is being held for a specific management purpose and the consequences of that should be reflected in the current period.

Agricultural produce that is harvested for **trading or processing activities** within integrated agricultural/ agribusiness operations should be measured at **fair value** at the date of harvest and this amount is deemed cost for application of IAS 2 to consequential inventories.

Presentation in the statement of financial position

Agricultural produce should be classified as inventory in the statement of financial position and disclosed separately either in the statement of financial position or in the notes.

Government grants

An unconditional government grant related to a biological asset measured at its fair value less estimated point-of-sale costs should be recognised as income when, and only when, the grant becomes receivable.

If a government grant requires an entity not to engage in specified agricultural activity (eg the EU's set aside grant), an entity should only recognise the grant as income when, and only when, the conditions are met.

IAS 20 does not apply to a government grant on biological assets measured at fair value less estimated point-of-sale costs. However if a biological asset is measured at cost less accumulated depreciation and accumulated impairment losses then IAS 20 does apply.

The following should be disclosed:

- The nature and extent of government grants recognised in the financial statements

- Unfulfilled conditions and other contingencies attaching to government grants

- Significant decreases expected in the level of government grants

2 IFRS 6: Exploration for and evaluation of mineral resources

IFRS 6 is an interim standard. It is only a short-term solution to the problems of accounting in this area, and was issued so that entities had at least some guidance until a complete standard is issued in the future. Before IFRS, accounting practices varied greatly between national standard-setters, so it was important that, with more and more entities switching to IFRS, there was at least some IFRS guidance in the area. Since it had had to be specifically excluded from IAS 16 and IAS 38, the IASB developed and issued IFRS 6.

IFRS 6 is related to IAS 38's distinction between research and development phases, where research costs are expensed and development costs are capitalised. The problem is that the exploration for and evaluation of mineral resources is not quite research and not quite development – hence the need for IFRS 6.

The scope of IFRS 6 is intentionally very narrow. Entities must apply IFRS 6 to all exploration and evaluation expenditure incurred, but it does not address other aspects of their accounting.

IFRS 6 only applies **after** the entity has obtained legal rights to explore in a specific area and **before** technical feasibility and commercial viability of extraction have been demonstrated.

> **Exploration and evaluation expenditures** are expenditures incurred by an entity in connection with the exploration for and evaluation of mineral resources before the technical feasibility and commercial viability of extracting a mineral resource are demonstrable.
>
> **Exploration and evaluation assets** are exploration and evaluation expenditures recognised as assets in accordance with the entity's accounting policy.
>
> **Exploration for and evaluation of mineral resources** is the search for mineral resources, including minerals, oil, natural gas and similar non-regenerative resources after the entity has obtained legal rights to explore in a specific area, as well as the determination of the technical feasibility and commercial viability of extracting the mineral resource. *(IFRS 6: Appendix A)*

Recognition

Expenditure is recognised as an asset for IFRS 6 up to the point where the technical feasibility and commercial viability of extracting resources can be demonstrated. Note that this also means that the entity must have the necessary technical and financial means to extract the resources.

An entity can then choose its own accounting policy as long as it is line with IAS 8. Specifically, it must conform to IAS 8 paragraph 10, which states that **management should use its judgement** in developing an **accounting policy** that results in information that is **relevant** and **reliable**. After choosing their policy, entities must then **apply their policy consistently**.

Note that expenditure related to the **development** of mineral resources must not be recognised as exploration and evaluation assets under IFRS 6, as it comes under IAS 38.

Measurement at recognition

At recognition, exploration and evaluation **assets must be measured at cost**.

The following are examples of expenditures an entity might incur in the initial measurement of exploration and evaluation assets:

(a) Acquisition of rights to explore

(b) Topographical geological, geochemical and geophysical studies

(c) Exploratory drilling

(d) Trenching

(e) Sampling

(f) Activities in relation to evaluating the technical feasibility and commercial viability of extracting a mineral resource

An entity should also recognise the cost of any obligations for removal and restoration, in line with IAS 37.

Measurement after recognition

Entities must apply either the cost model or the revaluation model (taking the revaluation model either from IAS 16 or IAS 38).

Classification and reclassification

Exploration and evaluation assets are classified as **tangible or intangible according to the nature** of the assets acquired. For example, drilling rights would be intangible; vehicles or drilling rigs would be tangible. The classification must be applied consistently.

They should no longer be classified as exploration and evaluation assets when the technical feasibility and commercial viability of extracting a mineral resource are demonstrable. Any impairment loss on the assets must be recognised before classification.

Impairment

Exploration and evaluation assets must be **assessed for impairment when facts and circumstances suggest that the carrying amount of an asset may exceed its recoverable amount. Any resulting impairment loss must be measured, presented and disclosed in accordance with IAS 36.**

The following **factors** suggest exploration and evaluation assets should be tested for impairment:

(a)   The period for which the entity has **exploration rights has expired** or is due to expire in the near future and is not expected to be reviewed.

(b)   **Substantive expenditure** on further exploration in the specific area is **not budgeted** or planned.

(c)   Exploration in a specific area has **not** led to the discovery of **commercially viable quantities** of mineral resources, and the entity has decided to discontinue activities in this area.

(d)   Sufficient data indicates that whilst a development in a specific area may proceed, the **carrying value of the exploration and evaluation asset is unlikely to be recovered** from successful development and sale.

For impairment purposes, each cash generating unit or group of units to which an exploration and evaluation asset is allocated must not be larger than a segment as determined by IFRS 8 *Operating segments.*

Disclosures

These must identify and explain the amounts recognised in the accounts. Specifically, entities must explain:

- Accounting policies

- The amounts of assets, liabilities, income and expenses, and operating and investing cash flows

Index

Index